BEST LITTLE STORIES
from the
WILD WEST

Other Books by C. Brian Kelly

BEST LITTLE STORIES FROM THE AMERICAN REVOLUTION
with "Select Founding Mothers" by Ingrid Smyer

BEST LITTLE STORIES FROM THE CIVIL WAR
with "Varina: Forgotten First Lady" by Ingrid Smyer

BEST LITTLE IRONIES, ODDITIES & MYSTERIES OF THE CIVIL WAR
with "Mary Todd Lincoln: Troubled First Lady" by Ingrid Smyer

BEST LITTLE STORIES FROM THE WHITE HOUSE
with "First Ladies in Review" by Ingrid Smyer

BEST LITTLE STORIES FROM WORLD WAR II

BEST LITTLE STORIES
from the
WILD WEST

C. Brian Kelly

with "Fascinating Women of the West" by Ingrid Smyer

CUMBERLAND HOUSE
NASHVILLE, TENNESSEE

Copyright © 2002 by C. Brian Kelly and Ingrid Smyer-Kelly

Published by
CUMBERLAND HOUSE PUBLISHING, INC.
431 Harding Industrial Drive
Nashville, Tennessee 37211
www.cumberlandhouse.com

Cover design by Bateman Design, Nashville, Tennessee.

Library of Congress Cataloging-in-Publication Data

Kelly, C. Brian.
    Best little stories of the Wild West / C. Brian Kelly. With Fascinating women of the West / by Ingrid Smyer.
        p.   cm.
    ISBN 1-58182-263-4 (alk. paper)
    1. West (U.S.)—History—Anecdotes. 2. West (U.S.)—Biography—Anecdotes.
3. Women—West (U.S.)—Biography—Anecdotes. 4. Frontier and pioneer life—
West (U.S.)—Anecdotes. I. Smyer-Kelly, Ingrid, 1927– Fascinating women of the
West. II. Title: Fascinating women of the West. III. Title.
F591.K38 2002
978—dc21
                                                                            2002006891

Printed in the United States of America.

1 2 3 4 5 6 7 8 9 10—05 04 03 02

For Eugenie, Harald, Joanie, Sharon, Shirley

Contents

Part 3: Emigration, War, and Gold

Part 4: Nation of Two Faces

Part 5: Cowboys & Indians, Lawmen & Outlaws

Part 6: Sliding into a New Century

Fascinating Women of the West *333*

Introduction and Acknowledgments

It truly has been said that any history written is writ to large degree on the backs of others, be they the creators of raw, primary data or the sifting, distilling historians of another moment in time. We have tried all along herein to give credit to our sources of either variety, and we do want to thank those who thus lent us their "backs," while also extending our apology to any whose name or title we may inadvertently have left out.

We wish also to give special thanks to some very helpful allies who went out of their way to answer questions and furnish background materials for several of our stories. In this regard we would like to cite and thank Jeb Stuart Rosebrook, editor of the *William and Mary Alumni Magazine* and former associate editor for research at the magazine *Arizona Highways,* for his excellent advice and counsel (plus the very helpful books he lent us!); historian Matthew B. Wills for his encouragement, helpful book, and general information; and Harald Smyer and his wife, Mary, for taking turns showing us around Oakland, San Francisco, nearby Marin County, and the magnificent Pacific coastline below San Francisco, plus their gift of a most helpful history. In addition, we are most grateful for the help provided by the staff at the Stevens County (Kans.) Public Library; ranger Jill Harding and her ranger colleague Sally Freeman at the Fort Clatsop National Memorial, National Park Service, Astoria, Oregon; archaeologist Peggy McGuckian at the Bureau of Land Management field office in Winnemucca, Nevada; Victor Jones, librarian-in-charge, North Carolina Room, New Bern–Craven County Public Library in New Bern, North Carolina; and the staff at the Winchester Mystery House in San Jose, California. Archivists and other staffers at the state historical societies of North

Dakota, South Dakota, Utah, and Montana also were most helpful, and our thanks to them as well.

Steve Bell, our thanks to you too for hours spent over a hot computer helping to prepare our manuscript. And the same to our editor, Ed Curtis, at Cumberland House Publishing, along with president and publisher Ron Pitkin. And to our literary agent of note, Jenny Bent.

We also wish to thank the editors and publishers of *Military History* magazine for permission to reprint four Best Little Stories columns from that publication, titled herein as: 1836: Reunited at the Alamo; 1861: Civil War Intrusion; 1875: Model Indian Fighter; and 1887: "Stovepipe" Johnson Pursues His Dream. In addition, we owe our thanks to the editors and publishers of the *Country's Best Log Homes* magazine for permission to reprint the story 1884: Dude from the East.

Our Messages from the Past came from a variety of sources, some of them books, some carried on the Internet. In cases when it seemed relevant, we were able to mention the source in the accompanying text. Among those not so identified, Jack London's account of the San Francisco earthquake came from *A Treasury of Great Reporting,* edited by Louis L. Snyder and Richard B. Morris. In addition, those Messages from the Past consisting of quotes about the death of Jesse James (1882), White Bull's claim to have killed Custer (1876), John Wesley Powell entering the Grand Canyon (1869), and the last spike being driven to complete the transcontinental railroad (1869) all came from *Eyewitness to America: 500 years of America in the Words of Those Who Saw It Happen,* edited by David Colbert. Then, too, among the Internet sources furnishing our Messages from the Past, the San Francisco Museum's Internet site (www.sfmuseum.org) carries Ulysses S. Grant's impressions of the teeming city after the gold rush. Remaining Messages came from the books and memoirs cited or carried on the Internet. Meanwhile, the Lewis and Clark Trail Heritage Foundation's informative publication *We Proceeded On* served as a wonderful source for many of the facts in our stories about Lewis and Clark, as did the PBS Web site based on the eight-part 1996 documentary series *The West.*

Speaking of the Internet, anyone reading our book will notice a good many citations of Internet sources and perhaps wonder: How can we be sure they're reliable? To gather our facts, hadn't we better stick to books or other published accounts . . . in print? And one answer is, we do, to a large extent. But another is the fact that not all published-in-print accounts are necessarily reliable and accurate themselves. One has to sift, balance, and weigh one factor against another in the effort to determine what's correct and what's not. Our story on the death of George Armstrong Custer is a classic example of conflicting published-in-print accounts. Likewise, our story on mountain man John Colter's escape from his Blackfoot captors points out that our history of this event today largely is based upon the accounts given by two men claiming to have heard the story from the victim's own lips . . . and they report, in their own words, two very contradictory versions. One, for instance, says Colter's companion, John Potts, was riddled with bullets, and the other says he was riddled with arrows. And . . . guess what? Both accounts are reproduced verbatim on the Internet (as well as in a number of old-fashioned printed books). That's pretty close to primary material, right there. The only way to get closer to primary sources would be to have a sworn statement from an eyewitness or from Colter himself.

The fact is, the Internet actually provides quick and easy access to an incredibly wide-ranging world of primary materials such as first-person and eyewitness statements in short or long form, up to and including entire books. It also is a world of ex parte but contemporary third-person accounts, written or compiled at roughly the same time period as the events described. Still another Internet resource consists of traditional oral histories and various historical statements and/or publications produced sometime between the event and the present day. For instance, our story about Abraham Lincoln and Jefferson Davis serving at the same time and place in the Black Hawk War came from a history published about seventy years after the fact, so the historian author actually knew some of the participants and witnesses while he was young and they were old. He had access to documentation that families and others still held on to; he reproduced many letters and like statements verifying that the future U.S. president and future president of the Confederacy really were there, together, and all this material is available and easy to see on the Internet. Do a search under the heading "Black Hawk War," and it should turn up . . . just like that.

But, yes, just as in the case of printed material from either past or present, not all information on the Internet is reliable, and the reader or historical writer must make his or her own judgments. There are fools and knaves in both worlds as well as a lot of rank amateurs. So one must try to divine and judge the source. Thus any researcher on the history of Texas hardly can go wrong by calling up the *Handbook of*

Texas Online (www.tsha.utexas.edu/handbook/online), an encyclopedic reference work produced by the University of Texas and the Texas
State Historical Association and boasting more than twenty-three
thousand entries. Or searching for primary materials on the history of
San Francisco? For a raft of first-person statements by people who were
there from the start, check out the City of San Francisco Museum site.
For almost anything American, consult the various state historical societies. Moreover, hundreds of cities, towns, and counties have Web sites
of their own with histories, even memoirs, included. Many publications—newspapers and magazines—offer access to their archives,
sometimes for a fee, often not. On a more national scale, the Library of
Congress and many colleges and universities and hundreds of museums and history-minded organizations offer historical materials once
only available in printed form and requiring a trip to a bricks-and-
mortar building *somewhere,* be it bookstore, library, or museum.

The Internet is rife also with genealogical research, often by amateurs simply digging into their own family histories, but their findings,
on view for all to see, may sometimes be of interest to outside
researchers as well. Meanwhile, even the so-called amateurs or hobby-
ists, like some self-publishers of yore, can be both helpful and reliable as
historical sources. You can hardly beat Duncan, Oklahoma, newspaperman Glen Seeber's Along the Chisholm Trail Web site (www.
texhoma.net/~glencbr) for attractive display and complete historical
coverage of the item in question. The same goes for the voluminous
Sons of DeWitt Colony Web site (dewittcolony@swbell.net) on early
Texas history, maintained by Wallace L. McKeehan, who proudly
explains (on the Web site) that his forebears include a defender of the
Alamo and other early Texans.

Researchers of American history also will find a gold mine of information in the publications, ranging from newsletters to full-blown, full-
color magazines, issued by various state historical societies and specialty
organizations. Already mentioned here, one such publication is the
Lewis and Clark Trail Heritage Foundation's quarterly magazine *We Proceeded On,* an excellent source for anyone interested in the great Lewis
and Clark Expedition, especially during its bicentennial years of 2003–6.
Finally but far from least, and with the bias of personal association, we
would like gratefully to cite as additional invaluable sources for our stories herein, the Primedia historical magazines *Wild West, Military History,*
and *American History* and their Web site (http://history.about.com).

In sum, without being able to stand on the backs of all those mentioned in the foregoing and on the many additional sources cited in our text throughout, this book would not have been possible. And so we thank one and all, and we hope our readers will be moved, in some cases at least, to dig more deeply by delving into the sources cited, whether in print as books or magazines or accessible electronically on the Internet. Either way, have a good time. History can be fun.

C. Brian Kelly
Ingrid Smyer-Kelly
Charlottesville, Virginia
May 2002

The Vanishing West

MESSAGE FROM THE PAST: At Charleston, South Carolina, on March 31, 1902, one hundred years ago, Owen Wister, author of the quintessential western, *The Virginian,* wrote these sad and chilling words:

> Had you left New York or San Francisco at ten o'clock this morning, by noon the day after tomorrow you could step out at Cheyenne. There you would stand at the heart of the world that is the subject of my picture, yet you would look around you in vain for the reality. It is a vanished world. No journeys, save those which memory can take, will bring you to it now. The mountains are there, far and shining, and the sunlight, and the infinite earth, and the air that seems forever the true fountain of youth—but where is the buffalo, and the wild antelope, and where the horseman with his pasturing thousands? So like its old self does the sagebrush seem when revisited, that you wait for the horseman to appear.
>
> But he will never come again. He rides in his historic yesterday. You will no more see him gallop out of the unchanging silence than you will see Columbus on the unchanging sea come sailing from Palos with his caravels.
>
> And yet the horseman is still so near our day that in some chapters of this book [*The Virginian*], which were published separately at the close of the nineteenth century, the present tense was used. It is true no longer. In those chapters it has been changed, and verbs like "is" and "have" now read "was" and "had." Time has flowed faster than my ink.

After a hundred *more* years, we come to the season in which *this* book was written, and the mountains still remain, shining at that, but so much more time has flowed past, so much more has changed, so many of those heady days and sights, with their incredible characters, have long since gone by, and all so very fast. Exploration and settlement of the West, the end of America's frontier life, took up the better part of a century, the nineteenth century, and yet it all happened so fast . . . in just the blink of an eye.

BEST LITTLE STORIES
from the
WILD WEST

★ Part 1 ★
First Explorations

Come Work for Me

The young army officer had been in Detroit, pretty far west the way the country's map looked in those days—you could even say *way out west*, real frontier territory. So he didn't see the letter and its beguiling, come-work-for-me message until he returned to base at Pittsburgh. That was on a Friday, too late to make that day's outgoing mail. Even so, he wasted no time in answering, and . . . did he ever want that job! "I most cordially acquiesce, and with pleasure accept the office," he fired back on March 10, 1801, to the man in Washington, D.C. No further "motives" were needed, he hastily added, than to be considered of service to his country or useful to his prospective employer.

He in fact already was making arrangements with his commanding officer in the First Infantry Regiment "to get forward to the City of Washington with all possible despatch."

Asking first for the use of three pack horses, a few packing boxes, and some extra lash rope, he set out right away. But beset by a lame horse and roads turned into mud by spring rains, he didn't slog into the federal capital until April 1. His new boss, unfortunately, had just left the day before for his home in Virginia.

Since they already knew each other, no great matter . . . the honorable captain had a few lingering matters to take care of in the capital anyway. For one, as departing paymaster of his regiment, he had to turn over his records to a successor, a Lt. Ninian Pinkney. And certainly he could count upon his former neighbor from Albemarle County, Virginia, to return soon to resume his own duties in Washington. More specifically, in the President's House . . . today known as the White House.

There Thomas Jefferson, inaugurated on March 4 as third president of the United States, had promised in his offer of employment that young Meriwether Lewis would earn a small salary (five hundred dollars a year) as Jefferson's private secretary, plus food and lodging "as you would be one of my family."

Despite a shared background in Virginia, they of course weren't quite "family." Lewis, only in his late twenties, had been raised at Locust Hill, a plantation bordering Ivy Creek, some miles away from the older Jefferson's mountaintop estate, Monticello. They in fact presented quite a contrast in style—Jefferson, now in his late fifties, was tall, slim, elegant, sophisticated, and Lewis, bowlegged, introspective, sometimes moody, was a bit unpolished in manners and lacking in grammatical and spelling skills. As historian John Bakeless noted, "Most people would have said that a worse private secretary for the President of the United States could hardly be imagined."

Clearly that's not what Jefferson thought. Even though others had been pleading for the post in Jefferson's intimate circle, it seems none but Lewis would do. Jefferson wrote that his rivals for the job "will have no answer till I hear from you."

But why the blue-eyed, fair-haired lad from Albemarle? Was it just a case of neighborly nepotism that moved Jefferson? The president's own response to such questions was stated in his offer. Writing to Lewis on February 23, 1801, Jefferson had said he wanted a secretary with a "capacity" to help "in the private concerns of the household" while also contributing to "the mass of information which it is interesting for the administration to acquire."

There perhaps was an early, if unconscious hint of what yet was to come . . . of the grand and noble purpose to which Jefferson eventually would assign his Albemarle protégé. Indeed, Jefferson went on to say: "Your knoledge of the Western country, of the army and all it's interests & relations has rendered it desirable for public as well as private purposes that you should be engaged in . . . [this] office."

Obviously, it was not a glorified clerk's job that Jefferson had in mind. As the third president surely knew, Lewis since childhood had been an outdoorsman, a lover of the wild, a happy wanderer in wood and field. Further, he had served in the army for the past seven years. He had joined the Virginia militia as a private in 1794 at the age of twenty, served in the abortive Whiskey Rebellion staged by angry Pennsylvania farmers, then had become an officer in the regular army, ultimately serving as paymaster for the First Infantry Regiment. Ironically, he once was in a rifle company commanded by Lt. William

Clark, also with family ties to Albemarle County, Virginia, both of them serving the frontier army under the overall command of Gen. "Mad" Anthony Wayne of Revolutionary War fame. Then, too, just the year before Jefferson's call, Lewis had commanded the infantry elements of Capt. Isaac Guion's expedition into future Mississippi to take over posts being given up by the departing Spanish.

While Lewis the military careerist achieved good marks in general, he had fallen afoul of a court-martial along the way, and it is not known today if Jefferson was aware of this. Either way, and quite fortunately for Lewis, he had been exonerated of charges that he had engaged in ungentlemanly (and drunken) conduct toward a fellow officer, even challenging him to a duel. Had a conviction appeared on his record, Jefferson likely would have known . . . and likely would have passed over his young Albemarle colleague for the great venture to come.

As it was, the exonerated Lewis suited Jefferson to a T. No matter that he would come up short in terms of normal secretarial skills (Jefferson himself had those in abundance). "None of these things really mattered," wrote historian Bakeless in 1947. "This particular secretary was going to have duties—some very special duties—in the next year or so, though Mr. Jefferson was not yet ready to admit all that he was planning." Perhaps, added Bakeless, "it was not all quite clear yet" even to Jefferson.

Nor did Jefferson and Lewis plunge immediately into the great "Discovery" scheme that makes Lewis so famous today.

Since the former paymaster knew the small American army and its officers quite well, the president first put Lewis to work identifying officers with Federalist political views, in contrast to Jefferson's own Republican politics of the day. That done, with consequent dismissals in more extreme cases, Lewis really did spend time on clerical-secretarial duties. He copied and hand-delivered Jefferson's first State of the Union message to Congress as simply that, a written message. He also stepped out of the President's House many an early morning to shoot game for the presidential table—wildlife still was abundant in the wooded terrain surrounding the brand-new federal capital by the Potomac.

Inside the still roughhewn presidential mansion, Lewis lived in a cavernous, unfinished chamber where Abigail Adams used to hang her laundry—the resplendent East Room of today. The education that now came the young man's way was, however, far from rough-hewn or unfinished. For in the future White House he lived alone, except for a handful of slaves and servants, with America's widowed Renaissance man as constant companion. As a result, young Lewis for two years met Jefferson's visitors of all kinds, dined with his friends and associates, ran his errands among the fledgling nation's high and mighty, shared the great man's library, and of course spent time in conversation with him on a daily basis.

And surely, such exposure, such a "growing" experience, had its beneficial effects.

Among other new attributes, biographer Stephen Ambrose suggests in *Undaunted Courage,* Lewis learned a crucial skill that still commands our attention today. "[F]rom someone—who else could it have been but Jefferson?—he learned to write." No doubt, says Ambrose. "A distinct difference is evident between Lewis's writing before 1800 and after 1802. His sense of pace, his timing, his word choice, his rhythm, his similes and analogies all improved. He sharpened his descriptive powers. He learned how to catch a reader up in his own response to events and places, to express his emotions naturally and effectively."

No doubt, too, Lewis was still learning, still growing when an electrifying book made its way across the Atlantic from England and into Jefferson's hands. It was Canadian explorer Alexander Mackenzie's account of his overland passage in 1793 through the Rocky Mountains to the West Coast as the first white man to cross the North American continent to the Pacific. Jefferson, long fascinated with the notion of exploring the virginal western empire beyond the Missouri and Mississippi Rivers, had ordered the book as soon as he heard of it. He and Lewis were both at Monticello in Charlottesville when it arrived in the summer of 1802. And, says Ambrose, "They devoured it."

The Mackenzie book openly urged the explorer's sponsoring North West Company and the British to colonize the Northwest and develop a dominant fur trade in the region. His words hit the two Virginians like a bombshell. Adds Ambrose: "[Mackenzie] thought big and he thought like a businessman," but "the fire he lit . . . was not under the company, or the British government." Rather, the fire was "under Jefferson."

Indeed, Mackenzie's book "galvanized Jefferson into manic activity" . . . and changed Meriwether Lewis's life "overnight."

Now came a crash course for Lewis in geography, botany, astronomy, and the navigational arts, all at the feet of the remarkable savant of Monticello. Soon traveling to Philadelphia, Lewis would learn even more of mapmaking, astronomy, topography, field medicine, and similar sciences from top professionals. In Jefferson's personal library he would find all there was to know—in writing—about the western frontier.

Physically, too, he was well prepared for the combination ordeal and adventure that lay ahead. Just over six feet in height and lean, he was in excellent condition. Moreover, both as a youth in Virginia and as an army veteran, he had learned how to take care of himself in the wild.

Naturally, too, he was used to discipline and could be considered fiercely loyal—especially to Jefferson, a mentor since Lewis's boyhood.

It of course was the decision to mount an expedition across the Rockies to the Pacific that had spurred all this sudden activity by Jefferson's protégé, a decision made sometime in the late summer or early fall of 1802, with the Mackenzie book as catalyst. As Ambrose relates, however, it is not known who initiated that fateful decision—Jefferson or Lewis. Either Jefferson told Lewis to prepare for the expedition, "Or Captain Lewis talked President Jefferson into giving him command." Further: "We don't know when or how Jefferson made his decision that there would be an American answer to Mackenzie and that Lewis would lead it. Evidently he consulted no one, asked no one for advice, entertained no nominees or volunteers, other than Lewis. This was the most coveted command in the history of exploration of North America. Jefferson was confident he had the right man under his roof."

Thus, just two centuries ago, America was about to begin discovery of her vast and remote West, not only the eight hundred thousand square miles of the new Louisiana Purchase, but far beyond as well. But first there was the matter of finding the second half of the historical equation known today as the Lewis *and Clark* Expedition.

1 8 0 3
Essential Partner

He couldn't quite spell the word ocean, but he found the Pacific and described it as an "emence Ocian" anyway. He served as an officer in the army of the "Untied" States. He and "Cap Lewers," as co-captains of the Corps of Discovery, would make sensational history together.

They were west of the Mississippi and traveling along the path of the Missouri, but exactly which river did he mean when he made note in their journals of the "Missopie"?

What the heck . . . not everybody in those frontier days had time or opportunity to learn how to speak and spell "good." Even the unusually learned Thomas Jefferson could commit a gaffe or two in his writings.

Laugh as we may today over William Clark's inventive mangling of the English language of his own day, the important point about his role in the great Lewis and Clark Expedition is the fact that his contributions to its success were on a par with those of Lewis, who had been pampered, doted over, and groomed for the venture over a two-year period by none other than Jefferson himself. Clark entered the picture with no such advantage . . . but he had others that counted very well on his behalf.

For one thing, born in 1770, he almost was a native of the same Albemarle County that produced both Jefferson and Lewis (born in 1774). As another legacy in his favor, Clark was the youngest brother of the Revolutionary War hero George Rogers Clark, conqueror of the Old Northwest (the Illinois country). As was well known to the contemporary Jefferson, George really had been born in Albemarle, but the Clark family had moved to Caroline County, also in Virginia, before William was born. They in fact had moved on to a plantation near Louisville, Kentucky, when young William was fourteen. And soon after, William, the youngest of six brothers in all, began to earn his own credits.

By 1789 he was to be found among the militiamen fighting hostile tribes in the Ohio Valley. By 1792 he had become a regular army officer, a lieutenant destined to serve under the command of Gen. "Mad" Anthony Wayne for the next four years. As one result, Clark took part in the benchmark 1794 battle of Fallen Timbers in northwestern Ohio, during which Wayne, two thousand regulars, and one thousand militiamen battled thirteen hundred or more Indians pinned against the Maumee River. The result was the greatest victory of the campaigns against the Indians of the Old Northwest. All this time, too, Clark was expanding, sharpening, polishing, and exhibiting the leadership skills that would stand him in such good stead as co-leader of the Corps of Discovery just a decade or so later.

When a young Lewis, fresh from his court-martial acquittal, was assigned to Clark's company of sharpshooters, he spent roughly the first half of 1796 under an amiable fellow Virginian also standing about six feet tall, but marked by a distinctive thatch of red hair. As Lewis quickly realized, William Clark was a man of impressive accomplishments in areas of considerable interest to Lewis himself. "Clark was a tough woodsman accustomed to command; he had been a company commander and had led a party down the Mississippi as far as Natchez," noted Stephen Ambrose in his book *Undaunted Courage*. "He had a way with enlisted men, without ever getting familiar."

Of considerable importance ten years later, Clark "was a better terrestrial surveyor than Lewis, and a better waterman." Clark also proved to be a whiz at mapmaking. In sum, adding to their all-important compatibility, the two men together offered a combination of skills that augured well for their remarkable partnership. Various historians have noted that each possessed strongpoints that compensated for the other's shortcomings. Together they made a seamless partnership.

Not much is known about the interaction of the two Virginians during their six months of frontier army duty together, but clearly, added Ambrose, "in that six months together they had taken each other's measure," and "they liked what they saw."

Meanwhile, Clark resigned from the army in mid-1796, partly because of ill health and partly so he could spend time with his aging parents at their Mulberry Hill plantation in Kentucky. They died soon after, leaving the Clark homestead to young William, but he sold it to a brother in 1800. William then joined older brother George in Clarksville, Indiana—across the Ohio River from Louisville—in an effort to help the older Revolutionary War hero salvage his sinking finances and seek compensation for his military services, which he had often financed from his own pocket. Unfortunately—if not yet evident—the older Clark brother had a drinking problem that was no boon for his financial or physical well-being in his later years.

Thus the youngest Clark, William, spent the next several years tending to family and personal business. He still was so engaged when, out of the blue in the early summer of 1803, came a letter that changed his life . . . and the history of the nation. It of course was from his old friend Meriwether Lewis, and in it, Lewis extended an invitation for Clark to join him as co-leader of Jefferson's proposed expedition up the Missouri River and across to the Pacific Ocean.

As Lewis described the mission: "My plan is to descend the Ohio in a keeled boat thence up the Mississippi to the mouth of the Missourie, and up that river as far as it's navigation is practicable with a keeled boat, there to prepare canoes of bark or raw-hides, and proceed to it's source and if practicable pass over to the waters of the Columbia or Origan River and by descending it reach the Western Ocean."

To this, Lewis added the highly personal note that "believe me there is no man on earth with whom I should feel equal pleasure in sharing [all the thrills of the enterprise] as with yourself."

For an adventurous spirit like Clark, still young, more vigorous and healthy, probably a bit restless by now, it was an incredible offer—not only an opportunity to go along, but the promise of co-leadership with his former army friend . . . and all with President Jefferson's enthused blessing as well! Indeed, wrote Lewis also, the president "expresses an anxious wish that you would consent to join me in this enterprise." Not only that, Jefferson authorized Lewis to offer Clark a captain's commission.

The promised captaincy fell through and would prove to be an embarrassment when the two men joined up later in 1803, but Lewis generously insisted that Clark go by the rank of "captain" without letting their men know that his official rank was lieutenant. And so they proceeded, equal in all matters for the more than two years and more than eight thousand miles spent as partners in one of the greatest exploratory trips ever undertaken . . . with more than fifty Indian tribes encountered, multiple volumes of journal notes produced, various new plant and animal species found, uncharted terrains traversed, surprising climatology observations made, new rivers and new mountains discovered, a continent crossed.

And through it all, Clark proved his unwavering mettle at every step. As Robert B. Betts wrote in the November 1980 issue of the Lewis and Clark Trail Heritage Foundation's publication, *We Proceeded On:* "William Clark was a fearless and resourceful man. In an extremely tense confrontation with the Teton Sioux, when warriors of that tribe threatened to attack the . . . party, he boldly drew his sword, signaled his men to prepare for action, and faced the Tetons down."

Similarly, and yet differently too, Clark later found the right answer when he needed to seek food from "some sullen Indians along the Columbia River." Recalled Betts of this instance: "[H]e adroitly won them over by using a magnet to make the needle of his compass spin and by throwing an artillery fuse into a sleeping fire, making flames magically flare and change color."

Never mind that Betts also noted Clark's twenty-seven different spellings of the five-letter word "Sioux" in his journals, along with his fifteen variations of the girl-woman Sacagawea's common-law husband Touissant Charbonneau's last name, none of them right. Never mind, because as Betts himself also wrote, a bit less lightheartedly, "Throughout the long journey across the trans-Mississippi West during the years 1804–1806, Clark exhibited these qualities [of fearlessness and resourcefulness] time and again."

Additional note: After the Teton Sioux backed down, the Americans spent three uneasy days with the tribe. One must wonder what Clark's thoughts were when his men at one point carried him from the riverbank to the Indians' council fire—"seated on a buffalo robe . . . as a sign of respect," wrote Geoffrey C. Ward in the companion book to the PBS television series *The West.* Whatever Clark's thoughts, he certainly did not leave with any friendly feelings for these particular Indians, who remained suspect both for their apparent ties to the British and their propensity to intervene with any passing Missouri traffic and demand tribute like the Barbary pirates of the same era. Wrote Ward: "[T]he Indians made no promises of future peace, and the Americans were in no position to force them to abandon the British." For months after, Ward noted, Clark was still calling them "the vilest miscreants of the savage race" and predicting that until stopped by American military power, they "must ever remain the pirates of the Missouri."

1804
Tyrant of the Omahas

"After the rain was over," wrote William Clark on August 11, 1804, "Capt. Lewis myself & 10 men asssended the Hill where the Mahars King Black Bird was burried 4 years ago. A mound of earth about 12 feet Diameter at the base, & 6 feet high is raised over him turfed, and a pole 8 feet high in the center on this pole we fixed a white flag bound with red blue & white."

For all his misspellings, Clark was right on target, for indeed buried in the mound just four years before had been the legendary Omaha chief Blackbird, along with his favorite horse. One has to wonder how much either Clark or Lewis really knew about the once-great and, it seems, thoroughly Machiavellian Omaha chief, since much of his story is legend, hearsay passed along and passed along . . . stories of widespread fame, power, cunning, streaks of humanity . . . and cruelty.

Blackbird apparently held sway late in the eighteenth century in a village of earth lodges on Omaha Creek in today's Nebraska. Home for an estimated eleven hundred Indians, the village was called Tonwantonga ("large village"). More generally, the Omahas tended to live in earth lodges along the Missouri River from the mouth of the Platte River north to the Little Bow River, observed Nebraska historian Addison Erwin Sheldon in his *History and Stories of Nebraska* (see http://www.ukans.edu/~kansite/hvn/books/nbstory). The Omahas and the closely related Otoe (or Oto) and Ponca tribes spoke similar languages and had moved up the Missouri from the Southeast a few hundred years before, Sheldon noted. "All three belonged to the great Sioux family of Indians and were relatives of the Sioux nation living northwest of them. The Otoe and Omaha tribes numbered about 3,000 each and the Ponca between 1,000 and 2,000."

If the Omahas "belonged" to the great Sioux family, however, that didn't mean they got along with the Sioux who lived nearby. These Sioux made up a nation of ten to twenty thousand who, following the buffalo herds, roamed the country north and west of the Omaha. Throw in the Pawnee, Cheyenne, and Arapahoe who also lived or wandered in future Nebraska, and the result is an Indian population of perhaps forty thousand when the white man first appeared in their territory in the 1700s. As the first white visitors discovered, added Sheldon: "The Sioux, the Cheyennes and the Arapahoes dwelt in skin tents, or tepees, and hunted for a living. The Omahas, Otoes, Poncas and Pawnees built large houses, called earth lodges, out of sod and poles, but also used tepees. They raised crops during certain seasons and hunted at other times."

While the Nebraska tribes at first were friendly to their early white visitors, "especially to the French," they were at constant war among themselves, with the hunting, or "wild," tribes usually fighting the crop-raising tribes. "How these wars would have ended if the white men had not come cannot be told, but the wild Indians were gaining ground at that time," Sheldon noted.

Into this evolving, turbulent mix was born, sometime early in the eighteenth century, the future tyrant of the Omahas, Blackbird—"the first Nebraska Indian whose name we know," said Sheldon. And if this was somewhat of a war zone, Blackbird seemed to fit right in . . . as a boy he was captured by the Sioux, but he escaped. Later he would fight them so fiercely that "they feared his name."

But he also was a scourge to his cousins the Pawnees, the Otoes, and the Poncas. After becoming a chief, "He led his warriors against the Pawnees and burned one of their large towns. He took scalps from the Otoes and from the Kanzas tribes."

When the Poncas conducted a raid against his precincts, Blackbird went after them, too. Gathering his warriors and pursuing the raiders, he caught up to the Poncas and "drove them" into a primitive "fort" of hastily thrown-up dirt walls. Since the Omahas greatly outnumbered the raiders, they sent out an emissary with a peace pipe, perhaps hoping to survive by negotiating the return of the horses and women they had taken in the raid.

But Blackbird wasn't interested. He killed the emissary on the spot. "Another herald was treated in the same way. Then the head chief of the Poncas sent his daughter, a young girl, in her finest Indian suit of white buckskin, with the peace pipe."

This time, Blackbird liked what he saw. He took the pipe, smoked it, "and there was peace between the tribes." Moreover, the Ponca girl became his favorite wife.

If Blackbird was hard on his enemies, he was absolutely unconscionable in his treatment of his own people.

When the first Spanish and French traders traveled up the Missouri to barter for furs, Blackbird was more than willing to deal with them— and to cheat his fellow tribesmen at the same time. He had a favorite hill overlooking the river, from which he could see up and down the shining water for miles. He or his lookouts could spot the approaching traders far in advance of their arrival. For their part, the traders, struggling upriver against the current, always welcomed the sight of the great hill, noted Sheldon, "for they knew great springs of cold water gushed from the sandstone rock at the foot of the hill, and there were rest and food and friendship for the white men in the lodges of the Omaha village."

When the traders arrived, in fact, they were taken to Blackbird's lodge, where they were asked to spread out all their trade items. "Blackbird then selected the things he wished—blankets, tobacco, whiskey, powder, bullets, beads and red paint—and laid them to one side, not offering any pay for them."

Next, the chief's tribesmen were asked to bring in their furs to trade with the white visitors. "No one was allowed to dispute the prices fixed by the white trader, who was careful to put them high enough to pay five times over for all the goods taken by the chief." Thus Blackbird never paid for his favorite items; his people did. "Blackbird and the traders grew rich together, but his people grew poor and began to complain."

Complaining turned out to be a deadly mistake for his subjects, because one of the traders, noticing the restlessness, gave the chief a supply of arsenic and taught him how to use it. "After that the terror of Blackbird and his mysterious power grew in the tribe. He became a prophet as well as a chief. When anyone opposed him Blackbird foretold his death within a certain time and within that time a sudden and violent disease carried the victim off in great agony. Before long all his rivals disappeared and the people agreed to everything Blackbird wished."

He claimed to have powerful "medicine" in other ways, too. "Once when following the trail of a hostile war party across the prairies he fired his rifle often into the hoofprints of their horses, telling his band it would cripple them so that they would be overtaken." Powerful "medicine"? More likely he was shrewd enough to see that his war party was overtaking the enemy party and decided to take advantage of the fact. To wit: "He did overtake and kill them all and his tribe looked upon the fact as proof of the wonderful effect of his 'medicine.'"

His bad temper, however, brought him personal grief. Remember the Ponca maiden who became his favorite wife? She for some time "had great influence over him," but not enough. One day, in a violent temper, he killed her with a knife. Then he was grief-stricken. "He covered his head with a buffalo robe and sat down by the dead body, refusing to eat or sleep. He answered no one. The tribe feared that he would starve to death. One of them brought a child and, laying it on the ground, put Blackbird's foot upon its neck. This touched the chief's heart. He threw off the buffalo robe, forgot his deep sorrow and resumed his duties."

But now came the real curse of the Omahas, a tyrant more deadly even than Blackbird with his arsenic . . . and there was nothing that he could do about it. "This was the smallpox, the white man's disease which the Indians had never known. They could not understand how it traveled from lodge to lodge and from village to village. The fever and the fearful blotches drove them wild. Some of them left their villages and rushed out to the prairies to die alone. Others set fire to their houses and killed their wives and children."

All told, smallpox killed two-thirds of the Omaha tribe, Sheldon reported in his Nebraska history. And one of the victims, toward the end of the epidemic, was Blackbird himself. "His friends gathered around his dying bed to hear his last word. He ordered them to bury him on the top of the great hill which rose several hundred feet above the Missouri and from which he could see up and down the river for thirty miles."

Blackbird Hill of course. "On the top of this hill Blackbird desired to be buried, seated on his favorite horse so that his spirit might overlook the entire Omaha country and first see the boats of the white men as they came up the river."

And so it was done. The unfortunate horse "was led to the summit of the hill with the dead chief firmly fastened upon his back." Next, presumably, the horse was killed. "Then the sod and dirt were piled about them in a great mound until both were buried from sight. A pole was set in the mound and upon it were hung scalps Blackbird had taken in battle. From time to time food for the spirit of the dead was placed upon the mound by the few Omahas who survived the smallpox scourge of 1800."

When Lewis and Clark visited Blackbird Hill on their way up the Missouri in 1804, the mound and the pole were still there. The mound remained intact for some time. "All the early writers mention the mound," wrote Sheldon. "It was the great landmark of the Nebraska shore." Eventually, though, it eroded away, to leave behind only the legends and stories about Blackbird the Omaha chief. "Stories told in this way," Sheldon also noted, "are often changed in the telling. We cannot say how far they are changed, but whether much or little, they are all we are ever likely to know of the life of the first noted Nebraska Indian."

1 8 0 6
Jefferson's Forgotten Expedition

His neighbors in New Bern, North Carolina, knew him simply as a small-town physician with a somewhat peppery disposition . . . and yet his name as an early American explorer so easily could have been added to those of Lewis and Clark, Zebulon Pike, John Wesley Powell, John C. Frémont, and so many others. As it was, Virginia-born Peter Custis's brief moment in the historical sun is largely forgotten. Even today, who has ever heard of President Thomas Jefferson's ambitious Freeman and Custis Expedition? Jefferson's once-vaunted "Grand Excursion" into the American Southwest is a widely forgotten footnote.

That largely was the case even in New Bern during Peter Custis's day. There the riverside townspeople knew him as a widowed doctor who later married a colleague's daughter. They knew him as the father of six, two of them saucy sisters destined to give the occupying Yankees fits during the Civil War. They knew him, wrote one contemporary, as "somewhat blunt and caustic" in manner but also as "the life of all social companies in which he appeared."

Presumably, the good townspeople of New Bern also would have been aware of his birth on Virginia's Eastern Shore as a member of the distinguished Custis family that gave young America the familiar name Martha Custis Washington . . . stemming from the widowed Martha Dandridge Custis's marriage to George Washington.

As they knew also, Peter Custis arrived in town about 1808, lived nearly all his adult life there, took care of his patients, married, fathered his children, died, and was buried there in 1842. All in all, a quiet, constructive but historically unremarkable life.

But that wasn't the full story. For Peter Custis came to New Bern from a dramatic brush with history as an explorer and naturalist who, on an expedition mounted by Jefferson, had ventured into western territory so new to Americans it was thought to be inhabited by tigerlike creatures, possibly even by unicorns.

Custis, a twenty-five-year-old medical student at the time—but also America's first academically trained naturalist—didn't find anything quite so exotic, but he did catalog 267 species, including 22 new to scientists of the day.

The still-youthful Custis was destined to wind up an unrequited explorer for a combination of reasons. First and foremost, the Freeman and Custis Expedition—planned by Jefferson as a southwestern counterpart to the more northerly Lewis and Clark Expedition—was turned back by the Spanish, who were still aggressively occupying the American Southwest. Then, too, the very success of the same Lewis and Clark eclipsed the abortive, nearly simultaneous venture up the Red River in the Southwest. Finally, the official government report of the young naturalist's findings condensed the text and botched his Latin descriptions.

In sum, he and expedition leader Thomas Freeman have gone down in the annals of Americana as historical nobodies, their ambitious probe of the virginal American Southwest widely overlooked today.

And yet, at the start, it had seemed so logical, so auspicious, so full of promise. At least that's what Jefferson thought when he summoned an eager young man to dinner at the President's House in Washington, D.C., in November 1805. And surely the air crackled with barely subdued excitement as the president laid out the broad parameters of a trip into uncharted western territory, a first-class expedition that would require a leader with just the right stamina, command skills, and scientific knowledge for the job. And, yes, that leader would need a partner or two at the head of the expedition; he also would need a naturalist, and together they would need a party of hardy souls to accompany them into the wild and potentially hostile country west of the lower Mississippi.

It all was so similar to the instructions Jefferson had given Lewis and Clark just months before! But Jefferson this time was making plans, discussing possibilities—in effect brainstorming—with Freeman, an Irish-born surveyor and civil engineer who had done survey work in Washington, D.C., Florida, and Louisiana. Especially in the wake of the Louisiana Purchase of 1803, it seems that Jefferson was anxious to clarify conflicting boundary claims in the Southwest and to begin a study of the region's scientific parameters—its geography, geology, wildlife and plant life.

Jefferson also considered it vital to establish friendly trade relations with the region's native tribes, already rumored to be unhappy with their Spanish neighbors.

Figuratively speaking, Jefferson wanted an exploratory package similar in shape, size, and goals to the Lewis and Clark Expedition, at that point already under way. Jefferson's southerly "Grand Excursion" would run parallel to the Lewis and Clark northerly exploration of the Missouri River corridor into the Northwest and on to the Pacific Coast.

As early as April 14, 1804—a moment when Lewis and Clark were only preparing to commence their historic mission—Jefferson had composed a seven-page letter of instruction for the as-yet-unchosen leader of the southwestern expedition. Amazingly, Jefferson's "grand excursion" letter was never published until 1984, according to University of Montana historian Dan Flores. Elaborating upon the letter's historical importance in the spring 2000 issue of *Montana* magazine, Flores wrote, "Jefferson's letter was based closely upon his June 20, 1803, letter of instructions to Meriwether Lewis, a letter often praised as a classic expression of Enlightenment scientific instruction."

At first, however, Jefferson's new letter of instruction languished for lack of an addressee—for lack of a potential expedition leader. "[A]pparently there existed in America few men who could combine leadership qualities, the requisite scientific education, and a woodsman's physique," Flores further explained in his book *Jefferson & Southwestern Exploration.*

For this alternate exploration of the Louisiana Purchase territory and beyond, incidentally, Jefferson already had done a good deal of the necessary groundwork. Rarely lacking in extensive resources, he had been in touch with the Scottish émigré scientist Sir William Dunbar, then in Natchez, Mississippi. Dunbar answered Jefferson's questions with a letter surmising a huge length to the Red River, mentioning its possible sources in mountains of pure or partial salt, and repeating trader stories of unicorns and giant water serpents abounding in unexplored river reaches.

In reality also, the allegedly uncharted territory abounded with its own Indian peoples, and it already had been crossed and recrossed for more than two centuries by European interlopers—Spanish and French explorers, missionaries, traders, and settlers. The fact was, exploring the mysterious Red River would take "Americans threateningly close to Spanish settlements and dangerously accessible to Spanish presidios," wrote Flores.

Then, too, Jefferson and his fellow Americans had an entirely incorrect notion of the topography involved. Rather than flowing from the "Stony Mountains," as the southern ranges of the Rockies then were called, the Red River in reality emanated from the desert plateau in the southern high plains called the Llano Estacado. Originally, Jefferson also wanted his explorers to chart the Arkansas River on their way home, but it soon became clear that crossing overland to the sources of the Arkansas River far to the north and east of the Red River would have been totally impractical.

At Jefferson's behest, Dunbar and Philadelphia chemist George Hunter made plans for an expedition up the Red River in 1804, but they wound up making a much more limited survey of a tributary, the Ouachita River, and central Arkansas. The middle-aged, sometimes ailing Dunbar simply wasn't up to the far more demanding Red River foray, while Hunter returned to more homebound interests back in Philadelphia. So the way was cleared for Jefferson to recruit Thomas Freeman, young Peter Custis, and company.

Custis at the time was a medical student at the University of Pennsylvania, but his blue-blood family connections in Virginia—the Byrds, the Randolphs, the Lees, and by Martha's marriage, George Washington—certainly did no harm to his chances of appointment to the expedition. He would serve as its naturalist for the outstanding wage of three dollars a day plus expenses.

As other pieces of the endeavor fell into place early in 1806, Capt. Richard Sparks, a veteran woodsman and soldier, took his place on the roster as commander of the expedition's military section, but the exploratory party of fifty or more still would be known as the Freeman and Custis Expedition, because field leader Freeman and the young naturalist Custis were the expedition's only journal-keepers. Custis, it might also be mentioned, came on board as the new nation's first academically trained naturalist assigned to a government mission. The mission itself, costing eleven thousand dollars in government funds, would be the largest exploratory party the fledgling American government had sent into the field thus far.

The group set out from the mouth of the Red River on the Mississippi in Louisiana on May 1, 1806, well aware there would be repercussions once they entered Spanish-claimed lands to the west. As the Americans knew, the Spanish knew they were coming. Custis himself wrote, "This expedition seems to have thrown their whole Country into commotion."

What Freeman, Custis, and company did *not* know was the fact that the Spanish had been "tipped off" by an American, Maj. Gen.

James Wilkinson, governor of the Upper Louisiana Territory and, just three years before, a participant in negotiations completing final details for the Louisiana Purchase itself. As a result of Wilkinson's news, the Spanish would attempt to intercept both the Lewis and Clark foray to the north and the southwestern venture led by Freeman.

As part of the scheming Wilkinson's double game, oddly enough, the general himself had urged Jefferson to authorize the exploration of the vast lands included in the Louisiana Purchase. He also, for a time, apparently was a coconspirator in former Vice President Aaron Burr's schemes to create a private mini-empire in the Mississippi Valley. Wilkinson, however, later turned on Burr and testified against him in Burr's trial for treason.

While it's a complex story, a mysterious episode in American history not fully understood even today, it appears that Wilkinson may have wanted to stir up a war between New Spain and young America in hopes of personal gain, perhaps a huge land grant from a grateful benefactor . . . the Spanish.

In any case, in May 1806 the men of the Freeman and Custis Expedition were on their way, knowing that the potentially hostile Spanish would be awaiting them somewhere upriver. They were, however, quite ignorant of Wilkinson's machinations.

With Jefferson's "grand excursion" plan now limited to the Red River alone, the explorers were to follow the meandering stream to its source, a journey expected to take a year and extend for thirteen hundred miles. Not so incidentally, it seems that Jefferson considered the Red "next to the Missouri the most interesting water of the Mississippi."

Proceeding up this "interesting water" from central Louisiana, Jefferson's explorers poled their barges where the water depth would allow and negotiated portages on foot when rocks and rapids blocked the river, all without major incident. As they entered an ecoparadise replete with buffalo, bear, two-foot woodpeckers, and flocks of brightly colored parrots, Custis happily collected specimens and jotted down careful notes. Still, the real treasure trove for him—and the most interesting geographic feature the party encountered—was the "Great Raft."

This was not a real raft, but a huge, centuries-old logjam that dammed the river for a hundred-mile stretch and created a "Great Swamp" for miles around.

After examining then skirting the bottleneck's many channels and bayous—a laborious process consuming fourteen days—the Americans pressed on, more or less expecting interception by the Spanish at some point soon.

The fact is, not one but two Spanish military forces were searching for Freeman and Custis. And finally, on July 28, 1806, one of the Spanish patrols caught up to the American party—at Spanish Bluff in today's Bowie County, Texas, six hundred miles upriver from the expedition's starting point. Keeping in mind Jefferson's clear order to avoid hostilities at any cost, Freeman and his men offered no resistance and complied with the Spanish demand that they turn back.

Except for the reports to be made later, so ended Jefferson's largely forgotten southwestern expedition, which under better circumstances might have been as successful and well known today as the northwestern travels of Meriwether Lewis and William Clark. Despite the abrupt ending, however, the Freeman and Custis probe still serves as a reminder of Jefferson's farsighted dreams for the nation he was so instrumental in creating. He had hoped to find a viable waterway possibly leading all the way to Santa Fe or the southern Rockies. Then, too, as per his instruction to Lewis and Clark, he wished to establish friendly relations with the tribes encountered along the way west. Further, as a scientist, Jefferson expected his exploratory parties to report exciting new discoveries in the geography and among the flora and fauna to be found along the Red River corridor.

Interestingly, too, whether intended or not, the president had indulged in a bit of brinksmanship to test the resolve of New Spain to maintain the integrity of its territorial claims west of the Mississippi. This was a prickly and unresolved issue since the Southwest had been Spanish-controlled for more than two centuries. Only recently were portions ceded—in secret—to France, which in turn had just sold the Louisiana Territory to the United States as a sudden and unhappy surprise for the Spanish. Since much of the sold territory had never been surveyed properly, many related border and jurisdictional questions were to be tested and "settled" over the next forty years by treaties and additional American expeditions, both private and governmental, as well as an alternately encouraged then stoutly resisted flood of American settlers. Add to this the Mexican revolt against Spain, the Texas revolt against Mexico, and finally, the Mexican War.

In the meantime, not a few historical ironies transpired:

• The man who succeeded the nefarious James Wilkinson as governor of the Upper Louisiana Territory was . . . Meriwether Lewis.

• When Lewis mysteriously died at a one-horse tavern on the Natchez Trace in 1809, an apparent suicide, the man sent to retrieve his personal effects—plus his latest journal writings—and deliver them to an anxiously waiting Jefferson in Virginia was . . . Thomas Freeman.

• When Wilkinson later was prosecuted (and acquitted), his old friend Thomas Freeman testified in his behalf . . . presumably unaware that it was Wilkinson who had torpedoed Freeman's expedition of five years before by ratting to the Spanish authorities.

• Meanwhile, not only had Wilkinson been a mentor at one time to Thomas Freeman, he once had been a far more famous explorer's commanding officer in the Indian campaigns leading up to the battle of Fallen Timbers. That is to say, a young lieutenant serving under Major General Wilkinson in the 1790s was . . . William Clark, later a leader of the celebrated Corps of Discovery.

New Spain's "Agent 13"

In the annals of American history, was there ever a more ungrateful, self-serving backstabber like the American army officer who held sway over the lower Mississippi during the days of America's first explorations of the lands acquired by means of the Louisiana Purchase? Was there ever a betrayer who so consistently combined effrontery with repeated perfidy?

Perhaps Benedict Arnold comes to mind. Ironically, it was under Arnold that future American general and Spanish spy James Wilkinson began his military career during the American Revolution. Born in Calvert County, Maryland, in 1757, Wilkinson was studying to become a doctor when the Revolutionary War broke out in 1775. He interrupted his studies to join the Continental army and quickly found himself serving under Arnold in the disastrous campaign against Quebec and Montreal in the winter of 1775–76.

After participating in the crucial battles of Trenton and Princeton in 1776–77 under George Washington, Wilkinson showed his true colors when he took credit for another officer's intelligence coup at the battle of Saratoga, New York, in the fall of 1777.

His commanding officer, Gen. Horatio Gates, was so pleased with aide-de-camp Wilkinson's alleged coup, he dispatched the young lieutenant colonel to Philadelphia to inform the Continental Congress of the great victory over the British. Gates also recommended promotion for Wilkinson to brigadier general.

Wilkinson had to wait a few weeks for an only-temporary promotion, but by January 1778 he had emerged as secretary of the Board of War. Soon after, he and his mentor Gates were up to their necks in the so-called Conway cabal, the attempt by some malcontents to usurp Washington as overall commander and replace him with Gates.

When that palace conspiracy fell through, Wilkinson and Gates were no longer allies . . . by some accounts there was a challenge to a duel involved in their falling out. Benedict Arnold himself by this time had no use for Wilkinson, either. And Wilkinson had to resign from his key position at the Board of War.

He would bounce back quickly, however, in 1779, emerging as the Continental army's clothier general. Just a year later, though, he had to leave that job as well. It seems the books didn't quite balance.

Having married Ann Biddle in Philadelphia, he next spent a couple of years as a farmer in Bucks County, Pennsylvania. He was elected to the state legislature in 1783 and served as a brigadier general of militia . . . but his true calling soon emerged far to the south.

As a first step toward an eventual career as New Spain's "Agent 13," he struck out for Kentucky, where he quickly became involved in local campaigns to split the region off from Virginia and become a separate state. He even founded the town of Frankfort, the future state capital. By some accounts, the smooth-talking Marylander usurped Revolutionary War hero George Rogers Clark, among others, in the jockeying for leadership of the statehood drive.

He buttressed both his claims in that endeavor and his own shaky finances by floating a barge of goods downriver to New Orleans and talking the Spanish authorities there into allowing the Kentuckians to ship their produce and trade goods from there to the outside world. The catch was his "fellow Kentuckians" would have to use him as their agent—he had acquired a monopoly on the primary shipping route into the Spanish territory. In return, he apparently led the Spanish to believe he could talk Kentucky's statehood adherents into splitting off entirely from the United States and perhaps joining the Spanish in some sort of western confederation.

Wilkinson even took an oath of allegiance to Spain.

Returning to Kentucky, he tried to take advantage of frustrations over slow or inattentive congressional reaction to Kentucky's statehood aspirations—he did his best to nudge Kentucky leaders in the direction of independence from the United States, but thankfully they resisted. As Spain's spy-lobbyist, some sources say, he received an annual pension of two thousand dollars.

By 1791, however, the Mississippi trade had been opened to others—his monopoly days were over. As both his so-called Spanish Conspiracy and his own finances failed, Wilkinson rejoined the U.S. Army. After leading a volunteer group against marauding Indians in the Ohio country, he managed to obtain a lieutenant colonelcy in the regular army. He then served in the Old Northwest country under "Mad" Anthony Wayne, with Lt. William Clark, brother to George Rogers. "While serving under Gen. Anthony Wayne he conducted both open and covert campaigns to discredit him," noted Robert McHenry in his *Webster's American Military Biographies* (1978). By some accounts, young Clark himself reported Wilkinson once held up a supply movement simply to make Wayne look bad.

Taking possession of Detroit in the absence of the British in 1796, the brazen Wilkinson, now a brigadier general, became the senior officer in the U.S. Army after the death of Wayne in December of that year.

With the Louisiana Purchase unexpectedly negotiated in 1803 by Napoleonic France and the United States, Wilkinson and Mississippi Territory governor C. C. Claiborne took possession of the vast territory at New Orleans on December 20, 1803. Wilkinson was named governor of the Upper Louisiana Territory (those lands north of 33 degrees north), with headquarters at St. Louis. If not before, the fox really was in the henhouse now . . . with no one close by to watch over his activities.

While he sent off exploratory parties, most notably that of Lt. Zebulon Pike, into uncharted western lands, Wilkinson also was in a position to inform the Spanish about the Jefferson administration's two major exploratory probes of the West—the Lewis and Clark and the Freeman and Custis expeditions of 1804 and 1806, respectively. As a result, the Spanish tried to intercept both, but they succeeded in stopping only the Red River probe headed by Freeman and Custis.

But Wilkinson's machinations didn't stop there.

During these same years he had met from time to time with former Vice President Aaron Burr, apparently as a fellow conspirator in Burr's mysterious scheme to break off part of the western United States as some sort of private reserve.

Perhaps fearing exposure, Wilkinson turned on Burr and sounded the alarm. Occupying New Orleans and declaring martial law, "He arrested scores of persons in the next few months for alleged complicity in Burr's scheme," added McHenry. "Burr's men and eventually the fleeing Burr himself were arrested, and in May 1807 Wilkinson, already replaced as governor by Meriwether Lewis, was called east as the principal prosecution witness in Burr's treason trial before Chief Justice John Marshall. He narrowly escaped indictment himself and was subsequently tried and acquitted of wrongdoing by a military court of inquiry."

Returning to his command at New Orleans, Wilkinson then survived both a congressional investigation of his activities and a formal court-martial. As the saying goes, so far nobody had laid a glove on him . . . but his reputation certainly had taken a beating.

Still, he remained an active duty U.S. Army general as the United States entered the War of 1812 with the British. After seizing Mobile and Fort Charlotte in Spanish West Florida on the grounds that those areas harbored British forces, he was promoted to major general and reassigned north . . . to take part in an American incursion into Canada with the seizure of Montreal the goal. Fighting the British to a draw at Chrysler's Field, he retired to winter quarters in Upstate New York.

Reemerging in the spring of 1814, Wilkinson ran into disaster at Lacolle Mill, where a mere two hundred British repulsed his command of four thousand. Another court-martial quickly followed, but he was acquitted of all charges. Still, Spanish Agent 13's U.S. Army days by now were very much numbered . . . a year later he was honorably discharged and sent back into the civilian world.

Unsurprisingly, Wilkinson returned to the New Orleans area. In 1816, he turned out a three-volume set of memoirs. He remained near New Orleans at least until 1821 then traveled to Mexico to negotiate a land grant in future Texas. He died near Mexico City on December 28, 1825. By some accounts, his failing health could be blamed on the effects of smoking opium.

So passed the U.S. Army officer whom historian Frederick Jackson Turner once called "the most consummate artist in treason the nation ever possessed."

Christmas at Fort Clatsop

MESSAGE FROM THE PAST: For most members of the Lewis and Clark Expedition, December 1805 meant a Christmas away from home for the second year in a row. Just moving into their newly built log fort on the Pacific Coast, Fort Clatsop, they did what they could to mark the occasion. As William Clark noted in his journal, Christmas Day began with gunfire . . . celebratory gunfire.

> At day light this morning we were awoke by the discharge of the fire arm of all our party & a Selute, Shouts and a Song which the whole party joined in under our windows, after which they retired to their rooms . . . were chearful all the morning. after brackfast we divided our Tobacco which amounted to 12 carrots one half of which we gave to the men of the party who used tobacco, and to thoes who doe not use it we make a present of a handkerchief, The Indians leave us in the evening all the party Snugly fixed in their huts. I recved a present of Capt. L. of a fleece hosrie Shirt Draws and Socks, a pr. Mockersons of Whitehouse a Small Indian basket of Gutherich, two Dozen white weazils tails of the Indian woman, & some black root of the Indians before their departure. Drewyer informs me that he saw a Snake pass across the path to day. The day proved Showerey wet and disagreeable.
>
> We would have Spent this day the nativity of Christ in feasting, had we any thing either to raise our Spirits or even gratify our appetites, our Diner concisted of pore Elk, so much Spoiled that we eate it thro' mear necessity, Some Spoiled pounded fish and a fiew roots.

Food, the weather, gunfire salutes—and Christmas gifts—also were on the mind of Sgt. John Ordway that same Christmas day of 1805. So was the fact that this was a red-letter day in the travels of the Corps of Discovery. They now had shelter for the winter days ahead! And, also important, they had their good health.

> Wednesday, 25th Decr. Rainy & wet . . . Disagreeable weather. We all moved into our new Fort, which our officers name Fort Clatsop

after the name of the Clatsop nation of Indians who live nearest to us. The party Saluted our officers by each man firing a gun at their quarters at day break this morning. They divided out the last of their tobacco among the men that used and the rest they gave each a Silk handkerchief, as a Christmast gift, to keep us in remembrance of it as we have no ardent Spirits, but are all in good health which we esteem more than all the ardent Spirits in the world. we have nothing to eat but poore [spoiled] Elk meat and no Salt to Season that with but Still keep in good Spirits as we expect this to be the last winter that we will have to pass in this way.

Note: The unfortunate Clatsops ("dried salmon people") no longer were much of a "nation," since a smallpox outbreak had thrown the tribal population into decline two to three decades before. In the years after the Lewis and Clark Expedition's visit, the surviving Indians married into the coastal area's growing white society until the tribe lost its identity, according to the National Park Service, although "many" descendants of the Clatsops still live in the area today.

★

1 8 0 6
Sharing in the Acclaim
★

Appearing in 1839, a little-known pamphlet relating *The Adventures of Zenas Leonard* reported that the wandering Leonard found a black man living in a Crow village at the confluence of the Bighorn and Stinking Rivers. He claimed to have traveled to the Pacific Ocean and back with the Lewis and Clark Expedition as Clark's slave York. . . . but York, by most other accounts, was dead.

As the obscure reference suggests, both York and the expedition were well-enough known in the world of whites and their slaves to engender wild claims or erroneous reportage. York, more specifically, although William Clark's slave, had been the first African American to cross the American continent. As such, he was especially well known in another world, that of Native Americans—not for crossing the continent, but for his black skin and curly hair. Everywhere the expedition went, he aroused great interest, even amazement, among the Indians. And if he had made a legendary impact upon them, blame the often high-spirited York himself. A tale is told—by Clark himself—of the first meeting of the Corps of Discovery and the Arikara in October 1804 and their "astonishment" at seeing "my black servant," who, it seems, was quick to demonstrate impressive feats of strength before the Indian audience.

Much more impressive, no doubt, was York's own wry tale that he once lived in the wild like an animal before being caught by Clark. Embellishing the story even more, York added that he found "young children was verry good eating." On this occasion, Clark's journal entry noted that York "made him self more turrible in thier view than I wished him to Doe."

As Clark of course knew, there was nothing "turrible" about York. Nor was there anything mysterious or unusual about him. While slave and master by 1804, the two men had grown up together as members, you might say, of the Clark family. York ultimately became William's slave as a bequest. As adults in 1803, they were living in Clarksville, Indiana Territory, across the Ohio River from Louisville, Kentucky, when Meriwether Lewis invited Clark to join the pending expedition.

Since York was Clark's manservant, it was a near automatic conclusion that he would be joining the expedition, too. It's not known if he had any real choice in the matter, but he later did have a vote in the decision made by the Corps in late 1805 on determining a site for its winter quarters at the mouth of the Columbia River.

York isn't often mentioned in the expedition's journals, but enough is said from time to time to reveal that, unlike some of the other men of the corps, he could swim. He also figured in hunting forays. One time Clark and York went off to hunt buffalo. At other points in the journals, York is called a "waiter"and noted as waiting upon the two officers. But he also was assigned to work parties from time to time . . . thus, not all his energies were spent acting as a personal servant to Clark.

If his appearance excited the curiosity of the tribes encountered, he also impressed one and all with his feats of strength. Endurance, though, may have been another matter, and he may have been a bit overweight. Clark in one summer's day journal entry noted that on a long hike, York was dragging from the heat, thirst, and fatigue, "he being fat and unaccustomed to walk as fast as I went being the cause."

On the occasional long haul between the opportunities for river travel, he suffered from sore feet and was allowed to ride a horse briefly. When the expedition drew close to the Pacific, however, he joined a party led by Clark on a nineteen-mile hike to the beach.

Not long after, he pitched in on the building of Fort Clatsop as a winter quarters . . . but apparently he suffered for the effort. Clark wrote that York was "verry unwell from violent colds & strains carrying in meet [meat] and lifting logs on the huts to build them."

That he was a compassionate men seems evident from a short reference by Clark at the time of Sgt. Charles Floyd's appendicitis. York attended the dying man more closely ("principally" was Clark's word) than anyone else. Another time, when Clark and the Charbonneau family were endangered by a flash flood during a storm, York at some risk to himself went out looking for them. Clark and the Charbonneaus reached safety at the top of the river canyon in question, where they encountered York. Wrote Clark, "I found my servant in serch of us greatly agitated, for our wellfar."

As recalled by the Internet materials relating to the PBS documentary series *Lewis and Clark* (http://www.pbs.org/lewisandclark/inside/york.html), the list of the men left at Fort Clatsop by the expedition leaders included, for all posterity to see, "York, a black man of Captain Clark's." Says the Web site's profile of York as well: "One [list] was posted on the fort and copies were given to local Indians, one of which was passed to a ship's captain, who carried it around the world."

The same source also notes that Clark named a tributary of the Yellowstone "York's Dry River," and the last mention of York in all the expedition journals and diaries was Clark's entry from August 3, 1806, on the return from the Pacific Coast. After following the Yellowstone River to its meeting with the Missouri, Clark said, he next floated downriver for 636 miles "in 2 Small Canoes lashed together in which I had the following Person. John Shields, George Gibson, William Bratten, W. Labeech, Tous' Shabono his wife & child & my man York." (Shields, about thirty-five, was the expedition's blacksmith; Gibson, also in his midthirties, was a hunter, salt maker, and boatman; Bratton, about twenty-six, made salt and helped build canoes; Francois Labiche, midthirties, was an interpreter and hunter; "Shabono" was Clark's spelling for Charbonneau.)

Not long after, the explorers reached St. Louis, and "York publicly shared in the warm welcome," noted the PBS site. "By one account,

'Even the Negro York, who was the body servant of Clark, despite his ebony complexion, was looked upon with decided partiality, and received his share of adulation.'"

But York received no recompense for his part in the expedition—he simply remained Clark's slave. He asked for his freedom or at least to be "hired out" to be closer to his wife in Louisville, but Clark at first refused. In 1811, however, Clark freed all his slaves, York included, then provided York with a wagon and a team of six horses that would allow his lifelong companion to start a freight-hauling business. The sad ending is that the business failed. York planned to rejoin Clark, but along the way he contracted cholera and died, possibly as early as 1823 but no later than 1832. Depending on the year, he would have been in his forties or fifties.

Additional note: Stephen Ambrose goes into considerable detail in *Undaunted Courage* on the altered relationship between Clark and York upon the expedition's return in late 1806, a scenario supported by the many sources. Essentially, one might conclude, both men were creatures of the slavery culture of their day. "York was demanding his freedom as his reward for his services on the expedition," related Ambrose. Clark refused to let him work in Louisville but did allow a visit of a few weeks, while telling his brother Jonathan in a letter, "I am determined not to Sell him, to gratify him, and have directed him to return . . . to this place, this fall."

When York still pressed Clark to grant his freedom, Clark wrote his brother again: "I did wish to do well by him, but as he has got Such a notion about freedom and his emence [immense] Services [on the expedition] that I do not expect he will be of much Service to me again." Clark at times threatened to sell York or hire him out to a "severe" slave owner. A climax to the festering situation came after York returned to Clark's side in St. Louis in May 1809. Wrote Clark, somewhat starkly to be sure: "York brought my horse. He is here but of very little Service to me, insolent and sulky. I gave him a Severe trouncing the other Day and he has much mended."

As Ambrose noted: "Much of the evil of slavery is encapsulated in this little story. . . . York had helped pole Clark's keelboat, paddled his canoe, hunted for his meat, made his fire, had shown that he was prepared to sacrifice his life to save Clark's, crossed the continent and returned with his childhood companion, only to be beaten because he was insolent and sulky, and denied not only his freedom but his wife and, we may suppose, children."

Lewis, added Ambrose, held a somewhat softer attitude about York but was unlikely to urge Clark to free York. "Lewis could no more escape the lord-and-master attitude toward black slaves than Clark could—or, come to that, than Jefferson could. . . . No wonder Jefferson could write, 'I tremble for my country when I reflect that God is just.'"

★

1 8 0 9
Meriwether Lewis, RIP

★

When Meriwether Lewis was five years old, his father died of pneumonia two days after barely escaping death in Virginia's icy, flood-swollen Rivanna River, not many miles from their friend and neighbor Thomas Jefferson's mountaintop plantation home, Monticello. The father was returning to duty after a short furlough at home from his Revolutionary War service in the Continental army. Half a year later, the boy's mother remarried. In 1809, three decades after these events, Lewis, thirty-five years old and unmarried, was himself engaged in an ill-fated trip back to old haunts in the East.

In recent months, the collaborative hero of the Lewis and Clark Expedition had been drinking heavily. Appointed governor of the Upper Louisiana Territory shortly after a Christmas 1806 visit to his mother in Albemarle County, Virginia, he wouldn't return to St. Louis to take up his duties as governor until March 1808, a full year after his appointment. In the meantime, he had visited many publishers and editors in Philadelphia to discus publication of the journals he and William Clark had compiled . . . but he never came up with the manuscripts. Apparently thoughts of marriage were on his mind . . . to no avail. It is said that his relationship with his old mentor and boss, Jefferson, suffered from the drinking as well.

Perhaps he would have been happier, more settled, back in the wild. After all, as one of the leaders of the great expedition he had been superb as a rugged frontiersman, as a knowledgeable and dutiful explorer, as a firm disciplinarian with his men, and as a generous partner with Clark.

Successful in most cases, Lewis had fulfilled his diplomatic role as an ambassador to the many native tribes he and Clark encountered on the expedition. Like the soldier that he basically was, he also had reacted quickly and decisively when a band of Blackfoot tried to steal his rifles and horses. He had endured danger, accident, illness, and other threats to life and limb with near equanimity. When he fell twenty feet or so at Tavern Cave on the lower Missouri early in the journey, he somehow managed to stop his fall with his knife. When, at another time, it appeared a strange ore he tasted might have poisoned him, he used "salts" to purge it from his body. He naturally suffered the same vicissitudes of the cross-continental journey that afflicted all members of the Corps of Discovery, from squadrons of mosquitoes to carpets of rapacious fleas at some sites, to scrapes with bears, to weather extremes, to near starvation at times. But Lewis alone also had to endure a nonlethal but painful gunshot wound in a rear "thye" as a result of a hunting accident.

Returning to St. Louis at the end of the epic journey. Lewis immediately submitted his preliminary reports to Jefferson through a series of letters. In one of them, as recalled in the Internet materials stemming from the PBS television series *Lewis and Clark* (http://www.pbs.org/lewisandclark/inside/mlewi.html), he wrote: "In obedience to your orders we have penetrated the continent of North America to the Pacific Ocean, and sufficiently explored the interior of the country to affirm with confidence that we have discovered the most practicable route which does exist across the continent by means of the navigable branches of the Missouri and Columbia Rivers."

Based upon the expedition's findings, Lewis added, the best route entailed 2,575 miles up the Missouri River by boat to the Great Falls of the Missouri. Travelers of the future then would portage the 18 miles required to circumvent the falls and resume boat travel for another 200 miles by river. Then would come the tough, 140-mile trek across the Bitterroot Range in western Montana—"[T]remendous mountains which for 60 miles are covered with eternal snow," Lewis wrote. Next would come the same 640 miles of travel downstream on the Snake, Clearwater, and Columbia Rivers that the expedition took. Relating all this, Lewis assured Jefferson that game was plentiful and the potential trade in furs would be most profitable.

By the end of 1806, Lewis was spending Christmas at his mother's home on Ivy Creek in Albemarle County, Virginia, not ten miles from Jefferson's own Monticello. Always introspective, often moody, even melancholy in the past, the sometimes "deranged" Lewis was not easily recognized as the well-organized, take-charge leader seen during the twenty-eight months of the great expedition.

He of course still was busy . . . very busy. After that Christmas visit with his mother, noted the PBS site, "he went to Washington to receive his rewards for successfully completing the expedition: double pay while on service with the Corps (amounting to $1,228), a warrant for 1,600 acres of land, and a naming as Governor of the Territory of Upper Louisiana, which was put into effect in early March 1807."

Another necessary—indeed, compelling—chore was the trip to Philadelphia to discuss publication of the journals. But now a "new" Meriwether Lewis emerged. "At the same time, other efforts to publish the accounts of Sergeant [Patrick] Gass and Private [Robert] Frazer discouraged Lewis, and he never followed through with providing the publishers with the manuscript."

Meanwhile, more problems. "The following summer, a couple of attempts at marrying were unsuccessful, and his alcoholic consumption became more prevalent." Sadly too, "His relationship with Jefferson became problematic, due to his drinking and his delay in returning to St. Louis to take up his duties as governor." Then, too, an anxious Jefferson in the months ahead wondered aloud about the publication of the journals . . . when would that take place?

When Lewis finally did return to St. Louis in March 1808, he had lost a full year from the time of his appointment in 1807. By now, "The city was awash with opportunists, land speculators, eager traders, and Native Americans, who were becoming increasingly restless in anticipation of the changes that were to come."

The pressure was on, and quite likely Lewis wasn't really cut out to be a stellar administrator. Then, with Jefferson gone from the presidency in 1809, Washington questioned some of Governor Lewis's official expenses. As the word spread around St. Louis, it didn't help that Lewis was personally short of cash, although he, in fact, owned quite a bit of real estate in Virginia and elsewhere. He made arrangements to sell the sixteen hundred acres of land that Congress had granted him just two years earlier and, somewhat bitterly, decided he must go to Washington to defend himself against any implication of misappropriating government funds. It was time, in any case, to take the all-important journals east and see to their publication. For that matter, Clark would make the journey east as well, but by an alternate route.

Clark, still his expedition partner's close friend, was concerned both about the accusations and Lewis's state of mind. "I took my leave of Govr. Lewis who Set out to Philadelphia to write our Book (but more particularly to explain Some Matter between him and the Govt.)," Clark wrote to his brother Jonathan. "Several of his Bills have been protested, and his creditors all flocking in near the time of his Setting out distressed him much, which he expressed to me in Such terms as to Cause a Cempothy [sympathy] which is not yet off—I do not beleve there was ever an honester man in Louisiana, nor one who had pureor motives than Govr. Lewis. if his mind had been at ease I Should have parted Cherefuly."

The troubled Lewis left town in early September 1809, apparently planning to travel down the Mississippi to New Orleans then take ship to Washington . . . thus going by water all the way. Instead, his riverboat carried him only as far as Fort Pickering, the future site of Memphis, Tennessee. Once on board, it seems, he drank continually, fell into a deep depression, and twice tried to kill himself. Significantly or not, for medicinal purposes common to his era, he carried a small supply of opium pills, according to his own account book. In any case, he was landed at Fort Pickering on September 15 "in a state of mental derangement," noted the fort's commanding officer, Capt. Gilbert Russell, in a statement two years later. "On discovering his situation, and learning from the Crew that he had made two attempts to kill himself, in one of which he nearly succeeded," Russell added, "[I] resolved at once to take possession of him and his papers, and detain them there untill he recovered, or some friend might arrive in whose hands . . . [he] could depart in safety."

Lewis, who reportedly had written a will while aboard the riverboat, showed no "material change" for about five days, but on the sixth or seventh day "all symptons of derangement disappeared and he was completely in his senses," albeit "considerably reduced and debilitated." He remained that way for another "ten or twelve days."

In the meantime, Maj. James Neelly, Indian agent to the Chickasaws, had stopped by on his way to his agency near later Houston, Mississippi. Arrangements were made for Lewis to travel a ways with Neelly, who, by his own account, would furnish Lewis with a horse "to pack his trunks &c. and a man to attend to them." As a result, Russell allowed Lewis to continue his journey to Washington in the company of Neelly and his personal servant plus a servant named John Pernier and "some of the Chiefs." The party left on September 29, "with his [Lewis's] papers well secured and packed on horses," Russell also recalled.

After three days' travel in sultry weather and only a hundred miles covered, Neelly later reported to Jefferson, Lewis again "appeared at times deranged in mind." They had reached the Chickasaw Indian agency by then, and Neelly insisted they rest there for two days. In case anything happened to him, Lewis asked Neelly to forward the trunks containing the journals to "the President" (presumably Jefferson rather than his successor, James Madison).

The party set out again on October 6, apparently without the "Chiefs." In two or three days, they crossed the Tennessee River. On October 10 members of the small party awoke to find that two of their horses had strayed during the night. It was mutually decided that Neelly would stay behind to find and round them up while Lewis and the two servants would proceed along the Natchez Trace, but would stop at the "first houses he came to that was inhabited by white people," Neelly recounted.

The trio traveled until late afternoon before coming across a tavern about seventy miles southwest of Nashville, Tennessee. It was operated by a couple named Grinder (Griner by some accounts), but the husband apparently was away as Lewis settled in.

Now arises the still-debated issue of Lewis's subsequent death by gunshot wounds. Who, or *what*, killed Meriwether Lewis?

Historian Stephen Ambrose, author of *Undaunted Courage* and a student of the Lewis and Clark story, believes that Lewis committed suicide that night at Grinder's Stand. He relies heavily upon Scottish-born ornithologist Alexander Wilson's interview two years after the fact with Mrs. Grinder. And, one may well say, why not?

By this account, Grinder reported that Lewis had arrived about sundown and the two servants arrived shortly behind him. It wasn't long before Lewis began to act oddly. According to the Wilson version of her story, Lewis sometimes walked up to her but "would suddenly wheel around and walk back as fast as he could."

Then: "Supper being ready, he sat down, but had eaten only a few mouthfuls, when he started up, speaking to himself in a violent manner. At these times, she says, she observed his face to flush as if it had come to him in a fit."

And yet he could be quiet, even friendly at moments too. "He lighted his pipe, and drawing a chair to the door, sat down saying to Mrs. Grinder, in a kind tone of voice, Madame, this is a very pleasant evening." Then he jumped up and paced about the yard again. Just as suddenly, he sat down again, "seemed again composed, and casting his eyes wistfully toward the west, observed what a sweet evening it was."

At bedtime, he stopped her from making up a bed for him, saying he would sleep on the floor on his bear skins and buffalo robes.

Soon the servants retired to a nearby barn, and Grinder went to bed in the separate kitchen structure of her log cabin hostelry.

All during the night, Lewis paced in his room, continually talking aloud, "like a lawyer." After several hours of this, Grinder heard a shot and the thump of something falling "heavily" onto the floor, with both sounds followed by the discernible gasp: "Oh, Lord."

It appeared that, like many of his activities of recent months, Lewis had botched his latest suicide attempt. The ball created only a head wound.

Still apparently determined, though, Lewis turned a second pistol on his chest and fired again, the ball this time coursing through his torso and out his lower back. She heard that shot also.

He still lived, however, and was able to call out: "O Madame, give me some water, and heal my wounds!"

Looking through the chinks between the logs of the kitchen structure, the terrified woman "saw him stagger back and fall against a stump that stands between the kitchen and the [his] room," related Wilson. "He crawled for some distance, raised himself by the side of a tree, where he sat about a minute. He once more got to the room; afterwards, he came to the kitchen door, but did not speak; she then heard him scraping the bucket with a gourd for water; but it appears that this cooling element was denied the dying man."

After a while, the two servants, alerted by Grinder's children, hurried over from the barn and found Lewis sinking fast but busily cutting himself with a razor. Displaying his second gunshot wound, he allegedly said, "I am no coward; but I am so strong, so hard to die." He asked them to shoot him in the head with a rifle and end it. They refused. Lewis finally, a little after sunrise, died.

What to make of this inexplicable change in the Meriwether Lewis of expedition leadership . . . of so tragic an end for this early icon of the American West?

Many have wondered if he was murdered on the Natchez Trace. Then, too, was he possibly suffering from the final ravages of syphilis? Neither speculation has ever been proven, and most historians today—like the major figures of the explorer's own time—accept the premise that a deeply disturbed Lewis took his own life.

Some have suggested that Lewis's demise was a self-inflicted death that was not, in fact, suicide. Thomas C. Danisi suggested as much in the February 2002 issue of the Lewis and Clark Trail Heritage Foundation's quarterly publication *We Proceeded On* in an article titled "The 'Ague' Made Him Do It." Ague is better known these days as malaria. And the essence of Danisi's very convincing argument is this: "I believe that Meriwether Lewis suffered from untreated malaria, a condition that can lead to the kind of erratic behavior he exhibited in the weeks before his death. Malaria has been known, literally, to drive its victims crazy, causing them to mutilate and even shoot themselves in a desperate attempt to rid their bodies of pain."

Consider, argued Danisi, that Lewis was reported in the *Missouri Gazette* to have been suffering from "fever" when he left St. Louis. Then, too, he left in September, "a time when outbreaks of malaria (a.k.a. 'the autumnal fever') often occurred." Further, the "waxing and waning" of his periods of so-called derangement are typical of advanced malaria. Finally, how could someone as astute as Lewis in the use of firearms possibly, "at point-blank range," miss such "large" vital organs as the brain or heart. And if "cutting himself head to foot" with a razor, why not simply slash a vital spot like his wrists?

"I have done the business," Lewis is said to have told his servant Pernier. "But," summed up Danisi, "that 'business' was a strange and tragic form of self-surgery, not suicide."

In the same issue of *We Proceeded On,* not so incidentally, historian John Guice reported there was no moonlight that fateful night, thus he asks, How could Grinder have seen the things she alleged that she did see? He argued, "It is not likely that Mrs. Grinder could have witnessed the actions of Lewis through the cracks of her log cabin with the door bolted shut." Guice further noted that Mrs. Grinder over many years "offered several different versions" of her story.

However muddy the waters at this late date, whatever the cause of the still-young explorer's death, his passing in such a bizarre manner of course was a shock to the two men closest to him, but it may not have been totally unexpected. In a letter to the helpful Captain Russell of Fort Pickering, an undoubtedly grief-stricken Thomas Jefferson, Lewis's chief mentor and sponsor, acknowledged that the Lewis he had known was "much afflicted & habitually so with hypocondria." More lately, Jefferson seemed to imply, "This was probably increased by the habit into which he had fallen & the painful reflection that would be necessarily produced in a mind like his." Similarly, when William Clark first read of his close friend's death in a newspaper, he wasn't quite convinced of the report's veracity, but he nonetheless feared that "the weight of his mind has overcome him."

As for the precious journals, they were received by Jefferson, and he and Clark agreed that Clark would take them to Philadelphia to arrange their publication. After a bit of shopping around, Clark found Nicholas Biddle, who, with the copyediting help of Paul Allen, edited and reworked the journals kept by the two leaders of the expedition for publication in 1814 as the *History of the Expedition of Captains Lewis and Clark.* Down through the years, other, more complete versions of the journals have found their way into print as well.

Additional note: Indian agent James Neelly arrived at the Grinders' roadside inn later on the morning of Lewis's death, October 11, 1809, and buried the great explorer "as decently as I could." Added Stephen Ambrose as a footnote to his account of Lewis's final days: "Lewis is buried today at the site of Grinder's Inn, along the Natchez Trace. Alexander Wilson saw to preparing a proper plot and putting a fence around it. A broken shaft, authorized by the Tennessee legislature in 1849 as symbolic of the 'violent and untimely end of a bright and glorious career,' marks the spot." Today, the site, near Hohenwald, Tennessee, is encompassed—and protected—within the bounds of the Natchez Trace Parkway.

★ Part 2 ★
Mountain Men
and Texans

1 8 0 9
Running to Live

Running like a deer through the wilderness near the three forks of the Missouri River, and naked as a deer at that, John Colter didn't lose a step when the blood burst out of his nose and poured down his bare chest. He didn't . . . he couldn't if he valued his life.

Running for survival itself, he paid little heed to the prickly pear thorns tearing into his bare feet. He just ran . . . and ran.

Also silent and running, no longer whooping and shouting, heads also bent to their task, was a virtual crowd behind Colter. Many of them encumbered by weapons but lithe and athletic, in marvelous physical condition, they had begun the footrace expecting to catch their quarry and kill him in short order. Instead, Colter had managed to stay ahead of his Blackfoot pursers for two or three miles now.

Even so, how long could this white man last? Could he reach the finish line in this deadly contest? But . . . what finish line? For Colter, alone in the wilderness, Indian captive, often called America's first mountain man, veteran of the Lewis and Clark Expedition, there was no finish line. When he could run no more, the Blackfoot warriors would kill him. It was that simple. They already had killed his trapping partner, John Potts, riddling him with arrows.

For the two mountain men the day had begun inauspiciously enough. In the early dawn, they glided along a creek in their canoe and checked their beaver traps, about six miles from the Missouri River branch called the Jefferson—named just four years before by the leaders of the Lewis and Clark Expedition in honor of expedition sponsor Thomas Jefferson. Colter, a native of the Staunton (pronounced Stanton) area of Augusta County, Virginia, by most accounts—had accompanied the Corps of Discovery all the way from Kentucky to the Pacific and back as far as the Hidatsa and Mandan villages north of today's Bismarck, North Dakota. At that point, with the permission of his fellow explorers, he had left the group to join two trappers from Illinois who wanted to gather beaver pelts in the Yellowstone River area that the corps had passed through.

That partnership fell through in just weeks, but Colter was hooked . . . this roaming and trapping in areas never seen by white men before was the life for him. He is credited, in fact, with being the first white man to discover the natural wonders today encompassed by Yellowstone National Park. In addition, his reports of steaming geysers and hot springs near Cody, Wyoming, led many to call that area "Colter's hell."

He of course had been with the Lewis and Clark Expedition when Lewis and a small party had had a run-in with eight hostile Blackfoot on the Marias River in July 1806 and killed two of them. But historians today doubt that the Blackfoot really held that incident against all Americans, since the same tribe indicated a willingness to trade only a year or two later. The incident that really set their teeth on edge involved Colter himself . . . by pure chance and no fault of his own. In 1808 he was traveling with a party of Crow and Flat Head on the lower Gallatin River near Three Forks when they suddenly were attacked by a large band of Blackfoot. A number of them saw the white man Colter fighting with their traditional enemies, the Crows. He continued to fire his rifle even after being wounded in the leg and crawling "to a small thicket," wrote Colter's friend and traveling companion Thomas James in *Three Years Among the Indians* (1846).

Thus Colter himself, even while acting in self-defense, may have soured the Blackfoot on all white Americans. At least that's what Burton Harris suggested in his 1952 biography of Colter. "The Blackfoot," wrote Harris, "saw Colter, a white man, fighting side by side with their detested enemies the Crows; they also suffered the effects of his deadly shooting. They did not pause to consider that Colter had no choice but to fight for his own life and that of his friends, but rather construed it as proof that the Americans were allied with their implacable foe [the Crows]. . . . During the half century that followed, the Blackfoot attacked all Americans they encountered, and took an appalling number of American lives by vicious, remorseless fighting on every possible occasion that presented itself, or could be created."

Meanwhile, Colter is presumed to have recuperated from his leg wound behind the log walls of Manuel's Fort, established by fur trader Manuel Lisa at the mouth of the Bighorn River in 1807 as the first permanent building in the future state of Montana. Ironically, Lisa, organizer of the Missouri Fur Trading Company of St. Louis, had sent Colter as an "ambassador to the Blackfoot," Harris noted. Instead, the Virginian inadvertently became their enemy.

Still, he would go out into their country again. In 1809 he and Potts, also a former corps member now working with Col. Andrew Henry's fur-trading party, willingly set off into the face of danger. But wisely they were cautious. According to British botanist John Bradbury, Colter personally told him, "They set out their traps at night, and took them up early in the morning, remaining concealed during the day." One morning, while gliding along a creek in their canoe and checking their beaver traps, "They heard a great noise resembling the trampling of animals." Colter said it must be Indians, "and advised an instant retreat," recounted Bradbury in his book *Travels in the Interior of America* (1819). But Potts, calling Colter a coward, insisted the noise was made by a herd of buffalo instead. "And they proceeded on."

Their argument was settled minutes later when "five or six hundred" Blackfoot appeared on either side of the creek. The Indians "beckoned" them, and with no escape possible, Colter obligingly turned the canoe into the shore. "At the moment of its touching," wrote Bradbury, "an Indian seized the rifle belonging to Potts, but Colter, who is a remarkably strong man, immediately retook it and handed it to Potts."

Potts then pushed the canoe back into the river, leaving Colter among the Indians on the embankment. Seconds later an arrow flew. Potts, struck in the hip, cried out, "Colter, I'm wounded!"

Colter, seeing that they couldn't escape and possibly hoping they still could treat with the Indians, urged Potts to come ashore. But Potts leveled the rifle at an Indian "and shot him dead on the spot."

That was the trapper's last act. "He was instantly pierced with arrows so numerous that, to use the language of Colter, 'He was made a riddle of.'"

With the Blackfoot outraged by the death of one of their own, Colter fell victim to their wrath. "They . . . stripped him entirely naked, and began to consult on the manner in which he should be put to death." (According to the sometimes differing, sometimes conflicting account in Thomas James's book, the Blackfoot hacked Pott's body to pieces and threw them in Colter's face. Thomas described Colter as bearing "an open, ingenious, and pleasing countenance of the Daniel

Boone stamp" while also noting the mountain man's "hardy indurance of fatigue, privation and perils.")

The Blackfoot asked Colter if he were a good runner, and he, guessing their intent, said no. Like the Indians surrounding him, though, Colter—five foot ten inches, blue-eyed, still in the prime of life at age thirty-five or so—was himself in excellent condition. Among his white brethren, he happened to be a very good runner. But . . . how would he fare in a footrace with these men born and raised in the wilderness?

Once Colter said that he wasn't a very good runner, that seemed to decide the issue of his fate, Bradbury added. "The chief now commanded the party to remain stationary, and led Colter out on the prairie three or four hundred yards and released him, bidding him to save himself if he could. At that instant, the horrid war whoop sounded in the ears of poor Colter, who, urged with the hope of preserving life, ran with a speed at which he was himself surprised."

Running for all he was worth, Colter did have a goal in mind, a "finish line" of sorts. The Jefferson River (or Fork), a good five or six miles away.

Fortunately for him, but also for his pursuers, the terrain ahead was largely flat, a plain, albeit often covered with the prickly pear.

A mile then two, perhaps three, were consumed as the silent race proceeded. Colter hadn't dared to miss a step by looking back . . . but at last he did. "He ran nearly halfway across the plain before he ventured to look over his shoulder, when he perceived that the Indians were very much scattered, and that he had gained ground to a considerable distance from the main body," wrote Bradbury.

But one Blackfoot warrior, carrying a spear, was "much before all the rest." In fact, he lagged only a hundred yards behind Colter.

Galvanized by the sight, Colter summoned a last burst of energy and ran all the harder, but the added effort "was nearly fatal to him, for he exerted himself to such a degree, that the blood gushed from his nostrils, and soon almost covered the fore part of his body."

The river lay perhaps another mile ahead. He might make it. But he heard "the appalling sound of footsteps behind him, and every instant expected to feel the spear of his pursuer."

Glancing over his shoulder, he saw the Blackfoot warrior "not twenty yards from him."

It was Colter's moment of truth. The unnamed warrior's as well.

In a flash, Colter whirled around to face his adversary, arms spread.

Taken by surprise, perhaps startled by the sight of the blood-covered white man, quite exhausted himself, the pursuing warrior tried to stop, stumbled, tried to throw his spear, but fell and drove the point into the ground with such force that the shaft broke in his hand. In an instant Colter snatched up the weapon and "pinned him to the earth."

Colter loped onward with no further delay, still intent on reaching the river, while, behind, the first Indians to reach their comrade's body "set up a hideous yell."

In minutes, himself exhausted and feeling faint, Colter was among the cottonwood trees lining the river "through which he ran, and [then] plunged into."

He found refuge under a great raft of timber piled up at the end of a small island just downstream. Like a beaver entering its lodge, he had to duck under the water, find an opening giving him air, then squeeze into it. "Scarcely had he secured himself," said Bradbury, "when the Indians arrived on the river, screeching and yelling, as Colter expressed it, 'like so many devils.'"

More wrathful than ever, the Blackfoot began a systematic search for Colter, even scrambling about on his pile of logs while he watched them "through the chinks." The frightening thought suddenly struck him that they might set his raft afire and flush him out . . . but they didn't.

Still, at any moment, they could have. "In horrible suspense he remained until night, when hearing no more of the Indians, he dived from under the raft, and swam silently down the river to a considerable distance, when he landed, and traveled all night."

For the moment he was safe, yet here he was, deep in Blackfoot country, utterly naked, and, as Bradbury recounted, "under a burning sun: the soles of his feet were entirely filled with the thorns of the prickly pear; he was hungry, and had no means of killing game, although he saw an abundance around him, and was at least seven days journey from Lisa's Fort." Still, living on roots and berries, he completed the distance to the trading post . . . and safety.

But he wouldn't be staying long. When he and Potts first were accosted by the Blackfoot, it seems, Colter, quite unnoticed, quietly had placed his traps in the water on one side of the canoe and allowed them to drop down to the creek bottom. He wanted those traps, which were worth a good ten dollars each. So back he went that winter when the Indians presumably would be in "winter quarters," back to the spot where he and Potts had encountered the Blackfoot.

Well, not quite all the way back . . . since sitting over the campfire one night near the Three Forks, he heard the cocking of guns, leaped beyond the fire's circle of light, and fled into the night as guns boomed behind him.

After one or two more scrapes involving the Blackfoot over the next couple of years, Colter decided he had exhausted his quotient of good fortune and headed down the Missouri for a farm, marriage, and a much quieter life outside St. Louis (population then fourteen hundred). On the way, according to Thomas James, Colter and a companion were attacked by the ubiquitous Blackfoot and only escaped by hiding in a thicket. After that, noted Harris in his Colter biography, the Virginian's small party successfully ran the two-thousand-mile gauntlet presented by the Missouri River as a watery pathway to St. Louis—a gauntlet because it ran through "the territory of the Arikara, Sioux, Pawnee, and other tribes with similar piratical habits." Added Harris: "There were few Indians along the Missouri at that time who could resist the temptation to rob a small party, and no one knew this better than John Colter."

Sadly, for all his narrow escapes and wilderness adventures, John Colter died in the relative safety of Franklin County, Missouri, of yellow jaundice in 1813, just three years after his return to civilization.

☆ ☆ ☆

Additional note: While Bradbury and James essentially relate the same story about Colter's soon-to-be legendary race for survival, each of them reporting that Colter told him the story in person, there are some striking differences in the detail.

James, for instance, wrote that Colter and Potts were in two canoes when accosted by the Blackfoot. They were on the Jefferson River itself. The Indians appeared just on one shore. Potts was riddled with bullets, rather than arrows. Potts was mutilated, with pieces of his body thrown into Colter's face. The warrior who Colter killed near the end of the footrace carried a blanket as well as a spear that broke. He had begged for mercy before Colter killed him. Colter kept the blanket when he ran on, to plunge into the Madison River rather than the Jefferson, a run of five miles, rather than six. Further, it was a beaver lodge that Colter hid in, rather than a pile of timber. Finally, the blanket kept the naked

Colter warm after he climbed to the top of a snow-covered mountain that night and then hid there through the following day. It took him eleven days, rather than seven, to reach refuge . . . at Manuel's Fort rather than Lisa's Fort.

Whom to believe? Biographer Harris, while acknowledging that Bradbury's is the "classic" and more literary account of the episode, concludes that James tells a story that is "more realistic and logical" . . . except for one small item. Can a man really fit inside a beaver lodge?

1 8 1 1
Upheaval

It was shortly after 2 A.M. on a Monday. Aboard a keelboat on the Mississippi River, British botanist John Bradbury was shocked to feel the heavy boat suddenly rise then drop down with a jolt. To either side, the riverbanks were caving in and trees were toppling. Through it all, he and his companions were assailed by an incredible noise—"the noise of the most violent tempest of wind mixed with a sound equal to the loudest thunder, but more hollow and vibrating," he later recalled.

Such huge chunks of the shoreline fell into the river, said Bradbury, "as nearly to sink our boat by the swell."

Elsewhere along the path of the "Father of Waters," islands disappeared, mighty waves swept back and forth, and the riverbed was sucked dry, only to be inundated moments later by walls of water running *backward.*

In the St. Louis, Missouri, area, a newspaper editor was roused from his sleep "by the clamor of windows, doors and furniture in tremulous motion, with a distant rumbling noise, resembling a number of carriages passing over pavement."

Another Mississippi traveler at the same time was roused by "a violent shaking of the boat." Even in distant Pittsburgh and Norfolk, Virginia, people felt the mighty earthquake of December 16, 1811, that spread from the Mississippi River Valley. The dissipating concentric waves reached as far as the Gulf Coast to the south and Quebec,

Canada, to the north. More frightening for those near the epicenter, it was an upheaval that just kept on heaving. A series of quakes continued through the night and only ended in the daylight hours with one final powerful jolt like the one that had struck at 2:15 A.M. or so.

And these were only the first in a series of intermittent earthquakes lasting for more than a year. Three of them would be among the most powerful quakes to strike North America in recorded history. Before it was all over, noted Larry E. Morris in the May 2001 issue of *We Proceeded On*, witnesses reported "violent whirlpools, spontaneous waterfalls, and geyser-like fountains, and the Mississippi actually flowed upstream."

The epicenter for one of the more powerful jolts was tiny New Madrid, Missouri, population about four hundred. "[T]he grounds burst and threw out water as high as the trees and it threw down part of our houses," said New Madrid resident Elizabeth Robison, according to the Morris account in an article titled "Dependable John Ordway." Added survivor Eliza Bryan: "[T]he earth was horribly torn to pieces; the surface of hundreds of acres was from time to time covered over with various depths by the sand which issued from the fissures."

Another Mississippi River traveler that first day said he could hardly believe his eyes when he saw "the rising of the trees that lie in the bed of the river." He went on to explain: "I believe that every tree that has been deposited in the bed of the river since Noah's flood, now stands erect out of the water; some of these I saw myself during one of the hardest shocks rise up eight to ten feet out of water. The navigation has been rendered extremely difficult in many places in consequence of the snags being so extremely thick."

Clearly, there were injuries and deaths among area residents and travelers, but no one knows how many. Where millions live today, only hundreds lived back in 1811, so the casualties would have been relatively few—a few hundred by best estimates today. Damage to man-made structures was relatively limited also, since most settlers lived in log cabins that emerged unscathed except for their chimneys. Brick and masonry structures did suffer extensive damage if not total destruction.

The initial shock of the early morning of December 16, 1811, says the National Earthquake Information Center, "inaugurated what must have been the most frightening sequence of earthquakes ever to occur in the United States."

The quakes were to last for days, weeks, even months. "Intermittent strong shaking continued through March 1812 and aftershocks strong enough to be felt occurred through the year 1817," says the Earthquake Center Web site (http://wwwneic.cr.usgs.gov/neis/states/missouri/1811.html). "The initial earthquake of December 16 was followed by two other principal shocks, one on January 23, 1812, and the other on February 7, 1812. Judging from newspaper accounts of damage to buildings, the February 7 earthquake was the biggest of the three."

The quakes left their mark over a wide area. "The scene was one of devastation in an area which is now the southeast part of Missouri, the northeast part of Arkansas, the southwest part of Kentucky, and the northwest part of Tennessee. Reelfoot Lake, in the northwest corner of Tennessee, stands today as evidence of the might of these great earthquakes. The stumps of trees killed by the sudden submergence of the ground can still be seen in Reelfoot Lake."

More dramatic were the effects along the rivers of the region. "Entire islands disappeared, banks caved into the rivers, and fissures opened and closed in the river beds. Water sprouting from these fissures produced large waves in the river. New sections of river channel were formed and old channels cut off. Many boats were capsized and an unknown number of people were drowned."

The shocks are called the New Madrid earthquakes because the epicenter of the big jolt on February 7, 1812, apparently was near that Missouri town. The epicenters for the other quakes, however, while in the same region, are not precisely known.

What *is* known is the frightening fact that a similar earthquake or series of earthquakes today would wreak widespread havoc in an area populated by millions of persons, most of them living or working in vulnerable buildings and cities such as St. Louis or Memphis. "This," says the Earthquake Center, "would result in a much greater loss of life and property today because of the much larger amount of people and man-made structures in the region."

While the frequency of earthquakes like those of 1811–12 "is very low," warns the Center, "continuing minor to moderate seismic activity in the central Mississippi Valley area is an indication that a large magnitude tremor can someday be expected there again." How soon? As soon as right now or several thousand years from now, says the Earthquake Center.

☆ ☆ ☆

Additional note: To make matters a bit more discouraging for Missouri settlers early in the nineteenth century, added Larry E. Morris in his article on John Ordway, the area four years later went through a "year of no summer." As he explained this phenomenon of 1816, "Survivors of the earthquake experienced snow or frost repeatedly through the months of May, June, and August."

Reason? "Cold weather in many parts of North America during the summer of 1816 is generally attributed to the volcanic explosion of Mt. Tambira, Sumbawa, Indonesia, the previous year." Thus volcanic debris in the atmosphere apparently blocked enough sunlight to create the abnormal cold-weather conditions experienced at ground level below.

Sioux Hunter's Busy Night

There was a young Santee Sioux originally named Mysterious Medicine but later called Big Hunter, Long Rifle, and White Footprint. Not a bit handsome, he was, however, very strong, tall, and very brave. And he was out hunting one day, armed with bow and arrows as well as a favorite Kentucky rifle he called *Ishtahbopopa,* or "Pops-the-eye."

"It was at the time of the fall hunt," he later told a young nephew named Ohiyesa. "One afternoon when I was alone I discovered that I was too far away to reach camp before dark, so I looked about for a good place to spend the night. This was on the Upper Missouri, before there were any white people there, and when we were in constant danger from wild beasts as well as from hostile Indians. It was necessary to use every precaution and the utmost vigilance."

If his language does not sound like "Indian talk," that's because little Ohiyesa grew up to enter the white man's world, acquire a university education, take on the name Charles A. Eastman, and recall his Santee Sioux background in the book *Indian Boyhood* (1902). His uncle's account of a dramatic night alone in the wilderness is presented in *Ohiyesa*—Eastman's book—as a true story told by White Footprint many years after the fact.

The dangers he encountered that night in the upper Missouri region were all of the four-footed variety, it seems, rather than hostile Indians. Before the next day dawned, White Footprint related, he was to be visited at his lonely campsite by coyotes, porcupines, wolves, a mountain lion, and a grizzly bear—all of them hungry.

Earlier in the day, he had killed and dressed two deer. Before bedding down for the night, he hung great chunks of the deer meat at various distances around his camp. Wolves and perhaps a bear might come no closer than the hanging meat, he explained to his nephew. Mountain lions, on the other hand, would be bolder and might attack with no warning. Perhaps they would be deterred by his campfire . . . perhaps not. In any case, he had a fire, and a full moon overhead aided his visibility. "Having cooked and eaten some of the venison, I rolled myself in my blanket and lay down by the fire, taking my *Ishtahbopopa* for a bed fellow. I hugged it very closely, for I felt that I should need it during the night."

It wasn't long before a disturbance interrupted any thoughts of sleep. "I had scarcely settled myself when I heard what seemed to be ten or twelve coyotes set up such a howling that I was quite sure of a visit from them."

Right after that came what sounded like "the screaming of a small child." As a hunter familiar with the ways of the wild, White Footprint knew that the cry signaled the arrival of a porcupine lusting after the hanging meat.

But now a coyote openly appeared on a flat rock fifty yards away. The coyote proceeded to howl and bark in so many "keys" that White Footprint realized, "What had seemed to be the voices of many coyotes was in reality only one animal."

A mate briefly appeared, then both coyotes vanished from sight.

No matter, the porcupine hove into view. Indeed, "He had climbed up to the piece of meat nearest me, and was helping himself without any ceremony."

This, actually, could be a welcome development because the porcupine would be a handy watchdog. "Very soon, in fact, he interrupted his meal, and caused all his quills to stand out in defiance. I glanced about me and saw the two coyotes slyly approaching my open camp from two different directions."

A couple of arrows from White Footprint's bow sent them pelting off "with howls of surprise and pain."

Now there arrived a second porcupine—he climbed to a tree branch close by another piece of meat, "a splendid ham of venison," and "began his supper."

Far more ominously than anything the Sioux hunter had seen or heard yet, however, was a frightening noise from the canyon walls above him. "It sounded much like a huge animal stretching himself, and giving a great yawn which ended in a scream."

Recognizing the screech of a mountain lion, White Footprint made hasty preparations for a truly unpleasant visit. Taking his weapons with him, he climbed the nearest large tree—"but first I rolled a short log of wood in my blanket and laid it in my place by the fire."

Not long after, a hissing by one of the busy porcupines warned of a nearby intruder. Instead of the mountain lion, though, it was not one but two gray wolves.

They also wanted the deer hams, which were hanging a good eight feet off the ground. They began to leap in the air, trying to reach the fragrant meat, "although evidently they proved good targets for the quills of the prickly ones, for occasionally one of them [the wolves] would squeal and rub his nose desperately against the tree."

Finally, one wolf managed to bury his teeth in a ham, but that left him dangling in midair, "kicking and yelping, until the tendon of the ham gave way and both fell heavily to the ground." Another pair of arrows took care of that wolf. The other ran off a short distance . . . "and remained there a long time, as if waiting for her mate."

Meanwhile, White Footprint had not forgotten the mountain lion . . . nor had it forgotten him. "As I had half expected, there came presently a sudden heavy fall, and at the same time the burning embers were scattered about and the fire almost extinguished. My blanket with the log in it was rolled over several times, amid snarls and growls."

The "assailant," apparently realizing he had been tricked, plunged back into the thick underbrush, but not before the watching Indian was able to pierce his side with an arrow. "He snarled and tried to bite off the shaft, but after a time became exhausted and lay still."

The busy night was not yet over, even though the dawn's first light was visible to the east. Groggy from lack of sleep but still concerned about some grizzly bear tracks he had seen in the vicinity the day before, White Footprint tied himself to the trunk of his tree with a length of rawhide, settled himself on a hefty, right-angle branch, and finally fell asleep.

But not for long. The sharp crack of a rifle shot very close by "rudely" woke him up with a terrible start. Not only that, he realized the tree was shaking—it felt like someone was trying to shake him out of the tree. And "someone" was trying to do just that, a big grizzly!

This time, White Footprint reached for his rifle rather than his bow and arrows. But the weapon was gone. He realized it had fallen from his relaxed grasp when the bear started shaking the tree. Already cocked and ready for action, it went off when it hit the ground. That had been the rifle shot. And the grizzly in no way had been deterred by the loud noise. "The bear picked up the weapon and threw it violently away; then he again shook the tree with all his strength."

White Footprint had told his young nephew that bold shouting at some animals encountered in the wild often would scare them away. But a grizzly? He tried it anyway. "I shouted: 'I have still a bow and a quiver full of arrows; you had better let me alone.'"

When the bear only answered with an angry growl, the treed Indian was ready to act. "I sent an arrow into his side, and he groaned like a man as he tried to pull it out. I had to give him several more before he went a short distance away, and died."

It was full daylight now as White Footprint descended from his perch in the tree, so stiff he hardly could walk. He discovered the bear had killed both of his "little friends" the porcupines and eaten most of the hanging meat. But no great matter—at least he had survived the night. And what a night it had been! As he acknowledged to his young and wide-eyed listener Ohiyesa, even for an experienced hunter in a wilderness thick with game, it had been "an unusual experience to see so many different animals in one night."

1823
Grizzly Bear Encounters

For any mountain man—any wilderness wanderer any time, any place—it would be one thing to survive a close encounter with an angry grizzly bear, but . . . to be badly mauled and then left for dead in hostile Indian country two hundred miles from the nearest outpost of civilization? What then?

Originally Glass was a sailor, but he was captured and forced to join Jean Laffite's pirates in the Gulf of Mexico. After escaping the pirates on Galveston Island, he was a captive of the Pawnees in Kansas. Glass eventually, in 1822, wriggled back into civilization . . . and only then, not yet through with the *adventurous* life, he became a mountain man and trapper for the Rocky Mountain Fur Company. In August 1823 he and a party of trappers led by Andrew Henry traveled along the Grand River in South Dakota, heading toward the Yellowstone.

They were tense and alert since they already had had painful meetings with the region's Arikara (often called Rees). Not long before, fifteen trappers had been killed in a fight with the Rees—then, too, just in recent days, two men in Henry's current party of thirteen had been killed in yet another ugly skirmish with the Indians.

Briefly off alone and looking for game, Hugh Glass poked into a thicket and stumbled across a mother grizzly and her cubs . . . the predictable followed. Firing one quick shot into her chest, then taken in her grip before he could load and shoot again, Glass stabbed and stabbed at the beast as she raked and mauled him mercilessly. Drawn to the scene by his screams for help, his companions shot the she-bear after Glass fell to the ground, inert. The bear finally collapsed as well.

Unsurprisingly, the onetime sailor's companions found him to be more dead than alive—with one broken leg, chunks of flesh torn away to expose the white bones of crushed ribs, his face flayed, and his throat torn in one place. He surely couldn't move, he was likely to die, and they still were in hostile Indian country. What to do?

They bandaged his terrible injuries as much as possible and, while waiting and expecting his death at any moment, discussed their options. After a time, Henry asked for two volunteers to stay and bury him when the time came. The rest of the party would move on. The two who stayed were a young Jim Bridger, only nineteen, later to become one of the most famous mountain men and western guides, and an older, more experienced John Fitzgerald.

Thinking ahead, they began digging a grave.

But Glass didn't cooperate and die. Not right away, anyway. After a few days, with their patient still seemingly unconscious, still barely clinging to life, fear of attack by the Rees had eaten away at the two watchdogs. Finally gathering up not only their belongings but also their patient's rifle, knife, and other equipment (he wouldn't be needing them, they apparently rationalized), they quietly stole away.

The episode took place close to the site of today's Lemmon, South Dakota, a small city of sixteen hundred with a Web site citing the Hugh Glass story as a memorable milestone of "stamina, strength and raw courage" from the days of the plains frontier. And of course, Glass did *not* die. "Hugh eventually woke—to a grim situation," notes the online historical sketch (http://www.lemmonsouthdakota.com/about/history/hughglass.htm). "His companions had abandoned him, and he vowed he would kill them. He was alone, unarmed, without even a knife and two hundred miles from Ft. Kiowa [on the Missouri River], the nearest settlement. His leg was broken. His wounds were festering. So much flesh had been torn from his back that he could touch bare ribs."

To move at all, he had to reset his broken leg, then fashion some sort of carriage to hold it while he dragged himself forward "on two elbows and one knee." That is, crawled.

His only "equipage" beyond his torn clothing was a bearskin his so-called friends had left behind to cover, hide, and protect his supine body as they departed.

It was September 9 when he began crawling. Destination: the Cheyenne River, a hundred miles away. He didn't dare try rafting down the nearby Grand, for fear the Rees would spot him.

Two months later, he pulled up on the banks of the Cheyenne, halfway back to civilization.

It was a rough passage, but one this time *blessed* by a grizzly bear encounter . . . the second such meeting in the woods for Glass. "Fever and infection took their toll and frequently rendered him unconscious," says the online history. But soon came what may have been his salvation. "Once he passed out and awoke to discover a huge grizzly standing over him. The animal had evidently been attracted by Hugh's bearskin. While Hugh lay perfectly still, the grizzly flicked the bearskin off Hugh's back and began licking his maggot-infested wounds. This may have saved Hugh from further infection and death."

Then, too, it may have been his burning thoughts of revenge that propelled Glass on and on.

In any case, he "fashioned a crude dugout from a fallen tree, shoved it into the water and began floating down the Cheyenne, and then the Missouri." And what luxury that must have been! After crawling for a hundred miles, after two months on the forest floor, he was safe now from most predators, and he had water, all the water he could possibly need or want, at his very fingertips.

Glass finally reached Fort Kiowa. He then gradually recovered from his injuries . . . and his lengthy deprivation of normal foods. "He recuperated and then sought the two men who had left him for dead."

He first tracked down Bridger "at a fur trading post on the Yellowstone River near the mouth of the Big Horn River," but took pity on the future frontier legend's youthfulness and inexperience in such matters as they had shared in the wild. "He [Glass] then sought out Fitzgerald and found him some time later, discovering that he had joined the U.S. Army. Hugh likewise did not kill Fitzgerald because the killing of a U.S. soldier carried severe consequences."

Perhaps in each case he simply realized it was not his nature to kill merely for the sake of revenge.

The experience did *not* send the onetime sailor back to sea, by the way. He stayed on in the West, returning to the upper Missouri country in 1828 "and remaining there until the end of his life," the online history says. "That life came to an end in the early days of 1833, when Hugh and two companions started down the frozen Yellowstone River on a hunting and trapping excursion. They had proceeded only a few miles . . . when a roving band of Arikaras jumped them from the bank, and Hugh Glass, who had become a legend in his own time, at last fell dead beside his two comrades."

★

1 8 3 0 s

Way It Once Was

★

Traveling to Texas in the 1830s, Davy Crockett and his party were puzzled about noon one day by a rumble in the distance. It sounded a bit like thunder, yet the sky was clear—no clouds, no storm in sight.

They had crossed the Trinidad River the day before and now had just stopped by a copse of trees rising from the prairie to rest their horses. As the famous Tennessee woodsman and his companions lolled on the grass, Crockett said he sorely would like to hunt buffalo.

The distant rumble all the while grew more and more distinct, even somewhat ominous. The rumble came from the west, and there, on the horizon, arose a large cloud of dust.

No, no, his companions said, you don't want to hunt buffalo. Too dangerous.

The deep distant rumble grew louder and louder. The dust cloud advanced toward them.

"What can all this mean?" Crockett asked.

"Burn my old shoes if I know," said one of his companions.

It wasn't a tornado, as they thought just possibly for a moment or two. But it *was* coming directly toward their resting spot . . . and now the horses began to show signs of alarm. The men quickly rounded them up and rode them in among the trees.

And just in time, for now, no dust, no cloud, the oncoming juggernaut had taken shape and revealed itself as an immense herd of buffalo—big, thick, hoary animals racing across the plain and, Crockett later wrote, "roaring as if so many devils had broken loose."

With the stampeding buffalo soon abreast of the travelers, Crockett realized he and his companions could have been trampled to death if they hadn't taken shelter among the trees. As it was, his horse shook with fear.

Crockett, though, was fascinated. At the head of the racing herd, he saw, was a black bull. "He came roaring along, his tail straight on end, and at times tossing up the earth with his horns," said Crockett, according to an autobiography he wrote in 1834 with U.S. Rep. Thomas Chilton of Kentucky.

A hunter all his life, Crockett hardly could resist such a challenge. His trusty rifle "Betsey" sprang to his cheek almost automatically. "I never felt such a desire to have a crack at anything in all my life," he recalled. "He drew nigh the place where I was standing. I raised my beautiful Betsey to my shoulder, took deliberate aim, blazed away, and he roared and suddenly stopped."

The black bull's halt threw the beasts behind into great confusion. When the bull stopped, "Those that were near him did so likewise, and the concussion occasioned by the impetus of those in the rear was such that it was a miracle that some of them did not break their legs or necks."

The wounded bull "stood for a few minutes pawing the ground," but then "darted off around the cluster of trees and made for the uplands of the prairies."

The herd followed, "sweeping by like a tornado."

It was a sight to remember all right—"I never witnessed a more beautiful sight to the eye of a hunter in all my life."

After a few moments, Crockett spurred his horse into pursuit. He followed the wide swath of the buffalo herd for two hours or more— "by which time the moving mass appeared like a small cloud in the distant horizon."

And still he followed, completely caught up, "absorbed by the excitement of the chase," until finally all signs of the buffalo herd were gone, "entirely lost in the distance."

Additional Note: Disgusted with his defeat while seeking a fourth congressional term from Tennessee, Davy Crockett decided to chuck it all and head for Texas to help its American settlers fight for their independence from Mexico. By some accounts, the woodsman-legislator started west after telling the voters, "You may all go to hell, and I will go to Texas."

He unfortunately didn't live to see Texas become either independent or an American state, since he was among the nearly two hundred defenders of the Alamo in San Antonio who died fighting the overwhelming numbers that Mexican strongman Antonio López de Santa Anna sent against the old mission in March 1836. Historians still wonder, however, whether Crockett was among those who fought to the death or if he was among the small number of defenders captured as the bastion finally fell and summarily executed. Either way, he died a bona fide American hero soon to be raised to the status of frontier legend.

1832
Old-timer's First Rendezvous

Rejected as too old to participate in the battle of New Orleans (1815), Canadian-born mountain man Jacques "Pino" Fournaise was quite fit and able at the time of the famous wilderness battle of Pierre's Hole seventeen years later, was spry enough to elude angry Bannock Indians while out in the wilderness a year after that, was healthy enough at nearly one hundred years of age to retire (in 1846 or so) and to dwell alone in his cabin near the mouth of the Kansas River (possibly the first "house" in the future Kansas City, Missouri) . . . and was remarkable enough to keep on going for another quarter-century.

Contemporaries in Kansas City fondly recalled the old man with blue eyes, a full head of silvery white hair, stooped shoulders, and an odd, shuffling walk due to knees that "seemed always to be at variance with each other."

Perhaps the shuffle was a memento of his run-in with a wounded buffalo back in the decade after the battle of New Orleans. On that occasion, wrote Frederic E. Voelker in *The Mountain Men and the Fur Trade of the Far West*, "He had set his traps in a mountain stream, gone down afoot into the nearby plains for some buffalo meat and, with one shot, badly wounded a big, crumple-horned bull."

Like so many of mountain men of the Old West, Pino Fournaise trapped beaver for their valuable pelts and wandered far into the unsettled wilderness, either alone or in parties of fellow trappers. In this case the Canadian, probably in his seventies, was trapping in the Black Hills of the Dakotas with a group of fellow mountain men. But he had gone down onto the flat prairie alone. And now he was in trouble. Seemingly only stung by Pino's shot, the enraged buffalo bull turned and charged so quickly that all Pino could do was drop face-down on the ground and hope for the best.

Fortunately for the old-timer, the bull couldn't gore him with its damaged horns. Less fortunately, it found another way to punish its tormentor—the great animal, big as a small automobile, "danced" on Pino's flattened form. The pummeling was so severe that Pino passed out. He awoke sometime later to realize his back was "a mass of wounds and bruises" and his right shin bone was broken. Floating in and out of consciousness, he eventually noticed the buffalo was still with him. The ponderous animal was lying nearby, quite motionless. Pino's only shot had been a deadly one after all.

Still, Pino was twenty miles from his campsite, badly hurt . . . and alone.

Obviously, he had to find help; he must hobble back to his party's camp in the hills as best he could with a broken leg unable to bear any weight. Other than sheer, gritty will, his only resources would be his rifle and hunting knife . . . and both indeed were mentioned by his good friend Bernard Donnelly in a memoir written years later. "[W]ith painful efforts he cut down a sapling with his knife by the aid of which and his rifle he walked or rather crawled the whole distance of twenty miles to his camp, which took him twenty-two days to accomplish," wrote Father Donnelly.

"His comrades," added the priest, "did all they could for him, but [with] no surgeon living at hand, his broken leg was imperfectly set and bandaged." Thus he was left lame for life.

But what a life still to come! Pino's buffalo encounter occurred when he was sixty-eight. Still to come would be many more years of wanderings and trapping in the wilderness north and northwest of the future Kansas City, of brushes and outright battles with hostile Indians, even a close encounter in the bush with a grizzly bear.

For that matter, what a life already lived! Born Jacques Fournaise about 1747 on the north side of the St. Lawrence River, somewhere between Quebec and Montreal, in French Canada, he later recalled that he had been splitting fence rails with his father near Quebec on the day—September 14, 1759—that the British defeated the French on the Plains of Abraham. Thus ended French control of Canada.

Jacques still was in Canada two decades later as the American Revolution effectively ended British power in the future United States . . . and he then headed south, traveling down to Fort Niagara, Lake Erie, and finally Fort Pitt. Finding the future city of Pittsburgh to be "only a miserable village of about a dozen houses," he moved on.

His travels—as a hand on a river flatboat—next took him down the Ohio and Mississippi Rivers until he reached New Orleans. Now almost seventy years in age, he was working there, Voelker noted, "until late in 1814, when General Andrew Jackson prepared to defend the city against the expected attack by the British under General [Edward] Pakenham." Still a skilled rifleman, the Canadian was among the first to volunteer their services against the British, "but was rejected because of his age."

With the British once more driven out of America as a result of the war, Fournaise joined a party of thirty or so Canadians in an Indian-trading expedition taking them up the Missouri River from St. Louis to a campsite a mile or so southeast of the mouth of the Kansas River. "There he built a cabin," wrote Voelker, with a footnote citing an early settler's statement "that when he went to Kansas City, Mo., as a boy in 1868, Fournaise's cabin, on 13th St., just west of Summit, was known as the first house there, that it stood until the 1880s, and that he met Fournaise in the 1870s."

Added Voelker: "It must have been about this time [1815 or thereabouts] that he became well known as 'Old Pino,' a *sobriquet* bestowed by his Canadian companions."

By this time, too, Lewis and Clark had returned from their explorations of the Rockies and the far West; in 1806 their expedition member John Colter had parted company with them and struck off into the wilds of the Yellowstone region as one of the first of a long line of mountain men. Now other hardy souls were continuing the tradition. One of them being the remarkable old-timer Pino Fournaise.

The historical record says little about Pino for the seven or eight years after he arrived at the mouth of the Kansas River in or about the year 1815, noted Voelker, "but the probability is that for some time he trapped and hunted the excellent game country surrounding his 'headquarters' cabin." Somewhat paradoxically, it was during this same period that he encountered his wounded buffalo while trapping beaver in the distant Black Hills.

Although "it required many years for his wounds to heal," Pino soon was out in the untamed wilderness again. First, he probably "was with Etienne Provost's party which went up from Taos, New Mexico, in the fall of 1823, worked the streams of the Colorado Rockies, continued northwestward, and wintered in the mountains." The next year, they moved on west, crossing the Green River and proceeding up the Strawberry to Utah Lake. "At a point about northeast of the lake, probably between the Provo and Jordan rivers, only Provost, Pino and a few other trappers survived a bloody attack by a prowling band of Bannock Indians and escaped across the Wasatch Mountains. They wintered near the confluence of the White and Green rivers."

But that would be only one of the old-timer's Indian fights. After more trapping and, in 1825, attending the first annual summertime rendezvous of mountain men (at Henry's Fork of the Green River), Pino traveled with the famous Jedediah Smith and William Sublette in one trading operation, survived a fight with the Blackfoot near Bear Lake while on another wilderness trek in 1828, and then was present for the fateful rendezvous of 1832 at Pierre's Hole, just west of the Teton Mountains in today's Teton County of southeastern Idaho.

The better-known drama of that gathering was the battle that ensued between the mountain men and raiding Gros Ventres ("Big Belly") Indians, with twelve of the trappers and some Indian allies killed. Lesser known but a fateful moment for Pino in a very personal way was the birth of a baby girl at Pierre's Hole, almost at the same moment as the Indian fight. Born to trapper Andrew Drips and his Otoe wife, the infant Catherine, reported Voelker, became the old man's pet. "He called her '*ma petite* Catherine,' and happily exhibited her around the trappers' camps."

Catherine Drips twenty years later married William Mulkey. The young couple then lived near her father, Andrew, and the retired Pino Fournaise in Kansas City. Seventeen years after that, in 1869, Pino finally accepted their invitation and left his old cabin for a small brick house his "pet" Catherine and her husband had built just for him.

Long before those quieter, more peaceful years, however, Pino continued to tramp around the mountains and valleys of the glorious, untrammeled West. Still ahead, in fact, lay another life-threatening encounter with hostile Indians, an ordeal he again endured alone.

Surprised by Bannock warriors while tending his traps along Henry's Fork of the Snake River (in today's Idaho counties of Fremont and Madison), he dove into a thicket of willows and somehow eluded their search for him. Returning to camp later, he found the Indians had raided it. Moreover, his two companions from the same trapping foray had disappeared. This was in September 1833, by the way, with Pino now in his mideighties.

Determined to "harvest" the beavers in his traps, he revisited them the next morning, took away two more beavers—thus adding to the pair he had salvaged the day before—then continued on with his perambulations in the forest . . . only to be spotted by the Indians again. Once more disappearing among some handy willows, undiscovered even when the Bannock warriors "systematically" beat the thick foliage around him, he this time was dismayed to see the Indians set up camp on the spot. "To Pino's horror, they pitched camp on the bank immediately below him and began to play games," wrote Voelker. "So close were they that one Indian brushed Pino's body."

Lying absolutely still to avoid discovery was excruciating for the elderly trapper. Even so, he remained immobile in his thicket all day long and into the evening, not daring to stir until his Indian foes had fallen asleep. But moving then also was an excruciating exercise. "His aged, lame limbs, for hours painfully cramped, refused to function, and he had to drag himself by his hands and what help he could coax from his crooked knees to a safe spot on the Snake River Plain, where he consumed precious time rubbing his legs until circulation returned and he was able to begin a night march toward a designated rendezvous with his partners on Snake River."

The Indians never caught on, it seems. By good fortune, too, a grizzly bear Pino encountered in the bush allowed him to pass, "unmolested."

Not even now did the old man quit his adventuring. To be sure, he had an emotional and thankful reunion with his two companions, but undeterred by his latest scrape, he spent a good part of the next six years with trapper-trader Andrew Drips, Catherine's father. Then in 1839 Pino set off with his old friend Etienne Provost and John C. Frémont, the "Pathfinder," on an exploration of the area between Fort Pierre on the Missouri River, Devil's Lake, and "the Renville trading post at Lac Qui Parle, on the waters of the Minnesota River," a seven-month sojourn partially accomplished by steamboat.

After that it was back into the mountains again . . . but keeping in close touch with Drips. By 1845 both mountain men were living at "what was called Drips' Trading Post on the North Platte River," twelve miles east of Fort Laramie in present-day Goshewn County, Wyoming. And now, finally, both men were ready to call it a day and retire to Kansas City.

Thus at nearly one hundred years of age, "Pino apparently reoccupied his old cabin, near Drips' house, but he insisted on living alone and expertly cultivating 'his little garden planted with choice vegetables, berry bushes, beautiful flowers and a few tobacco plants,' sleeping on a buffalo robe bed, and swapping yarns with the surviving old French trappers who still haunted the river bluffs near his home."

Thus, too, "Old Pino" Fournaise could remain close to Catherine Drips Mulkey. His friend Andrew Drips (her father) died in 1860.

By 1869, however, four years after the end of the Civil War, Old Pino finally was ready to take up residence in the small brick house the Mulkey couple had built for him. Two years later, in 1871, he suffered an apparent sunstroke and died the next day, "comforted by his beloved Catherine and old friend Father Bernard Donelly." The best guess is that he was 124 years old. (Drips, before he died, recorded his friend Pino's birth date as 1747, and Father Donnelly recalled that Pino was said to be one hundred years old in 1845.

1 8 3 2
Star-crossed Indian Lovers

As Washington Irving once observed, not all Indians—and perhaps not any, for that matter—were as stoic, without personal passion in their lives, as the white man tended to think. Irving, the great storyteller ("Rip van Winkle," "The Legend of Sleepy Hollow") had gone west for a spell. Later he pointedly told the tale of two Indian lovers who were as star-crossed as Romeo and Juliet, albeit in a slightly different way.

However different, though, theirs likewise was a tale replete with senseless death, with real tragedy . . . with roses among thorns, thorns among roses.

For the easterner from Tarrytown, New York, this apparently true tale began with a displaced Blackfoot warrior restless as a caged hawk because he and his stolen paramour, also of the fierce Blackfoot, lived among the far more tranquil Nez Perce ("Pierced Noses") to the west of Blackfoot country.

The wandering Capt. Benjamin Bonneville of Irving's nonfiction book *The Adventures of Captain Bonneville* knew the displaced couple and observed the restless pacing of the Blackfoot warrior Kosato among the Nez Perce.

Going by Bonneville's tale, Irving wrote that Kosato was a "fiery, hot-blooded youth who, with a beautiful girl of the same tribe, had taken refuge among the Nez Perces."

But here he was a wolf among sheep. "Though adopted into the tribe, he still retained the warlike spirit of his race, and loathed the peaceful, inoffensive habits of those around him. The hunting of the deer, the elk, and the buffalo, which was the height of their ambition, was too tame to satisfy his wild and restless nature. His heart burned for the foray, the ambush, the skirmish, the scamper, and all the haps and hazards of roving and predatory warfare."

To make matters worse, his native Blackfoot, traditionally hostile to the neighboring Nez Perce, had been busy in 1832 repeatedly stealing Nez Perce horses and harassing their fugitive warrior's Nez Perce camp when Bonneville came across him. As a result of his people's "nightly prowls," their "daring and successful marauds," Kosato was constantly "in a fever and a flutter, like a hawk in a cage who hears his late companions swooping and screaming in wild liberty above him."

Again and again, the renegade Blackfoot urged his hosts to attack the intruding Blackfoot. "He drew the listening savages round him by his nervous eloquence; taunted them with recitals of past wrongs and insults; drew glowing pictures of triumphs and trophies within their reach; recounted tales of daring and romantic enterprise, of secret marches, covert lurkings, midnight surprisals, sackings, burnings, plunderings, scalpings, together with the triumphant return, and the feasting and rejoicing of the victors."

But never did they rise to his bait. Not even when he beat a drum, gave vent to the war whoop, or plunged into a war dance, all normally "so inspiring to Indian valor." No, there was hardly a smidgen of reaction. "All . . . were lost upon the peaceful spirits of his hearers; not a Nez Perce was to be roused to vengeance, or stimulated to glorious war." The visiting brave's frustration in time gave way to bitterness, and he "repined at the mishap which had severed him from a race of congenial spirits, and driven him to take refuge among beings so destitute of martial fire."

Entering now to query Kosato was Bonneville, who was curious to learn why the warrior had left his people "and why he looked back upon them with such deadly hostility."

Shakespeare, had he known the facts, probably could have answered that last question, understanding as he was that triumph could begat guilt, that guilt could begat anger, that even love could begat guilt . . . even when love succeeds.

Kosato consented to tell Bonneville the story, and as Irving commented, "It gives a picture of the deep, strong passions that work in the bosoms of these miscalled stoics."

The warrior explained that his situation had to do with his wife. "You see," he began, "she is good; she is beautiful—I love her. Yet she has been the cause of all my troubles. She was the wife of my chief. I loved her more than he did; and she knew it. We talked together; we laughed together; we were always seeking each other's society; but we were as innocent as children. The chief grew jealous, and commanded her to speak with me no more. His heart became hard toward her; his jealousy grew more furious. He beat her without cause and without mercy; and threatened to kill her outright if she even looked at me."

Kosato, of course, was devastated to see his true love treated in such a manner. But he, too, would be an object of the chief's wrath. "His rage against me was no less persecuting," he related to Bonneville (but, true, most likely in somewhat simpler language than seen in the version served up by the storyteller). "War parties of the Crows were hovering around us. Our young men had seen their trail. All hearts were roused for action; my horses were before my lodge. Suddenly the chief came, took them to his own pickets, and called them his own. What could I do? He was a chief. I durst not speak, but my heart was burning. I joined no longer in council, the hunt, or the war-feast. What had I to do there? An unhorsed, degraded warrior. I kept by myself, and thought of nothing but these wrongs and outrages."

In short, Kosato remained aloof, vengeful, a brooding menace to the chief . . . who should have foreseen. What could have been on *his* mind as he strolled one evening, quite alone, among his horses, that is, among both his and Kosato's horses? Was he deliberately tempting fate?

On a knoll overlooking the meadow where the horses were pastured, sat Kosato, brooding. He told Bonneville he pondered "the injuries I had suffered, and the cruelties which she I loved had endured for my sake, until my heart swelled and grew sore, and my teeth were clinched."

As luck, or fate, would have it, Kosato chanced to look down on the meadow as the villainous chief happened to walk into view . . . the moment of retribution was at hand. In mere seconds the hero of the piece—and his lovely heroine—would be freed of their burden but consigned to the retribution imposed by implacable fate. "I fastened my eyes upon him as a hawk's; my blood boiled; I drew my breath hard. He went among the willows. In an instant I was on my feet; my hand was on my knife—I flew rather than ran—before he was aware I sprang upon him, and with two blows laid him dead at my feet."

And now, to hide the dread deed, "I covered his body with earth, and strewed bushes over the place."

Next he told his one true love. "I hastened to her I loved, told her what I had done, and urged her to fly with me."

She of course was stunned, fearful . . . unsure. "She only answered me with tears. I reminded her of the wrongs I had suffered, and of the blows and stripes she had endured from the deceased; I had done nothing but an act of justice."

But was it? She had her doubts. "I again urged her to fly; but she only wept the more, and bade me to go."

This was not what he had expected.

"'Tis well," he said, heavy in heart. "Kosato will go alone to the desert. None will be with him but the wild beasts of the desert. The seekers of blood may follow on his trail. They may come upon him when he sleeps and glut their revenge; but you will be safe. Kosato will go alone."

He turned to go, but that was too much for her to bear. "She sprang after me, and strained me in her arms. 'No,' she cried, 'Kosato shall not go alone! Wherever he goes I will go—he shall never part from me.'"

And so they departed, "stealing quietly from the village" and mounting "the first horses we encountered." They traveled night and day as speedily as possible until reaching the Nez Perce camp where Bonneville had come across the star-crossed lovers.

While not happy with his new situation, the Blackfoot brave readily conceded that the Nez Perce had "received us with welcome, and we have dwelt with them in peace." Further, "they are good and kind; they are honest," but, by Kosato's Blackfoot standards, their hearts were the hearts of women.

His story, Washington Irving paused to say, "is of a kind that often occurs in Indian life; where love elopements from tribe to tribe are as frequent as among the novel."

While that may be so, contrary to the stereotype of the stoic warrior, the gods of love and war were not yet quite through with Kosato the renegade Blackfoot who had killed his chief and loved his wife.

Not long after, for instance, the Nez Perce village as a body went on a buffalo hunt, Kosato included. They still were "haunted and harassed by their old enemies the Blackfoot, who, as usual, contrived to carry off many of their horses." After a time, a small body of Kosato's hosts separated from the larger group to find good pasturage for their remaining horses. The Blackfoot, on the other hand, pulled together their smaller bands to produce a large war party of three hundred. The Blackfoot then approached the camping ground where Bonneville had first heard Kosato's story, found its lodges deserted, and hid themselves in nearby willows and thickets, Irving wrote, in hopes that some "straggler" would appear and lead them to the absent Nez Perce.

"As fortune would have it, Kosato, the Blackfoot renegade, was the first to pass along, accompanied by his blood-bought bride. The Blackfoot knew and marked him as he passed; he was within bowshot of their ambuscade; yet, much as they thirsted for his blood, they forebore to launch a shaft; sparing him for the moment when he might lead them to their prey."

Unaware that he was being followed, Kosato did lead the Blackfoot to the small party of Nez Perce, only twenty men and even fewer, just nine, armed with firearms. Outnumbered when the Blackfoot attacked, the Nez Perce "showed themselves . . . as brave and skillful in warfare as they had been mild and long-suffering in peace."

Like soldiers of later centuries, they dug in, digging holes in their lodges, and fought back "desperately." Soon, several of the attacking Blackfoot lay dead . . . but not a single Nez Perce had been killed.

The Blackfoot, meanwhile, ran out of ammunition and resorted to throwing stones.

Not to be denied a role of their own, it seems, the gods of war had decreed a great irony in the affair. The leader of the attacking Blackfoot was a renegade Nez Perce! And soon, having "no vindictive rage against his native tribe," the Blackfoot chief called off the attack and led his warriors away—together with seventy Nez Perce horses, the prize sought all along.

And what of the fiery Kosato? Was he not heard from at all?

He hardly was, but not through any fault of his own. At the start of the engagement, he had fought hard—"with fury rather than valor, animating the others by word as well as deed." But then he was laid low by a bullet to the head, falling "senseless" to the ground. "There his body remained when the battle was over, and the victors were leading off the horses." His pretty wife, once their chief's wife, "hung over him with frantic lamentations." When the departing Blackfoot urged her to leave with them and return to her own people, she refused.

Instead she stayed by her fallen warrior's side, "giving way to passionate grief." But also studying his face . . . suddenly she detected a tremor. Was it real? A shuddering breath? Yes, no mistake—he indeed was breathing! "The ball, which had been nearly spent before it struck him, had stunned instead of killing him. By the ministry of his faithful wife, he gradually recovered, reviving to a redoubled love for her, and hatred of his tribe."

With his recovery, Kosato resumed his old exhortations for the Nez Perce to take action, to show themselves to be real men by retaliating against the troublesome Blackfoot. And finally they did.

With Kosato himself as the leader, a band of Nez Perce warriors set off for Blackfoot country and soon came upon a large Blackfoot band.

"Without waiting to estimate their force, he attacked them with characteristic fury, and was bravely seconded by his followers. The contest for a while was hot and bloody; at length, as is customary with these two tribes, they paused, and held a long parley, or rather a war of words."

This was psychological warfare, pure and simple. If it's fighting you want, the Blackfoot chief warned, you had better return to your villages and prepare to defend your homes. "The Blackfoot warriors have hitherto made war on you as children," he said. "They are now coming as men. A great force is at hand; they are on their way to your towns, and are determined to rub out the very name of the Nez Perce from the mountains. Return, I say, to your towns, and fight there, if you wish to live any longer as a people."

Kosato, realizing the chief meant what he said, persuaded his comrades to rush back to the Nez Perce territory and prepare for the attack. But his hosts, as before, paid little attention. When three hundred Blackfoot appeared, the Nez Perce were in a panic. With many of their young men off finding new horses, those left behind were too few in number to give the Blackfoot much of a fight in the open.

They jumped at the offer of a chief—"named Blue John by the whites"—to take a small party, circle behind the Blackfoot through a hidden defile, then stampede their horses, allowing all the Nez Perce to fight an unmounted enemy while mounted on their own horses. Unfortunately, the Blackfoot discovered the attempted flanking movement and themselves outflanked the band in the defile. In the bloody fight that followed, thirty Nez Perce died—only one escaped the carnage, by leaping upon a slain Blackfoot's horse and galloping off.

Back in the Nez Perce camp, the rest of the grieving Indians prepared for the worst, but, for reasons of their own, the surviving Blackfoot turned away and left the area. Perhaps they had suffered too many casualties of their own.

The Nez Perce, of course, were left prostrate by their losses—"the women with piercing cries and wailings, the men with downcast countenances, in which gloom and sorrow seemed fixed as in marble." As the mutilated bodies were carried from the defile to the village, "the scene of heart-rending anguish and lamentation that ensued would have confounded those who insist on Indian stoicism."

Kosato, meanwhile, had not taken part in Blue John's brave flanking attack. Along with the other defenders, he had stayed in the village. As his only parting note, Irving tells us that, last seen or heard, Kosato "was again striving to rouse the vindictive feelings of his adopted brethren, and to prompt them to revenge the slaughter of their devoted braves."

Additional Notes: Although he apparently never set foot there, Utah's Bonneville Salt Flats—so flat you sometimes can see the earth's curvature there—were named for Capt. Benjamin Louis Eulalie de Bonneville (1796–1878), French-born explorer-adventurer and hero of Washington Irving's book. So was the 197-foot-high Bonneville Dam in Oregon and so was nearby North Bonneville, Washington, a bedroom community for the dam's construction workers. Although born in Paris, Bonneville graduated from West Point and served for many years as an officer in the U.S. Army. He and his family in France were close friends of the Revolutionary War pamphleteer Thomas Paine and the Marquis de Lafayette, also of Revolutionary fame. Bonneville, in fact, accompanied the marquis in his American tour of 1824–25 as an aide.

Bonneville took leave from 1832 to 1835 to try his hand as a trader during the mountain-man era of the West, with a base on the Green River in Wyoming. While his venture, involving New York financing and a party of a hundred men, failed commercially, his exploratory travels gave the army information about British activities in the Northwest and provided fresh details on the geography of the region. He also is credited by some with conducting the first wagons over the South Pass in the Rockies. For overstaying his leave, he was dismissed from the army, but with the support of President Andrew Jackson, he was reinstated.

1832
Unlikely Comrades in Arms

Picture this: Jefferson Davis and Abraham Lincoln sitting down to the same officers mess with perfect amiability. Unlikely as it may seem, it did happen . . . at a time early in their lives when they both served the American flag as comrades in arms.

As young men the future presidents of the Confederacy and the Union of Civil War years served together in an Indian war, one as a lieutenant in the regular army, the other as an elected militia captain . . . served together and likely knew each other, even to the point of messing together at a frontier post called Dixon's Ferry on the south banks of the Rock River in Illinois.

They were there as participants in the Black Hawk War of 1832, and therein is to be found a tale or two about each of the historic figures. Not only were Jefferson Davis and Abraham Lincoln from time to time on the same premises, engaged jointly in the same military venture, so was another historical luminary destined to become a president, Zachary Taylor . . . and all taking part in a campaign boding no good for the Indian chief Black Hawk and his followers. Also present, it bears mentioning, were two young officers destined to become leading Confederate generals in the Civil War: Albert Sidney Johnston and Joseph E. Johnston. The camp also included Col. Nathan Boone, son of the famous frontiersman Daniel Boone.

The setting for those hours, even days, that so many significant figures spent together was the pioneering John Dixon's rambling, ninety-foot log cabin and associated grounds, and his ferry, which carried travelers across the Rock River as an integral segment of an early trail west.

"This famous old trail was then the route pursued by the argonauts of all the southern country in search of sudden wealth in the mines," wrote Frank Stevens in his 1903 history, *The Black Hawk War.* "It was the great thoroughfare from Peoria, then more commonly referred to as Fort Clark, to Galena, sought by those from the St. Louis country on the southwest and the old Vincennes country to the southeast, and followed on northwesterly past Dixon's Ferry to Galena, where the crowds dispersed and scattered for the lead 'diggings' over northwestern Illinois and southwestern Wisconsin, then a part of Michigan Territory."

According to Stevens, "White men and Indians alike made their pilgrimages along that trail, stopping over with Mr. Dixon to strengthen the inner man and replenish their stock of supplies."

The affable Dixon had established his friendly outpost by the river in 1830, the same year, ominously, that the federal government ordered the Sauk Indians of Illinois to make way for an ever-swelling tide of white settlers by moving to designated lands in today's Iowa. There the

Indians tried to continue their farming practices in strange surroundings until the harsh winter of 1831–32. In the spring, the charismatic leader Black Hawk led a thousand or more Sauk and Fox Indians back into northern Illinois with the naive hope of once again growing corn on what they considered their land. Apparently Black Hawk hoped other tribes, such as the Winnebago, would join in his revolt against the white man's fiat.

Alarmed when he observed the settlers organizing militia units in response to his people's reappearance in Illinois, Black Hawk tried to surrender to one such militia group. But the poorly disciplined volunteers fired on the Indians in the face of a peace flag. The Indians returned fire . . . the militia retreated. The Black Hawk War was on.

As the Sauk retreated northward into Wisconsin by way of the Rock River, nine hundred militiamen joined four hundred regular army troops in pursuit of the Indians, who now raided frontier villages and farms along their pathway. For a time, the military fetched up at Dixon's Ferry, where, reported historian Stevens, "Officers of the militia were invited to mess with the regulars, and vice versa, and . . . Abraham Lincoln and Jefferson Davis were brought together for the first time and 'messed' at Mr. Dixon's table."

Lincoln, riding a borrowed horse, was there as captain of "a company of militia composed of sixty-nine as intractable and headstrong men as could be found at that very independent period, extravagantly opposed to discipline, acknowledging no superior, yet managed with skill and credit to all by the captain."

The young Lincoln, only twenty-three but a towering six foot four, had been "elected" his company's captain. The vote was conducted by having the men line up behind their choice for the honor of command. At the conclusion of the process, the inexperienced Lincoln stood at the head of the longer line . . . by two men or by two-thirds, according to conflicting accounts. In later years he called this one of his proudest moments.

The neophyte company commander was noted for his good humor as well as his readiness to take part in a good footrace or wrestling match. "Captain Lincoln was magnetic and his men were drawn toward him from admiration and not alone because they knew he was a man of courage and strength," wrote Stevens. In the sporting environment that thrived among the militiamen in their idle hours, Lincoln was well known for his athletic abilities and readiness to compete. "There were close upon two thousand horses in camp," wrote Stevens also, "and when off duty no time was allowed to lapse without a horse race, a foot race or a wrestling match. Into those contests, Captain Lincoln did not obtrude himself, but he was always counted on as 'being ready' and on the spot. His men knew his prowess and were proud of it. . . . They were alert to advertise that prowess at all times and willing to stake their last earthly possession on his success."

Fortunately, their captain was willing to do his part. "To oblige his men, and likely his own inclination, [he] took on wrestling matches and vanquished his antagonists one after the other to the end of his service as a soldier."

He may have defeated all comers, that is, except a "burly" challenger from another "section" named Thompson. Their match before an excited crowd of onlookers began slowly enough. "The combatants grappled and it soon became evident that Thompson was qualified to bear championship laurels," reported Stevens. "The tussle was long and uncertain and keyed all the men up to a high tension, as each contestant was being cheered to a victory; but Thompson, after a hard battle, secured the first fall."

For the next round, Lincoln changed his strategy, explaining to his friends: "This is the most powerful man I ever had hold of. He will throw me and you will lose your all [wagers] unless I act on the defensive."

Accordingly, Lincoln first tried a "crotch hold" on his opponent, then, when that didn't work, a "sliding away" maneuver. "In this Captain Lincoln was more successful, for in the scramble for advantage both men went to ground in a heap, which according to the ethics of frontier wrestling, is denominated a 'dog fall,' hence a draw."

When Thompson's partisans claimed victory, "a storm of protest went up from Captain Lincoln's backers," and for a moment it appeared a brawl might break out between the two groups. But Lincoln himself ended that threat by loudly telling his fans, "Boys, the man actually threw me once fair, broadly [obviously] so, and the second time, this very fall, he threw me fairly, though not apparently so."

It was a generous way to settle the issue, although, said Stevens, the term *dog fall* "was frequently repeated during the remainder of the campaign by the Captain's partisans." In fact, "That defeat and the acknowledgment of it in no sense diminished the influence or standing of Captain Lincoln with his men or those who were beginning to know and like him."

Meanwhile, Beardstown, site of the state mustering-in ritual for Lincoln and his company, gave birth to a famous anecdote. Lincoln's men were marching toward a fence with a gate, and he couldn't remember the orders that would rearrange the men in files so they could march through the gate . . . on the other hand, their present marching formation couldn't possibly squeeze through the gate. And yet the fence had to be traversed.

Lincoln's solution? He halted his men, dismissed them on the spot, and ordered them to fall in on the other side of the fence. They leisurely walked through the gate.

Speaking of mustering in, Stevens dismissed the allegation that Lt. Jefferson Davis personally administered the oath of federal service to Lincoln, although that would have been a wondrous irony had it been true. It pained Stevens to discredit this long-held belief, but Lincoln had already been sworn into *state* service in Beardstown.

Just as surely, it seems, the Lincoln of 1832 was known for his dignity, his loyalty to his men, and his quiet but firm leadership. Some of the Illinois militiamen one night broke into the officers quarters, stole some whiskey, and got rollickin' drunk. Lincoln, unaware, had nothing to do with it, but some of his men did . . . Lincoln had to share a measure of their punishment with them. Thus for two days he had to wear an embarrassing wooden sword.

"This he did 'for the boys' with grim humor. As the men sobered up and gradually straggled into camp . . . , they realized what their disgraceful behavior had brought to their captain. Remorse, or some equally powerful agency, made Captain Lincoln's company a model one from that hour."

In a more serious incident, Lincoln may have saved an old Indian from possible harm. According to Stevens, "[T]he story is told of an old Pottawatomie Indian who came into camp, tired and hungry." He was not exactly welcomed with open arms He pulled out of his "garments" a safe conduct pass signed by the appropriate authority, but that didn't mollify the trigger-happy militiamen in the slightest. "Make an example of him," came a shout. "The letter is a forgery," shouted others. "[S]till others," added Stevens, "called him a spy, and the poor old fellow was in danger of death, when Captain Lincoln, 'his face swarthy with resolution and rage,' stepped forward, even between the cowering Indian and the guns pointed at him, and shouted, 'This must not be; he must not be shot and killed by us,' and the men recoiled.

'This is cowardly on your part, Lincoln,' one man said; to which Captain Lincoln instantly replied, 'If any man thinks I am a coward let him test it.' Still defiant, another cried, 'Lincoln, you are larger and heavier than we are,' but that miserable objection was quickly disposed of by the rejoinder from the Captain: 'This you can guard against; choose your weapons.' It is needless to add that no one chose a weapon and that the Indian departed in safety."

Stevens has stories to tell about future Confederate president Davis's service in the Black Hawk War as well. For one thing, the young army officer broke off a prearranged furlough and reported for duty the moment he heard of the Indian "troubles" in Illinois and adjoining Wisconsin. Thus he was in and out of John Dixon's trading post and ferry station many times during the largely springtime campaign of 1832, but Stevens has no real interplay to report between the two future political principals of the Civil War. The historian does cite a number of eye-witnesses to Davis's presence to show that the Mississippian really was on hand, despite the War Department's records indicating he was on leave. Apparently the cancellation of his furlough never caught up to the approval granting his application for leave.

Not only did Davis report immediately, he served throughout the campaign, up to and beyond the battle that broke the back of Black Hawk's resistance, the battle of Bad Axe (River) on August 2, 1832, in the future state of Wisconsin. In the meantime, though, West Point graduate Davis had been greatly impressed with the Indian tactics he witnessed in the battle of the Wisconsin River on July 21 near today's Sauk City, Wisconsin.

In that affair, Davis told an Iowa historian late in the nineteenth century, "We were one day pursuing the Indians, when we came close to the Wisconsin River. Reaching the river bank, the Indians made so determined a stand, and fought with such desperation, that they held us in check." During the fight, the tribal women "tore bark from the trees, with which they made little shallops, in which they floated their papooses and other impedimenta across to an island, also swimming over the ponies."

Half the warriors then plunged into the water and swam across, "each holding his gun over his head, and swimming with the other."

From the island, they opened a galling fire on the white troops as cover while the second half of the warriors "slipped down the bank and swam over in like manner."

Davis, destined to fight in the Mexican War and lead the Confederacy in the bloody Civil War, never forgot the Indians' fighting withdrawal on the Wisconsin River in 1832. "This was the most brilliant exhibition of military tactics that I ever witnessed—a feat of consummate management and bravery, in the face of an enemy of greatly superior numbers," he told his Iowa contact, identified by Stevens as "curator of the Historical Department of Iowa."

Like Lincoln, Davis apparently adhered to his duties and responsibilities and was well liked by those around him. . . . even, it seems, by Black Hawk himself.

The Indian chief came to know Davis as the officer in charge of transporting a hundred of the captured Indians, Black Hawk and a son among them, aboard the steamboat *Winnebago* en route to Jefferson Barracks at St. Louis by way of the Mississippi River. "He is a good and brave young chief, with whose conduct I was much pleased," wrote Black Hawk in an autobiography the next year. When the steamboat carrying the newly taken prisoners stopped at Galena, Illinois, Black Hawk also observed that people "crowded to the boat to see us." But Davis wouldn't allow anyone to make a spectacle of his prisoners. "[T]he war chief would not permit them to enter the apartment where we were,"added Black Hawk, "knowing from what his feelings would have been if he had been placed in a similar position that we did not wish to have a gaping crowd around us."

One further anecdote stemming from this time that Lincoln and Davis spent in close proximity to each other:

Years later, wrote historian Stevens, an aging John Dixon, more than eighty years old by this time, sought a federal land grant as compensation for the many services he had provided during the Black Hawk War. A House-originated bill that would have granted him a warrant for 160 acres reached the U.S. Senate's Public Lands Committee but foundered there for lack of supporting testimony or documentation. When a friendly Illinois senator then asked Dixon if he had any more friends in the Senate, the old man thought a moment then said, "Why, yes, there is Lieutenant Davis."

Indeed, serving on behalf of his native Mississippi shortly before its secession from the Union, was Jefferson Davis, now a U.S. senator. And he, of course, did recall Dixon's role during the short Black Hawk campaign of 1832. "He was of great service in the settlement of the country," Davis now told the Senate, which was meeting as a committee of the whole. "He was of service at that time in furnishing supplies and giving information in regard to the country, and afterwards in taking care of the sick."

With these and a few other well-chosen words, Davis assured the bill's passage by the Senate . . . and thus assured Dixon his reward for vital services rendered.

Epilogue: The Black Hawk War, meanwhile, came to a tragic end for Black Hawk and his followers. In the battle of Bad Axe on August 2, 1832, the Indians were caught trying to ford the Mississippi near today's Victory, Wisconsin. An Internet summary by the Wisconsin Historical Society spells out the devastating outcome for the Indians: "Ignoring a truce flag, the troops aboard a river steamboat fired cannons and rifles, killing hundreds, including many children. Many of those who made it across the river were slain by the Eastern Sioux, allies of the Americans in the 1832. Only 150 of the one thousand members of Black Hawk's band survived the events of the summer of 1832" (http://www.wisc.edu/oss/lessons/secondary/blackhawk.htm).

Black Hawk himself was taken east to meet President Andrew Jackson and later was sent back west "to live with surviving members of the Sauk and Fox nation," notes the same historical society source.

★

1 8 3 6
Reunited at the Alamo
★

They both were born in South Carolina—in a section of today's Saluda County. Their families attended Red Bank Baptist Church. Only two and a half years apart in age, they surely knew each other and perhaps even played together as children.

But their lives took different paths . . . only to merge years later far from their mutual birthplace. To merge at a mutual hour of death.

Because of their fateful reunion, the South Carolina Hall of Fame in recent years gathered them into its ranks of renown. In addition, Saluda County boosters pridefully sell bumper stickers and T-shirts boasting, "Where Texas Began."

How's that again? Texas!

For many, one name alone should be the tipoff: William Barret Travis. But so should the other as well: James Butler Bonham.

And it indeed was in Texas, after two decades apart, that their paths came back together again—at a place called the Alamo. For there, Travis, a lieutenant colonel of cavalry, commanded to the bitter end. And there, Bonham also fought to the last after voluntarily returning to the besieged old mission from forays as a courier for Travis to the world outside.

What separate paths brought these two South Carolinians together in the crucible of the Texas Revolution? For Travis, born in 1809, the better-known of the pair and the first to join the American settlers and adventurers pouring into Mexican Texas, it was a journey that began with a family move to Alabama in 1817. After normal schooling, then apprenticeship with a lawyer in Claiborne, Alabama, young Travis became an attorney himself. He married at age twenty and fathered a son, launched a newspaper, the *Claiborne Herald,* and became an adjutant of a local militia regiment.

Not so happily, he soon left his wife, whose second pregnancy he apparently suspected was not his doing. He may even have killed a man over the issue, according to various historical sources. In 1831 he turned for Mexican-owned Texas and set up a law practice in Anahuac on Galveston Bay. Technically an illegal immigrant, he soon allied himself with a group of restive American settlers chafing under Mexican rule, "Eventually this group became known as the war party as tension increased between the Mexican government and American settlers in Texas," notes the encyclopedic *Handbook of Texas Online.*

As one event led to another, Travis briefly was arrested then freed. He led two dozen men in an attack against a Mexican military garrison at Anahuac in 1835—and, no surprise, was branded an outlaw as a result. Late the same year, as a militia cavalryman, he joined the American settlers besieging the Mexicans holding San Antonio de Bexar. But he wasn't present for the final Mexican collapse because he was closeted with leaders of the Texas Revolution at San Felipe.

For Travis those consultations would prove fateful indeed. He emerged as a newly appointed lieutenant colonel of cavalry and chief recruiting officer for the Texan army. Ordered to gather one hundred men as a reinforcement for Col. James C. Neill at recently captured San Antonio, he could only round up twenty-nine before setting off for his place of destiny.

Events there already were unfolding at an inexorable pace. Mexican dictator Antonio López de Santa Anna was marching on San Antonio to wrest it back from the outrageous Texan rebels. Neill was called away in response to a family illness. Command of his few men fell to Travis, who threw himself into finishing Neill's conversion of the old mission into a fort on the edge of San Antonio. Meanwhile, James Bowie had arrived with about thirty additional defenders in tow (Davy Crockett soon appeared as well). Travis and Bowie, a quarreling pair, agreed to share command until, with Santa Anna virtually at the Alamo gates, Bowie fell ill. At that point, Travis assumed overall command.

Meanwhile, what of his childhood acquaintance and possible play-mate, James Butler Bonham? Well, here was a rebel from the word go. Born in 1807 then attending South Carolina College (now the University of South Carolina) in 1823, this hotheaded young man was expelled for leading student protests against the school's food and against the requirement to attend class in bad weather as well as good. Taking up the law as his vocation (like Travis), Bonham soon made a name—of sorts—for himself by caning a fellow lawyer in court then threatening to tweak the protesting judge's nose. That little contre-temps earned Bonham ninety days for contempt of court.

Apparently undismayed, militia Lieutenant Colonel Bonham turned up next as an aide to South Carolina Governor James Hamilton during the Nullification Crisis of the early 1830s. Also briefly serving as an artillery captain in Charleston but still a practicing attorney, Bonham moved on to Montgomery, Alabama, in 1834. Edging ever westward, he popped up next in Mobile, Alabama, where in October 1835 he led a pro-Texan rally in the Shakespeare Theater.

But that wasn't enough for Bonham. He next organized the volun-teer Mobile Grays to serve in the Texas Revolution and by November 1835 was himself in Texas. Volunteering to serve the cause without pay or land grant in return, he was appointed a second lieutenant in the Texas cavalry. By January 1836 no less a personage than Sam Houston recommended a major's rank for Bonham, saying, "His influence in the army is great—more so than some who 'would be generals.'"

That same month Bonham rode into San Antonio for his pending reunion with Travis, probably arriving January 19 with Bowie. It wasn't long before Bowie, Bonham, Crockett, and Travis—along with nearly two hundred additional defenders—were trapped behind the Alamo walls by Santa Anna's overwhelming forces.

Bonham was one of several messengers to leave the adobe mission with pleas from Travis to the world outside for help in resisting the Mexican siege. In one of his messages, addressed to the "people of Texas & all Americans in the world," Travis vowed no surrender or retreat. "Victory or death," he bravely declared.

But along with the defiance there was a note of desperation. "I call on you in the name of Liberty, of patriotism & everything dear to the American character, to come to our aid, with all dispatch." Few would come in time, but one who did, apparently returning more than once to the besieged Alamo—and a sure death—was Bonham.

Both Carolina-bred heroes were destined to die on March 6, 1836, the day that Santa Anna finally, after nearly two weeks of siege and artillery fire, launched an all-out attack against the old mission. Alamo commander Travis was one of the first to die, from a bullet in the head. Bonham went down later in the day, probably while serving a cannon in the Alamo chapel.

For each man it had been a relatively short, albeit often dramatic interlude between birth and a hero's death so far from their starting place at Saluda, South Carolina . . . where, incidentally, some still wonder if they hadn't kept up with each other over the years, where some still speculate that Travis might have written Bonham and asked him to join the still-aborning Texas Revolution, which of course did succeed despite the setback of the Alamo.

Whatever the case there, the Saluda County Historical Society is quite firm in stating the claim that its Flat Grove, a restored eighteenth-century log structure, is the only still-standing house in America where an Alamo defender was born. Not Travis, but James Butler Bonham.

★

1 8 3 6
Day of Reckoning

★

Of the big three associated with the heroic American stand at the Alamo, the first to arrive was a Kentucky-born alligator rider, slave trader, land speculator, sometime gambler, knife fighter, Indian fighter, and veteran Mexican fighter for whom a popular frontier knife had been named. William Barret Travis and Davy Crockett may have done their bit at the Alamo (and many others, too), but James Bowie was the first of the famous trio to arrive at the mission-turned-fort on the edge of San Antonio, Texas.

The road leading Bowie to the Alamo had been a rocky one with many dramatic turns, some of them not the usual sort of thing that qualifies one for a hero's garlands, but all of them adding up to the Bowie legend. Born in Kentucky but raised in Missouri and south-eastern Louisiana, the young Bowie certainly could have broken wild horses, trapped bears, and ridden an alligator or two, as held by family stories. Surely he did a lot of hunting and fishing, like any frontier lad of the early nineteenth century. By the time he reached adulthood, he also knew how to handle himself among the men of his rough-and-ready environment.

About six feet in height by then (tall for his era), sandy-haired, and gray-eyed, he could be cool and smooth when he wanted, but violent and hot of temper, too.

Coming a bit later in his life, there is the story of the time he faced down the redoubtable Sam Houston . . . over nothing, really. As told by Walter Lord in *A Time to Stand*, Bowie was returning from "deep inside Mexico" and "fell in with Sam Houston." Bowie's horse was tired out, exhausted, and Bowie simply announced, as if entirely his due, "Houston, I want your horse."

The future president of the Republic of Texas and the conqueror of Santa Anna at the battle of San Jacinto replied, "You can't have him. I have only one and I need him."

Bowie calmly responded, "I'm going to take him." He then "left the room for a moment."

Houston turned to a friend and asked, "Do you think it right for me to give up my horse to Bowie?"

The friend, apparently familiar with Bowie's reputation, said, "Perhaps it might be proper under the circumstances."

"Damn him," said Houston, "let him take the horse."

"Yet," added Lord, "Houston liked the man. Unlike [Stephen] Austin, who always sniffed at Bowie as an impossible adventurer, Houston saw in him the admirable qualities of a born leader, a good friend."

Whether adventurer, leader, or good friend, Bowie was always a man of action. Of that there is no doubt. His thirst for action, beyond roping and riding alligators in the bayous of Louisiana, can be traced back to 1815, when he and his brother Rezin marched off to fight at New Orleans with Andrew Jackson. But it seems the War of 1812—and its belated battle of New Orleans—ended before they got there. Born in 1796 by most accounts, Jim Bowie was about nineteen years old at the time.

He and Rezin turned to slave trading, with the notorious Gulf Coast pirate Jean Laffite as their supplier of human cargo. The arrangement was based upon Laffite's seizure of slave ships in the Caribbean and the Gulf of Mexico. The pirate then sold the hapless slaves to people like the Bowie brothers, and they in turn sold them to planters and others in St. Landry Parish, Louisiana, some distance up the Vermilion River.

After amassing a nest egg of sixty-five thousand dollars, according to William R. Williamson in the *Handbook of Texas Online,* the brothers quit the tawdry slave business and indulged in land speculation. James, meanwhile, was engaged and about to marry when his betrothed suddenly fell ill and died just two weeks before the planned wedding.

That was in September 1829, by which time Bowie—and his knife—had become notorious up and down the frontier for his role in the so-called Sandbar Fight of 1827. This vicious affair began with a duel on a river sandbar in which the two principals fired at each other with no blood spilled then saw their observers pitch into a deadly brawl. An old enemy of Bowie's was there, Rapides Parish sheriff Norris Wright, who, doubling as a banker, had turned down a loan request from Bowie. When one observer shot and felled another man, Bowie fired at the first observer but missed. Wright then shot Bowie in the lower chest. Bowie nonetheless was able to pull out a butcher-sort-of-knife he usually carried and chased Wright. Another onlooker then shot Bowie in the thigh, and when the Kentuckian fell, Wright and a companion began stabbing him.

But Bowie still had his knife, which he "plunged into his assailant's [Wright's] breast," noted Williamson in his online profile of Bowie. He also severely slashed Wright's companion. "All the witnesses remembered Bowie's 'big butcher knife,' the first Bowie knife. Reports of Bowie's prowess and his lethal blade captured public attention and he was proclaimed the South's most formidable knife fighter. Men asked blacksmiths and cutlers to make a knife like Jim Bowie's."

Recovering from his wounds, Bowie spent the late 1820s "enjoying . . . [the] excitement and pleasures" of life in colorful New

Orleans, but he and two brothers, Rezin and Steven, also were busy establishing "the Arcadia sugar plantation of some 1,800 acres near the town of Thibodaux, Terrebonne Parish, where they set up the first steam-powered sugar mill in Louisiana." In 1831, however, they sold Arcadia, "other landholdings and eighty-two slaves to Natchez investors for $90,000." Jim Bowie, meanwhile, moved on to Mexican-owned Texas in 1830 and soon swore allegiance to Mexico, bought land, established a base at San Antonio, and began to win new friends. "Bowie, age thirty-four, was at his prime," notes the Williamson account. "He was well traveled, convivial, loved music, and was generous. He also was ambitious and scheming; he played cards for money, and lived in a world of debt."

Passing himself off as a well-heeled Anglo with a deep commitment to the future of Texas, Bowie ingratiated himself with San Antonio's truly wealthy Veramendi family, joined the Roman Catholic Church, and in April 1831 married their beautiful young daughter Ursula. He pledged a dowry of $15,000 and said his properties were worth $222,800, but some of the details he claimed were "fraudulent," says the Williamson account, as was his stated age of "thirty-two." He was thirty-five. Meanwhile, he still was owed $45,000 for his share of the Arcadia sugar plantation.

The Veramendis surely must have entertained some doubts about the man who married their daughter when he "borrowed $1,879 from his father-in-law and $750 from Ursula's grandmother for a honeymoon trip to New Orleans and Natchez."

Doubts or not, they soon advanced the financing he needed to mount a search for the legendary "lost" Los Almagres silver mine near the ruins of the Santa Cruz de San Saba Mission west of San Antonio. Riding off with brother Rezin and a party of nine additional men, Bowie began an amazing series of fights, skirmishes, and battles with Indians and Mexicans in which the other side always seemed to suffer disproportionate losses. Attacked by Indians near San Saba, Bowie and his men fought them off for thirteen hours from an oak grove, "reportedly" killing forty of their attackers and wounding another thirty while losing only one man.

In August 1832, with the Texan revolution against Mexican rule nearing its boiling point, Bowie took part in James W. Bullock's siege of the Mexican garrison at Nacogdoches, where thirty-three Mexicans died. Bowie and a few men then ambushed the withdrawing Mexican column. Rarely at rest, Bowie spent the years leading up to the full-blown Texas Revolution more or less bouncing from one land purchase deal to another, one adventure to another, one place to another. Thus he was in Natchez in September 1833, prostrate with yellow fever and unaware, when cholera struck his family back in Texas and took the lives of Ursula, both of her parents, and a child Bowie had fathered. (A second Bowie child may have died young, too.)

Recovering from his own illness, if not the great personal loss, Bowie in the midsummer of 1835 led a group of so-called militia in a raid against the Mexican armory in San Antonio and withdrew with a number of muskets. Technically speaking, some say the first engagement of the Texas Revolution was the seagoing battle between the Texan schooner *San Felipe* and the Mexican revenue cutter *Correo de Mexico* on September 1, 1835; others say the war began with the exchange of fire between Mexican troops and the Anglo settlers of Gonzales on October 1, 1835. Bowie, not one to be bothered with such technical niceties, was ahead of both dates.

Meanwhile, Bowie and Travis were already acquainted, not only as like-minded members of the War Party, but as lawyer and client. "Bowie had hired Travis as early as 1833 in San Felipe to prepare land papers," notes the Williamson account. Travis also represented Bowie and an associate in a lawsuit, and he "did legal work for Bowie's friend Jesse Clift, a blacksmith who is often credited with making the first Bowie knife."

With the revolutionary activities heating up in earnest in the fall of 1835, Bowie was appointed a colonel of volunteers on the staff of Stephen F. Austin, just back from twenty-eight months of imprisonment in Mexico, now ruled by Santa Anna. Travis joined the regulars of the revolutionary army, which was commanded by Sam Houston.

On October 28 Bowie was in charge of a mounted patrol ninety-two strong that was attacked near the mission of Nuestra Señora de la Purisima Concepcion de Acuña by three hundred Mexican horsemen and a hundred infantry, all rolling out of a heavy fog at dawn.

Once again, over a period of three hard-fought hours, the seemingly invincible Bowie prevailed, losing one man to sixteen Mexicans killed and at least as many wounded. Early Texas settler Noah Smithwick was present for this battle of Concepcion, and, as stated in his memoir *Evolution of a State,* he never forgot it. "His voice is still ringing in my old deaf ears as he repeatedly admonished us, 'Keep under cover boys and reserve your fire; we haven't a man to spare.'" In Smithwick's view, Bowie showed himself to be "a born leader never needlessly spending a bullet or imperiling a life."

While the Texan leadership was debating whether or how to drive the Mexicans from San Antonio de Bexar, as the locale of the Alamo was called in those days, Bowie, still strictly a volunteer, briefly visited San Felipe, center of Austin's original colony, then returned to the side of the Texan revolutionaries on the outskirts of San Antonio on November 18. "[O]n the twenty-sixth he and thirty horsemen rode out to check on a Mexican packtrain near town, while [Gen. Edward] Burleson followed with 100 infantry," recalls the *Texas Online* account. Meeting the supply column, which was delivering bales of grass for the livestock of the San Antonio garrison, Bowie led a charge into its cavalry escort then went after the Mexican infantry. In what went down in history as the Grass Fight, the Mexicans backed off with sixty lost this time.

Next dispatched to check on the condition of the Texan garrison at Goliad, Bowie was away while the Texas revolutionaries attacked and drove the Mexicans out of San Antonio in December, only to see most of their personnel pack up and return to hearth and family, rather than stay for any prolonged war. Col. James C. Neill was given the thankless job of guarding against a vengeful return by the Mexicans with only fifty or so men under his command at the old, ill-equipped, adobe-walled mission called the Alamo. Soon, on January 19, 1836, Bowie rode in with thirty men, this time to stay. Travis rode in next, on February 3, with another twenty-nine men. Davy Crockett appeared with a dozen or so volunteers on or about February 8.

All of them—Bowie, Travis, Crockett, and nearly two hundred others eventually crowding into the Alamo—were committed to Texan independence . . . the day of reckoning was drawing near.

For once, though, Jim Bowie, man of action, peripatetic and seemingly invincible warrior, would not be in the forefront of the fighting.

The first real crisis to strike at the heart of the Alamo garrison that winter had nothing to do with Santa Anna . . . although he indeed was on his way. Instead, it had to do with Colonel Neill's announcement that he was being called away. He cited an illness in his family and plans to find money for the Alamo's defense needs. Departing in the second week of February, he promised to be back in twenty days.

Neill's absence created a crisis of command, for Travis, inexperienced and only twenty-six, was the ranking man among the regulars of

the short-lived Texan army. The far more experienced Bowie, nearly fifteen years older, was the natural choice to command the volunteers on
hand, even if his colonel's rank more or less was an honorary one. The
question was, which of the two would be in overall command? Neill
selected his fellow army officer Travis, but the men holed up behind
the Alamo's adobe walls weren't having that. Travis was too young, too
new to most of them, too inclined to the melodramatic. Why take him
when they could have Bowie, "the best-known fighter in Texas"?

Why indeed, and chances were, they wouldn't. "Bowie did nothing
to discourage the mood," observed Walter Lord. "He had always gotten
along with Travis—but serving under the man was quite a different
matter. He didn't need his big knife to prove no one was his master;
those cold gray eyes and his quiet, firm manner took care of that."

A vote on February 12 only affirmed the obvious—the volunteers
wanted Bowie; the regulars stood by Travis. For the moment, the
Alamo had two commanders rather than one. Not good.

But Bowie, already feeling the weakening effects of an unknown
malady, didn't help his own cause—or his health—by rampaging
through town that night on a monumental bender. "He loudly
claimed command of the whole garrison," wrote Lord. "He stopped
private citizens going about their business. He ordered town officials to
open the *calaboose* and let everyone go. When one of the freed prisoners . . . was thrown back into jail, Bowie exploded with rage. He called
out his men from the Alamo, paraded them back and forth in the
Main Plaza. They were all drunk now, shouting and cheering, waving
their rifles."

An outraged Travis sent word to Gov. Henry Smith that he would
not be responsible "for the drunken irregularities of any man." But
Bowie and Travis now arrived at an arrangement defining how one
would command the volunteers and the other the regulars. Both men
would cosign all orders affecting the Alamo and its defense . . . at least
until Neill returned. Meanwhile, Travis was certain Santa Anna would
not reach the fortified Alamo until the Ides of March—the fifteenth.

In fact, with Neill still away and upwards of 150 defenders gathered in the Alamo, Santa Anna's army appeared at the gates on February 23.

The Mexican commander sent word to surrender, and Travis
responded with a cannon shot. Bowie sent a note saying perhaps the
cannon shot was premature . . . that is, if the Mexicans were seeking a

truce. But the reply was that the Mexicans would discuss no terms other than unconditional surrender. Meanwhile, Travis, furious at Bowie for acting unilaterally, sent out a messenger of his own with an offer to talk with a Mexican representative. Again, the answer was, Surrender first, no terms . . . except that we'll spare your lives and property.

Travis's emissary "trudged" back into the Alamo, Lord reported, "and the reply [from Travis] came in the form of another shattering blast from the big 18-pounder." Thus the siege of the Alamo was on. It wouldn't end until broken by a desperate and costly charge by an overwhelming number of Mexican troops on the morning of March 6.

More defenders slipped into the Alamo during the thirteen-day siege, and several times Travis sent out messages begging for help, for reinforcement, for supplies . . . but also pledging to fight to the very end. From February 24 until the end on March 6, 1836, Travis clearly was the man in charge. Bowie, a long-festering illness—tuberculosis, possibly—finally catching up to him, collapsed and spent the siege in bed, where, it is believed by most historians, he was several times shot in the head and killed by the Mexicans pouring over and through the old mission's walls the morning of March 6. All 188 known Alamo defenders (there may have been more, some sources suggest) were killed during the siege, in the final assault, or by outright execution as the smoke cleared that same morning, with William Barret Travis and Davy Crockett also included among the casualties.

☆

1 8 3 6
A Man and His Cannon

☆

What became of Col. James C. Neill, the absent commander of the Alamo who never returned? Apparently he *was* on his way back on the day the Alamo fell. He stopped in Gonzales to purchase medical supplies for the Alamo garrison, with a ninety-dollar outlay from his own pocket, according to Stephen L. Hardin in *Texas Online*.

That stop brought Neill full circle, since he had been present at Gonzales the previous October when the first *official* fighting—a minor skirmish, really—of the Texas Revolution broke out. And it may have been Neill who actually fired the town's only cannon—called the "Come and Take It" cannon, because that was the challenge the Texan settlers hurled at the Mexican troops trying to disarm them.

Neill then was placed in charge of a single artillery piece providing a diversion for the successful Texan assault against the Mexicans in San Antonio de Bexar that December. Adds the Hardin account: "On December 8 he commanded the battery that repulsed a Mexican attack on the Texan base camp. Had Neill's defense failed, the insurgents inside the town—cut off from their logistical support—would have been forced to abandon their assault."

It then fell to Neill, newly commissioned as a lieutenant colonel of artillery in the regular Texan army, to "hold the town with fewer than 100 men." Blessed with a new wealth of artillery pieces captured from the departing Mexicans, he installed them at key points in the Alamo and fortified the old mission as best he could with the materials and supplies on hand. Walter Lord called the first commander of the Alamo "somewhat pedestrian," but Jim Bowie clearly thought otherwise. At first persuaded that Sam Houston was correct in suggesting abandonment of the Alamo, Bowie changed his mind once he returned to San Antonio, saw the improvements in the Alamo's defenses and had a first-hand glimpse of Neill's performance as commander of the outpost. "No other man in the army could have kept men at this post, under the neglect they have experienced," Bowie declared.

If Neill missed the siege of the Alamo, he certainly contributed to Houston's stunning victory at San Jacinto. Left without cannons for a while after the fall of the Alamo, Neill soon took over the "Twin Sisters," a pair of 6-pounders the Texans obtained on April 11. The online account adds, "Since Neill was the ranking artillery officer, Houston named him to command the revived artillery corps. On April 20 Neill commanded the Twin Sisters during the skirmish that preceded the battle of San Jacinto. During this fight his artillery corps repulsed an enemy probe of the woods in which the main Texas army was concealed."

But Neill in the same action was badly wounded "when a fragment of grapeshot caught him in the hip."

He survived that setback and became both an Indian fighter and an Indian agent in the 1840s. A native of North Carolina and a once-wounded veteran of the battle of Horseshoe Bend in 1814, he died at his home in Navarro County, Texas, in 1845 at about fifty-five years of age.

1 8 3 6
Prisoner of Note

Looking for stray members of Antonio López de Santa Anna's shattered army after the battle of San Jacinto, six Texans on horseback had peeled off from their main detachment at Vince's Bayou and were working their way back toward camp. "We picked up two or three cringing wretches before we reached Vince's bayou, eight or nine miles from our camp," reported Joel Walter Robison (some sources call him Robinson). Riding captured Mexican horses, the six approached a ravine about two miles east of the bayou—the road crossing the ravine close to this spot led to the battlefield itself.

Suddenly, up ahead, another stray. "As we approached this ravine," wrote Robison, "we discovered a man standing in the prairie near one of the groves. He was dressed in citizen's clothing, a blue cottonade frock coat and pantaloons."

As the only one of the six who spoke Spanish, Robison questioned the man—and the Mexican answered "readily."

The most obvious and crucial question: Where was Santa Anna? Where was the cruel despot who had ordered the death of every man defending the Alamo just weeks before? The monster who had ordered the infamous Goliad massacre as well?

Gone . . . already gone to safe haven across the nearby Brazos River, the lone Mexican asserted.

What about any other Mexicans in the area? There might be some in the thicket along the ravine, the prisoner suggested.

A Texan named Miles (probably A. H. Miles) took the prisoner up on his horse, and they all set off at a placid pace for the road, about a mile away. But Miles then ordered the prisoner to dismount—"which he did with great reluctance."

The prisoner stumbled along slowly and in apparent pain. "Miles, who was a rough, reckless fellow, was carrying a Mexican lance, which he had picked up during the morning. With this weapon he occasionally pricked the prisoner to quicken his pace, which sometimes amounted to a trot."

In a short while, the prisoner begged for relief, "saying he belonged to the cavalry and was unaccustomed to walking."

The Texans stopped and debated what they should do with such a nuisance. "I asked him if he would go on to our army if left to travel at his leisure."

He said he would, but Miles said that if they left the prisoner, he would kill him.

That was when Robison agreed to take the prisoner on his horse and ride double. "He was disposed to converse as we rode along; asked me many questions, the first of which was, 'Did General [Sam] Houston command in person in the action of yesterday?' He also asked how many prisoners we had taken and what we were going to do with them."

When told that fewer than eight hundred Texans [nine hundred-plus, actually] had fought his fellow Mexicans at San Jacinto the day before, he couldn't believe it—"he said I was surely mistaken, that our force was certainly much greater."

Meanwhile, Robison had questions of his own. Why did the prisoner come to Texas to fight Texans—"to which he replied that he was a private soldier, and was bound to obey his officers."

But did he expect to see his family again? "His only answer was a shrug of the shoulders."

Soon the small party reached the Texan camp and rode on to the section holding the Mexican prisoners—"in order to deliver our trooper to the guard."

And then . . . a general shout rose up among the prisoners. *"El Presidente! El Presidente!"* Robison, Miles, and company unwittingly had captured the so-called Napoleon of the West, Santa Anna himself!

Naturally, the discovery of the prisoner's identity drew an excited crowd, and he was escorted immediately for a visit with Houston, the victor of the eighteen-minute battle of San Jacinto. According to one account, the Mexican commander told Houston, "I am Santa Anna and surrender myself to you."

Additional Note: A slightly different account of the capture of Santa Anna was offered long after the battle of San Jacinto, in 1872, by James Austin Sylvester, who apparently was the sergeant in charge of the group that encountered the fugitive dictator near the ravine. Sylvester confirmed the fact that none of the Texans realized they had come across Santa Anna himself, but he claimed that he alone spotted the wanderer from a distance and then captured him . . . before the rest of the Texan party rode up.

Sylvester stated that he rode up to find his quarry covered with a Mexican blanket. "I ordered him to get up, which he did, very reluctantly and immediately took hold of my hand and kissed it several times, and asked for General Houston and seemed to be very solicitous to find out whether he been killed in the battle the day previous."

According to Sylvester, he conversed with the Mexican prisoner and did the questioning—a point seemingly at odds with Robison's (or Robinson's) claim to have been the only man in the party able to converse with the prisoner in Spanish. But Sylvester, a Maryland native new to Texas in 1836, sent the *Austin Democratic Statesman* a message in 1874 repeating his claim to have been the first captor of the infamous Santa Anna. "[N]either Mr. Robinson [n]or any of the party was within five hundred yards of me when General Santa Anna was captured by myself." He added, "They joined me in a few moments after General Santa Anna had surrendered. I have always awarded the same credit to them that I felt was due to myself."

Oddly, it turns out that each participant in the capture of Santa Anna claimed to have given the Mexican strongman a ride back to camp on his horse.

Further note: Both the Robison and Sylvester accounts are reproduced on the in-depth historical Web site called *Sons of DeWitt Colony Texas* (http://www.tamu.edu/ccbn/dewitt/dewitt.htm), copyright by Wallace L. McKeehan.

Lake with a Past

Its undulating shoreline ever-changing, its beginnings an aberration of nature, its history colorful and often violent, Caddo Lake sprawls across the Texas-Louisiana border for miles on either side. A lake, yes, but also "a maze of sloughs, bogs, and bayous, guarded by looming cypress trees, bearded gray in Spanish moss," notes the promotional literature for the Caddo Steamboat Company of Uncertain, Texas, operator of a paddle-wheel steamboat, the *Graceful Ghost*, that plies the lake waters these days as a tourist attraction.

Back in the nineteenth century, a steady stream of heavily loaded steamboats plowed the same waters on the run from New Orleans to the port towns of Jefferson, Swanson's Landing, Port Caddo, and Uncertain. Once known as Uncertain Landing, the Uncertain of today may owe its quaint name to the difficulty some steamboat captains experienced in finding an adequate mooring for their big boats in the maze of waterways. On the other hand, the locals may have been *uncertain* whether they lived in the United States of the 1840s or the newly independent Republic of Texas, a quandary settled when Texas became a state in 1845.

Uncertain allegiances also were an issue in the once-booming frontier town of Port Caddo, which not only boasted frequent steamboat arrivals but also benefited from a stream of westbound wagons. Designated a port of entry for Harrison County, Texas, during the days of the Texas republic, Port Caddo refused to pay customs duties when it appeared Texas soon would become a state. Taxes were also a burning issue for the townspeople. According to a history developed by the Caddo Lake Area Chamber of Commerce and Tourism, the republic's second president, Mirabeau Lamar, ordered the Harrison County sheriff to collect the town's taxes, but "the townspeople shot the sheriff dead and burned the tax rolls he had been carrying."

Once Texas was admitted to the Union, the rebellion ended.

Meanwhile, Jefferson, Texas, on Big Cypress Bayou, "soon eclipsed every other port city on the Texas side of the lake." Good Texas cotton was shipped east, "and everything from furniture to gravestones came west on the steamboats which left the Port of New Orleans on the Mississippi and traveled up the Red River and into Caddo Lake," explains the chamber account (online at http://www.caddolake.org/history.htm).

Jefferson reached a post–Civil War population of thirty thousand, with as many as fifteen steamboats at a time moored at its docks, by some accounts. With the coming of the railroads, however, the riverboat traffic died . . . and Jefferson's star rapidly declined. The town fathers once refused an offer by railroad baron Jay Gould to run a rail line through Jefferson, and he "angrily predicted death for the city, and laid his tracks elsewhere" (see http://www.Instar.com/mall/txtrails/jefrson.htm). Ironically, Jefferson today offers both Gould's private rail-car, the *Atalanta,* and an excursion train pulled by a steam locomotive as tourist attractions.

Then, too, there was Swanson's Landing, a busy port on the south shore of Caddo Lake, sometimes alternately called Big Lake or Ferry Lake. Peter Swanson, a settler from Tennessee, set to work in the 1830s equipping his twenty-acre lake property on the Texas-U.S. border with a dock, warehouses, a general store, and a gristmill. "Soon settlers began arriving by boat, by oxcart, on horseback, and by foot," notes the *Handbook of Texas Online.* "Before many months had passed, the warehouses were filling with cotton, hides, and corn, all en route to New Orleans."

Statehood only enhanced the Swanson boom. By the time Swanson died in 1849, he and his wife owned "6,800 acres of land, slaves, and livestock." His son Thomas now carried on the family business, which experienced another boom with the coming of a local rail line in 1857. Swanson's Landing became the starting point for the Southern Pacific Railroad, "one of the earliest of all Texas railroads." The riverboats brought in the rail stock, and the Swansons made the railroad ties. Further, revelers from nearby Marshall, Texas, twenty-nine miles southwest of the center of Caddo Lake, discovered Caddo Lake's recreational amenities. "The young people of Marshall began riding the Southern Pacific to Swanson's Landing, where they would swim, dance, picnic, and go boating. At day's end, they would board the train for home."

But Caddo Lake had a dark side, too. Nearby Old Monterey once was known for its shady doings, saloons, brothels, rooster fights . . . and frequent homicides. A racetrack also was a big attraction.

Caddo Lake played a role in the so-called Regulator-Moderator War, an outgrowth of swindles, cattle rustling, land squabbles, and overzealous vigilanteism associated with the lawless neutral ground once set up between the Mexican and American borders. People were killed in this strictly parochial conflict, among them Moderator leader Robert Potter, formerly a U.S. House member from North Carolina, currently a Texas legislator, and recently secretary of the republic's navy.

By most accounts, he was killed in Caddo Lake itself while fleeing a Regulator gang that surprised him at his lakeside home, Potter's Point, on March 2, 1842. Only the day before, it also seems, Potter had led a posse trying to arrest the same gang's leader, William Pinckney Rose.

He, however, managed to hide under a pile of brush being raked up by a slave. A crowing rooster almost revealed Rose's hiding place. After the Potter group left empty-handed, the errant rooster paid the price of having its neck wrung.

It was that kind of "war."

That night, Rose and his men surrounded Potter's home on the lake. As leader of the Harrison County Regulators, incidentally, Rose was called both "Hell-roaring" Rose and "Lion of the Lakes" Rose.

When Potter discovered his threatening situation the next morning, he tried to swim to safety on a wooded island offshore but was shot in the attempt. Rose, his son Preston, a son-in-law, and several others were arrested. Some soon were released, and eventually the case against the Rose family members was dismissed for lack of evidence. Still, the Potter murder was so notorious that it was reported in newspapers around the country . . . and Charles Dickens, traveling in America at the time, made note of it in his *American Notes.* Many years later, twentieth-century Texas writer Lena Kirkland wrote a popular novel, *Love Is a Wild Assault,* based upon the memoirs of Potter's widow, Harriet Potter Ames.

Meanwhile, the slain Potter first was buried at his home, on a bluff overlooking the lake, but his remains were shifted years later, in 1936, to the Texas State Cemetery at Austin, the state capital. The state named Potter County in the far-off Texas panhandle for him, too.

With the coming of the Civil War, the riverboat traffic crossing Caddo Lake between the inland Texas ports and New Orleans was a conduit of military supplies and civilian goods reflecting the area's allegiance to the Confederacy. The steamboats still plied the New Orleans–Red River–Caddo Lake route in the years immediately following the war, but one night in 1869, at Swanson's Landing, there came a disastrous accident—the sidewheel steamboat *Mittie Stephens,* seven days out of New Orleans and bound for Jefferson, caught fire.

As the blaze swept through the forward half of the steamboat, men, women, and children fled aft and leaped into the lake waters at the stern. Most drowned or were sucked into the grinding paddlewheels. Ironically, the stern was in deep water, but the bow of the steamboat had grounded in just three feet of water. Many of the 61 who perished in the accident might have been able to wade ashore had they known refuge was so close at hand . . . and found a safer place to jump overboard. As it was, only 46 of the 107 aboard survived.

In later years, souvenir and treasure hunters squandered their time probing the lake waters by Swanson's Landing for the *Mittie Stephens,* which reportedly had burned and foundered three hundred yards off shore while carrying all kinds of cargo, passenger belongings . . . and a payload of gold for the Union troops still occupying postbellum Jefferson. They didn't realize the chameleon-like lake had been so changeable over the years that remnants of the *Stephens* actually crept up on land in the interim. According to the chamber of commerce history, historian Jacques Bagur found the wreckage in 1993. "Nothing much was left but twisted, melted window pane fragments and detritus; anything useful had been carried off years before."

All this history, and still we haven't reached the apparent origin of Caddo Lake as a phenomenon—an aberration, really—of nature.

After all, when Peter Custis and Thomas Freeman (see pages 18–24) slogged westward along the Red River in 1806, they didn't see Caddo Lake. They certainly didn't see a vast expanse of water covering an estimated 26,800 acres, thus easily one of the largest natural lakes in the South. What they did see was the "Great Raft," a huge logjam blocking the Red River for a hundred miles and creating a network of bayous, swamps, ponds, lakes, and alternate channels.

Over the next few years, as more and more debris—"snags" or "sawyers" to a river boatman—floated downriver, the Great Raft only grew and dammed anew, finally creating a series of lakes, blocking tributaries, flooding buffalo grasslands . . . and giving the world what became known as Caddo Lake, named for the Caddo Indians of the region. The Raft was so solid, Custis and Freeman reported, it rose three feet above water with perfectly healthy grass and bushes growing on top. Their men, they said, "could walk over it in any direction."

According to environmental historian Don Flores, their Great Raft was one of a kind in North America. "In terms of size and age, the gigantic logjam had no parallel on the rest of the continent's rivers," he wrote in his 1984 book *Jefferson and Southwestern Exploration.* "Just when or where the Great Raft first was formed never has been satisfactorily determined. Early Louisiana geologist A. C. Veatch thought it might have been formed about A.D. 1100 to 1200, but all we really know is that it was in existence long before the coming of the Europeans."

Interestingly, the region's Caddo Indians attributed the lake's formation to an earthquake brought about because a Caddo chief had angered the Great Spirit. And there really was, in 1811, a series of mighty earthquakes in the Mississippi Valley that did create one or more lakes . . . and even sent the Mississippi River briefly flowing backward. But Flores argued that neither the historical documents of the period nor the geological evidence can explain the lake's formation as a product of the New Madrid (Missouri) earthquakes, severe as they were (see pages 49–52). In 1806, Flores pointed out, Custis noted that the Great Raft was just below Twelve-Mile Bayou; by 1811, Louisiana border surveyor William Darby found "most of the northwestern corner of the proposed state of Louisiana flooded by a lake sixty to seventy miles long and eight miles wide." Thus, "At some time during the interval since 1806, the mouth of Twelve-Mile Bayou obviously had been blocked by the Raft."

Moreover, Indian agent John Sibley, long active in the area, wrote in 1812 that the lake had taken form "within about Twelve years."

Naturally, as early exploration west of the Mississippi gave way to settlement, the same blockage that created the lake also was an impenetrable impediment to navigation.

Enter now another historical figure with ties to Caddo Lake . . . and, more directly, to the Red River, the Great Raft, and the birth of Shreveport, Louisiana. He was the city's namesake, Henry Miller Shreve, a pioneer of steamboating on the Mississippi and creator-inventor of the steam-powered, windlass-equipped "snag-boat." Starting with his *Heliopolis,* Shreve's snag-boats used a windlass mounted at the bow to pull snags out of the river.

Shreve became the Army Corps of Engineers superintendent of western river improvements in 1826, and in 1832 he was ordered to begin clearing the Great Raft from the Red River. Shreve arrived on the scene in 1833 and spent the next five years at the Herculean task—his work camp on the banks of the Red River became the nucleus for today's Shreveport. Thanks to his pioneer adaptations of the steamboat for river use, along with his river-clearing work here and elsewhere, says the National Rivers Hall of Fame, Shreve probably did more than any other individual to make inland river travel a reality for America in the first half of the nineteenth century.

Thanks also to his assault upon the Great Raft, the steamboat route from New Orleans to Shreveport and even into Arkansas became a reality as well. As noted in Flores's book and in *The Red River in Southwestern History* by Carl Newton Tyson, however, Shreve's work was far from finished. It wouldn't be finished even in the 1870s, when army engineers once more returned to the assault in hopes of clearing the Red River of its notorious Raft once and for all. Now armed with nitroglycerin, they began blowing up more stubborn sections of the Raft. But no matter, with spring freshets forever bringing more logs, choking river bends to straighten out, and bayous to dam up, this was a project destined to drag on into the early twentieth century, at a total cost of more than two million dollars.

Still, the work of the 1870s and beyond had dramatic impact upon Caddo Lake and its port cities, another blow to once-bustling Jefferson. No sooner was the Red River channel opened up than Caddo Lake's water level fell markedly. No more steamboat traffic! Instead, freshwater pearling became a new Caddo Lake industry. Families camped on the shores and dug with their toes into the mud looking for the mussels containing the black freshwater pearls.

But then came the first of two dams once again raising the lake's water level. Meanwhile, oil had been found lurking far beneath its placid, lotus lily–covered waters. Gulf Oil conducted the first offshore oil drilling within the lake's parameters, adds the chamber of commerce history. In fact, "The techniques developed among the cypress trees of Caddo Lake are the same used today in the world's great oceans," notes the online historical sketch.

Today the lake is both a recreational boon to fishermen, boaters, and vacationers and an exceedingly rich wetlands site under study by researchers ranging from professional environmentalists to students in area schools. It is defined as a "wetland of international significance" by terms of the Ramsar (Iran) Treaty of 1971 identifying a worldwide network of wetlands deserving ongoing study and protection.

1 8 4 2

Bloodless War in Texas

The Black Hawk War, the Mexican War, the Regulator-Moderator War, the cattle range wars, the county seat wars, the Indian wars . . . so many wars out west. And, not to be forgotten (at least not in Texas), the Archives War, in which Sam Houston's boarding house proprietress Angelina Eberly fired the first and perhaps only shot.

To explain, and as the Texas State Library and Archives Commission itself notes, the Archives War of 1842 revolved around Houston, his namesake town of Houston, and the log cabin metropolis of Austin, with a few invading Mexicans and Eberly thrown into the same stew.

An old argument over the best site for the Texas capital also was in play. Houston, first president of the Republic of Texas, had rejected the hopes of the Texas Congress to establish a planned city in central Texas as the capital. Since Houston instead liked the idea of having the capital in his namesake city of Houston close to the Gulf of Mexico, the issue still was in doubt when Mirabeau B. Lamar succeeded Houston in 1839.

With Lamar adding his voice to the call for a centrally located capital, notes the archives commission (see http://www.tsl.state.tures/republic/archwar/archwar.html), "A site was chosen along the Colorado River near the tiny settlement of Waterloo." Hardly a year had passed before "Lamar had moved to the new capital, now called Austin, and Congress was meeting in log buildings in the frontier town."

Even back then, though, the government papers were piling up. It took forty to fifty wagons to carry the republic's archives from Houston to Austin.

In 1841, however, Sam Houston was back in the saddle again as the republic's latest president. Calling Austin "the most unfortunate site on earth for a seat of government," he refused to bed down in the official presidential residence. Instead, he took a room at the Eberly House, a hostelry operated by Angelina Belle Peyton Eberly. Just the year before, she had hosted Lamar and his cabinet at dinner.

For the moment, the archives rested comfortably in an Austin abode . . . but not for long. In 1842, the archives commission notes further, "The Mexican army invaded Texas and took control of San Antonio, Goliad, and Victoria," the defiant stand of 1836 at the Alamo and Sam Houston's crushing, eighteen-minute victory at San Jacinto notwithstanding.

With the renewed Mexican threat to Texas so perfectly clear in 1842, Houston "saw his chance to move the capital back to the city of Houston." He called for a special session of the Congress at Houston, "arguing that Austin was defenseless against Mexican attack."

Such a move, of course, would mean transferring the archives again to keep them out of danger.

Certainly, that seemed clear to Houston, who in December 1842 declared Austin was no longer the capital and ordered Col. Thomas I. Smith and Capt. Eli Chandler and a company of Texas Rangers to transfer the republic's most treasured documents . . . not to Houston, but to another occasional capital of Texas, Washington-on-the-Brazos.

Austin citizens formed a vigilante committee of safety. They "warned the heads of government in Austin that any attempts to move the official papers would be met with armed resistance."

As events turned out, Houston's own landlady discovered the two officers and twenty men loading the wagons for the transfer.

And it was she who sounded the alarm for her fellow citizens by firing a cannon kept loaded with grapeshot in case of Indian attack, notes *The Handbook of Texas Online.*

Adds the archives site: "Smith and Chandler fled with their wagons, with the vigilantes in hot pursuit. At Brushy Creek in Williamson County, just north of Austin, Chandler and Smith were forced to surrender at gunpoint." According to some accounts, another cannon shot or two might have been heard here. In any case, "The archives were returned to Austin, where the citizens celebrated with a New Year's Eve party."

And there the archives stayed, although the government itself did not return to Austin until 1845. Even then the final site of the Texas capital still remained an open question, an issue that wouldn't be settled until the Texas citizenry chose Austin by a majority vote in 1850, by which time the republic no longer was a republic but a state.

In the meantime, Eberly, twice widowed in her lifetime, had operated a tavern in future Port Lavaca and a hotel in Indianola, where she died in 1860, leaving an estate of fifty thousand dollars to a grandson.

In Defense of Buffalo

On a still night, wrote Washington Irving many, *many* years ago, their vast army simply crossing a river created a "roaring and rushing sound"

that could be "heard for miles." Much, *much* earlier, the Spanish explorer-conquistador Cortez, arriving in Mexico in the sixteenth century, was stunned when he found one of the huge beasts in a zoo maintained by the Aztecs. It looked, he said, like a "Mexican bull with a hump like a camel's and hair like a lion's."

Stubbornly reluctant to die and able to run nearly forty miles in a day, soon leaving the swiftest horses far behind, the American buffalo, or bison if you prefer, also had a *heart* like a lion's.

Once more than fifty million strong, they fed, housed, and even clothed the Plains Indians for generations. They fertilized the grasslands for those same generations. They created migratory trails that later guided the white man's railroads in the search for the shortest, easiest routes from here to there. Itchy in the summer months, they scratched and rubbed as best they could, and in their millions they affected the terrain of the West by creating saucerlike buffalo wallows in the ground, by rubbing against trees and killing them, even by wearing smooth huge boulders as they rubbed against them . . . by the million.

When they decided to travel, in a seasonal migration of three to four hundred miles north or south, a leader would start and the others would follow in single file. The file attracted more and more buffalo, and they became a herd. Soon the herd found another herd, and it was like an army, noted the 1949 book *American Wild Life Illustrated.* "In their travels," added the same Works Project Administration (WPA) study, "large numbers of bison fell victims to prairie fires, quicksand, and thin ice on rivers. Danger often caused immense herds to stampede and the animals trampled one another or anything that stood in their path. If the leaders tried to stop before a quicksand or other hazard, the momentum of the herd driving on behind frequently knocked them down to provide a living bridge for the remainder."

Still, this was no puny creature of the wild. Males could weigh two thousand pounds or more (females "half as much"), measure nine to ten feet in length and, from hoof to hump, stand taller than the average man of the nineteenth-century era (five foot five to five foot six). Both males and females sported horns, but they hardly ever fought each other to the death. The males did use their horns "in fighting among themselves for leadership in the herd," but the bulls used a "wrestling technique" that didn't kill. Enemies, however, were another question altogether. "Other animals . . . are gored by a powerful downward thrust, then thrown high as the bison raises its massive head."

Socially responsible and a "solicitous parent," the bulls would respond to danger by forming an outer ring "with lowered heads to guard against wolves and other aggressors."

For all his massive size, *American Wild Life* also noted, the buffalo "when pursued can tire out three sets of horses and run nearly forty miles in a single day," thanks to a "huge heart and lungs [that] seem to provide it with remarkable endurance."

Even so, the many tribes of the plains learned how to hunt down and kill these leviathans of the prairie, who, for Indians, were factories on four legs that supplied life-giving food for basic survival, sinews for bows, skins for clothing and tepees, robes for warmth. Before the introduction of the horse and then the rifle, which made things much easier, Indians often crept close to the buffalo herd covered with an animal skin as disguise. The Indians also were known to stampede the buffalo over a cliff or into corrals as hunting techniques.

If the great buffalo herds sustained the native tribes for so many generations without risk of extinction, the ubiquitous buffalo also gave the white man a "free food supply" as he advanced across the continent from the East. But then, noted *American Wild Life:* "As civilization pressed westward, the great herds began to disappear from their grazing grounds. By the early part of the nineteenth century those east of the Mississippi had been wiped out as a result of the spread of agriculture and the heavy demand for buffalo skins. The completion of the Union Pacific Railroad divided the western herd into a northern and southern half. The southern herd was totally exterminated, and by 1895 only eight hundred of the northern herd remained."

Incredible to contemplate, the buffalo at one time grazed across a third of the North American continent, from Canada to Mexico, from the Blue Mountains of Oregon to Pennsylvania, Virginia, the Carolinas, and western New York. The migratory trails they beat into the ground with their passing sometimes were several miles in width.

For Indian or white man, buffalo hunting up close was a high-risk business, to be sure. Even from a moderate distance, the hunter armed with a rifle risked the possibility of a stampede in his direction. The "experienced hunter," noted *American Wild Life,* "would pick off the leader of the herd. Leaderless, the creatures would stand still for a while, not knowing what to do, until a new leader stepped out of the ranks. The hunter would then pick off the new leader, and so on down the line."

What almost killed off the buffalo entirely were the vast numbers of rifle-toting white buffalo hunters pursuing a full-time, moneymaking business . . . all for the skins and the heck with the meat that had sustained the tribes (and the earliest white explorers) for so long. One result, as is well known today and understandable to boot, was Indian rage. And, typically, that was exactly the cause and the effect of a small but bloody skirmish in Texas known as the battle of Yellow House Canyon.

Enraged by the white man's wanton slaughter of the near-sacred buffalo, the Quahadi Comanche leader Black Horse was determined to do something about it. Leading a sizable band of 170 warriors from the reservation at Fort Sill, Oklahoma, across the Texas border and into the Staked Plains in December 1876, he scouted the Salt Fork of the Brazos River . . . just in time to observe buffalo hunter Marshall Sewell start to work on a buffalo herd on February 1, 1877, with a powerful Sharp's rifle. Firing again and again, Sewell brought down buffalo after buffalo until he ran out of ammunition, with Black Horse watching, waiting, all the while.

When the hunter turned for his nearby camp, the Indians struck, killing and scalping him in a moment's time.

They were seen, however, by three skinners and another buffalo hunter, who rushed to Rath City to report the murder . . . and, as it happened, to raise a posse of forty or more men.

Posse members rode to the scene, buried Sewell, then set off in pursuit of the Indians. In a brief fight that resulted, one of Black Horse's band was wounded, after which the posse retired to Rath City.

The Comanches, though, were not yet through with the buffalo-hunting fraternity. They stayed in the area, raiding and plundering the hide camps, including one belonging to Pat Garrett, later to become famous as the man who killed Billy the Kid. Traveling and fighting with Black Horse, meanwhile, was the strictly German- (and Comanche-) speaking white captive Herman Lehmann.

Back in Rath City, anger and demands for action swelled among the buffalo hunters. They finally, in early March, gathered another posse, this one forty-six men strong, and set off against the Indian raiders once again. Bolstered by a barrel of whiskey, the buffalo hunters traveled both on horseback and in wagons.

They tracked Black Horse to Yellow House Canyon (or Draw) in the Texas south plains, today the site of Lubbock, Texas, found a Comanche sentry near their entry point at today's Buffalo Springs

Lake, and killed him. They then left their wagons, slogged through an overnight march in hopes of surprising their foe in the predawn darkness . . . but instead took the wrong canyon fork and became lost.

Long after dawn, however, they finally found their quarry encamped in Hidden Canyon, at the site of today's Lubbock Lake. Despite the full-daylight hour, the posse divided into three parts and then attacked.

Taken by surprise after all, clearly shocked in fact, the Comanches quickly recovered and fought back fiercely, with their *women* at one point charging the mounted white men and firing at them with pistols. Badly outnumbered, two of their complement soon wounded, a third hurt when his horse fell, the buffalo hunters regrouped and withdrew to Long Water Hole. Their Indian foe then set the grass on fire, and out of the smokescreen came a Comanche warrior and the white captive Herman Lehmann in a kamikaze-like charge. A fusillade of shots killed the Indian and sent Lehmann scurrying back with a wound in his thigh.

By midafternoon, however, the buffalo hunters had seen enough. They retreated to Buffalo Springs, with their Indian "prey" now following *them*. But . . . only for the moment; Black Horse was happy enough to disengage. Alone now, but unsure what might come next, the whites were ready to give up the chase. "The hunters built a bonfire to the west to decoy the Indians, drove their wagons out of the canyon under the cover of darkness, and at daybreak set fires behind them to obscure their tracks," reports the *Handbook of Texas Online*. "On March 27, twenty-three days after they took the field, the buffalo hunters returned to Rath City." Their three casualties included one man dead.

As events turned out, it would take intervention by the U.S. Tenth Cavalry to write *finis* to the episode of Yellow House Canyon and buffalo hunter Sewell's murder. Riding out from Fort Griffin with seventy-two troopers, Capt. P. L. Lee caught up to Black Horse on May 4 at Quemado (Silver) Lake in today's Cochran County, Texas. After one Indian and his wife were killed in "a brief skirmish," reports *Texas Online*, "the Indians surrendered, accompanied the soldiers to Griffin, and were sent back to the reservation at Fort Sill."

In later years, two of the buffalo hunters recalled the Yellow House Canyon fight in their memoirs, while the captive Herman Lehmann told the Indian side of the affair in his autobiography *Nine Years Among the Indians*.

☆ ☆ ☆

Additional note: Meanwhile, it can be argued that not all the Plains Indians took up arms against the encroaching white man strictly because of the vanishing buffalo. As William Brandon wrote in the authoritative *American Heritage Book of Indians:* "The disappearance of the buffalo is generally emphasized as a cause of war on the plains, perhaps too much so. As early as the close of the 1850s, when the buffalo could still darken the earth and their gigantic mirages fill the sky, numbers of Indian leaders foresaw the finish of buffalo hunting. The question was not if the buffalo would vanish, but when. Some thought soon; some thought not for 100 years. It was the former who usually associated themselves with the treaty factions, anxious to make a deal for the sale of land and mineral rights that would subsist their people through the coming time of change."

That doesn't mean the buffalo weren't, and aren't, widely revered among the continent's Native Americans of the past—or of today. "To Native America," wrote Winona LaDuke, founder of the White Earth Recovery Project and the Indigenous Women's Network, in the May-June 2000 issue of *Sierra* magazine, "the buffalo is the elder brother, the teacher. In Lakota culture it is said that before you kill a buffalo you must perform the Buffalo Kill ceremony. You must offer prayers and talk to the animal's spirit. Then, and only then, can you kill the buffalo."

Fortunately, as LaDuke also points out, the buffalo are making their way back from the brink of extinction, thanks to the efforts of far-sighted wildlife managers in national or state parks, of Native Americans on their reservations or farms, of many other farmers and ranchers scattered across the nation, or of various organizations. Obviously, though, the midcontinent can never again see—or support—the likes of fifty million of the massive creatures wandering and feeding at will.

★ Part 3 ★
Emigration, War, and Gold

The Hastening Decade

Of all the decades of the nineteenth century, which, more than any other, hastened the development and settlement of the Old West? Can the argument be made that any single decade went further than any other ten-year period in creating the American West as we know it today? And if so, could it be the decade of the 1840s?

Just consider what all went on during those ten years.

Look first to the year 1840. What's happening?

Well, this was the year of "retirement," you might say, of the mountain men, those romantic figures of yore who for twenty years or so prowled the Rockies and environs in search of beaver pelts and fought off predatory grizzlies and the occasional hostile Indian band. Due both to the decline in the region's beaver population and to the genteel male population's switch to silk hats, rather than beaver, the mountain man era virtually ended with a last rendezvous on the Green River.

While a bookend in one respect, the year 1840 was a harbinger in another. Texas was on the outs with Mexico . . . the Republic of Texas, that is. The Texas navy, for instance—yes, navy!—was dispatched to blockade Mexican ports. Further, independent Texas supported antigovernment rebels in northern Mexico. Where would it all lead? To war . . .

But first, in 1841, a gentleman named John Sutter bought Fort Ross, thus dislodging a Russian toehold on the California coast above San Francisco. More significantly, Sutter cannabalized the thirty-year-old Russian facility and moved its best pieces to his own settlement at the junction of the Sacramento and American Rivers, Fort Sutter . . . and soon, fifty-four miles away, would come Sutter's Mill.

Keep that name in mind. *Sutter's Mill.*

In the meantime, more significant history was to be set in motion during the same year of 1841 as John Bidwell led the first sizable group of emigrants traveling overland into California. Bidwell, soon to become a member of Sutter's establishment, accompanied a wagon train of sixty-nine through the Rocky Mountains by way of South Pass. One party then veered northward to Oregon, but the remaining emigrants stuck with Bidwell for the final leg into California and its Sacramento Valley.

Bidwell's California party suffered all kinds of hardship on the way, but if anyone thought massive westward emigration by land was still years away, they would have to think again. Just two years later, in 1843, the zealous missionary Marcus Whitman guided what many still call "the Great Migration," an unprecedented party of one thousand souls traveling in more than one hundred wagons and bringing a herd of five thousand cattle across the Rockies, again through South Pass, onward to the Green River Valley, then on to the Snake River, and up the trail—now becoming the well-worn Oregon Trail—into Oregon, to the Columbia River, and into the Willamette Valley. Every year that followed, thousands more settlers would make the same two-thousand-mile overland trip to settle in the Northwest.

But that's getting ahead of the story . . . the story of the 1840s.

In 1842 a soon-to-be-famous name popped up. Lt. John C. Frémont of the U.S. Army's Topographical Corps of Engineers, the future "Pathfinder," with mountain man Kit Carson as his guide, took a scientific expedition through the Rocky Mountains—once again by way of South Pass—and then through the Wind River Mountain region in Wyoming, pausing long enough to plant a flag on a peak he named for himself. His report and maps would be published by Congress.

Far less noticeably, so far as the American public was concerned, but also in 1842, a man digging up an onion for his lunch one day in Placerita Canyon near Los Angeles found gold dust clinging to the onion's roots. When the word spread locally, there was a momentary rush by amateur gold seekers, but hardly any further excitement resulted. Still, wait until later in the same decade!

More attention, even excitement, was stirred in 1842 when word spread of an attack by Mexican troops against San Antonio—Dawson's Massacre, it was called. Texas moved its capital to Washington-on-the-Brazos from Austin . . . and attacked Mexican-owned Santa Fe.

That simmering brew hardly would cool the next year, 1843, as the bellicose Mexican dictator Antonio López de Santa Anna took power again. Already notorious for his massacre of the Alamo defenders (and for Goliad, where about three hundred Texan prisoners were summarily executed) during the Texas Revolution of 1836, he now threatened war if America annexed Texas as a state.

The year 1843 of course was to be remembered for its tremendous boost to the flight west in expansionist America . . . most visibly by way of the Oregon Trail. But 1843 also was to be marked by another major exploratory expedition with Frémont and Carson at the lead. This time they made their way from the Great Salt Lake into Oregon then turned southward to negotiate the stunning Sierra Nevada mountain range into California, followed by a crossing of the so-called Great Basin and the Wasatch Mountains into Colorado and on to the banks of its Arkansas River. Frémont's later report to Congress became a bestseller when published the very next year, 1844, only adding to still-young America's fascination with its largely uncharted western domains.

With the election of James K. Polk of Tennessee as president, however, other forces were set in motion in that same year of 1844. His campaign slogan of "54-40 or Fight" clearly signaled America's expansionist mood and meant that Polk would insist on a northern border to the Oregon Territory at 54 degrees, 40 minutes, on the map. If successful, such insistence would settle a long border dispute with the British to the north, but here also was a challenging signal to Mexico's Santa Anna to the south. And he certainly was not pleased that same year of 1844 to see John C. Calhoun succeed in negotiations presumably leading to the annexation of Texas as a full-fledged American state . . . *presumably* but not yet definitely, since, for the time being, abolitionist sentiment scuttled the ratification effort in the U.S. Senate.

Also during 1844, as presage to pending larger events, a visionary took charge of the affairs of the Mormon Church after its leader Joseph Smith and his brother Hyrum died at the hands of a rampaging mob in Carthage, Illinois. The new leader, Brigham Young by name, soon would be turning to the untrammeled West as refuge from the prejudice and outright hatred that seemed to dog his people wherever they went.

In the following year, 1845, halfway through this definitive decade of the nineteenth century, the geopolitical die was cast with departing President John Tyler's signature on a congressional joint resolution affirming the annexation of Texas as a state after all . . . followed by Mexico's severance of diplomatic relations with the United States . . . followed by newly inaugurated President Polk's two-pronged psychological offensive. On the one hand, he deployed troops under Gen. Zachary

Taylor into Texas, and on the other he sent a diplomatic envoy to Mexico City with an offer of forty million dollars to offset Mexico's probable loss of Texas and to purchase the California and New Mexico territories, all in one package.

Mexico's response was: Thanks but no thanks; we're preparing for war.

And so dawned a fateful year—1846, start of a year and a half of war, the Mexican War, in which 13,283 Americans would die and another 8,304 would be wounded. The dispute first focused on the territory between the Nueces River and the Rio Grande, with Mexico asserting the Nueces should be the border of Texas and the Americans saying that the Rio Grande was the real border. The military action began after Taylor was ordered to the American-claimed Rio Grande in February 1846, to be confronted by a cavalry skirmish April 25 near Fort Texas (the future Fort Brown) with a Mexican brigade that crossed the river. That minor action was followed more dramatically by a battle at Palo Alto May 8 between 2,200 Americans and 4,000 Mexicans, with the latter defeated—largely by American artillery. Accusing the Mexicans of invading American territory, Polk won a declaration of war from Congress five days after this first major battle of the Mexican War. In other early stages of the war, Stephen Watts Kearny swept through New Mexico and moved into California.

Later, and far to the south and east, Winfield Scott landed troops just below Vera Cruz on the Mexican Gulf Coast and drove inland toward Mexico City. To the north Taylor continued his own campaign against the Mexicans, including a stunning victory at Buena Vista on February 23, 1847, over a Mexican force outnumbering his by three to one. The war pretty much was over seventeen months after its start when Scott seized Mexico City on September 14, 1847. Santa Anna resigned as Mexican president and commander in chief.

The overall result was American acquisition of territories extending the southwestern frontier all the way to California and the Pacific Ocean. At the same time, the annexation of Texas and the victorious war solidified Southern strength in national politics, added a new slave state to the Union's roster, and gave a slew of future Civil War generals important combat experience. The war also made a hero of Virginia-born Zachary Taylor—who himself had never voted for president—just in time for him to succeed Polk as president . . . and to die unexpectedly in office in July 1850.

Back in 1846, incidentally, Abraham Lincoln of Illinois had been one of those House members casting a no vote and thus joining the considerable congressional sentiment against going to war.

Out west, meanwhile, other events, other personalities, had been on the move during the years 1846 and 1847.

In 1846, for instance, the Mormons under Brigham Young began their historic emigration to future Utah but stopped to winter near today's Omaha, Nebraska. Unfortunately, their best preparations for survival could not forestall the dire effects of a cholera epidemic and near starvation as rations dwindled—six hundred or more died. Even so, Young was able to recruit five hundred volunteers for the Mormon Battalion that marched off to join the Mexican War campaign in distant California. That endless trek through mountain and desert took so long, however, that the fighting in California was over by the time the battalion reached its destination.

If the Mormon Battalion found the going tough—and it did—the luckless Donner Party of the same winter of 1846 stumbled into a frozen hell as it tried to cross the Sierra Nevada into California at an ill-timed moment. Trapped for weeks by unexpectedly heavy snows in the Hastings Cutoff, starving members of the party resorted to cannibalism in their efforts to survive.

On another front, also in 1846, Britain and the United States had finally, and peaceably, settled upon a northern border for the Oregon Territory, at the forty-ninth parallel rather than presidential candidate Polk's 54-40 dictum.

Early in the same year, it should also be mentioned, Pathfinder Frémont had begun a third major expedition, stopping to raise the American flag over Monterey, California, and next setting out northward toward Oregon. Then learning that war was under way, he joined with other Americans in California in a localized revolt against Mexican authority supposedly establishing the territory as an independent republic, à la Texas, but under a bear-emblazoned flag—the so-called Bear Flag Revolt.

With U.S. Navy Com. Robert Stockton's arrival at Monterey in July 1846, however, American claims to California were reasserted, and now began a military campaign resulting in the seizure of key coastal points from San Diego in the south to San Francisco in the north with little to no bloodshed. Fighting did erupt in the Los Angeles area in the fall, briefly resulting in a setback for the Americans, but with Stockton,

Frémont, and Kearny all joining forces, they regained dominance of California in January 1847.

That development began a charade of rival command interests. Stockton appointed Frémont as governor of California . . . Kearny asserted that he had orders to act as governor . . . Kearny arrested Frémont . . . Frémont was court-martialed in Washington and dismissed from the army . . . he still would be heard from later.

With the year 1847 by now well under way, Brigham Young led his people into the Valley of the Great Salt Lake, establishing the Mormon Trail to his church's new refuge. Thousands would be following the advance party, whose members began sowing their crops the day they arrived, July 23, 1847. And Young himself wasted no time in planning the streets for future Salt Lake City.

In Oregon, meanwhile, a grim reminder of the perils inherent in the attempted coexistence of white and Indian cultures side by side—the Cayuse Indians, many of their people fatally stricken in a measles epidemic, reacted by killing fourteen whites at the Whitman Mission, among them the missionary Marcus Whitman and his wife, Narcissa.

To the south, on a quiet January 24, 1848, James Marshall, busy building a lumber mill for John Sutter, *Sutter's Mill,* on the American River in northern California, by pure chance happened to find gold. This single event changed the face of California through an explosion of emigration, of boom towns, of heartbreaks for some and riches beyond imagination for others. And yet at the time few knew of the discovery, no one suspected. By mid-March a short article appeared in a San Francisco newspaper, but few paid attention.

A Mormon storekeeper from the Sutter's Fort area really set off the California gold rush. Visiting San Francisco in search of more customers for his store, Mormon elder Sam Brannan walked up and down the city streets with a bag of gold dust and shouted: "Gold! Gold! Gold from the American River."

That did it. As the word spread, confirmed late in the year by President Polk, early-bird gold seekers rushed to the spot, but it was the huge rush of 1849, of fortune hunters from every corner of the country, of the globe even, that tripled California's population to eighty thousand in record time and created the reality and the legend of the forty-niners.

The 1848 Treaty of Guadalupe Hidalgo by this time had sealed the bargain gained by the Mexican War . . . Texas, New Mexico, California, and other areas of the Southwest now officially belonged to the United

States. Only Thomas Jefferson's purchase of the Louisiana Territory in the first decade of the nineteenth century was a larger addition to the continental United States, which now, thanks to the fifth decade of the century, truly stretched, both north and south, from the Atlantic Ocean to the Pacific.

✫

1 8 4 5
Achieving the Near Impossible

✫

A sometimes rough "road" west? Listen as William L. Todd of Springfield, Illinois, writes back home about his travel west in 1845 by wagon train. An articulate voice from the past, he was in a caravan of twenty-five wagons that struck what he called "the California mountains," a final impediment blocking the pathway to his ultimate destination in the fertile valleys of California. There, at the mountain range, he wrote in a letter to his father on April 17, 1846, "We met with tribulation in the extreme." There was no way, he added, that he could fully describe the "evils" that beset his party. From the time he and his fellow travelers left one unnamed lake on the north side of the mountains until they reached another lake "on the top," he said, "it was one continued jumping from one rocky cliff to another."

Still with their wagons, mind you.

Thus: "We would have to roll over this big rock, then over that; then there was bridging a branch; then we had to lift our waggons by main force up to the top of a ledge of rocks, that it was impossible for us to reduce, bridge or roll our waggons over, and in several places, we had to run our waggons broadside off a ledge, take off our cattle, and throw our waggons round with handspikes, and heave them up to the top, where our cattle had been previously taken."

He and his companions spent three days at their "vexatious" task, and at the end of that time, they still were only six miles beyond the northside lake he mentioned as a starting place. He recalled, "[Y]ou never saw a set of fellows more happy than we when we reached the summit. When night came, we were glad to take a blanket or buffalo robe, and lay down on the softest side of a rock, and were sorry to be disturbed from our sweet repose, when we were called in the morning to our labor."

But the outcome apparently was worth all that hard work. "On the top of the mountain we found a beautiful lake, but quite small, and few miles farther we came to a fine prairie, about three miles long by three fourths of a mile broad, full of springs of excellent water, and at the lower end a fine branch, which forms the head of Juba river, and the way we danced Juba there, as a caution to all future emigrants."

Fact is, they had achieved the near impossible. "Solomon Sublette, of St. Louis, who passed us at the Lake on the north side of the mountain, told us afterwards that he had no idea we could get through with our waggons. In some places [now going down the western side of the mountain] we found it necessary to lock all four of the wheels coming down hill, and then our waggons came very near turning over hind part before, on to the cattle. At last. . . . our hardships were ended by our arrival at Fort Suter [Fort Sutter], where we concluded to spend the winter in the mountains."

By Fort Sutter, he meant Swiss-born John Augustus Sutter's trading post at the confluence of the American and Sacramento Rivers in the Sacramento Valley, ultimately to become California's capital city, Sacramento. Todd added that he was writing from a spot just sixty miles from San Francisco and forty from the Pacific Ocean as the crow flies, with Bodega the nearest port. "It is a beautiful valley," Todd wrote, "about ten miles long and two wide, situated between mountains, which are 2,000 feet high, from the bed of Cache Creek, which runs through the valley. In the mountains, there are deer and bear in abundance and about 15 miles from here there are plenty of elk."

Rather then being pleased, however, he had a few bones to pick with any would-be promoters of California as an unmitigated paradise. So many bones, in fact, that he would advise the folks back east to stay home! "There you are well off. You can enjoy all the comforts of life, live under a good government, and have peace and plenty around you—a country whose soil is unsurpassed by any in the world, having good seasons and yielding timely crops. Here everything is on the other extreme—the [Mexican] government is tyrannical, the weather unseasonable, poor crops, and the necessities of life not to be had except at the most extortionist prices, and frequently not then."

Not a big problem today, the combination of climate and horses apparently could be a nettlesome thing to contend with in Todd's day.

"In the winter season," he reported, "it is impossible for a horse to go about—the soil being so loose that the first rains make a perfect mortar of it, and your horse frequently sinks down so much that you are compelled to jump off in the mud knee deep to help him out." As for that climate, he noted what any northern Californian can tell you today: "I should be more pleased with this country if the seasons were more favorable. From the 1st of May to the 1st of October, it is one continued drouth [drought]; and from the 1st of October to the 1st of May, it rains off and on, all the time."

He did go on to say, "I do not, however, believe there was ever a more beautiful climate than we have in this country. During the whole winter we have delightful weather, except when it rains. We do not need fire except for cooking—nor have I seen during the whole winter ice thicker than a window glass, although we are in sight of snow the whole year round. Most all day long, we could be seen in winter with our coats off walking in the neighborhood of our cabin—except when we were off hunting for a term of 4 or 6 days."

If he was ambivalent about the weather in California, he was adamant about one thing—he didn't like the Mexican government that then, before the conclusion of the Mexican War, still ruled California. For one thing, the Mexicans had imposed laws forbidding land grants to "foreigners" like himself. In fact, Todd added, "the laws are framed to prevent foreigners from coming to the country unless they have passports."

If by chance he were asked to show such a document, he declared, he would be "inclined" to "shew my rifle."

The Mexicans, he also said, "talk every spring and fall here of driving the foreigners out of the country." But he correctly predicted, "They must do it this year or they can never do it. There will be a revolution before long, and probably this country will be re-annexed to the United States. If here, I will take a hand in it."

And that is a fact . . . he did. With the Mexican War raging far to the south for the better part of 1846, he did take part in the Bear Flag Revolt of the same year that propelled California forward on its pathway to eventual statehood in the United States. "On June 14, 1846, he and other American settlers raised the Bear Flag in the plaza at Sonoma," reports the same Oregon-California Trails Association (OCTA) Web site (calcite. rocky.edu/octa/todd.htm) that carries the *Springfield (Ill.) Sangamo Journal*'s version of young Todd's letter home to his physician father.

Burrowing Through Mexican Walls

MESSAGE FROM THE PAST: Traveling as a general's aide with the American force of twenty thousand that plunged into central Mexico from Vera Cruz, against tremendous odds and in danger all the while of being cut off from resupply or reinforcement, was the newspaper entrepreneur George Wilkins Kendall of the *New Orleans Picayune*. Having been captured and imprisoned by the Mexicans while fighting on behalf of the Republic of Texas in 1841, he made no secret of his antipathy toward the Mexicans. Nor did it bother the cofounder of the *Picayune* that he was both a participating general's aide and a reporter covering the Mexican War . . . he just kept sending in his dispatches from the ultimately triumphant front, up to and including the capture of Mexico City.

> CITY OF MEXICO, SEPTEMBER 14, 1847—Another victory, glorious in its results and which has thrown additional luster upon American arms, has been achieved today by the army under General [Winfield] Scott—the proud capital of Mexico has fallen into the power of a mere handful of men compared with the immense odds arrayed against them, and Santa Anna, instead of shedding his blood as he had promised, is wandering with the remnants of his army no one knows whither.
>
> The apparently impregnable works on Chapultepec [a hotly defended height on the western outskirts of the city], after a desperate struggle, were triumphantly carried; Generals Bravo and Moulterde, besides a host of officers of different grades, taken prisoners; over 1000 noncommissioned officers and privates, all their cannon and ammunition, are in our hands; the fugitives were soon in full flight towards the different works which command the entrances to the city, and our men at once were in hot pursuit. . . . [T]he daring and impetuosity of our men overcame one defense after another, and by nightfall every work to the city's edge was carried.

A highly effective American tactic, both here and in other battles of the Mexican War, was to avoid the risks of street fighting by burrowing through the walls of the city's adobe houses. As Kendall reported, the Americans at one point faced musket and cannon fire, including grapeshot, that was "sweeping the street completely." Thus, "At this juncture the old Monterey game, of burrowing and digging through the houses, was adopted." A sappers and miners unit under Lt. G. W. Smith went to work, "and every minute brought our men nearer the enemy's last stronghold."

> In one house which they entered, by the pickax, a favorite aide of Santa Anna's was found. The great man had just fled, but had left his friend and his supper. Both were well cared for—the latter was devoured by our hungry officers; the former, after doing the honors of the table, was made a close prisoner. Just as dark had set in, our men had dug and mined their way almost up to the very guns of the enemy, and now, after a short struggle, they were completely routed and driven out with the loss of everything. The command of the city by the San Cosme [gate] route was attained.

More precisely, Kendall also reported that a delegation of Mexican officers appeared a bit after midnight to report "that Santa Ann and his grand army had fled, and that they wished at once to surrender the capital!" Although sporadic fighting still broke out here and there all through the next day, Winfield Scott at seven in the morning took possession of the national palace in Mexico City, "at the top of which the Stars and Stripes was already flying."

Additional note: During the preceding day, the Americans at one point had wrestled two mountain howitzers into a church cupola to achieve "a plunging and most effective fire." Credit the young U.S. Army officer and recent West Point graduate Ulysses S. Grant for that feat. Then, too, George Wilkins Kendall espied another young officer doing his bit during the assault on Chapultepec. "I never saw a man work as hard as young Jackson, tearing off harness and dragging out dead and kicking horses." Jackson, that is, as in Thomas J. "Stonewall" Jackson, also of Civil War fame. Not far away and of course also contributing to the American triumph of arms over Mexico were Robert E. Lee, George B. McClellan, and a host of other future Union and Confederate military leaders. To the north, serving under his onetime father-in-law (and future U.S. President) Zachary Taylor, for that matter, was the future president of the Confederacy, Jefferson Davis.

☆

1 8 4 7
Mormon Battalion Arrives

☆

"Tongues," she said, "were swollen and dark." And no wonder . . . they had just crossed the arid desert stretch from Yuma, Arizona, into lovely, verdant California. They had just spent the better part of six months on an incredible two-thousand-mile infantry "march" from today's Council Bluffs, Iowa, as the first party traveling across the Chuhuahan, Sonoran, and California deserts into California proper . . . with wagons. As an indication of how rough their road was, count those wagons. Thirty-seven when they started out, and by the time they reached their destination at San Diego, California, exactly eight left.

Consider, though, what this group, the Mormon Battalion, had done: beaten down a new southern pathway to California that could be used year round . . . or, in the more graphic words of its commander, Lt. Col. Philip St. George Cooke, U.S. Army, marched through deserts "where, for want of water, there is no living creature"; gone through a wilderness, "where nothing but savages and wild beasts are found"; and of course crossed the mountains . . . and, oh, the mountains! "With crowbar and pick and axe in hand, we have worked our way over mountains, which seemed to defy aught but save the wild goat, and hewed a pass through a chasm of living rock more narrow than our wagons."

Whether hewing a mountain pass or digging wells for the future traveler in those bone-dry deserts, he summed up, "marching half naked and half fed, and living on wild animals, we have discovered and made a road of great value to our country." In short, in Cooke's view, "History may be searched in vain for an equal march of infantry."

Cooke, though, was not present six months and two thousand miles *before* trail's end—and the start, back in Iowa, of the unparalleled infantry march had not been a pretty one. That start came, explains Clayton C. Newell (on the Mormon Web site http://www.lds.org/ gospellibrary/pioneer/12_Council_Bluffsin.html), when U.S. Army Capt. James Allen rode into a sprawling Mormon refugee camp at Mount Pisgah, Iowa, near today's Thayer, Iowa, on a recruiting mission, only to face "something less than enthusiam."

Passing through this "makeshift refugee camp," says Newell's online article "America's Longest March," were up to fifteen thousand members of the Church of Latter-day Saints (LDS) who just recently had been "driven from their homes and farms in or around Nauvoo, Illinois, by a citizenry that had turned vicious and a government—right to the top—that had turned the other way."

This was after a mob had killed Mormon leader Joseph Smith and his brother in 1844, with Brigham Young then taking the LDS leadership reins and now hoping to lead his followers to a fruitful Zion beyond the reach of government and enemies of the church. "The possibility of removing to 'a place of safety . . . away towards the Rocky Mountains' had been on the minds of Church leaders since 1840," writes Newell. The Smith brothers' assassination only proved "the time had come."

But money was a problem—"the Latter-day Saints were largely destitute."

They had sent President James K. Polk an offer to build "block houses and stockade forts" along the Oregon Trail on their way west, then turn them over for the benefit of all. The hope was that the government would pay the Mormons, who "would build, then politely abandon, a string of secure shelters on their way out of America."

Polk at first wouldn't accept the offer, even when the Mormon leaders sent a second message declaring their patriotic loyalty despite their complaints of persecution and a governmental cold shoulder to their troubles. With the start of the Mexican War in May 1846, however, Polk suddenly was more interested in the goals of the Mormon Church. His diary of June 2, 1846, mentions that he had authorized Stephen Watts Kearny "to receive into service as volunteers a few hundred of the Mormons who are now on their way to California, with a view to conciliate them, attach them to our country, and prevent them from taking part against us."

It was the very next month when Captain Allen showed up at the Mount Pisgah refugee camp with a request for five hundred able-bodied men willing to join the war against Mexico.

At first, "he was regarded with something between ambivalent distraction and outright disdain."

And yet, "within days," he "had his five companies, plus laundresses, helpers and a passel of kids." The exact number setting out July 20 for far-western climes—and, presumably, for war with the Mexicans—would be 513 men, 34 women, and 51 children.

What had happened? Brigham Young, it seems, recognized the financial reality involved and passed along the word—join up. The military pay for battalion members—their clothing, shoes, and supplies—all could benefit the much larger flock he still intended to lead farther west, to the Great Salt Lake of future Utah. The way it worked out, most of the forty-two-dollar clothing allowance paid in advance to the battalion's one-year enlistees went to a general church fund helping to finance the planned exodus to Utah. In addition, wages paid to battalion members over the next year would amount to nearly thirty thousand dollars, and most of that money would be diverted to Mormon coffers as well.

While benefiting from the badly needed material help, suggests Newell, Young's "overriding" motive was "to win the confidence of—and independence from—a capricious and to-date uncaring U.S. Government." Even so, Brigham Young later would pronounce the enlistment of the battalion in the service of the United States, "indeed the temporal salvation of our camp."

And so the battalion set out, with Fort Leavenworth, Kansas, its first major destination . . . and right away there were setbacks. Captain Allen, it turned out, was deathly ill: He died within days of the large party's arrival at Fort Leavenworth. Now the battalion was taken over by Lt. Andrew Jackson Smith, with Santa Fe, New Mexico, to be the next major stop. Unfortunately for all, the Mormons and Smith did not always see eye to eye . . . safe to say, he was hardly disliked by his neophyte troops. "Presumably annoyed with the nature of his force," says Newell's account, "Smith employed frequent forced marches and other inequities with a dictatorial demeanor. One chronicler of the events stated that any other body of people not already accustomed to being herded from one place to the next "would have mutinied rather than submit to the oppressions.'"

Before reaching Santa Fe, a fair number of battalion members, including most of the women and children, along with the sick, were detached and sent to Fort Pueblo, Colorado.

Happily for those remaining on the historic march, a new commander, Colonel Cooke (later known in army circles as, ironically, "Father of the Cavalry," and later to become father-in-law of the future Confederacy's great cavalry leader Jeb Stuart), was awaiting them in Santa Fe, and he would be taking them the rest of the way to San Diego.

Them at this point consisted of 340 men, 4 officer's wives (commissioned as privates), and a handful of children.

As events turned out, the Mormon Battalion never did fight any battles against any enemy but the elements, which at times were severe enough. Instead, the battalion faced down and scared off the Mexicans holding Tucson, Arizona, and survived a scary moment of its own called the "Battle of the Bulls," aptly described by Newell as "a wild cattle stampede that resulted in the death of fifteen bulls (shot), two mules (gored), and three wounded men."

Still, there were many difficult moments, and one of them was that last desert crossing from Yuma, with no fresh water seen for days. "The men were so used up from thirst, fatigue, and hunger," wrote Melissa Burton Couray in her journal on January 18, 1847, "there was no talking. Some could not speak at all; tongues were swollen and dark."

Fortunately, the battalion now was encamped at Vallecito Creek in the Anza-Borrego region of California. Its members now could have all the water they want; they washed clothes and rested. "An Indian from a nearby village brought a letter from the alcade [leading official] in San Diego welcoming the Battalion to California. In the early evening there was singing and fiddling with a little dancing."

By January 29, the battalion was at San Diego, its mission of joining Kearny's minuscule Army of the West satisfactorily completed . . . but the force had no military significance since the Americans already had taken over California with hardly a fight. Still, the Mormon Battalion had a lot to be proud of. Its personnel had mapped terrain surrounding their march, notes the Newell account, "an effort which played prominently in the Gadsen Purchase of 1853." They had opened the southerly wagon road into California "and established a U.S. Presence that would, two years later, be officially recognized with the . . . Treaty of Guadalupe Hidalgo (giving the United States possession of California, New Mexico and Arizona)."

Stated another way, notes Kent Duryee in "The Mormon Battalion in the Desert Southwest," appearing in the online magazine *DesertUSA* (http://www.desertusa.com/mag00/oct/papr/mormbat.html) the east-west trail blazed by the Mormon Battalion soon would become the route of choice "for thousands of pioneers, treasure seekers and others who would follow the lure of California and gold." It also would become a leg on John Butterfield's southern overland mail route, Duryee's account notes.

As Duryee also suggests, the outcome could have been far different if the battalion had not crossed the final desert stretch in the relatively cool month of January—otherwise, "history may well have been very different."

Meanwhile, with the historic march completed, according to Newell, fifteen battalion members escorted Kearny on a march back to Fort Leavenworth, 81 reenlisted in the army, "and the rest (about 245) were discharged." At least 6 of the latter group were working at Sutter's Mill when gold was discovered there in January 1848. Others contributed to the construction of the adobe Fort Moore at Los Angeles soon after its capture by U.S. troops in early 1847. Still others, Duryee notes, were the first to find the bodies of those who died in the Donner Party disaster "and buried the remains." Further, the group returning to Brigham Young's side forged a new trail eastward from California to Salt Lake City.

☆ ☆ ☆

Additional note: Today a massive monument commemorating the Mormon Battalion stands on the Utah state capitol grounds in Salt Lake City. Inspired by the Daughters of the Mormon Battalion and created by sculptor Gilbert Riswold, it was dedicated on May 30, 1927. A bronze tablet on the north side of the monument lists the names of battalion members, including the four women who completed the entire march (one of whom died, however, shortly after her arrival in California, where she also gave birth to a child).

Incidentally, two more historically prominent figures who took part in the long march were:

• Lt. George Stoneman, who later served as a major general in the Civil War and, from 1883 to 1887, as governor of California

• Jean Baptiste Charbonneau, best known as little "Pomp," the infant son of Sacagawea who accompanied Lewis and Clark to the Pacific Ocean and back to the Dakotas in 1805–6. Fully grown by 1846–47, Jean Baptiste traveled with the Mormon Battalion as a guide. Lured by the gold rush two years later, he stayed on in California for some years.

By ironic timing, the returning battalion soldiers arrived at Salt Lake just five days behind Brigham Young and his pioneering entourage.

---

1 8 4 8
The Gold Found

★

You never know who just stepped off the latest wagon train. In 1844 it was James Wilson Marshall, New Jersey–born farmer, mechanic, carpenter, wheelwright, and all-round handy fellow. Stepped off in Oregon Territory but then, the next year, drifted down to California and found a job at Sutter's Mill on the Sacramento River. Nothing special about him . . . except that now, in hindsight, it's hard to say what other single individual, other than Meriwether Lewis or William Clark, had a greater impact on the development of the West.

His statue stands tall in a state park today, and that same state park's online history says the single thing he did on January 24, 1848, "led to the greatest mass movement of people the world had ever known."

That's saying an awful lot, but then isn't it true that California's non-Indian population of 14,000 in 1848 would shoot and soar to 223,000 in just four years? Can't we say that without this huge influx, California wouldn't have become a state as early as 1850? That there wouldn't have been quite the same hurry to build the transcontinental railroad right after the Civil War? Couldn't we also say that without the new state's best known product, the Union would have had a much more difficult time financing the Civil War? That San Francisco might have remained some sort of hick town for a while longer?

Poor fellow, for all that, he personally wouldn't be getting much good or wealth out of his great discovery, his chance finding of . . . *the gold!*

Leaving his hometown of Lambertville, New Jersey, on the Delaware River, just a bit above George Washington's famous crossing place, Marshall took the long route to California, you might say. He stopped for six years in Missouri, where he operated a farm on the Missouri River and did spot work as a carpenter. But the bottomland fevers were getting to him, and he had heard about the wonderful climate of California. He pulled up stakes in 1844 at age thirty-four and joined a wagon train headed for Oregon. The next year he was at Sutter's Fort and working for its proprietor and impresario, John Sutter.

Still a farmer at heart, Marshall bought himself a ranch, continued working for Sutter, then plunged headlong into the Bear Flag Revolt and the American conquest of California. During his yearlong absence, his cattle disappeared—"strayed or stolen," according to the Marshall Gold Discovery State Historic Park at Coloma, California. "Nearly penniless—he collected the princely sum of $36 for his army service—he went back to Sutter's Fort looking for work."

Delighted to have Marshall's wide-ranging talents again available, Sutter commissioned the displaced rancher-farmer to find an appropriate site for a sawmill that they could build and operate in partnership together. Marshall found just the right spot on the south fork of the American River in the Sierra Nevada's foothills, fifty-four miles to the northeast, a site soon to become the town of Coloma, named for the local Cullumah tribe. With Sutter's consent, he began building their planned sawmill in September 1847. Working for him were a number of local Indians and a few veterans of the recently dispersed Mormon Battalion.

By January 1848 all was ready except for the channel (called the millrace) under the big mill wheel. The millrace would carry water from the adjoining river through the mill. "The lower part, the tailrace, carried water away from the mill and back into the river," notes the park's Web site (see http://www.windjammer.net/colomas/briefhist.htm). But the tailrace was too shallow, with the result that the water "was backing up, [and] the big mill wheel would not turn properly." Therefore, Marshall had his workers and Cullumah laborers deepen the tailrace ditch, clearing it of boulders by day and running water through it at night to wash out the debris.

"On the morning of January 24, 1848 [there is *some* argument over the exact date], while inspecting the tailrace, Marshall spotted some shining flecks in the water. He scooped them up and, after testing them with his fingernail and pounding them with a rock, he placed them in the crown of his hat and hurried back to announce his find to the others. 'Boys,' he said, 'by God, I believe I have found a gold mine.'"

Well, he had, and he hadn't. Not for himself, anyway . . . but not for lack of trying.

Meanwhile, Marshall raced back to Sutter's Fort to tell his senior partner the stupendous news. Bursting into Sutter's quarters, John Sutter recalled later, Marshall declared he had information that "would put both of us in possession of unheard-of-wealth—millions and millions of dollars."

Sutter quite naturally thought "something had touched Marshall's brain."

But then his partner in the sawmill scheme "was flinging on the table a handful of scales of pure virgin gold." Sutter was convinced, especially after they tested the sample bits.

In the meantime, Marshall was telling Sutter that out of sheer laziness, he almost did *not* lean over and pick up the shiny, glittering flakes in the tailrace. Recalled Sutter: "'Do you know,' said Mr. Marshall to me, 'I positively debated whether I should take the trouble to bend my back to pick up the pieces and had decided on not doing so when farther on, another glittering morsel caught my eye—the largest of the pieces now before you. I condescended to pick it up, and to my astonishment found that it was a thin scale of what appears to be pure gold.'"

On another, more crucial point, according to one Sutter account of that startling day, Marshall told him he had not told anyone about the discovery. "I . . . was glad to hear he had not spoken to a single person about it," wrote the impresario of Sutter's Fort. But Sutter at another time wrote: "He told me that he had expressed his opinion to the laborers at the mill, that this might be gold; but some of them were laughing at him and called him a crazy man, and could not believe such as a thing." For both accounts, see the San Francisco Museum Web site (http://www.sfmuseum.og/hist2/gold.html).

Far better for both had they been able to keep the discovery a secret while they organized and made plans to exploit Marshall's discovery. As it was, both men hurried back to the sawmill site the next day, according to Sutter's account. They arrived just in time to poke around in the stream bed for a short while before sundown. In that time, they collected more than an ounce of gold. Exploring farther the next day, up both the north and south forks of the American River, they kept finding more and more of the gold. When they returned to the mill, however, they found the big secret was out. "[W]e noticed by the excitement of the working people that we had been dogged about," said Sutter.

Worse, one of the Indian laborers displayed gold samples of his own while crying out, "*Oro! Oro! Oro!* [Gold! Gold! Gold!]."

While the word quickly spread within the Sutter's Fort community, ironically, it was months before the discovery of gold in California generated the smallest bit of excitement in the larger world beyond the confines of the Sacramento and American Rivers. After all, gold had been found in California before . . . with limited results. As historian Richard H. Peterson wrote in *Wild West* magazine in 1997, "California Indians gave gold to the [Spanish] mission padres in return for trading goods." Then, too, Padre Luis Antonio Martinez at San Luis Obispo operated "a modest gold mine in his district in 1829." Further, Baptiste Ruelle, a French-Canadian fur trapper with the Hudson's Bay Company, apparently found gold near Los Angeles in 1841. And finally, in 1842 vaquero Francisco Lopez pulled up some wild onions in Placerita Canyon, also near Los Angeles, "to season his lunch of dried beef or jerky," and discovered "glittering gold flakes clinging to the roots."

Six years before James Marshall found *his* gold, twenty ounces of gold from the same Placerita Canyon was the first gold sent from California to the U.S. Mint in Philadelphia.

As history also records, however, word of the Marshall discovery in 1848 finally did get out and take hold . . . with a vengeance. Sam Brannan, chief purveyor of the news, was a Mormon elder and co-owner of a store close to Sutter's Fort. He heard about the discovery from the Mormon workers at the sawmill site. "[T]hey readily gave him a tithe of the gold they had obtained in their spare time," says the Marshall State Park's online history. Then, visiting San Francisco in May 1848, "Brannan paraded through the streets waving a quinine bottle containing the gold and shouting, 'Gold! Gold! Gold from the American River!'"

By various accounts, that did it. Locally and then regionally at least, the California gold rush was on. "By June 1, San Francisco was reported to be 'half empty' as the able bodied males departed en masse for the mines. This scene was repeated up and down California as people everywhere responded to the irresistible cry."

And now, instead of themselves reaping the greatest reward of all from the gold found at their sawmill, both Marshall and Sutter suffered for it. Sutter quickly became a victim of the effects as his work force melted away . . . gone to search for the gold. Even worse, as recalled in Geoffrey C. Ward's companion volume to the PBS television series *The West:* "Squatters arrived on his land and refused to move. He lost town sites he'd owned in Sacramento. Creditors dogged him. 'Stealing began,' he wrote. 'Land, cattle, horses, everything began to disappear.'"

Soon no one was visiting Sutter's Fort, once "the gateway" to California. "A meatpacking company made a fortune rustling his cattle and he seemed powerless to stop them. Finally, someone burned his house down."

For James Marshall, it was much the same sad story. He tried to assert his own claims to Coloma Valley land where the gold was found, but the flood of gold seekers pouring into the valley was far beyond his control. By July the estimated population of tiny Coloma had jumped to four thousand. It was a scene of total insanity. "Gold seemed to be everywhere," wrote Ward in his book, "lodged among rocks, glittering in sandbars, swirling in pools and eddies. Some made fortunes using nothing but spoons or jacknives to scoop it up. Others brought in crude machinery and hired Indians to do the work: seven men employing fifty Indians dug out 273 pounds of gold in just two months. 'My little girls can make from 5 to 25 dollars a day washing gold in pans,' a miner wrote home to Missouri. 'My average income this winter will be about 150 dollars a day.'" As one discovery followed another, reported Col. R. B. Mason, military governor of California, and his subordinate, Lt. William Tecumseh Sherman, to Washington that summer, four thousand men were at work in the gold fields—"and they were pulling out $30,000 to $50,000 worth of gold a day," Ward noted.

Apparently overwhelmed from the beginning of the rush, Marshall at first hired himself out to hopeful prospectors, but he soon found he was being followed everywhere by all kinds of strangers expecting he would take them straight to additional gold strikes.

Foolishly, he claimed "special powers of divination" in finding sources of gold. When he couldn't, or wouldn't, make good on such promises, there were threats of violence, even a lynching. "Fearing for his life, he stayed away from Coloma for six months," notes the online park history. For a time, he still was harassed by miners wherever he came to rest.

In short order also, disputes over management of the sawmill left it idle—it would be abandoned by 1850. In the meantime, President James K. Polk had announced the discovery of gold in California to the world, and in 1849 the real California gold rush began. The initial flood of newcomers transmogrified itself into an avalanche.

Far from striking it rich himself, Marshall spent the next few years combining largely unsuccessful prospecting attempts with part-time carpentry work to eke out a living. He had to sell off his ranch to settle piled-up debts.

He eventually returned to Coloma, bought some land at rock-bottom price and began a vineyard, notes the state park history. "He and a partner . . . made furniture, saddle trees, rockers, wheels, and coffins. He spent a lot of money on new and exotic varieties of grapevines, dug a long cellar and began to make wine for sale." His vineyard won an award at a county fair. Like many of those who rushed to California, he found there was a living (and for some, a real fortune) in providing goods or services for others, "but in the late 1860s a lessening demand for fruit, high taxes, and increased competition sent him prospecting again."

He and partner William Burke invested in a quartz mine near Kelsey, not far from Coloma, but they needed money to develop it further. Marshall was persuaded—as the man who had discovered the California gold—to go on a lecture tour to raise money, and Burke contributed a biography to their joint fund-raising effort. Neither effort worked. While a curiosity, Marshall apparently was no public speaker. "The tour ended in Kansas City where Marshall found himself penniless and unable to continue."

Coming to his rescue was California's railroad magnate Leland Stanford, who advanced Marshall railroad fare for a visit to his mother and sister back in Lambertville, New Jersey. To their chagrin, by various accounts, he arrived broke, rife with odd habits, bad-tempered, and a thriving alcoholic. After a few months, the famous discoverer of gold returned to Kelsey, where he lived out his life in the Union Hotel.

For his "contribution to California's gold-crazed growth," wrote historian Peterson, Marshall won a two-hundred-dollar-a-month pension from the California State Assembly in 1872. He then paid off some debts and opened a blacksmith shop next to his hotel. After two years, however, the legislature cut the pension in half. It finally was "allowed to lapse in 1878 after sharp criticism of Marshall's personal habits—especially his weakness for liquor."

When Marshall went to the lawmaking body in person in 1878 to appeal the cutback, legend has it, a brandy bottle fell out of his pocket and rolled across the floor. Legend or not, his appeal failed. "Over the next few years, Marshall continued to work his blacksmith shop and in . . . two small gold mines he owned near Kelsey," adds the state park history. "He was a regular at the local saloon and sometimes walked from Kelsey to Coloma or Georgetown to visit friends, drink, and socialize."

His life, though, went no farther. Noted Peterson: "During his last years, Marshall . . . an obvious alcoholic, was forced to live by handyman jobs, handouts and the sale of his autograph on special cards for 50 cents each." He died virtually a pauper in August 1885, two months shy of his seventy-fifth birthday. Peterson recalled an epitaph-like comment by one of Marshall's friends, Margaret A. Kelly: "Probably no man ever went to his grave so misunderstood, so misjudged, so misrepresented, so altogether slandered as James W. Marshall."

☆ ☆ ☆

Additional note: The Marshall Gold Discovery State Historical Park at Coloma offers visitors a full-sized, operational replica of the sawmill that James Marshall built for John Sutter, along with a Gold Discovery Museum and a major portion of Coloma itself, including a few buildings harkening back to the gold rush days. Marshall is buried on a hill overlooking the site where he first found the gold, his grave marked by a monumental statue showing him pointing to the discovery site below.

Meanwhile, noted Richard H. Peterson, the nugget that Marshall found now belongs to the Bancroft Library at the University of California in Berkeley. Rather than have Marshall as its namesake, however, it's the *Wimmer* Nugget, after Peter L. Wimmer, Marshall's assistant in supervising the Indians and others who dug the tailrace of Sutter's Mill. Explained Peterson, "Wimmer's wife tested the metal by boiling it with homemade soap to assure it would emerge untarnished."

The discoverer of gold also is recalled these days in New Jersey, where he grew up as the great-grandson of a signer of the Declaration of Independence; where, wrote Peterson, he learned his father's trade of carpenter and wheelwright but clashed "with his stern Baptist father"; and where also he suffered rejection by not one but two young women he had hopes of marrying. The historic, Federal-style brick home where Marshall lived from age six to his leaving town at the age of twenty-one now serves both as a museum and as headquarters of the Lambertville Historical Society. Right across the street stands the First Baptist Church, with nuggets of gold—Marshall's own gold—trapped unseen in the church cornerstone.

Epilogue: John Augustus Sutter, Geoffrey Ward noted in his book *The West,* came to California early and at first seemed so successful with the establishment of his Sutter's Fort and the colony he called *Nueva Helvetia* ("New Switzerland") that he lived like a king or baron of old. Never mind that he left a family of six behind in Switzerland or was in flight from a flock of creditors. Having obtained a fifty-thousand-acre land grant from California's Mexican government, "Sutter ran his sprawling domain like a European barony—drilling an army of Indians, dispensing a crude kind of justice, encouraging his workers to plant fields and orchards and harvest timber, and taking very young girls to bed." At the same time, he was indispensable as a supplier of goods, shelter, and helpful advice to the first Americans filtering through and over the mountain barriers separating California from the rest of the future United States.

After the gold rush swept through his "barony" like a hurricane, Sutter was ruined financially . . . personally, as well. "He turned over what was left of his fortune to his son, John Jr., who promptly lost it." Further, Sutter senior began to drink heavily. And "He haunted Congress for years before he died, seeking compensation he said he was owed for having come to the aid of so many American emigrants and for having once owned the land on which gold was found."

☆

1 8 4 9
Argonauts in Search of Gold

☆

We still call them Argonauts, that crazy, mixed-up collection of hardy trekkers, wagoneers, entrepreneurs, thieves, pioneers, heroes, and knaves . . . the Argonauts who in 1849 went after the gold, the California gold, and often by the overland route through northern Mexico.

The original Argonauts sailed with Jason in search of the Golden Fleece . . . and one of *our* latter-day crowd did, indeed, "sail" even while taking an overland trail to the promised land beyond desert, mountain range, river, and desert again, all, of course, far to the west of his native New England.

One was **Lewis Birdsall "Boat-Wagon" Harris,** and his saving grace was a tightly caulked wagon that could ford a river . . . like a boat. First testing his amphibious conveyance on the Pecos River in western Texas virtually unnoticed, he astonished onlookers when more visibly crossing the Rio Grande at populous El Paso.

Before starting west from San Antonio in the spring of 1849 with his wife, Jenny; their two black slaves, Bob and Jane; Capt. Herman Thorn, Cal Thorn, and other Thorn family members; plus a good friend named Cornelius, Texas settler Harris had anticipated the obstacles ahead by creating an overland wagon shaped like a river flatboat.

Traveling mostly in the wagon mode, the Harris party not only reached El Paso without disastrous incident but moved on northwestward from there with its boat-wagon fully loaded with fresh supplies. They moved on through rough, isolated country to Santa Cruz in the Mexican state of Sonora and then on to Tucson, Arizona.

But then came the wide Colorado River, to be crossed where it and the Gila River came together. Although Harris had "sailed" his boat-wagon down the Gila to the intersection of the rivers and then, for the price of sixty dollars had agreed to ferry some Mexicans across the Colorado, Captain Thorn and three of his men tried crossing the latter river to California Territory by lashing two log canoes together. They were swept downstream by the swift current and drowned.

Harris, in the meantime, turned down a seventy-five-dollar offer from U.S. Army Lt. Cave Johnson Couts for the boat-wagon. So Harris took the remaining members of his party across the river and moved westward . . . by wagon mode once again. Couts had hoped to turn the boat-wagon into a permanent ferry since so many California-bound emigrants were finding the river crossing difficult and often deadly. When Harris, understandably, clung to his main means of transportation, Couts hastened to establish a ferry service with a real ferryboat anyway.

Harris eventually settled in California's future state capital of Sacramento, wound up as a county sheriff, the mayor of Sacramento, and deputy secretary of the state of California, recalled historian Ferol Egan in his book *The El Dorado Trail.*

Meanwhile, there also was "**The Great Western,**" as *she* was known, more than six feet in height, red-haired, blue-eyed . . . and all female. Sick with fever, left behind at El Paso by his California-bound party, an overland traveler named Augustus Knapp couldn't believe his eyes when this legendary angel of mercy appeared in the doorway of his grass-and-reed hut . . . that is, filled the opening that passed for a doorway.

"This guardian angel at Knapp's doorway was not a Calamity Jane wearing man's clothing and looking more masculine than feminine," wrote Egan. "On the contrary, she wore a dress that she filled out with ample endowments in all the right spots. She was all woman, much woman, and there was no mistake about it."

The true name and origin of the Amazonian who then nursed Knapp back to health, first in his hut, then at her saloon in town, were a mystery to her contemporaries on the southwestern frontier, even though she was a well-known figure to the soldiers, miners, Indians, and others populating the Great Southwest . . . or, like Knapp, merely passing through. "She might have come from Missouri or Tennessee," wrote Egan. "Her maiden name possibly was Bourgette, Bouget, Bourdette, or Borginnis. She may have once been Mrs. Davis or Mrs. Foley."

What *was* known was her recent background as a cook for the U.S. Seventh Infantry officers mess at Fort Brown, then Fort Texas. Further, during the Mexican War, according to historian Egan, "She did assist wounded men during and including the battles up to Buena Vista. And she did go along with Maj. Lawrence P. Graham's battalion of Second Dragoons as they headed out of Monterrey, Mexico, in 1848, and began their long march to California. However, she became sick at Chihuahua City and remained there when the troops moved on."

Recovering, she had moved on to El Paso by the time Knapp met her in 1849. She later married—"a man named Bowman"—and operated a saloon in Yuma, Arizona, where she died in 1866. First buried—with the trappings of a military funeral—at the Fort Yuma cemetery, she later was transferred, along with 158 soldiers, to the Presidio at San Francisco, for reburial under a headstone bearing the name **Sarah A. Bowman.**

Then, too, still back in New York City in 1850, there was short, stocky **Parker H. French,** a confidence man busily advertising a sixty-day "pleasure trip" to California by sea and by land, with pots of gold possibly to greet his clientele even before journey's end—potential riches awaiting them at the Gila River in Arizona. Unscrupulous in his pursuit of a dollar, French promised a relatively easy stagecoach trip from the Texas port of Lavaca to El Paso, when in fact there was no stagecoach service on the "road" to El Paso . . . there was no road.

This is not to say that Parker H. French meant to cheat his paying customers and send them off on their own. No, he traveled with them.

Their rigors would be his rigors as well. Still, not even French himself could have imagined his pending transformation into a gun-slinging, one-armed gang leader . . . and then as a district attorney and a California legislator.

But first, returning to the various perils he failed to advertise back in New York (as recalled by historian Egan), there not only was the tough trek from Lavaca to El Paso, but after that, long dry stretches without water, plus dangerous exposure to hostile Apaches . . . and to scores of venomous rattlesnakes. There was the risky river crossing at the Colorado. Additionally, even after all that, came the high sand dunes of the Colorado desert, plus negotiation of the still-obscure trail through Guadalupe Pass in the Sierra Madre Occidental, a trail forged just a few years earlier by the Mormon Battalion—"a trail," wrote Egan, "that was hard to find and hard to travel if a man did find it."

As events turned out, the French expedition, more than two hundred strong, began to fall apart almost from the day, June 4, 1850, the entourage reached Lavaca by steamship, after stops in Cuba and New Orleans. "Wagons, supplies and mules were supposed to be waiting and ready to go," added Egan. But they weren't. And worse, "To compound the difficulty for these city men, French purchased unbroken mules, and turned over the taming of these wild animals to one vaquero and the greenhorn gold seekers."

The result naturally was chaos, to say nothing of delay piled upon delay. Already three weeks in transit from New York, the French party now spent an entire month just trekking to San Antonio, 150 miles from Lavaca. This was in summer heat punctuated by frequent rains that were accompanied by "a constant swarm of large mosquitoes."

In San Antonio, French displayed a letter of credit to obtain drafts he then used to buy additional supplies at a U.S. Army post. When it turned out his letter of credit was "worthless," a warrant was issued for his arrest. By then, though, he and his expedition were "well on their way" to El Paso. And still more troubles lay ahead, added Egan: "The party had a long list of complaints ranging from the dreadful summer heat and shortage of water to delays caused by Comanches who wished to trade with them and the constant worry about rattlesnakes which were striking their livestock on a daily basis."

At one point, the forage ahead was burned up in a grass fire set off by lightning. Further, "equipment was beginning to wear out . . . accidents were beginning to take their toll." Among the latter, one man accidentally was shot and killed; another fell under the wheels of a heavy wagon and suffered serious injury.

Soon, an unbridgeable schism developed between the expedition's more unhappy campers and French, who nonetheless managed to cling to an assortment of faithful cronies. Matters came to a head at the Rio Grande in the vicinity of El Paso. With expedition members finally restored to American territory after two and a half months of hard overland passage, warrant-bearing officers turned up in hopes of arresting French for his transgressions back in San Antonio. They were stymied, however, when he fled across the Rio Grande into Mexican territory, leaving both supplies and his clients behind.

They, in turn, wasted no time selling the supplies, dividing the proceeds, and setting out for California on their own. One mistake, though, was breaking up into small parties and picking various routes to the promised land.

The penalty for such fragmentation came hardly a month later, as one of those independent parties was surprised and attacked at Corralitos, a Mexican silver-mining town in Chihuahua, by a gang of gunmen . . . and who should be leading them but a vengeful Parker H. French! When the gunsmoke cleared, several men on each side had been killed or badly wounded. French, though, had been driven off, with one arm shattered from hand to elbow.

Seeking refuge nearby, he insisted upon having his arm amputated just above the elbow and under truly primitive conditions that "would have killed most men." And yet, just ten days later he was back in the saddle, headed south for Durango and a crossing of the Sierra Madre Occidental en route to Mazatlan.

This was a dangerous trail fraught with the possibility of attack by Indians or bandits.

For French, however, neither one was exactly his nemesis since he had joined the outlaw ranks . . . and soon would be jailed at Durango under a death sentence for robbing a mail coach.

Ever the glib one, One-Armed French, as he now was called, convinced a local priest to become his advocate by telling the cleric he had been orphaned at a young age and then "fallen into evil ways without parents to guide him." French's plea was that he was "a man more sinned against than sinning." Further, he and his men could, and should, spend their time protecting the good citizens of Mexico from hostile Indians.

Unbelievably, the gullible governor of Durango placed French in command of Mexican troops plus his own motley crew. And, true to form, French and his gang deserted the Mexicans at the first opportunity, next appearing—together with many of his recently fleeced clients—at the port of Mazatlan. There, unbelievably again, French convinced some of them to raise the funds needed to charter a ship able to carry them all to San Francisco . . . then sailed off without his now twice-duped investors!

Imagine their surprise, when and if they ever reached the California nirvana, to find their old New York chum installed as district attorney of San Luis Obispo County—that is to say, as the local prosecutor of violators of the law. And from there to find Parker French moving up yet another notch, to that of a maker of laws—as an elected member of the California State Assembly.

Never short on effrontery, the same flimflam man flitted from "careers" as politician and newspaper editor, as a chief lieutenant in William Walker's revolutionary activity in Nicaragua, as a Civil War spy, both Confederate and Union (again fooling any wishful thinkers standing in the way). "Last seen in Washington, D.C., as an alcoholic who enjoyed a chloroform booster with his whiskey," wrote Egan, French "was one of those characters who turned up in one wild venture after another in the American West, and very few of his activities were truly within the law."

As for his ultimate fate, who knows? Egan observed that French simply "vanished into the nether land of history—for nobody ever reported his death."

☆

1 8 5 0
Wheelbarrow Man

☆

The trail to the California gold fields led westward across the plains, the mountains, and the rivers, with California always seeming still a far piece beyond. Along this trail in the summer of 1850, on and on, trudged a lone emigrant from Pennsylvania, pushing a handcart most of the way.

Out on the vast plains the traveler on foot had seen victims of cholera buried in shallow mass graves later torn open by wolves. But on he passed.

He had encountered the local native peoples—Indians—but walked on past, unharmed.

At the Weber River near Salt Lake City, he lost his handcart in a ferryboat accident . . . and was fortunate to avoid drowning. Resupplied with the help of Mormons, he pushed on.

In the Rockies, "Wheelbarrow (or Handcart) Man" James Gordon Brookmire saw lightning strike at his very feet, tearing up the ground, stunning him . . . but allowing him to live. And he pressed on.

At home, in Warren County, Pennsylvania, where he had begun his long, long journey, a wife and six children waited on the family farm at the community of Sugar Grove.

At forty years of age, he had decided to join the gold rush begun the year before, make his fortune in quick order, then return home a rich man . . . just like that.

No matter that thousands with the same dream were ahead of him, no matter that many thousands more were on their way to the same gold fields in 1850. No matter that, unlike most of those on the trail west, he was making his way alone and on foot with only the handcart to carry his personal possessions, supplies, and equipment. No matter . . . except that James G. Brookmire would become the first gold-seeking "handcart emigrant" west to be identified by name in histories of the period, according to Morris W. Werner at the *Kansas Heritage* Web site (http://history.cc.ukans.edu/heritage/werner/wheemigrant.html). "At least three other unnamed gold seekers using wheelbarrows were mentioned by travelers on the trail in 1850," Werner adds. "One of these started from St. Joseph [Missouri] and was reported at Ft. Laramie [Wyoming] twenty-five days later, a record matched by few, if any, horse or mule powered companies."

Meanwhile, Brookmire, an Ulster Scot from Northern Ireland, didn't actually begin his footmarch in Pennsylvania. It is thought that he first made his way to the village of Kansas, Missouri, site of the future Kansas City, by riverboat (possibly via the Allegheny to the Ohio, the Ohio to the Mississippi, and the Mississippi to the Missouri, then upstream to the still-small Kansas settlement). He joined a group from Kentucky setting out on June 27, 1850, to cross the plains. But there were problems of some kind, and at Fort Kearny on the south bank of the Platte River in Nebraska, he and the Kentuckians parted company. From then on, Brookmire was on his own, except for "a well-trained and faithful dog which he had befriended on the trail."

The homestead he left behind in Pennsylvania consisted of a 280-acre farm . . . minus the 50 acres he had sold "to finance his trip." His wife, Margaret, also a native of Ireland, and their six children, age six to fifteen, were left in "very indigent circumstances," according to a later article in the *St. Joseph (Mo.) Gazette* (March 24, 1852), and certainly the couple had not strolled down Easy Street quite yet.

Brookmire, going by the name Gordon rather than his first name James, had spent seven years as an apprentice in the textile industry, from age fourteen to twenty-one. He next had emigrated to the United States, worked in the Philadelphia textile industry for nearly three years, then returned to Ireland to marry Margaret. Three financially "difficult" years and two children later, they set out for western Pennsylvania and its beckoning farmland—in their case, just three miles from the village of Sugar Grove in Freehold Township, close to Jamestown across the nearby New York state line.

Their circumstances, Brookmire's dream of easily finding a fortune in California, his expectations of crossing a continent, of negotiating its deserts and mountain ranges alone and pushing a handcart, obviously were a recipe for impending disaster.

Still, he eventually did reach California and its gold fields, but just when is not clear. Surely, as stated by Morris Werner in his Internet article for *Kansas Heritage* (titled "Wheelbarrow Emigrant of 1850"), "it must have been late in the season."

But the important point is that he was there, and now he could try the second stage of his impossible dream—find the gold.

Amazingly, that is exactly what he did. And in quick order, too. "Within eighteen months he managed to wash out and save $15,000 worth of gold dust."

Not only that, he now learned that his wife, Margaret, had just inherited ten thousand dollars. Quite suddenly, they had between them a nest egg of twenty-five thousand dollars, a considerable sum, even a small fortune, by the standards of the mid-nineteenth century.

Brookmire could now turn for home . . . and he did, but this time he traveled by boat down the West Coast to Nicaragua, crossed the narrow Central American neck there, and then set out for home via boat again to New York. No more westward trekking with a handcart, thank you.

Back in Pennsylvania, he and Margaret added nearly two hundred acres to their original farm. They later lived with a married son and his family in nearby Jamestown, New York, for some years. Margaret died in 1887, and her husband, age ninety, joined her in death three years later. "Both are buried in Cherry Hill Cemetery, which is located on a steep hill overlooking the village of Sugar Grove," adds the Werner account. Perhaps, in view of the mountains he once climbed, the steep hill is fitting tribute to the "Wheelbarrow Emigrant" from Pennsylvania, Gordon Brookmire.

★

1 8 5 0 s
Moby Dick on Four Feet
★

Between the wars—the Mexican and Civil Wars, that is—a young Virginia officer serving in the American Southwest was startled one day to encounter a great white Leviathan of the wild. Like Ahab, the Virginian was determined to hunt the beast in its own habitat, to flush out his quarry, then to pursue, pursue, pursue . . . to the bloody end.

An accomplished hunter for most of his young life, U.S. Army Lt. Dabney Herndon Maury was intrigued by reports about the ferocity of the once-domesticated cattle living in the Texas wilderness of the 1850s on their own.

When Mexico withdrew its garrisons from the future state of Texas, Maury explained in a post–Civil War memoir, "The Indians then poured in upon the large ranches, murdered the people and turned the stock loose. These had increased and multiplied till the whole of the region between the Rio Grande and the Nueces [River] swarmed with wild horses and cattle."

Stationed at Fort McIntosh near Laredo, Maury, a West Point graduate and future Confederate general, was anxious to test his hunting prowess against the "fierceness and activity of the wild cattle." Perhaps difficult for us to believe today, he wrote that the Southwest's wild cattle were considered as great a challenge to hunters as the more traditional wild animals of the region, including the American bison.

They were, he said, "as wild and savage as any other wild beasts in that region."

In between occasional Indian skirmishes, he set out one morning with a guide, Juan Galvan, and two enlisted troopers from Maury's own mounted rifles regiment to hunt meat for his men.

"Juan soon found the fresh trail of an enormous bull," Maury wrote in his *Recollections of a Virginian in the Mexican, Indian and Civil Wars* (see http://metalab.unc.edu/docsouth/maury/maury.html). "His tracks were easily followed, for amidst the thousands his were larger than any."

The small hunting party progressed uneventfully for a time, simply following the tracks, never seeing the quarry ahead. But then Juan suddenly "threw up his rifle and fired." Out of the brush ahead burst a gigantic bull. Harmlessly for the moment, the beast then galloped off "at a rapid gait."

As everyone in the hunting party immediately noticed, their wild bull was white in color, all white.

Now began a chase lasting two or three hours before the hunters caught up to their "monarch of the herds," as Maury described the monster bull. Their intended prey had taken refuge in a fresh stand of shrubbery. There, Maury and the guide dismounted, ran to within thirty or forty paces, and "fired into his great, white body." The bull again ran off, but he now left a trail marked by gouts of blood.

Soon closing in again—for the kill, they thought—Maury and company placed two more bullets in the bull . . . and even then had to chase him down to a third patch of bushes.

Like Moby Dick, though, their quarry was ready to turn on its tormentors.

"I resolved to make a sure shot and, running closer to him than ever before, delivered it," wrote Maury.

Savvy old Juan, in the meantime, had been "too smart" to climb down from his horse . . . and Maury hadn't really noticed.

With the crack of the Virginian's rifle, he heard the bushes "rattling." The troopers cried, "Look out, Lieutenant! He's charging you!"

Maury turned for his horse but then saw "the bull was too close for me to stop to mount."

He made a quick and painful decision. With the raging bull right on his heels, the young officer flung himself into a large growth of cactus—"struggling through it and tumbling flat on the ground upon the other side."

Maury admittedly was terrified of the bull, but his new circumstances were no panacea either. "I was so tormented by the great cactus spikes which had pierced my body," he later wrote, "that for an instant I would have welcomed the bull or anything else that would have relieved me of my misery."

Since he couldn't stay all day in such uncomfortable circumstance, Maury eventually dared to rise to his feet and look for the bull.

Bad mistake.

"For he instantly saw me and made another dash for me, the men crying as he did so, 'He's charging again!' I whirled through another cactus, the twin of the one I had just left, and lay as flat and still as a dead man; and I almost wished that I was dead, for in my flight I had acquired a second supply of cactus spikes, which left no part of my body unprovided for. They are of the size of a large darning needle, with barbed points, and when one is pulled out it leaves the barb in to mark the place."

Again, however, the cactus saved Maury from a possibly fatal goring by the enraged bull.

Cautiously coming to his feet, Maury saw that he was alone. With Maury's horse in flight, Juan had dashed off to retrieve it. The two troopers also had retreated to a safe distance. "My rifle was empty, and all my friends were gone, and, utterly demoralized, I stood wondering what had ever induced me to imagine that I wished to hunt a wild bull. One cheerful fact gave me courage: the bull was gone with the rest, but, alas! the cactus spikes remained."

Reloading his rifle and plucking out some of the painful barbs, Maury tried to maintain a cheerful attitude as Juan returned with the errant horse. Painfully Maury resumed his saddle as the hunting party pressed on . . . soon to find themselves out of the chaparral and into a grassy glen filled with wild cattle. "We drew up all abreast, and fired into the herd. I struck a great brindled bull, but permitted him to pass on, for just then bulls were a drug in my market."

Juan, however, went after the wounded animal and returned ten minutes later saying, "We got him."

Meanwhile, two shots had struck "a beautiful, young sorrel cow, breaking her foreleg."

Cow! you may say, what's so special about shooting a helpless cow?

This cow, though, would prove just as troublesome for the hunters as the now-missing white bull—in fact, even more so.

Juan in short order had lassoed the young bovine and tied her to the "big, swinging limb" of a mesquite. He assured a somewhat dubious Maury that the cow would remain secure there while the party went on with the hunt for the great white bull. But Maury told Juan to examine the rope more closely to be absolutely sure. Still on their horses, the young officer and his guide gingerly approached the cow. "[S]he charged madly at us twice, but being thrown violently back upon her haunches, she ceased this and remained sullenly quiet."

As Juan then dismounted to circle the tree and draw closer, the cow followed in a circuit of her own. Nearby one of the troopers, Moran by name, also had dismounted. He stood "leaning against his horse, holding Juan's rifle and his own in his hand." His companion soldier, "Old Dewey, a very phlegmatic Vermonter, was sitting lazily in his saddle, his rifle across his pommel." Maury, for his part, alert for another charge, remained in his own saddle.

That's when all hell broke loose. The cow suddenly lurched forward. The rope snapped. She was free of all restraint. And her blood was up.

In quick order, she gored Moran's horse, then went for Dewey's mount. Moran, dropping the rifles, "sprang" up the nearest tree. "She then struck Old Dewey's horse, lifting him so that his rider pitched over his head and, turning a somersault, landed upon his feet, rifle in hand."

Dewey, no slouch after all, got off a quick shot in the cow's face, then raced toward another tree, "which he lost no time in climbing."

As Maury noted, the field now belonged to the maddened cow— "for by the time Dewey was safely ensconced, I was a rifle shot away, where a three-legged cow could not catch me."

Perhaps needless to say, Juan also had demonstrated impressive tree-climbing ability, but, with the cow looking the other way, he now slid to the ground and remounted his horse. Riding up behind the cow, he killed her with one quick shot and thus "ended the battle." After butchering the cow and sending the meat back to camp with the two enlisted men, Maury then set out with Juan to find his white bull . . . but to no avail. "We bounced him out of a thicket a little before sunset, ran him a mile, and then gave up the chase and set out for camp ten miles away."

It was ten o'clock before they reached the camp—"and I was occupied until a late hour getting rid of the cactus."

The next day, his body pocked with measlelike wounds, Maury didn't feel up to the chase. Instead, Juan and a new party went back to the bull's last known location and found him still full of fight. "He charged them many times, and finally fell by the nineteenth ball. He was an enormous beast, entirely white save his jet black horns and hoofs."

It had been, for Maury, an exciting contest, and from it he came away with two helpful lessons for hunting wild cattle: "I discovered that day that when a bull charges, he puts his head down, shuts his eyes, and goes straight for his enemy, but when a cow makes the attack, she keeps her eyes wide open and can't be dodged."

★

1 8 5 2
River Still Left Unexplored

★

By 1850, the middle of the nineteenth century, the gods on high must have wondered, would *anyone* among those superenergetic, expansion-minded Americans ever get around to tracing the Red River to its source?

After all, as early as Thomas Jefferson's presidency (1801–9), efforts had been made to track the elusive river to its lair . . . and so far, no American had succeeded.

After all, too, thousands had been emigrating to the Northwest on the Oregon Trail ever since 1843; thousands more flooded into California in response to the gold rush of 1848 and 1849. By now, the Mormons were in Utah, Texas had become a state, the Mexican War was all over, the mountain men long since had held their last rendezvous.

In short, ever since Jefferson's Louisiana Purchase of 1803, Americans had flooded across their new land from east to west, and were even well along toward building a great city, San Francisco, on the western edge of the continent that would rival those on the eastern edge. Still, regardless of all that explosive energy, noted Carl Newton Tyson in his 1981 book *The Red River in Southwestern History,* "[M]uch of the region stretching from the Mississippi to the Rockies and from Texas to the Dakotas country lay unknown and unsettled, guarding its secrets from white men."

Despite the efforts of explorers such as Lewis and Clark, Zebulon Pike, and "Pathfinder" John C. Frémont, "much of what Jefferson had bought in 1803 remained unknown to whites."

A stunning "unknown" so late in the western discovery process was the meandering Red River, its source or sources still a mystery despite Jefferson's sponsorship of two attempts at exploring the Red . . . despite Pike's later failure to find the river's headwaters . . . despite Stephen Long's later effort, in which he confused the Canadian River for the Red.

Thus, as 1850 dawned, "The upper reaches of the Red River remained the domain of Indians," noted Tyson. "That situation could not be allowed to continue. The Red River, once an important international boundary [separating New Spain from the young United States before 1803] and, in 1850, the northern border of Texas, could not remain unknown to its owners."

Enter now one of the most active and yet unheralded U.S. explorer-soldiers of the nineteenth century—just the man for the job, it so happens. As Tyson observed: "The task of making it [the Red River] known fell to Captain Randolph Barnes Marcy of the U.S. Fifth Infantry."

Here was a man, a West Point graduate and experienced frontier soldier, who just recently (1849) had led two thousand potential settlers west from Fort Smith, Arkansas, to Sante Fe, New Mexico, "blazing a trail along the South Canadian as he went." A man who then explored terrain around the headwaters of the Trinity, Brazos, and Colorado Rivers in Texas; a man who thought it "remarkable" that the Red River, "one of the largest and most important rivers in the United States," still had not been tracked to its source. "In a word," Marcy later wrote, "the country embraced within the basin of Upper Red River had always been to us a 'terra incognita.'"

Seeking to remedy that omission, Marcy set out on May 14, 1852, along the Red River in Texas with fifty-five men of his Fifth Infantry's Company D, a doctor, Indian guides, hunting dogs, and a second in command destined not only to become Marcy's son-in-law but also a major figure in the Civil War. Only a brevet (temporary) captain in 1852, he would later be a Union general (and a Democratic presidential candidate) . . . George B. McClellan.

The party hadn't gone upriver very far before it came across buffalo tracks and, more exciting, an eight-foot (nose to tail) cougar. Treed by the dogs, the cougar was easy prey for Marcy . . . who soon would be meeting another big cat that almost made *him* the prey.

Rough terrain forced Marcy's party away from the riverbanks the next day, and heavy rains soon made things uncomfortable. Continuing regardless, the U.S. Army expedition drew within sight of the Wichita Mountains by May 22. Nearby they named a tributary of the Red River in honor of its frisky population—Otter Creek.

Pressing on beneath rainy skies, they saw buffalo for the first time on May 26. More to the point of their explorations, wrote Tyson, "Marcy noted that the country changed near the mountains, and the river was different there; whereas it previously had been wide and slow moving, it now was a narrow rushing torrent."

On May 27 Marcy's company encountered a buffalo-hunting party of Wichita Indians. Marcy explained he was on a peaceful mission to find the source of the river but warned the Wichitas that with Texas having become a state as of 1845, any Indians committing depredations in Texas would be subject to punishment.

Meanwhile, the leader of the Wichita band told Marcy that once they passed beyond the mountains, in about two days' time, they would find little to no freshwater available for miles ahead. "The chief represented the river from where it leaves the mountains as flowing over an elevated flat prairie country, totally destitute of water, wood, or grass, and the only substitute for fuel that could be had was buffalo 'chips,'" Marcy later told Congress in his official report, *Expedition of the Red River of Louisiana in the Year 1852.*

But Marcy was not to be discouraged. His job was to find the source of the big Red, and that's exactly what he intended to do. He was determined, he said in his report, "without subjecting the command to too great privations, [to] push forward as far as possible into this most inhospitable and dreaded salt desert."

Pushing forward at that, the party on May 29 reached and crossed what was thought to be the one-hundreth meridian . . . only it wasn't. Explained author Carl Tyson: "Unfortunately [their lunar] observations were later found to be in error, probably because of the imperfections in the instruments used to calculate them, and the incorrect survey complicated a border dispute between Oklahoma and Texas many years later."

Proceeding on but unaware of the mistake, the party on May 30 reached a fork widening the Red River to 650 yards, bank to bank, at the confluence of the two streams. Turning up this North Fork, the party two days later reached the mouth of a brackish, salt-laden "Salt Fork" (today's Elm Fork) to the North Fork. Nearby was a mountain that Marcy and company named Mount Webster in honor of the secretary of state, Daniel Webster.

Moving on, the party stuck to the North Fork for the next eighteen days before finally reaching the fork's headwaters on June 16—after engaging in a buffalo hunt and encountering signs of recent Kiowa and Comanche parties. With that much accomplished—but the overall mission as yet incomplete—Marcy led a small group twenty-five miles overland to the Canadian River as a brief diversion. On June 20 he and the main party turned back southward, still intent upon finding the Red River's primary source.

Six days later they came upon an underground "city" covering several hundred square acres and boasting a population, Marcy estimated, "greater than [that of] any city in the universe." The inhabitants were prairie dogs, thousands upon thousands of them.

Saying adieu to the prairie dogs and now "skirting the edge" of the Staked Plains, also known as the Llano Estacado, the Marcy expedition continued on south until it again struck the big Red itself on June 24, close to its emergence from the higher ground of the Staked Plains. Here the river was nine hundred yards wide and flowed "over a sandy bed," noted Tyson.

Just ahead, the explorers discovered a day later, the Llano Estacado/ Staked Plains loomed as an escarpment rising eight hundred feet above the prairie floor. The steep slope proved impassable to the party's wagons, so Marcy decided he, McClellan, and ten other men would set off on their own by foot.

But first there would be another hunting break . . . one that could have been Marcy's last.

He and McClellan had spotted a herd of antelope grazing among the mesquite. Hoping to lure one of them closer, Marcy took out a deer-bleating device and gave vent to a series of pitiful sounds. Sure enough, one of the antelopes did approach. Careful not to alarm his prey, Marcy slowly raised his rifle and took aim.

He would have fired, but he was distracted by a "rustling in the grass" to his left.

Turning quickly, he was shocked to see "a tremendous panther [a cougar] bounding at full speed directly toward me, and within the short distance of twenty steps."

But Marcy was able to swing his weapon around and fire just in time to halt the beast in midcharge. As he later said, he "sent a ball through his chest, which stretched him out upon the grass about ten yards from where I had taken my position."

Exultant and yet relieved at the same moment, Marcy shouted in triumph. His shouts brought McClellan hurrying to the spot.

When Marcy attempted to show off his latest trophy to the man who would be his son-in-law, however, they found the big cat still very much alive . . . in fact, up on its feet "and making off."

McClellan emptied his own rifle at the wounded animal, then—rashly, to be sure—clubbed the beast with the stock of his weapon, "to give him his quietus," as Marcy put it.

That ended the animal's life—and a dangerous incident from which Marcy was able to take away a valuable lesson for future hunts. As he later reported (employing just a bit of understatement), "It occurred to me afterwards that it would not always be consistent with one's safety to use the deer-bleat unless we were perfectly certain we should have our wits about us in the event of a panther or large bear (which is often the case) taking it into his head to give credence to the counterfeit."

In short, "The panther had probably heard the bleat, and was coming towards it with the pleasant anticipation of making his breakfast from a tender fawn; but, fortunately for me, I disappointed him."

Fortunately also, Marcy was able to continue his exploration for the source of the Red River, a hunt of a different nature that was to prove fruitless . . . fruitless in the sense that there would be no one source. What Marcy and company were about to establish was the fact that the Red River sprung from two major forks—the North Fork, already explored just days beforehand, and the South or Prairie Dog Town Fork, which stretched for an unknown distance ahead as Marcy, McClellan, and their few men made their way up the escarpment on foot.

What they now found undoubtedly was the most exciting and dramatic geographic feature of their entire trip—the Texas Panhandle's awesome Palo Duro Canyon, at sixty miles in length, up to six miles wide, and sometimes eight hundred feet in depth, a gouge in the surface of the earth that is second in size in North America only to the Grand Canyon. It was the Prairie Dog Town Fork that over the centuries had created the deep canyon and its towering walls . . . walls that from the riverbed sometimes seemed to close over the traveler like the roof of a tunnel.

Marcy and his companions of course were struck by the beauty of their discovery. "We all, with one accord, stopped and gazed with wonder and admiration upon the panorama that was for the first time exhibited to the eyes of civilized man," he wrote in his report. Some of the walls towering above looked like the battlements of feudal castles, he added. Others resembled "a colossal specimen of sculpture representing the human figure, with all the features of the face, which, standing upon its lofty pedestal, overlooks the valley, and seems to have been designed and executed by the Almighty artist as the presiding genius of these dismal solitudes."

"Dismal" indeed was the hot, dusty Llano itself, with freshwater so scarce that Marcy, for one, dreamed at night of "swallowing huge draughts of ice water."

Imagine, then, his delight at the discovery July 1, about a week after the panther incident, of first one then another freshwater spring. Not only did the springs provide precious, thirst-quenching water, they also signaled that his quest was over. With these and another "thousand little riverlets" right there, "in the foothills of the Rockies," summed up Tyson, Marcy finally had found the birthing place of the thirteen-hundred-mile-long Red River.

Thus, it fell to the explorer-soldier Randolph Marcy at midcentury to find the long-elusive "main sources of the main channel and the north fork of the Red River," added Tyson. Moreover, with no loss of life, he and his party had traversed a thousand miles of terrain (now encompassed by Texas and Oklahoma) that was entirely new to Americans. He had found and documented both the Tule and Palo Duro Canyons as the first white man to explore either one; he had added significantly to the documentation of the hardly known Wichita Indians; he had located important mineral deposits; and he had unearthed twenty-five new species of mammals and ten previously unknown species of reptiles.

1 8 5 2
Grant Reaches San Francisco

To reach northern California and its gold fields in the mid-nineteenth century, there was the overland route by foot, horse, or wagon . . . two thousand miles minimum. Or there was the sea voyage around Cape

Horn by ship . . . months at sea, with real risks of foundering in violent storms off the tip of South America. Or one could sail down the American East Coast to a landfall on the Gulf of Mexico and proceed overland from there . . . with mountains and desertland ahead, no easy trip, either.

Or, finally, a compromise sea voyage to Panama, overland travel across the narrow isthmus and then back to sea again for the final leg into an awaiting California port. A fast and easygoing trip by comparison with the other choices? Not necessarily. Certainly not when Mexican War veteran and West Point graduate Ulysses S. Grant tried it in 1852.

Given orders to relocate to northern California, Grant and the Fourth U.S. Infantry Regiment were told to sail on July 5 for Panama from New York aboard the commercial steamer *Ohio,* already loaded with civilian passengers. Counting the families of Grant's fellow soldiers, this meant squeezing more than seven hundred additional personnel aboard the old steamer. As the future Civil War hero and president wrote in his memoirs, "The addition of over seven hundred . . . crowded the steamer most uncomfortably, especially for the tropics in July."

No doubt, and in the days ahead, conditions did not improve to any great degree. In eight days, the steamer arrived at Aspinwall on the east coast of Panama (today's Colón, Panama). It was a relief to leave the overcrowded steamer, but it happened to be the "height of the wet season" in Panama. Thus, "The streets of the town were eight to ten inches under water, and foot passengers passed from place to place on raised foot-walks."

With monsoonlike rains pouring down one minute and a "blazing, tropical summer's sun" bursting forth the next, Grant observed, "I wondered how any person could live many months in Aspinwall, and wondered still more why any one tried."

Still ahead, of course, was the crossing to the Pacific side of Panama. With the rail line of the day complete only as far as the Chagres River, Grant noted, everybody planning to reach the city of Panama on the Gulf of Panama had to embark upon primitive boats poled against the river current at the rate of a mile or a mile and a half an hour, with Gorgona as their destination. "Those who traveled over the Isthmus in those days will remember that boats on the Chagres River were propelled by natives not inconveniently burdened with clothing," Grant wrote years later. "These boats carried thirty to forty passengers each. The crews consisted of six men to a boat, armed with long poles. There were planks wide enough for a man to walk on conveniently, running along the sides of each boat from end to end. The men would start from the bow, place one end of their poles against the river bottom, brace their shoulders against the other end, and then walk to the stern as rapidly as they could."

Not all was easygoing when they reached Gorgona, either, for now came a twenty-five-mile journey by mule. Trouble was, on this Panama crossing anyway, there weren't enough mules to accommodate all the passengers and military personnel who had stepped ashore from the overcrowded *Ohio* at Aspinwall. "Some of the passengers paid as high as forty dollars for the use of a mule to ride twenty-five miles, when the mule would not have sold for ten dollars in that market at other times," noted Grant.

To make matters worse (and, for Grant and his companions, it was an ominous delay as well), the government contractor—"an impecunious American" who was engaged to transport the regimental baggage—failed to produce a single mule for the task. Grant, as regimental quartermaster, was left at a town called Cruces with the baggage and those soldiers who were accompanied by their dependents.

After a short time and a lot of empty promises, Grant realized the contractor "could not procure the animals at all at the price he had promised to furnish them for."

Far worse for Grant's entourage, however, cholera had broken out, "and men were dying every hour."

Here was a real crisis—and for Grant a test of courage far different from anything on the battlefield. But he apparently never hesitated in answering his duty to his men. "To diminish the food for the disease," he sent his healthy men—and the regimental doctors—ahead to Panama, while, in his own words, "I was left alone with the sick and the soldiers who had families."

He was at Cruces for about a week, and then, still untouched by the disease himself, he set out for Panama. Either at Cruces or on the way to the Pacific side of the Isthmus, he related almost laconically, "about one-third of the people with me died." In fact, after spending a total of six weeks on the narrow neck of land called Panama, he recalled that about a hundred, or "one-seventh of those who left New York harbor with the 4th Infantry on July 5," were left buried in Panamanian soil.

The cholera outbreak, of course, had contributed not only to the deaths but also to delays in leaving the pestilent spot. Even when men of Grant's regiment reached the port city of Panama, they couldn't leave "until the cholera abated." The dread disease also had made its way to that city, where it struck down some of the men who had gone ahead of Grant's company. Fortunately, the regiment's still-healthy personnel could find some sanctuary from Panama's primitive conditions aboard a waiting steamer that eventually would carry them north to San Francisco, while the sick could go to a nearby "hospital" established "on an old hulk anchored a mile off." There also were hospital tents on Flamingo Island in the bay.

Back at Cruces, Grant finally had taken the bull by the horns and hired a local man to provide transportation for the stalled baggage train "at more than double the original price." That propelled him at least as far as the city of Panama, but then came the long wait until the cholera outbreak seemed to have died down.

Added Grant: "The disease did not break out again on the way to California, and we reached San Francisco early in September."

Additional note: Arriving in San Francisco in 1852, three years into the California gold rush, Grant found the bustling, still a'building northern California city to be a "lively place." Here's the way it looked to him:

> Gold, or placer digging as it was called, was at its height. Steamers plied daily between San Francisco and both Stockton and Sacramento. Passengers and gold from the southern mines came by the Stockton boat; from the northern mines by Sacramento. In the evening when these boats arrived, Long Wharf—there was but one wharf in San Francisco in 1852—was alive with people crowding to meet the miners as they came down to sell their "dust" and to "have a time." Of these, some were runners for hotels, boarding houses or restaurants; others belonged to a class of impecunious adventurers, of good manners and good presence, who were ever on the alert to make the acquaintance of people with some ready means, in the hope of being asked to take a meal at a restaurant. Many were young men of good family, good education and gentlemanly instincts. Their parents had been able to support them during their minority, and to give them good educations, but not to maintain them afterwards. From 1849 to 1853 there was a rush of people to the Pacific coast, of the class

described. All thought that fortunes were to be picked up, without effort, in the gold fields on the Pacific. Some realized more than their most sanguine expectations; but for one such there were hundreds disappointed, many of whom now fill unknown graves; others died wrecks of their former selves, and many, without a vicious instinct, became criminals and outcasts.

Grant also noted, "those early days in California brought out character." He noted the fact that just getting there was difficult and expensive. "The fortunate," he wrote, "could go by Cape Horn or by the Isthmus of Panama; but the mass of pioneers crossed the plains with their ox-teams. This took an entire summer. They were very lucky when they got through with a yoke of worn-out cattle." And then, arriving as strangers in a strange land, they had to find a means of subsistence.

Meanwhile, after months spent on the Columbia River to the north, Grant returned to San Francisco in 1853. In just a year, the city had changed.

This gave me a good opportunity of comparing the San Francisco of 1852 with that of 1853. As before stated, there had been but one wharf in front of the city in 1852—Long Wharf. In 1853 the town had grown out into the bay beyond what was the end of this wharf when I first saw it. Streets and houses had been built out on piles where the year before the largest vessels visiting the port lay at anchor or tied to the wharf. There was no filling under the streets or houses. San Francisco presented the same general appearance as the year before; that is, eating, drinking and gambling houses were conspicuous for their number and publicity. They were on the first floor, with doors wide open. At all hours of the day and night walking in the streets, the eye was regaled, on every block near the water front, by the sight of players at faro. Often broken places were found in the street, large enough to let a man down into the water below. I have but little doubt that many of the people who went to the Pacific coast in the early days of the gold excitement, and have never been heard from since or were heard from for a time and then ceased to write, found watery graves beneath the houses or streets built over San Francisco Bay.

But more change was on the way, he observed.

As the city grew, the sand hills back of the town furnished material for filling up the bay beneath the houses and streets, and still further out. The temporary houses, first built over the water in the harbor, soon gave way to more solid structures. The main business part of the city now is on solid ground, made where vessels of the largest class lay at anchor in the early days. Gambling houses had disappeared from public view. The city had become staid and orderly.

★

1854
Hole in His Head

★

In Santa Cruz County, California, just west of State Highway 17, rises and falls Mountain Charlie Road, an undulating pathway named for the colorful Irishman who once owned and operated sections of the same mountainous route as a toll road.

Born in Ireland in 1825, Charles Henry "Mountain Charlie" McKiernan arrived among the virginal Santa Cruz Mountains after a military sojourn in Australia and a brief fling under the spell of California gold fever. Tired of the mining game, Charlie pulled up stakes after a year and made his way into the coastal mountains in 1851, possibly as only the second Anglo settler to establish a lasting homestead in the area. "He hunted, tried raising beef and even did some gold mining [but] without luck," noted Richard Beal in his book *Highway 17: The Road to Santa Cruz.*

In those days, the Santa Cruz Mountains were bordered by giant redwoods and teemed with deer, wildcats, mountain lions, coyotes—and grizzlies, lots of grizzly bears. "Grizzly bears were numerous, prowling about in herds, like hogs on a farm," wrote a Spanish missionary many years earlier. To this, Lyman Burrell, a settler of the 1850s, added, "It seemed like a vast, solitary wilderness—no houses, no roads. I knew that bears and [mountain] lions dwelt there, but I feared them not."

Burrell's recollection and more local lore can be found in Stephen Michael Payne's book *A Howling Wilderness.* The same book reports that Mountain Charlie McKiernan was known far and wide for his prowess as a hunter who killed "hundreds" of bears in the area.

Twice, though, they almost killed him.

In one incident related by Payne, Mountain Charlie spotted a sleeping bear, rode up close on his mule, dismounted, and fired a shot into the back of the animal's head. "Assuming that the bear was dead, he was slowly reloading his weapon when the bear rose up and charged him."

As he tried to remount, his mule "threw him" and galloped off in terror. But the bear had cubs nearby and, for the moment, returned to their side. As Charlie then started looking for his musket, his movements stirred up the angry bear anew . . . and with pure mayhem in her eyes, she charged. "He took to his heels, and never man ran as he did until he reached home. The bear got pretty close to him at times, and would doubtless have caught him had she not been mortally wounded."

The next day Charlie found her dead and took her two orphaned cubs back home in hopes of raising them, "but four months later the cubs killed some hogs and he was forced to destroy them."

Until 1853 Charlie apparently had been living alone, but his life was about to take a dramatic turn—one that would lead him into the ministering arms of his future wife.

First, though, he fell into the cruel embrace of a second murderous she-bear—said to be a grizzly at that.

Charlie and neighboring pioneer John Taylor were surprised by the huge animal while hunting one day in 1854. It again was a mother with two cubs, fearful, protective—and of course enraged at their trespass.

By Payne's account, Taylor got off a quick shot that missed then ran for the nearest big tree. Charlie, too, managed to fire, a shot that struck the bear above an eye and stunned her . . . momentarily.

Seeing that more punishment was needed to stop the creature and unable to reload quickly enough to fire again, Charlie resorted to hitting the bear on the head with his rifle, beating the animal so hard the weapon at last shattered in his hands.

Undeterred by the blows and no longer dazed, the she-bear lunged at Charlie with a bite that took a wedge three by five inches out of his skull above his left eye. Throwing up his arms as protection for his head was no great help to Charlie, since the bear simply bit through his arms, her fangs completely passing through one of them . . . but without hitting bone.

By now, Taylor's dog was attacking the mother bear's cubs, so she "dropped" Charlie and lumbered off to their aid. "Taylor, thinking that McKiernan was dead, left for McKiernan's home to get a horse to pack his friend's body home," wrote Payne

While he was gone, the outraged she-bear returned and dragged the hapless Charlie into a nearby clearing, "pawed over him" for a while then left.

By the time Taylor returned, Charlie was sitting up. He had been fully conscious the whole time, he told Taylor. He was paralyzed from the waist down, perhaps due to shock and only temporarily so in any case. Far worse, the front of his head had been crushed and a significant piece of his skull was gone altogether.

Working as fast as he could, Taylor took Charlie back to his house, then rushed into fairly distant San Jose to find a doctor. It would be sunrise the next morning before he and Dr. A.W. Bell could return, and then there would be even more delay. Dr. Bell had to send for an associate, Dr. T. J. Ingersoll, who didn't arrive until nine o'clock that night. Still, he came prepared—almost.

His preparation was a "silver plate hammered out of two Mexican pesos."

But it wasn't big enough to cover the hole in Charlie's head. It took another full day for Ingersoll to go back to San Jose, obtain a larger plate and return to Charlie's side. He was back by eight o'clock the evening of the third day since Charlie's mishap and then the two doctors operated until eleven o'clock to clean and cover Charlie's wound—"without benefit of anaesthetics."

As time went on, two more surgeries were needed before Charlie recovered completely. The first came a week after the initial operation—the silver plate had been irritating the wound and had to be removed. A year later, the wound became infected. Ingersoll and a third physician cleaned out an abscess caused by a "wad" of hair still in the wound. "During this surgery," wrote Payne in his *Howling Wilderness* book, "chloroform was used to put McKiernan to sleep. This was the first reported local instance of the use of the new anaesthetic."

Also important, Charlie was being nursed back to good health by Barbara Berricke Kelly, the young lady destined to become his wife—and, soon enough, mother of his seven children.

Of course, her husband's face now was disfigured for life, but Charlie always covered the scars when out in public with a large-brimmed hat "pulled down to his eyebrows," Payne reported.

A historical plaque standing alongside today's Mountain Charlie Road near the Summit Road Overpass explains the hardy Irishman's connection with the hilly route. In 1858, it notes, Charlie and Hiram

Scott were given a six-thousand-dollar contract by the Santa Cruz Turnpike Company to build a toll road up the mountain from nearby Scotts Valley—later the McKiernan Toll Road.

Twenty years later, Santa Cruz County paid Charlie another six hundred dollars to take over the road as part of the county road system.

Meanwhile, Charlie had opened a successful stagecoach business making good use of "his" road. Explained Richard Beal: "McKiernan's cabin near the summit was often a stopping spot and became known as Halfway House or Station Ranch. Barbara cooked meals for the stagecoach passengers while Charlie helped change horses on the wagons."

But then came the railroads, a blow to the toll road business. In the 1880s Charlie and Barbara moved to San Jose, where Charlie died in 1892. So passed one more of the often unknown men and women who contributed to the history of the West, this one still memorialized by his own toll road. As noted by Beal, some of the road still remains in place. What's left of Mountain Charlie Road, he wrote, "is a 5.2 mile section of a beautiful narrow road that goes from the Summit to Glenwood Highway, and a 2-mile section that goes north from the Summit to the old Santa Cruz Highway."

1 8 5 6

Let Them Foot It

One of the greatest disasters—and possibly the greatest rescue effort—ever to be recorded during the years of westward migration had nothing to do with Indian attacks, broken-down wagons, starving oxen, the Donner Party, or lost guides. No, the combined disaster and rescue instead had everything to do with hundreds of people pushing or pulling handcarts over a fourteen-hundred-mile course between Iowa City, Iowa, and Salt Lake City, Utah.

Pushing and pulling, unfortunately, a bit late in the season.

The year was 1856, and the Mormon leader Brigham Young had put out a great call. Let the poor among our new converts in Europe come to our new, western Zion cheaply . . . by ship across the Atlantic

Ocean, by train to Iowa City, Iowa, and then . . . then pile the belongings in handcarts and finish the pilgrimage to a new land *on foot.*

For historian LeRoy R. Hafen's Swiss-born mother, the low-cost scheme of several years' standing worked out fine. "There were six to our cart," she once recalled. "Father and mother pulled it; Rosie (two years old) and Christian (six months old) rode; John (nine) and I (six) walked. Sometimes, when it was down hill, they let me ride too."

Her family's memorable tramp westward was a happy result of Brigham Young's plan to help new Mormon converts from Europe, chiefly from England, make their way to the still relatively new Mormon home in Utah's Great Basin, with Salt Lake City the focal point. According to Hafen, writing in a 1956 issue of the *Utah Historical Quarterly,* many of the converts "were from the underprivileged classes, whose means were insufficient to pay for an overseas voyage and a long journey to the far interior of a distant land."

But their new church stood ready to help out.

Brigham Young's first response to the problem had been a helping financial hand called the Perpetual Emigration Fund, established in 1849. By the mid-1850s, however, it was clear the fund simply was "unequal to the calls for help," Hafen noted. That was when Young turned to an old idea of a mass emigration by handcart. "Make handcarts," he proposed, "and let the emigrant foot it."

It made sense, he argued. Give the handcart emigrants the necessary supplies, along with a cow or two for every ten persons, and, "They can come just as quick, if not quicker, and much cheaper."

Brigham Young's proposal caught fire immediately. A Mormon publication in Liverpool, England, greeted his idea with an enthusiastic editorial saying, "The system of ox-teams is too slow and expensive and must give way to the telegraph line of handcarts and wheel barrows." Hafen noted that official church approval of the scheme came in the fall of 1855. "[L]et them come on foot, with hand-carts or wheel-barrows," said the Mormon General Epistle of October 26; "Let them gird up their loins and walk through, and nothing shall hinder or stay them."

And at first, as the plan went into action the very next spring and summer, nothing did hinder or stay the handcart emigrants.

"Plans developed rapidly," Hafen observed. "Sailing vessels were chartered; Church agents were sent to the frontier to procure handcarts and supplies for the on-coming emigrants." There would be nineteen hundred of them that first spring. They would sail from Liverpool, "intending to cross the plains and mountains to Utah with handcarts." They first would land at Boston or New York, then travel by train to Iowa City, the railhead on the eastern edge of Iowa.

"The Saints who were to comprise the first three handcart companies sailed in good time, arrived at the outfitting place [Iowa City] in due course, and were able to set out on their overland trek in June," Hafen wrote. They sang as they traipsed across Iowa. They sang a cheery chorus to their *Handcart Song:*

> Some must push and some must pull
> As we go marching up the hill
> As merrily on the way we go
> Until we reach the Valley, oh!

The three-hundred-mile stretch across Iowa, with its occasional towns and settler farms, was not absolutely terrible, despite the summer heat and the dusty roads. Even so, a relative few gave up the handcart effort before reaching Florence on the Missouri River, the jumping-off place for a much rougher trek of a thousand miles across desert and mountains. The first two companies reached Florence on July 17, with the third company less than two weeks behind them. All three caravans set out on the lengthy final leg of their journey as soon as they could catch a breath in Florence.

It was September 26, a red-letter day indeed, when the emigrants making up the first two companies trudged into Salt Lake City, weary but safe and sound. They were greeted by "Church officials, a brass band, lancers on horseback and most of the inhabitants," wrote Hafen.

And what an omen the grand arrival of the first two handcart companies seemed to signal—"the first hoisting of the floodgates of deliverance to the oppressed millions," said Wilford Woodruff, a Mormon leader who witnessed the event. "We can now say to the poor and honest in heart, come home to Zion, for the way is prepared."

To one and all, meanwhile, the subsequent appearance of Company Three on October 2 seemed but added confirmation of the handcart scheme's great potential. For here, wonder of wonders, were delivered another three hundred or more souls to the promised land, these all from Wales.

But far back on the long pathway to Zion in Utah, disaster was in the making.

Two more companies, a thousand strong, were on their way. After inordinate delays, they had left England on ships departing from Liverpool May 3 and May 25, dates that would haunt the Mormons for years to come. Even more delays stacked up at Iowa City and at Florence . . . and looming over all, unbeknownst thus far, were the opening rounds of an early winter season.

"It was June 26 [1856] when the first group reached Iowa City; and the second came in twelve days later," Hafen noted. "Upon arrival, they found that the handcarts were not yet ready." As a result, "Captain Willie's" Company Four and its five hundred pusher-pullers were delayed in leaving Iowa City until July 15—"being detained nineteen days." Just as bad, worse even, "The Fifth Company (Captain Martin's), with 576 members, departed on the twenty-eighth, after a wait of twenty days—precious time that could have seen them far along their perilous journey."

After both groups made the relatively easy Iowa crossing and reached Florence, yet more delay ensued as repairs were made to the handcarts. "Now the question was raised whether the emigrants could safely continue their journey so late in the season."

After lively debate on the issue, Captain Willie's company, hoping for "special divine favor," headed out for the mountains on August 17, with Captain Martin's company following suit an entire ten days later . . . almost at the very end of August.

Arriving in Florence just in time to assist the Martin group's departure, emigration director Franklin D. Richards and fellow veterans of the pathway west realized the last two handcart companies were liable to run into wintry weather before they could reach Salt Lake City. All too obviously, with a thousand miles lying ahead, they could be in mortal danger.

Realizing this, Richards and his companions took to light, speedy wagons hauled by first-class teams and rushed on to Salt Lake City ahead of the struggling handcarts to warn of a possible calamity in the offing. Interrupted on the eve of a Mormon General Conference, Brigham Young and his fellow Mormons were stunned at the news but responded immediately. Young halted the conference activities "to recruit and organize relief parties, to assemble and forward food and clothing." He of course was shocked to learn a thousand or more emigrants had been allowed to set out for Salt Lake so late in the season, and on foot at that. The rescue teams set off to the east as soon as supplies and volunteers could be rounded up.

"In the meantime," observed Hafen, "the two belated handcart companies made their way up the valley of the Platte River. As they reached the higher altitudes beyond Fort Laramie [Wyoming], their supplies ran low and individuals began to weaken and die."

As feared, the early winter's blizzards then descended—"Struggling caravans were brought to a complete standstill in the midst of white desolation." Now caught east of South Pass and three hundred or more miles from any settlement at any point of the compass, many would die.

To be sure, help was on its way . . . but it was also slowed and even stalled at times by the heavy snows. Still, help it was, perhaps even, as Hafen wrote, "the most heroic mass rescue the frontier ever witnessed."

Unfortunately, the death toll among the two companies would combine, in Hafen's words, as "the most appalling migration tragedy in the history of the West."

Even though the arrival of rescuers with food and clothing did save a majority of the foot travelers, Captain Willie's company arrived at Salt Lake in rescue wagons on November 9 with 67 emigrants lost; Captain Martin's company appeared at the city gates on November 30, nearly three weeks later, with 135 souls lost.

Such an outcome was a terrible blow to the Mormon community . . . but it did not stop the handcart emigration project. With church president Brigham Young warning against any more late starts, the Mormons organized a reverse trek by foot and handcart in the spring of 1857—from Salt Lake to Florence—as a demonstration that it could safely be done. The seventy missionaries who hiked the thousand miles to the Missouri River with handcarts achieved their feat in forty-eight days, with seven and a half days of rest interspersed.

That summer the handcart emigration resumed, with 480 persons successfully completing the trip—and no major problems. As other events, such as the Colorado gold rush, intervened over the next couple of years, the handcart "traffic" continued to decline, with the final handcart companies making the long journey in the summer of 1860. "In the last two companies—350 persons with 65 carts—there were fewer deaths than on any previous journey," wrote Hafen.

Hafen's mother, then only six years old, was one of those 350.

Overall, Hafen also noted, 10 handcart companies consisting of nearly 3,000 persons employing 662 carts made the incredible journey between 1856 and 1860. Despite its one spectacular failure of 1856, he argued, the handcart scheme—with proper and adequate planning—

was "an economical, effective, and rather beneficent institution." Further, "It enabled hundreds, who otherwise could never have come to America, to emigrate and become productive United States citizens."

Those nearly three thousand new Americans, by the way, had produced an estimated half million progeny by the time Hafen wrote in the 1950s, a century after the handcart migration. By the 150th anniversary of the first handcart trek to Salt Lake, in the year 2006, those half million by the most conservative estimate will have doubled . . . to one million, all descended from what Hafen called "the womb of the handcart."

☆ ☆ ☆

Additional note: One of the most famous women of the West was among the handcart trekkers caught by a killer blizzard. Twenty-one-year-old Emma Batchelor, a Mormon convert from England, later said the ground was too frozen to bang in the tent pegs—or to bury the dead. As a happier highlight of her fourteen-hundred-mile journey west, she helped another woman deliver a baby, then hauled the new mother in a handcart for two days.

Arriving safely at Salt Lake City, Emma soon met and married the notorious Mormon John Doyle Lee as his seventeenth wife, apparently unaware that he was accused of being a leader in the massacre of 140 California-bound emigrants at Mountain Meadows, Utah, just months before. After Lee was excommunicated from the church, he established a ferry crossing on the Colorado River near the Utah-Arizona border, calling the new home Lonely Dell.

And lonely it was, except for the occasional ferry customers, among them the explorer John Wesley Powell, generally considered the first white man to pass through the Grand Canyon on the Colorado River. Often left alone in their six-room log home by her frequently traveling husband, Emma Lee delivered their sixth child there with only their twelve-year-old son Billy able to help out with severing the umbilical cord. Lee not long after that was arrested for his alleged role in the massacre, convicted, and executed by firing squad.

Two years later, in 1879, Emma married Franklin French, a Civil War veteran and prospector who had helped her move from Lonely Dell after she sold the ferry business to the Mormon Church, reported Leo W. Banks in *Stalwart Women.* "French and Emma settled at

Brigham City . . . but harassment forced them to leave," Banks commented. "Their next home, in the White Mountains, was burned in an 1882 Apache uprising. Eventually, she opened a restaurant at Hardy Station, the terminus of the Atlantic and Pacific Railroad, then under construction."

Now she became "Doctor" French, Banks explained. Emma was an "unofficial physician" to railroad workers, cowboys, and many others living in isolated venues across the northern Arizona terrain. "Many times the railroad company sent a single car to pick her up, take her to a sick worker living in a remote line shack, and bring her home the same day."

Moving to Winslow, Arizona, with Frank, Emma continued her "doctor's" work and midwifery as "Grandma French." She delivered so many babies in a birthing room in their home that it came known as the "baby farm."

Sadly, Emma lost the daughter she had delivered virtually by herself at Lonely Dell fourteen years before. Named after Queen Victoria, the teenager committed suicide . . . possibly in reaction to lifelong taunting for being the daughter of such a notorious father. In another family tragedy, a son was murdered by a rival for his wife's affections.

Emma's own end was soon to come—she died a natural death in November 1897 and was buried with nearly every resident of Winslow following her casket to its final resting place in the city cemetery. She had been, said the local *Winslow Mail*, "filled to overflowing with the milk of human kindness . . . [and] always ready to respond to the call of the afflicted, whether rich or poor."

1 8 5 6
Mailman of the Mountains

Trapper James Sisson couldn't have been in a more perilous situation shortly before Christmas of 1856. His feet already burned by frostbite, he had been holed up for twelve days in an empty cabin in the snow-covered Sierra Nevada, stuck there with no food or firewood. And this in an isolated mountain range where the snow depth builds rapidly—ten feet, twenty feet, thirty feet, and drifts even higher!

But along came an apparition, an unexpected angel of mercy, on homemade ten-foot skis—the legendary wintertime mailman of the Sierra, Norwegian-born John A. "Snowshoe" Thompson, original name Jon Torsteinson-Rue.

Snowshoe quickly chopped some wood for the stranded Sisson then skied to Genoa, Nevada, on the east side of the Sierra to fetch help. There, reports Jill Beede in an article on Thompson for *Tahoe Country.com,* the Norwegian had to fashion skis and "give lessons" to those volunteering to return with him to the remote cabin to bring out the stranded trapper.

Even then, there still would be more to the rescue effort . . . and again Snowshoe would be the key figure. With the rescuing party and Sisson safely back in Genoa, "the doctor reported that Sisson's feet needed to be amputated, but he had no chloroform." Now the trapper's chief rescuer turned westward—his regular mail run, really—to Placerville, California, on the far side of the mighty Sierra range. But there was no chloroform available there, either. On he went then to Sacramento for a supply of the anaesthetic . . . and returned to Genoa. "In all," wrote Beede, "he traveled 400 miles in 10 days and saved Sisson's life."

Certainly the Sisson rescue was a highlight, a peak, among Snowshoe Thompson's many exploits, but it wasn't a bit out of character for this Norwegian immigrant bestriding the snow-clogged mountain range like some sort of Colossus on skis. "When I cross-country ski under the moonlight through the back country of the Sierra Nevada mountains," Beede reflected, "I often think of Snowshoe Thompson, one of the most intriguing heroes in California's history. From 1856 to 1876 he made legendary ninety-mile treks over snowdrifts up to fifty feet high and through blizzards with up to eighty-mile-per-hour winds, to deliver mail to those living in isolation. He was the sole link between California and the Atlantic states during the long winter months."

Imagine! For two decades, or "two to four times a month for twenty winters," as Beede puts it, "regardless of weather, Snowshoe Thompson set out at the appointed hour."

For the next three days, when headed east, he skied the mountain slopes from Placerville on the California side of the High Sierra to Mormon Station, Utah (which became Genoa, Nevada, when Nevada achieved statehood), on the east side. Going back to Placerville only took two days. Either way, Beede noted: "The people of the pioneer settlement knew when to expect his arrivals. Baking was left in the oven and abandoned meals grew cold. Everyone ran outdoors looking to the top of Genoa Peak to watch as the tall blond Norseman descended, streaks of snow flying in his wake."

And what a pretty picture he made, too. "He flew down the mountainside," wrote Dan de Quille of the *Virginia City (Nev.) Territorial Enterprise* back then. "He did not ride astride his pole or drag it to one side as was the practice of other snow-shoers, but held it horizontally before him in the manner of a tightrope walker. His appearance was graceful, swaying his balance pole to one side and the other in the manner that a soaring eagle dips its wings."

The Sierra pioneer who soared like an eagle once upon a time had learned to slide through the snows of Norway's Telemark region as a child mounted on "ski-shaped snow-shoes (called ski-skates)," reported Beede. When he was ten, his father having died, Thompson and remaining family members emigrated to a farm in Illinois. They then moved on twice more—to Missouri and next to Iowa. Nearing manhood, Jon moved in with a brother settling in Wisconsin. "Then gold fever struck."

Determined to reach the gold fields, Jon at age twenty-four "drove a herd of cattle to California." He settled in Placerville, smack dab in the area of action, and soon was mining gold in Kelsey Diggings, Coon Hollow, and Georgetown. He earned enough to buy a small ranch in Putah Creek in the Sacramento Valley but still had to chop firewood to make ends meet. One day late in 1855 he saw a headline in the *Sacramento Union:* PEOPLE LOST TO THE WORLD; UNCLE SAM NEEDS CARRIER."

Now there, he realized, was both a job . . . and a need. Once the snow came, usually October to April, Genoa and environs would be cut off from the outside world. And Jon well knew what it was like to miss out on the mail, Beede observed, since he once had received "long-delayed news of a flu epedemic which claimed his mother's life."

Of course he immediately volunteered, offering to try the wintry mountain range on his home-fashioned skilike "snowshoes" of green oak, ten feet in length and weighing a startling twenty-five pounds. Even for the rangy six-footer from Norway, however, the mountain crossing would be a dangerous challenge. As everyone in town knew, no local postman in woven Canadian or Native American snowshoes had been able to cope with the massive snow cover hiding the Sierra's steep mountain slopes. "A crowd formed in Placerville for his first mail run in January, 1856," Beede reported. "Few had faith that he would make it over the 7,500-foot passes. . . . But one optimistic voice in the crowd called out: 'Good luck, Snowshoe Thompson,' and he set out to become a legendary postman and father of California skiing."

After successfully completing his first mail run, he soon settled into a routine. "Thompson always wore a Mackinaw jacket, a wide-rimmed hat, and covered his face in charcoal to prevent snow blindness," Beede discovered. "He carried no blankets, but he did carry matches to start fires, and his Bible. He snacked on dried sausage, jerked beef, crackers and biscuits." He took very short rest breaks.

In case of a snowstorm—a blizzard more likely—he would seek shelter then wait long enough for a crust to form on the new-fallen snow before setting off again. As for other risks, he refused to carry a weighty weapon, preferring simply to whiz by possibly dangerous animals before they could react. "On one trip he came upon a pack of wolves feeding on a deer carcass. When they noticed him, they sat on their haunches and howled. Snowshoe kept his pace, expecting them to attack at any moment, and flew right by them. When he looked back, they had returned to their meal."

The Norwegian apparently had no fear of becoming lost in the silent, often dark wilderness, its dangerous rocks and dips obliterated from sight by the snow. Noting near the end of his career that he had found "dozens of men" who indeed were lost, he said it never happened to him. As in the case of the trapper Sisson, the Norwegian often came to the rescue of men less able to cope with the conditions of the wintertime Sierra. Whenever he came across these snowbound wanderers, writes Beede also, he simply "would carry them out on the back of his skis as they held their arms around him."

A contemporary who came to know Snowshoe quite well was the postmaster of Genoa, S. A. Kinsey—"Most remarkable man I ever knew, that Snowshoe Thompson," Kinsey once said. "He must be made of iron. Besides, he never thinks of himself, but he'd give his last breath for anyone else—even a total stranger."

After a storm in the winter of 1867–68 stranded visitors to Meadow Lake City, Snowshoe carried in their mail for a time, too. One recipient of those mail deliveries wrote that the amazing postman would sail downhill "at great speed, cross the ice-frozen river, throw our mail toward the house, and glide out of sight, up and over a hill, by the momentum gathered in the three-mile descent."

On his regular Placerville-Genoa mail run, the intrepid Norwegian often carried up to one hundred pounds of mail or various necessities for his snowbound clientele. "Once he brought in a pack of needles and a glass chimney for a kerosene lamp so a widow, Mrs. Franklin, could continue her winter sewing," Beede also ascertained. He carried type and newsprint, bit by bit, for the *Territorial Enterprise,* which went into business the winter of 1858 as Nevada's first newspaper.

On one return trip he carried a newly discovered bluish rock to Sacramento to have it assayed. It contained rich silver ore—welcome to the Comstock Lode!

After this, thousands of fortune seekers switched their attention from California's gold fields to Nevada's silver lode. As a result, noted Mark McLaughlin in his book *Sierra Stories:* "Thompson expanded to horse drawn passenger sleighs over the upper elevations of the Sierra. Over the years Thompson continued to provide newspapers, mail and essential medicines for the snowbound residents of the Eastern Sierra mining camps."

Meanwhile, Thompson married Agnes Singleton, an English-woman, in 1866. He raised grains, hay, and potatoes and tended cattle of his own and for others on his ranch. He served on Alpine County's board of supervisors and served as a delegate to California's Republican State Convention in 1871. He was still delivering wintertime mail across the Sierra up until 1876, the year he died of complications from appendicitis at age forty-nine—without ever being fully paid for his services as a mail carrier.

The couple's only child, a son named Arthur, died two years later of diphtheria and was buried next to his father in Genoa. Agnes remarried in 1884 but a year later placed a marble headstone at Snowshoe's grave saying "Gone but not forgotten" and embossed with a pair of crossed skis.

Additional notes: A highlight (of sorts) in Snowshoe Thompson's life came when he set out to appear before Congress in Washington with a plea for six thousand dollars in back pay as the High Sierra's wintertime mail carrier. Armed with a petition signed by all kinds of Nevada state officials, he boarded an eastbound train in Reno, Nevada, on January 17, 1864.

But that was only the beginning to an odyssey that would prove incredible even by the Sierra mailman's standards. Three days after its start, Snowshoe's train was held up thirty-five miles west of Laramie, Wyoming, by a blizzard.

He and a fellow passenger, Rufus Turner, walked the rest of the distance into Laramie, where they found another eastbound train and continued their journey . . . but only seemingly so, it turned out. When the second train also was stalled by heavy snow, Snowshoe took to his feet once more. "The storm had grown worse, temperatures ranged from fifteen to thirty degrees below zero," wrote McLaughlin. The Norwegian's traveling companion returned to the stalled train, but Snowshoe pressed on, alone. "In two days he walked another 56 miles to Cheyenne, Wyoming, where he boarded a waiting eastbound train."

This one managed to carry Thompson all the way to the nation's capital—as "the first man to arrive from the Pacific Coast in two weeks."

Despite all his effort, despite a flurry of press attention as the "first man to beat the 'iron horse' on such a long stretch," Snowshoe Thompson had to return home empty-handed. Congress did *not* grant his petition for back pay.

1857
Three Times an Emigrant

Most of the westward-ho emigrants of the nineteenth century were happy to make the forbidding cross-continental trip just once. Most who succeeded, that is. Very few emigrants chose to make the taxing trek west twice, a notable exception being the missionary Marcus Whitman, who safely completed two wagon train journeys from east to west only to die in an Indian massacre sometime later at the mission he and his wife, Narcissa, had founded in Oregon.

Notably, too, Whitman on his second trek westward was a leader of the "Great Migration" of 1843 in which a thousand persons took to the Oregon Trail, the first such massive number to travel overland to the far West at one time.

Aside from Whitman, safe to say, only a relative handful of the half million emigrants who completed the westward trek ever considered making the difficult, often dangerous overland journey a second time. But three-time travelers? Before stagecoach travel and the transcontinental railroad, did any sane and reasonable settler voluntarily chose to make three continental crossings? Well, yes, and leave it to an Englishman to have accomplished that daunting task . . . accomplished it, that is, at such shocking cost the third time out that he wouldn't talk about the experience for forty or more years thereafter.

To be utterly honest, Daniel Tickner was more a transplanted Englishman than one raised British to the core, since he was removed from Gravesend, Kent, England, to young America in 1823 at the age of eleven. By 1840 his father had carried his family, Daniel included, to Albion, Illinois, where Daniel, a blacksmith by trade, married a local girl, Mary Wood, in 1844. Three years later, they had a daughter, Ellis Sarah Tickner.

So far, they experienced no more than ordinary family excitements in their lives . . . but with the California gold rush of 1849, nothing for the Tickner couple would ever be quite the same again.

A brother of Mary's had gone west to join the gold seekers, according to the story related at the Oregon-California Trails Association (OCTA) Web site (http://calcite.rocky.edu/octa/tickner.htm). Tickner's in-laws in 1850 prevailed upon him to go west to retrieve the "foolish" brother-in-law. With a friend, A. Freeman, as a companion, Tickner did exactly that, traveling west by horseback and returning— "with the errant brother-in-law"—by steamer ship.

Tickner found a new infant child awaiting him at home in Albion, a son named Leon Francisco Tickner.

After a short time home, however, he found *he* had restless feet, restless for the California he had just left behind. In 1852, just two years after his first trip west, he bundled his wife and children into a covered wagon and, with two of her brothers, set out for California a second time. They reached San Leandro, where Tickner purchased a Spanish land grant and built a home of local redwood. "Being a blacksmith, Tickner made his own nails and front door hardware," notes the OCTA

Web site account—based, it says, upon information submitted by Tim Newcomb. The couple's kitchen, fittingly, was "papered with the London Times."

After a third child, Frank Semor Tickner, was born to the couple in 1854, Mary became so homesick the couple headed back to Illinois . . . by steamer.

But again, a revised situation wouldn't do for the growing Tickner family. California still beckoned. In 1857 they set out for the distant West again, a third and final time for Daniel Tickner and, of course, a second time for his wife, Mary. With Omaha, Nebraska, serving as a jumping-off place, it was a large family group that began the journey on June 5 in four wagons.

Traveling with English-born Tickner this time were Mary; her two unmarried brothers, William and Benjamin Wood; her married brother, James, and his wife, Catherine Gleason Wood; and Mary's married sister, Martha, and her husband, John West—eight adults in all, plus various children.

While the risks of overland travel west were known to all, especially anyone who had made the crossing beforehand, none in the Tickner-Wood party could have foreseen the horrors that awaited them on the trail ahead.

On their very first night on the road beyond Omaha, it seems, "Indians attempted to stampede their mules." The travelers thus found it necessary from the start to post a guard at their campsites every night. Not long after, they needed the help of another party—"oxen drivers"—to help them cross the Platte River.

They managed to cross the Rockies at easygoing South Pass with no further unhappy incidents, but then a white man dressed, oddly, as an Indian, warned them of the so-called war between the Mormons in Utah and the federal government, which was sending troops to deal with the situation. After passing Thousand Springs Valley on their way to the Humboldt River, widely detested by most California-bound emigrants for its sluggish, alkaline waters, the Tickners parted company with the West couple, Mary's sister Martha and brother-in-law John, due to a falling out. "West and his family took one of the four wagons and joined a nearby train."

The Tickner-Wood party struggled on, reached the Humboldt in northern Nevada, but not far from Gravelly Ford, was attacked on August 12 at a bend in the river by a band of seventy-five to one hundred "Indians," says the OCTA account. Apparently, there was considerable doubt as to their real identity. "About thirty of the 'Indians' were on horseback while the rest pursued the group on foot. They fired a mixture of guns and bows and arrows. This party of Indians was in league with renegade white men, presumed to have been members of [Mormon leader] Brigham Young's following."

Whoever the attackers were, the results for the innocent travelers were disastrous. Catherine Wood, who was pregnant, was killed, as were her unborn child and her infant son, Ellis. Her husband, James, was shot in the joint of the elbow but survived. His brother William suffered gunshot wounds in the back and arm, while the third Wood brother, Ben, was shot in the foot.

Young Ellis Sarah Tickner, Daniel's first child, would for the rest of her life remember being rolled up in protective feather mattresses with a brother in a wagon during the battle. Likewise, her mother Mary wouldn't forget "the hum of bullets as they tore through the canvas wagon-tops and passed all around me."

Fortunately, the attackers eventually desisted. The wounded men in the party were treated by a woman from another wagon train whose deceased husband had been a doctor.

In the meantime, a distraught Daniel Tickner returned to the battle scene with two men to bury Catherine Wood and her infant son.

Now joining up with the ox-team party that had been so helpful, the surviving Tickners and Woods successfully crossed the desert leading to the Truckee River at the foot of the Sierra Nevada. But it seems they still were in danger. "The Indians and white men continued to follow the injured Wood brothers. . . . In 1917 Ben said that one of the white men was captured and was taken to Carson City . . . [but] he escaped. He was followed by one of the ox-drivers, overtaken and shot."

The combined party next crossed the High Sierra into California, where the Tickners returned to San Leandro but then settled in Richmond. Their fourth child, Catherine Elena, was born there in 1858, so named for her aunt who had been killed on the trail. Also back on the trail, Daniel Tickner later said, William Wood "lost everything except the clothes on his back." The implication, according to the OCTA account, was that William "had lost a large sum of money with which he planned to buy land in the San Francisco area."

As the years rolled by, both William and Benjamin married in California, James settled in the Hayward Hills near San Leandro, young Ellis

Sarah Tickner married a Pony Express rider, and in 1874, California-born Catherine Tickner, only a teenager, also married.

In the meantime, Daniel Tickner, now the family patriarch, returned once to the battle scene to search for the graves of Catherine Wood and her son, Ellis, but to no avail. Thus, he a traveled a goodly part of the trail west a fourth time.

It was his third crossing, of course, that forever would be etched in his memory. He was so stunned by its searing events, says the OCTA account, "that for years he refused to discuss their 1857 crossing—even with members of his family." But then, "finally, on his 93rd birthday, he relented and a local newspaper recorded his painful recollections as he was honored as California's oldest living Mason in 1905."

★

1 8 5 9
Fifteen Wives

★

In appearance, wrote Horace Greeley, the man he interviewed on July 13, 1859, was "a portly, frank, good-natured, rather thick-set man . . . seeming to enjoy life, and be in no particular hurry to get to heaven." He was plainly dressed, and his "associates" seemed to be "plain men, evidently born and reared to a life of labor, and looking as little like crafty hypocrites or swindlers as any body of men I ever met." Greeley, famous founder and editor of the *New York Tribune,* was traveling west, all the way to California, but he had a few questions he'd like to ask of that portly and good-natured man he found in Salt Lake City. The result was a question-and-answer interview published in the *Tribune* and based upon Greeley's reconstruction of their two-hour conversation. The questions were blunt, and the answers by Brigham Young, leader of the Church of Latter-day Saints, did not mince words either.

H.G.: Am I to regard Mormonism (so-called) as a new religion, or as simply a new development of Christianity?

B.Y.: We hold that there can be no true Christian Church without a priesthood directly commissioned by and in immediate communication with the Son of God and Saviour of mankind. Such a church is that of the Latter-day Saints, called by their enemies the Mormons; we know no other that even pretends to have present and direct revelations of God's will.

H.G.: What is the position of your church with respect to slavery?

B.Y.: We consider it of divine institution and not to be abolished until the curse on Ham shall have been removed from his descendants.

H.G.: Are any slaves now held in this territory?

B.Y.: There are.

H.G.: Am I to infer that Utah, if admitted as a member of the Federal Union, will be a slave state?

B.Y.: No, she will be a free state. Slavery here would prove useless and unprofitable. I regard it generally as a curse to the master. I myself hire many laborers and pay them fair wages. I could not afford to own them. I can do better than subject myself to an obligation to feed and clothe their families, to provide and care for them in sickness and health. Utah is not adapted to slave labor.

H.G.: Can you give any rational explanation of the aversion and hatred with which your people are generally regarded by those among whom they have lived and with whom they have been brought directly into contact?

B.Y.: No other explanation than is afforded by the crucifixion of Christ and the kindred treatment of God's ministers, prophets, and saints in all ages.

H.G.: How general is polygamy among you?

B.Y.: I could not say. Some of those present [other Mormon leaders were present during the interview, Greeley explained at this point] have each but one wife; others have more; each determines what is his individual duty.

H.G.: What is the largest number of wives belonging to any one man?

B.Y.: I have fifteen; I know of no one who has more; but some of those sealed to me are old ladies whom I regard rather as mothers than wives, but whom I have taken home to cherish and support.

A few more questions and answers filled the column, and Greeley ended with the explanation that, "such is, as nearly as I can recollect, the substance of nearly two hours' conversation." Young, he also said, "spoke readily, not always with grammatical accuracy, but with no appearance of hesitation or reserve, and with no apparent desire to conceal anything." Further, he gave Greeley no impression of "sanctimony or fanaticism."

Young's views, plainly stated or not, would be controversial beyond the bounds of Mormon-founded Salt Lake City . . . and were not simply reported without comment by Greeley. By 1859 slavery, of course, was the subject of hot nationwide debate soon leading to the Civil War, but the Mormon practice of polygamy also was a matter of great controversy. Just three years after the Greeley interview, editors Louis L. Snyder and Richard B. Morris commented in their book *A Treasury of Great Reporting,* "Congress prohibited polygamy for the future in the territories, and ultimately the Mormons bowed to the sentiment of the country [although even in recent years, some Mormons have been known to maintain the old tradition]."

What really stirred Greeley's ire in his visit to Salt Lake City, though, was the general lack of consideration he found for women's rights . . . in general. "[T]he degradation (or, if you please, the restriction) of woman to the single office of childbearing and its accessories is an inevitable consequence of the system here paramount," he wrote. "I have not observed a sign in the streets, an advertisement in the journals, of this Mormon metropolis, whereby a woman proposes to do anything whatever. No Mormon has ever cited to me his wife's or any woman's opinion on any subject; no Mormon woman has been introduced or has spoken to me; and though I have been asked to visit Mormons in their houses, no one has spoken to me of his wife (or wives) desiring to see me, or his desiring me to make her (or their) acquaintance, or voluntarily indicated the existence of such a being or beings."

Greeley included Young in his condemnation. "One remark made by President Young I think I can give accurately, and it may serve as a sample of all that was offered on that side. It was in these words, I think exactly: 'If I did not consider myself competent to transact a certain business without taking my wife's or any woman's counsel with regard to it, I think I ought to let that business alone.'"

That remark, added Greeley, "fairly displayed" the "spirit with regard to woman of the entire Mormon, as of all other polygamic systems."

Added the newspaper editor: "Let any such system become established and prevalent, and woman will soon be confined to the harem, and her appearance in the street with an unveiled face will be accounted immodest. I joyfully trust that the nineteenth century tends to a solution of the problem of the woman's sphere and destiny radically different from this." Even if the American woman's political suffrage wasn't granted until the *twentieth* century, Greeley must have been looking into a crystal ball.

☆ ☆ ☆

Additional notes:

• Before his death in 1877, Brigham Young had "possibly as many as twenty-seven" wives and fifty-six children, reported Snyder and Morris.

• Greeley later put together his dispatches to the *Tribune* from the West as a book, *An Overland Journey.* A one-term congressman from New York, he helped to found the Republican Party and served as a delegate in the Republican National Convention that nominated Abraham Lincoln for the presidency in 1860. Greeley then ran for president himself in 1872 but was soundly defeated by Ulysses S. Grant. When Greeley died just a few weeks later, "thousands thronged the streets of New York to mourn his passing," noted Frederick R. Rinehart, editor of the book *Chronicles of Colorado* (1993). Quite an unusual—and enviable—accolade for a newspaperman. Meanwhile, as Rinehart also noted, it may *not* have been Greeley who uttered those famous nineteenth-century words, "Go west, young man, go west." More likely, the quote came from an editorial by John L. Soule in the *Terre Haute (Ind.) Express.*

1859
Questions Even After Death

Questions, questions, questions. All about the life and even the death of the pioneering Peter Lassen. And all those prominent landmarks named for this early trailblazer . . . this widely hated trailblazer, it so happens. Lassen Volcanic National Park, Lassen Peak, Lassen Creek, Lassen's Emigrant Trail, Lassen's National Forest, Lassen Monument, Lassen County, California . . . the list goes on and on. Indeed, say the authors of an unpublished study on the mysterious death of Peter

Lassen, "Of the multitude of pioneers who participated in the settlement of the west, few have left their name on as many prominent landmark sites as the Danish-born immigrant Peter Lassen."

And another question: Who killed, or possibly murdered, Peter Lassen and a companion in Black Rock Desert?

Then, too, did he deliberately send gold rushers on a bad trail into California, two hundred miles out of the way, just to guide them past his own ranch and trading post? "Travel along . . . [his] cutoff turned out to be a trip through hell," according to archaeologists Amy Dansie of the Nevada State Museum and Peggy McGuckian of the Bureau of Land Management (BLM) field office at Winnemucca, Nevada.

And yet, unsuspecting of the pitfalls ahead, "Approximately one half of the 1849 gold rush traffic heeded Lassen's advice."

What they found, instead of an easy shortcut, was a longer route with "much" of the grass and water "exhausted early in the season," and the "eagerly anticipated water holes frequently . . . muddy quagmires littered with the bodies of dead and dying animals."

Who to blame but the trail's namesake himself, Peter Lassen? "Thinking that their journey's end was a mere 100 miles distant, emigrants frequently dumped excess provisions at Lassen's Meadows and suffered serious shortages as a result," added Dansie and McGuckian in the joint paper they presented before the Great Basin Anthropological Conference of 1992. "Exorbitant prices at Lassen's trading post and the mysterious disappearance of emigrant stock while left in the care of Lassen's employees (blamed on the Indians of course!) led many to believe that they had been bambozzled by Lassen."

No surprise then that there was "a lot of hard feeling toward Lassen in the Sacramento Valley because of the hardships endured along the trail."

Who was this Peter Lassen? How did he get there to begin with? Did he really try to establish a republic named Nataqua in the mountains between Nevada and California?

In the first place, his name didn't quite start out as Lassen. More likely he was born in Denmark to a father named Lars Niesen then became Peter Larsen, then became Larssen . . . and finally Lassen. So say Ole Lysgaard and Holger J. Bladt in the online *Danish Journal* (see http://www.geocitiesd.com/lysgaard_2000/nyTheFounder.htm). Picking up the Lassen story from there, Richard Hughey in the *Mountain Democrat* of Placerville, California (see http://www.mtdemocrat.com/

columnist/hughey28.shtml), wrote that Lassen, a blacksmith in Denmark, arrived in America in 1831, then nine years later "trekked to the northwest over the Oregon Trail."

He grabbed a boat ride to the Russian-established Fort Ross on Bodega Bay, then worked for a time as a blacksmith at Sutter's Fort. "In 1843, with [John] Sutter's help, he secured a 26,000-acre grant of land from Mexican Gov. Micheltorena for a rancho in the upper Sacramento Valley." Here, at what he called *Rancho Los Bosquejo* ("ranch of the wooded places") he established a trading post—"at what is now Vina, about 18 miles south of Red Bluff." Located at the far end of his namesake trail, the trading post in time would "cater to the starved and exhausted pioneers who reached it."

First, though, Lassen returned to his earlier American stop of Missouri to lead a "large" wagon train to the far West, ultimately taking the pioneers along his new trail all the way to his ranch. In fact, he hoped to see these emigrants settle there, to help create a town to be called Benton City—"named for Sen. Thomas Hart Benton, the great expansionist politician who was Lassen's idol." Lassen and his settlers soon established the first Masonic Lodge in California, and all apparently was well . . . until gold was discovered at Sutter's Mill in January 1848. For John Sutter the discovery of gold had been a signal for wholesale desertion of workers; for Lassen, it meant the sudden loss of would-be Benton City colonists.

With his followers deserting him for the gold, Lassen began selling off portions of his vast land. He sold a large piece in 1852 to Henry Gerke. "Thirty years later," Hughey noted, "Gerke sold 9,000 acres of the original Lassen grant to Leland Stanford for a vineyard, which the early California mogul later donated to Stanford University." Returning to the story of Lassen's trail, however, it sometimes was known as the Applegate-Lassen Trail. "In 1846," explained Hughey, "Jessie Applegate blazed a trail from the Humboldt River in Nevada to the southern Willamette Valley in Oregon as an alternate route to the northern section of the Oregon Trail. Lassen used Applegate's Oregon Trail and the Truckee River emigrant trail to create an alternate route into California."

As described earlier, Lassen's trail, entering the upper Sacramento Valley near Los Molinos, north of Vina, "was no short cut." It instead was "a long, round-about cut-off through steep mountain country infested with hostile Indians, Paiutes in the east and Modocs in the west. The way was especially long for those '49ers heading for Sutter's

Fort; they had another 130 miles to travel after reaching Lassen's trading post at Vina."

The added distance meant more time spent reaching California than expected and, thus, a risk of being caught in the mountains by rough wintry weather. Then, too, after spending so much time covering the extra miles at the tail end of their long treks, both the emigrants and their animals would be "especially vulnerable to harsh weather conditions."

In late 1849, wholesale disaster threatened as "a large number of wagon trains" diverted from the Truckee River route to the more northerly Lassen Trail because the cattle traveling with earlier groups had denuded the Truckee route of grass. Disaster only was averted, Hughey noted, by a relief expedition sent into the mountainous terrain "to distribute food and supplies as needed and to help the emigrants get through the mountains, especially the women and children." One result of such problems: "By the end of the 1850 migration season few wagon trains followed Lassen's trail. It had developed a very bad reputation."

In 1851, meanwhile, William Nobles found a better shortcut from Nevada's Humboldt River that led to Shasta City at the north end of the Sacramento Valley, a much shorter and easier trek than Lassen's Trail. Nonetheless, travelers on the Noble Trail would be making their way through future Lassen County, California . . . the territory that might have been, that briefly was declared, the Territory of Nataqua, with Lassen as cofounder.

Lassen County historian Tim I. Purdy tells that part of the Lassen story on the county Web site (http://www.psln.com/pete/history.htm): "Of the thousands that passed this way," he says, "some choose to remain in the Honey Lake Valley. Among these, Isaac Roop [a young widower only thirty-two] established a trading post where travelers on the Noble Emigrant Trail could stock up with provision, before crossing the Sierras.

"First known as 'Rooptown,' the settlement later became Susanville, for Roop's daughter Susan."

By 1856 Lassen also was an ingrained member of the community, so much so that he and Roop became leaders of local citizens "unhappy over efforts of Plumas County [California] . . . officials to levy and collect taxes in this isolated and sparsely populated region." But they also were uninterested in becoming a part of Utah Territory, "a vast region that included parts of what were to become several western states." As a result, "Roop, Lassen and their followers opted to form a separate territory which they called 'Nataqua.'"

The valley they settled just west of today's California-Nevada line was so beautiful, the game so plentiful, the soil so rich, its early settlers were called the "Never-Sweats." Roop, though, worked hard at his trading post as the valley's unofficial greeter and general factotum. "He kept the register, lent money to the down and out, acted as land recorder, gave advice, greeted newcomers in the name of the valley and functioned as an all-around arbiter, indispensable to settlers and emigrants alike." Lassen, too, was well regarded, despite the poor reputation of his trailblazing days. "Old Pete Lassen stood solidly in the background, a sort of elder statesmen. Like Roop, he had immense prestige among the settlers, and like Roop, he had little material gain to show for it. Lassen had discovered gold at last, along and above the little creek where he had settled, but others were doing the actual mining and reaping the rewards."

The separatist idea behind the territory of Nataqua was all for naught. Roop, in fact, became governor of the territory of Nevada when it was formed. Then, too, "A few years later, surveys of the area established that Susanville was actually a part of the state of California; the county of Lassen was established in 1864."

But first, there had to be a "war" . . . the two-day Sagebrush War of February 1863. The so-called war—actually, a skirmish in Susanville— came about because Plumas County still claimed the area and assessed taxes on the residents, and they fought back. As Purdy notes, they lost the battle but won the war—they got their own Lassen County.

By now, however, county namesake Peter Lassen was dead, murdered while prospecting in the unforgiving Black Rock Range and Desert in 1859 with two companions.

They had gone there in April to search for a silver deposit reported by an emigrant ten years before. The party—composed of "Old Pete" Lassen, fifty-eight; a heavyset man named Lemericus Wyatt, about sixty; and a younger man, Edward Clapper—was supposed to meet in a certain canyon with a party of four led by a captain named Weatherlow.

Taking the story from there, the Dansie-McGuckian paper of 1992 reported: "Lassen's party arrived at what they *believed* to be the designated meeting place on April 24. Finding no trace of Weatherlow's party, they set up camp." They set up by a creek at the mouth of the canyon near some large rocks overlooking the site. The next day, they circled the area but saw no sign of the Weatherlow group. Clapper did find the footprints of two white men and two shod horses. A part of Weatherlow's party? They didn't know.

They had a brief visit that evening from an Indian, probably a Paiute, and heard a rifle shot while he was still there. "[T]he Indian indicated that it had been fired by one of the Paiutes from his party, of which there were five members."

The three men bedded down that night, side by side, next to a large boulder . . . and only Wyatt lived to tell the tale.

The sound of a rifle shot woke him at daybreak the next morning. Throwing off his blanket, he saw blood spurting from Edward Clapper's temple. Wyatt jumped to his feet and started to run. Nearby, Lassen was on his feet also. Wyatt shouted, urged him to run, too. But rifle in hand, peering at the nearby rocks, Lassen remained standing, his hand over his eyes to block the sunlight while he searched for the unknown sniper. A second shot then took him down. Wyatt ran back, saw that Lassen was nearly dead, done for, then went after their horses. Picketed nearby during the night, the panicked animals ran off.

But Wyatt's "usually elusive" horse returned and stood docilely while he mounted, with no stirrup or saddle horn to help—and "not before a third bullet had ripped through the fabric of his trouser leg." Added the Dansie-McGuckian account: "Wyatt then rode bareback without sleep or water for four days until he reached Honey Lake Valley—a distance of some 140 miles. This was a pretty impressive feat, given the man's weight and age."

Fearing for the safety of Weatherlow and his companions, a search party rushing back to the scene found them to be perfectly safe and wondering about the whereabouts of Lassen and *his* friends. The two groups apparently had camped in canyons about a mile apart. Continuing on to the murder scene, the searchers found the bodies of Lassen and Clapper to be so badly decomposed they thought it best to bury them on the spot.

They hadn't figured on the loyalty of Lassen's fellow Masons, however.

After all, he "had brought the charter for the Masons to California," said Dansie and McGuckian. He "thus was held in high esteem by the Masons of Honey Lake Valley"—such high esteem that a party of local Masons traveled back to the murder site that November to retrieve both bodies for a proper and fitting burial.

For unknown reasons, however, the only remains they carried back were those of Lassen. "While there was much public outcry at the time over the fact that Clapper's remains had been left at the murder site, no one ever returned to retrieve Clapper's body and over time the location of the site was lost."

Lost, that is, until a twentieth-century "rock hound" poking around the Black Rock Range (mountains protruding into the Black Rock Desert) on Memorial Day 1990 "came across human remains eroding out of a stream bed wall." Immediately, people wondered if this was the long-lost Clapper. With modern forensic tools at hand, here was an opportunity to solve "the most famous murder in Nevada's history." Since there had been some question about whose badly decomposed body the Masons had retrieved, could Lassen now "rest in peace" below the monument to his memory back in Honey Lake Valley?

After a forensic study by the local sheriff's office, the FBI, various anthropological and archaeological experts from the Bureau of Land Management and the Nevada State Museum (among them Dansie and McGuckian), and the Smithsonian Institution, it was determined that the Black Rock Desert remains indeed were those of a man taller and ten years younger than Lassen. He clearly had been shot in the head while lying down, just as Wyatt had described. Thus, this was Clapper, and the remains buried near Susanville were those of Lassen.

Another conclusion was that the killer was an expert rifleman, a supposition casting doubt on the long-held belief of some that an Indian had killed the two men. "Would an Indian be likely to have developed such skill in 1859, or is it more likely that an experienced military man would?" Dansie and McGuckian asked. Further, Lassen "was renowned for his good relations with the Paiutes."

Was the killer someone from the Weatherlow party? Weatherlow himself blamed Indians for the murders.

Was robbery the motive? "Only Lassen's rifle was taken, as far as the historical records document; none of the food or blankets were disturbed, and a single assailant is indicated by all the facts."

Oddly, in 1862 Weatherlow recovered Lassen's rifle, noteworthy for its handsome walnut stock . . . and retrieved, he claimed, from a slain Paiute accused of killing two other prospectors. "Had two men been murdered for an attractive firearm? Was it mere coincidence that Weatherlow had not only the opportunity to kill Lassen but also was the one who had found Lassen's gun in the hands of a dead member of the group toward which he attempted to redirect suspicions?"

Question, questions . . . even now, nearly a century and a half since his death, Lassen poses questions.

Meanwhile, the Lassen County Historical Society arranged in 1992 to have murder victim Edward Clapper reburied next to Peter Lassen in a "lush valley near Susanville," Dansie and McGuckian noted. "This event provided some historic justice for Edward Clapper, now with his own grave marker, and historic justice for the Native Americans, who are no longer blamed for the murder, as we still do not know 'who dunnit.'"

★ Part 4 ★
Nation of Two Faces

Accolades for a Job Well Done

MESSAGE FROM THE PAST: It had a great run but a short run. Carrying the mail west from the lower Missouri River to California in sometimes less than ten days, the Pony Express, one of the most romantic and colorful icons of the American West, lasted only a few months, overtaken in that short time by progress—and to some extent, by the Civil War, which utterly consumed the East. An editorial writer named McClatchey publicly shed a tear or two over the pending demise in the *Sacramento Bee* of October 26, 1861.

FAREWELL PONY: Our little friend, the Pony, is to run no more. "Stop it" is the order that has been issued by those in authority. Farewell and forever, thou staunch, wilderness-over-coming, swift-footed messenger. For the good thou hast done we praise thee; and, having run thy race, and accomplished all that was hoped for and expected, we can part with thy services without regret, because, and only because, in the progress of the age, in the advance of science and by the enterprise of capital, thou hast been superseded by a more subtle, active, but no more faithful, public servant. Thou wert the pioneer of a continent in the rapid transmission of intelligence between its peoples, and have dragged in your train the lightning itself, which, in good time, will be followed by steam communication by rail. Rest upon your honors; be satisfied with them, your destiny has been fulfilled—a new and higher power has superseded you. Nothing that has blood and sinews was able to overcome your energy and ardor; but a senseless, soulless thing that eats not, sleeps not, tires not—a thing that cannot distinguish space—that knows not the difference between a rod of ground and the circumference of the globe itself, has encompassed, overthrown and routed you. This is no disgrace, for flesh and blood cannot always war against the elements. Rest, then, in peace; for thou hast run thy race, thou hast followed thy course, thou hast done the work that was given to thee to do.

Employees working for Russell, Majors and Waddell—the firm operating the express on a 1,966-mile route threading through Kansas, Nebraska, Colorado, Wyoming, Utah, Nevada, and California—had to meet high moral standards. Each one was required to take this oath:

I,_____, do hereby swear, before the great and Living God, that during my engagement, and while I am an employee of Russell, Majors & Waddell, I will, under no circumstances, use profane language; that I will drink no intoxicating liquors; that I will not quarrel or fight with any other employee of the firm, and that in every respect I will conduct myself honestly, be faithful to my duties, and so direct all my acts as to win the confidence of my employers. So help me God.

Once the newcomer took his oath, he was presented with a company Bible embossed with the company name in gold lettering.

★

1 8 6 0 - 6 1
A Ride Like "Greased Lightning"

★

The legendary Pony Express mail service, inaugurated in April 1860, was halted in November 1861, thanks *not* to railroad development but to the completion of coast-to-coast telegraph lines. During its eighteen-month lifetime, the express delivered 34,753 letters carried over a total distance of 616,000 miles, according to Raymond W. Settle in the *Utah Historical Quarterly* of April 1959. (Or 650,000 miles, according to the Pony Express Museum in St. Joseph, Missouri.) Of all those letters, the majority, some 23,356, originated in California, while only 11,397 went west from the East. Noted Settle: "From the very start it was evident that the people of California prized the Pony Express more highly than did their countrymen in the East. Everybody on the Pacific Coast wanted rapid communication with the rest of the country, but most of the people east of the Missouri River, being preoccupied with the daily unfolding tragedy of the Civil War, were unconcerned. If they wrote to California at all . . . they were content to send the missive by stagecoach or by sea, even though it took ten or twelve days longer."

Riding hell-for-leather hour after hour aboard relays of horses, the cross-continental "mail-men" had to be young, daring . . . and light in weight (no more than 125 pounds). Mark Twain, who witnessed the Pony Express firsthand, described the riders as "usually a little bit of a man," reports the National Pony Express Association's Web site (http://www.xphonestation.com/npea.html). According to the same informed source: "Approximately 80 young riders were in use at any one time. In addition, some 400 other employees included station keepers, stock tenders and route superintendents. Riders were paid $100 to $125 a month."

One of those station keepers, Jay G. Kelley, based at the Sand Springs, Nevada, station as assistant keeper, inadvertently became a rider himself.

"The war against the Pi-Ute Indians was then at its height and as we were in the middle of their country," he later wrote, "it became necessary for us to keep a standing guard night and day." One night he saw an Indian behind a wall and took a shot at him but missed. The next day, Kelley and his colleagues found "many tracks" and Indian campfires on a nearby mountain. The day after that, an express rider came in with "a bullet hole through him from left to the right side, having been shot by Indians while coming down Edwards Creek in the Quaking Aspen Bottom."

The wounded rider, a Mexican, died. And since he died, the lightest man at the station had to take over the route . . . and that was Kelley, who weighed a hundred pounds. According to the story carried on the National Pony Express Association Web site (taken from the Raymond W. and Mary Settle's book *Saddles and Spurs*), Kelley was on the return run just two days later, and confronting him, he reported, was the unavoidable ride through "the forest of quaking aspen where the Mexican had been shot."

As Kelley knew: "A trail had been cut through these little trees, just wide enough to allow horse and rider to pass. As the road was crooked and the branches came together from either side, just above my head when mounted, it was impossible for me to see ahead for more than ten or fifteen yards, and it was two miles through the forest."

Expecting trouble, he cocked his Sharp's rifle and kept his spurs digging into his pony's flanks. The pony, for its part, raced through the forest "like a streak of greased lightning."

At the top of a hill just beyond, Kelley dismounted to rest his steed, "and looking back saw the bushes moving in several places." With no cattle or game to be found in the immediate area, the rider wrote, "I knew the movements to be caused by Indians and was more positive of it when, after firing several shots at the spot where I saw the bushes in motion, all agitation ceased."

As if to confirm his worst suspicions, added Kelly, two soldiers riding through the same aspen grove several days later "were shot and killed from the ambush of those bushes, and stripped of their clothing by the red devils."

Kelley in later life became an "eminent mining engineer and lived in Denver," reports the Web site.

Meanwhile, one of the greatest Pony Express rides ever reported had to be James Moore's feat of June 1860. He was at Midway Station, "half way between the Missouri River and Denver," reports the Web site, when a westbound rider "arrived with important Government dispatches to California." Taking over, Moore rode 140 miles to "old Julesburg." And stopped . . . almost.

He had done his duty, but . . . "Here he met the eastbound messenger, also with important missives, from the Coast to Washington."

Normally, "Moore should have rested a few hours at this point," and perhaps he would have, but the express rider scheduled to take the mail pouch and ride east from Midway "had been killed the day before." What now? "The mail must go, and the schedule must be sustained. Without asking any favors of the man who had just arrived from the West, Moore resumed the saddle after a delay of only ten minutes, without even stopping to eat, and was soon pounding eastward on his return trip."

His, it turned out, was a world-class run. "He made it . . . in spite of lurking Indians, hunger and fatigue, covering the round trip of two hundred and eighty miles in fourteen hours and forty-six minutes—an average speed of over eighteen miles an hour."

Not only that, "[H]is westbound mail had gone through from St. Joseph to Sacramento on a record-making run of eight days and nine hours." (The story also is told in *The Story of the Pony Express* by Waddell Smith.) Moore later became a rancher in Nebraska's South Platte Valley

On the other hand, the all-time record ride, says the Pony Express Museum Web site (http://www.ponyexpress.org./history.htm), was a 370-mile round trip by Bob Haslam. The average ride was a more sane 75 to 100 miles, with a change of horses every 10 to 15 miles. The average delivery time over the 1,966 miles from St. Joseph, starting point for the westbound mail, was ten days. The fastest run ever accomplished apparently was seven days, seventeen hours . . . to carry Lincoln's inaugural address to the West Coast. The riders ranged in age from "Bronco Charlie" Miller's possibly apocryphal eleven years to forty. They carried the mail in a specially designed saddlebag called a *mochila.*

Among the 225-plus names of onetime Pony Express riders gathered in recent years by the Pony Express Association is that of James "Dock" Brink, a native of Pennsylvania who later spent nearly thirty years as a butcher and restaurateur in St. Joseph. Oddly, he rarely mentioned his days as an express rider to anyone, nor did his obituary note it when he died in 1912. It did cite his eleven years as a scout in the Indian wars.

Curious descendants of Brink, reports the Pony Express Web site, began a genealogical hunt for facts relating to a family legend depicting their forebear as an express rider. Unfortunately, the facts pieced together with the help of staff researchers at the Pony Express Museum indicated that Brink, as a young Pony Express rider, had been at least present, if not directly involved, during an ugly murder scenario at an express station. He had been charged, tried . . . but *not* convicted.

To explain: Signing up early as an express rider on an eighty-mile route in today's southern Nebraska, from Rock Creek Station to 32-Mile Creek Station, Brink rode on the very first westbound mail run in April 1860. A year later, a young man named James B. Hickok was based at the Rock Creek facility as an assistant stock tender (i.e., stablehand); his boss was stationkeeper Horace Wellman. The station, also a stop on the Oregon Trail, actually was owned by David McCanles, but he was in the process of selling it to the express sponsors. McCanles appeared one day in July 1861 to collect a payment for the station site from Wellman. With McCanles were his twelve-year-old son and two men. With Wellman were Hickok and, perhaps waiting for his next run, Brink.

An argument flared up, then Hickok shot McCanles. As the McCanles boy ran for his life, his father's two companions were chased down and shot as well.

Hickok—later to be widely known as "Wild Bill" Hickok—Wellman, and Brink all were found innocent in a subsequent trial. The boy, the only witness available, was not allowed to testify.

The Pony Express Association credits the James Brink story to a museum newsletter article by Jackie Lewin, curator of history at the St. Joseph Museum. She also mentions that the Rock Creek Station has been restored to its 1860 appearance and is open to the public.

★

1 8 6 1
Civil War Intrusion

★

Talk about circles within circles, how about the case of two fathers-in-law, each a distinguished U.S. Army officer with notable service in the West, whose respective sons-in-law became central figures in the Civil War? That is, fathers-in-law who served on the same side, but sons-in-law who fought on opposing sides . . . even against each other.

All four men in question were graduates of West Point, all four served in the West on the expanding American frontier . . . but those factors did not deter one of the two younger men from joining the "secesh" states and becoming a legendary star of the Confederate firmament. So dedicated was this famous cavalry leader, in fact, so zealous was his fervor on behalf of the Southern cause, that he expressed hopes of personally meeting—and besting—his father-in-law on the field of battle. Indeed, said this angry young man, his father-in-law would "regret" his decision "but once, and that will be continually."

When a captured officer told him of the great improvements his father-in-law had brought to the Union cavalry, wrote Emory Thomas in his biography *Bold Dragoon,* the son-in-law responded: "I know he has command, and I propose to take him prisoner. I married his daughter, and I want to present her with her father; so let him come on."

Taking his strong personal feelings quite a step further, Virginia-born James Ewell Brown "Jeb" Stuart insisted upon renaming his own son as James Jr. rather than allow the child to be known any longer by his given name, Philip St. George Cooke (Stuart) . . . the name Jeb

Stuart and his wife, Flora, had given their newborn son in 1860 in honor of her distinguished father, Philip St. George Cooke.

Also Virginia born but a Union man through and through, Cooke suffered double and triple indignity at the start of the Civil War, as not only Jeb and Flora Stuart and not only another daughter and her husband, but Cooke's own son, John Rogers Cooke, joined the Confederate cause, as did a nephew, John Esten Cooke. As another aspect of a sad family split that was the talk of army circles on both sides of the war, a third daughter of Philip St. George Cooke and her husband did join her father in remaining loyal to the Union.

One can assume that relations among members of the distinguished Randolph Barnes Marcy's family were far more cordial. Like Cooke, Marcy was a well-known soldier-explorer and trailblazer from the West. During the abortive Peninsula campaign of 1862, he served as chief of staff to the Union general leading the intended assault against Richmond, his son-in-law George B. McClellan.

While theirs apparently were cordial relations, however, they had no great triumphs to savor in the war's aftermath, since McClellan was sacked when he failed to follow up on the Confederate retreat after the battle of Antietam. He then lost his bid to unseat Abraham Lincoln in the presidential election of 1864 (although the former general served as governor of New Jersey for three years, 1878–81, after the war).

West Point graduates McClellan and Stuart, of course, did directly—and quite famously—oppose each other in the Peninsula campaign of 1862. Stuart led his cavalry completely around McClellan's army after being ordered to reconnoiter the Union's right flank. For that matter, not only Marcy (as McClellan's chief of staff) but Stuart's father-in-law Cooke took part in the same campaign.

In far happier years a decade or two earlier, both Cooke and Marcy were outstanding soldier-explorers and trailblazers in the American West.

Cooke, born in Leesburg, Virginia, in 1812, was the older of the pair by three years. After serving in the Black Hawk War of 1832 and various duties in the West, he made history by leading the Mormon Battalion over the tough and then largely virginal miles across mountain and desert from Santa Fe to San Diego, California, in 1846–47 to provide reinforcements (unneeded, as events turned out) for the war against Mexico (see pages 120–25).

Also seeing frontier duty against Apache and Sioux outbreaks, Cooke helped in the army's efforts to stamp out the Kansas Border Wars of the 1850s. In 1861 he published *Cavalry Tactics,* a treatise destined to remain in long use among students of horse-soldier tactics. By now a brigadier general and soon a brevet major general in rank, Cooke at the age of fifty-two led a reserve cavalry division during the failed Peninsula campaign. He was engaged at Yorktown and Williamsburg, among other battles. That was his final service in the field . . . thereafter he was assigned to administrative activities such as courts-martial, department commands, or recruiting. He retired from the U.S. Army in 1873, eight years after the war, with more than fifty years of service behind him.

He outlived his son-in-law Jeb Stuart, who was fatally wounded at Yellow Tavern, Virginia, on May 11, 1864, and died in Richmond the next day, despite the ministrations of his brother-in-law, *Confederate* army surgeon Charles Brewer, previously an assistant surgeon in the *U.S.* Army . . . and Cooke's second defecting son-in-law. The general's only son, Confederate Brig. Gen. John Rogers Cooke, survived the war despite seven battle wounds, became a successful Richmond merchant, and helped to establish the Confederate Soldiers Home there before his death in 1891. His father, noted late in life for his memoirs on the frontier life, outlived him by four years.

In a western career remarkably similar to that of the slightly older Cooke, meanwhile, Massachusetts-born Randolph Marcy had begun his notable trailblazing by leading a party of a hundred or more settlers from Fort Smith, Arkansas, to Santa Fe in 1849. He made history also by leading the expedition through rough Texas and Oklahoma territory in 1852 that found the headwaters of the Red River, a prize that had eluded other American explorers of the Southwest for five decades.

Circles still within circles . . . both fathers-in-law, each a Union man to the core, served under Albert Sidney Johnston, a future Confederate general, in the expedition against the Mormons in Utah in the late 1850s. While the campaign resulted in no bloodshed, Johnston and his men passed a difficult winter at Fort Bridger. With the column's supplies and pack animals fast running out, Marcy came to the rescue—he and thirty-five men dispatched to find relief had to slog almost a thousand miles in wintry conditions to Fort Massachusetts, New Mexico, to achieve their goal. Leaving camp in November 1857, Marcy reappeared at Fort Bridger in June 1858 with reinforcements and fifteen hundred fresh animals. Johnston then was able to resume his march, enter Salt Lake City unopposed, and assert federal authority over the Mormons.

Marcy became so well known for his western ventures, the War Department asked him to return to the East to write a practical guide for emigrants and others traversing the often-violent, still largely uncharted West. His highly popular 1859 guidebook *The Prairie Traveler* was the result.

While the second in command to Marcy on that Red River expedition of 1852 was young Capt. George B. McClellan, Marcy's future son-in-law and, in the Civil War, commanding officer, it hardly needs saying which of the pair would wind up the ranking general. But it was Marcy who would remain in the army until 1881, finally retiring with the permanent rank of brigadier general after his closing-out service as the army's inspector general.

Like Cooke, for that matter, Marcy also was an author of popular frontier memoirs, and he, too, outlived his son-in-law before dying in 1887.

From Hannibal, Missouri, to Points West

MESSAGE FROM THE PAST: Samuel Clemens, alias Mark Twain, wrote in *Roughing It:*

My brother had just been appointed Secretary of Nevada Territory— an office of such majesty that it concentrated in itself the duties and dignities of Treasurer, Comptroller, Secretary of State and Acting Governor in the Governor's absence. A salary of eighteen hundred dollars a year and the title of "Mr. Secretary" gave to the great position an air of wild and imposing grandeur. I was young and ignorant and I envied my brother. I coveted his distinction and his financial splendor, but particularly and especially the long, strange journey he was going to make, and the curious new world he was going to explore. He was going to travel! I never had been away from home, and that word "travel" had a seductive charm for me. Pretty soon he would be hundreds and hundreds of miles away on the great plains and deserts, and among the mountains of the Far West, and would see buffaloes and

Indians, and prairie dogs, and antelopes, and have all kinds of adventures, and may be get hanged or scalped, and have ever such a fine time, and write home and tell us all about it, and be a hero.

What else was it that almost everybody thought about the West, even if here a wee bit exaggerated?

And he would see the gold mines and the silver mines, and maybe go about of an afternoon when his work was done, and pick up two or three pailfuls of shining slugs and nuggets of gold and silver on the hillside. And by and by he would become very rich, and return home by sea, and be able to talk as calmly about San Francisco and the ocean and the "isthmus" as if it was nothing of any consequence to have seen those marvels face to face. What I suffered in contemplating his happiness, pen cannot describe. And so, when he offered me, in cold blood, the sublime position of private secretary under him, it appeared to me that the heavens and the earth passed away, and the firmament was rolled together as a scroll! I had nothing more to desire. My contentment was complete.

Of course little brother would go!

At the end of an hour or two I was ready for the journey. Not much packing up was necessary, because we were going in the overland stage from the Missouri frontier to Nevada, and passengers were only allowed a small quantity of baggage apiece. . . . I only proposed to stay in Nevada three months—I had no thought of staying longer than that. I meant to see all I could that was new and strange, and then hurry home to business. I little thought that I would not see the end of that three-month pleasure excursion for six or seven uncommonly long years!

Foes Passing in the Night

A miserable night lay ahead for the three white men and their four horses traveling west through a tight pass in the Rockies in the early

1860s. One of the horses, exhausted by their pace all day, finally balked, wouldn't take a step more. Nighttime, with portents of a heavy snow, was coming on fast. They were stuck in a canyon not "ten rods" wide. To make matters worse, to render their lips tight with fear, this was Blackfoot country . . . and they wouldn't be friendly.

Anyone familiar with travel in these parts knew you should camp for the night a half a mile or more off the trail, to avoid detection by potentially hostile Indians. Boxed in by their canyon walls, these travelers couldn't take the well-known precaution. All they could do was bed down under their blankets in a gather of bushes atop a small rise on the canyon floor.

For what it was worth, too, they could also take turns as sentinels. As further precaution, they tied their horses to a single picket pin so they couldn't all gallop off in different directions if the Indians did strike during the night.

And so, in the dark, quiet descended and the snow fell—damp, heavy flakes.

The small party, its three members looking for work, had set out early in the day from Prickly Pear Creek, at the site of today's Montana City. They hoped to join gold miners working a new strike on a creek in Pikes Peak Gulch, sixty miles distant through the Rocky Mountain Range.

"Cornelius Bray, Patrick Dougherty and I started . . . on a horseback trip to the new camp in search of employment for the winter," recounted Nathaniel Pitt Langford. The intent, he said, "was to cross the main range on the first day and camp at the head of Summit creek, where there was good grass and water." But two miles short of the ridge top, Bray's horse "gave out and resisted all our efforts to urge him farther."

And so, at this "unpromising spot," there was "no alternative but to camp."

The campsite in the narrow canyon offered no feed for the horses. Worse, "our camp by the roadside could not escape the notice of any band of Indians that might chance to be crossing the range."

Preparing for the tense night, Langford and Bray crawled under their blankets, "they and the bushes being our only protection against a very heavy mountain snowstorm." Dougherty was the first to stand guard, with Langford due to take over the watch at midnight.

Amazingly, sleep came easily, Langford wrote, and he was dead to the world until awakened at midnight by Dougherty. "I crawled from under the blankets, which were covered to the depth of five inches with the 'beautiful snow,' and Dougherty fairly burrowed into the warm place I had left."

Silence still reigned in their narrow canyon, excepting the soft hiss of the falling snow, and all was well for the next three hours. As three o'clock approached, however, Langford noticed the horses were a bit uneasy—"for want of food," he assumed. Planning an early start up the trail, he threw caution to the winds and lit an immense fire from fallen pine branches. The effect was unforgettable. "It lighted up the canyon with a lurid gloom and mantled the snow-covered trees with a ghastly radiance," he wrote later. "The black smoke of the burning pitch rolled in clouds through the atmosphere, which seemed to be choked with the myriad snowflakes. So dense was the storm I could hardly discern the horses, which stood but a few rods distant."

But it now was time to awaken his companions, and that small action bemused the narrator afresh. "I could liken them to nothing but spectres as they burst through their snowy covering and stood half revealed in the bushes by the light of the blazing pines." Despite his "gloomy forebodings" earlier in the night, Langford now burst into a "fit" of loud laughter.

Chillingly, he was answered by the neigh of a horse "a few rods below"—a phony neigh that produced another one, "just above me."

Above and below, Indians!

"Bray and Dougherty grasped their guns, while I rushed to the picket pin, and, seizing the four lariats, pulled in the horses."

Just in time, too. For out of a thicket of willows just above the campsite, "there dashed down the canyon in full gallop forty or more of the dreaded Blackfeet."

And what a sight they made in the flickering firelight! "Their faces hideous with war paint, their long ebon[y] hair floating to the wind, their heads adorned with bald-eagle's feathers, and their knees and elbows daintily tricked out with strips of antelope skin and white feathery skunks' tails, they seemed like a troop of demons which had just sprung out of the earth, rather than beings of flesh and blood."

Next, with a small escort, came a herd of fifty or more horses—stolen, it later transpired, from a party of miners traveling toward the gold mining works at Bannack, future capital of the Montana Territory.

Both groups galloped past in a matter of seconds, and there the matter might have ended . . . except that the main body of Indians now stopped, turned, and formed a line facing the trio of whites.

Langford and his companions responded by hurriedly stepping behind their horses, "bringing our guns to an aim from behind them over their fore-shoulders."

And so the two groups stood opposite each other, "not twenty yards asunder."

For some tense moments nothing happened.

Then came an Indian chief to the front, a chief evidently furious with his warriors. He rode across their front with violent gestures and "vehement jargon." His braves "strongly expostulated" themselves. After a while, it dawned upon the onlooking whites that the Indians' guns were wet from the snowfall, the caps rendered useless. The braves were trying to persuade their chief to use the more traditional bow and arrow.

The chief still was so angry, his gestures so violent and manner so threatening, Langford later wrote, he expected "to see several of the Indians knocked off their horses."

But now they were putting away their firearms and taking out their bows. The three whites, of course, could only wait tensely behind their horses, guns still drawn. "Our guns were dry, and we knew that they were good for twenty-four shots and the revolvers in our belts for as many more." That meant, with absolutely perfect shooting, roughly one bullet for every Indian.

Suddenly, though, nearly half the Indians darted out of line and briefly vanished, only to reappear "emerging from the thicket on the opposite side of our camp." Cleverly, the three whites wheeled their four horses into a square. Standing inside the square they could unleash their firepower at either group of Indians.

This did not suit the Indians, who again hesitated. "As our horses were the booty they most wished to obtain, they were now restrained lest they should kill them instead of us," explained Langford.

Long moments of suspense now ensued until, at last, after brief consultation with his warriors, the chief evidently gave orders to withdraw. "They all wheeled into rapid line, and with the military precision of a troop of cavalry dashed down the canyon and we saw them no more."

Langford and his companions of course wasted no time also putting the canyon behind them, hurrying on to Pikes Peak Gulch "with all possible speed." On the way, they picked up two tired horses abandoned by the Indians and some days later came across a doctor who owned one of the steeds. "I have had seven horses stolen from me by these prowlers," he said, "but this is the first one that was ever returned."

Finding no work at Pikes Peak Gulch, meanwhile, Langford and his friends journeyed on to the gold town of Bannack, where he was destined to stay for some time . . . and become a noted chronicler of the area's vigilante movement of the 1860s.

☆

1 8 6 3
Ghost Town with a Past

☆

Here today, gone tomorrow was the fate of the extremely rough, tough miners' town of Bannack, briefly the first territorial capital of Montana and today possibly the most storied of all ghost towns in the West. Springing up after the discovery of gold in nearby Grasshopper Creek in July 1862, Bannack was the kind of town where a man named Jack Cleveland could swagger into the saloon in Goodrich's Hotel the following January to confront a number of citizens and accuse one of them, Jeff Perkins, of owing him money.

Oh no, said Perkins, he had paid off his debt to Cleveland.

The intruder said that was fine if true . . . but he kept handling his pistol in a threatening manner.

Looking on was Henry Plummer, a smooth-talking newcomer to the community who was destined in short time to serve as elected sheriff of Bannack and Virginia City, eighty miles away. Speaking firmly, Plummer told Cleveland to back off and behave himself. "Quiet was restored for the moment, and Perkins slipped off, intending to return with his pistols and shoot Cleveland on sight."

So wrote Nathaniel Pitt Langford, area merchant at the time and later author of a book, *Vigilante Days and Ways*, that painted Plummer as the murderous leader of a wide-ranging gang that preyed upon the miners and other relatively law-abiding citizens of the area.

The quiet described by Langford didn't last long. Cleveland, blustering and cursing, said he wasn't afraid of anyone in the room. That was more than enough for Plummer. "Filled with rage," Langford averred, the future sheriff of Bannack jumped up, pulled his pistol and, saying "I'm tired of this," shot Cleveland "below the belt."

And that wasn't all. Cleveland fell to his knees while trying to grasp his own pistol and "appealed to Plummer not to shoot him while he was down."

"No," said Plummer, still raging. "Get up."

Cleveland did, staggering—"only to receive two more shots, the second of which entered below the eye."

As Cleveland collapsed for good, Plummer returned his smoking gun to its holster and prepared to leave. He was met at the door by two men, pistols in hand, whom Langford identified as part of the area's criminal element. Grabbing him by the arms in a familiar way, they escorted him down the street in a manner suggesting "a variety of surmises as to the possible effect of the quarrel upon the public."

Soon after, Plummer was brought to trial before a "miners' court" in the slaying of Jack Cleveland, but he was acquitted upon his plea of self-defense.

By Langford's description, Bannack was that kind of town.

By his sometimes-challenged account also, not only Cleveland but the two men escorting Plummer down the street were old criminal associates of Henry Plummer. One of them, George Ives, soon after quarreled with a man named George Carrhart out on the main street of town. Both ran into a nearby saloon to grab their pistols, then engaged in an old-fashioned shootout on the street. "Facing each other upon the instant, both parties raised their pistols and fired without effect. After a second fire with no better effect, both parties walked rapidly backwards till they were widely separated, at the same time firing upon each other. Ives having emptied his revolver, stood perfectly still while Carrhart took deliberate aim and shot him in the groin, the ball passing through his body, inflicting a severe wound."

The amazing result was not so much that Ives later recovered, but that they "reconciled their difficulties," and Ives then spent the rest of the winter living with Carrhart on his ranch.

As events turned out, Ives would be a key figure in the still ongoing controversy over the Montana vigilante organization that evolved in response to the rampant lawlessness terrorizing both Bannack and Virginia City. Langford, now viewed as a chief apologist for the vigilantes, wrote that in Bannack's early days no one knew whom they could trust. With robbers controlling local affairs, "No one was safe," Langford wrote quite convincingly. "The miner fortunate enough to accumulate a few thousands, the merchant whose business gave evidence of success, the saloonkeeper whose patronage was supposed to be productive, were all marked as victims by these lawless adventurers. If one of them needed clothing, ammunition, or food, he obtained it on a credit which no one dared refuse, and settled it by threatening to shoot the person bold enough to ask for payment."

A leading example of the lawless element plaguing the town was George Ives, whose custom it was when needing money "to mount his horse, and, pistol in hand, ride into a store or saloon, toss his buckskin purse upon the counter, and request the proprietor or clerk to put one or more ounces of gold dust in it 'as a loan.'"

Said clerk or proprietor didn't dare refuse. But while the victim was complying with Ives's latest demand, "the daring shop-lifter would amuse himself by firing his revolver at the lamps and such other articles of furniture as would make a crash." This amusement "became so common that it attracted little or no attention, and people submitted to it, under the conviction that there was no remedy."

Even worse, miners and others leaving Bannack (or Virginia City) were likely to be robbed of their cash or hard-earned gold dust and possibly killed on the roads outside of either town.

One time, wrote Langford, Ives approached an informer on the road and shot him in the head. "The man fell dead from his horse, which Ives took by the bridle and led off to the hills. This cold-blooded murder was committed in open day on the most populous thoroughfare in the country, in plain view of two ranches, and while several teams were in sight. Travelers who arrived on the spot half an hour after its occurrence, aided by the neighboring ranchmen, paid the last sad offices to the still warm but lifeless body."

Not long after, with the discovery of yet another robbery victim's body out in the countryside, roused citizens of Nevada City, the victim's home, formed a posse and with little trouble tracked down George Ives among some men at a campsite close to where the body had been found. At the campsite also was a black mule belonging to the victim, a young German named Nicholas Tiebalt (or Tbalt). One of the men at the campsite said Ives had killed the young man.

Taken back to Nevada City, another gold mining community in Alder Gulch, Ives was "tried" by a jury of twenty-four men in an outdoor "courtroom" consisting of two wagons and several benches—since it was December and snow was on the ground, a roaring bonfire provided some warmth for participants and onlookers alike. In this rustic setting, the informer from the campsite testified that Ives had boasted of shooting his victim point-blank while he knelt in prayer. Convicted, as it were (with one "juror" dissenting), Ives was hanged, all the time protesting that he was innocent . . . and, at the very end, naming still another highwayman, Alex Carter, as the real killer.

Obviously taking its cue from the Ives incident, the vigilante movement of Bannack and Virginia City quickly took shape and in the next few weeks produced a frenzy of nearly two dozen hangings. The same vigilantes soon focused their wrath upon none other than the region's popular sheriff, one Henry Plummer, described both by Langford and by Oxford-born newspaper editor Thomas J. Dimsdale as chief villain of the area's criminal element.

The "charitable" outlook, wrote Langford in his treatise years later, had been to suppose that Plummer arrived in town "intending to reform, and live an honest and useful life" after earlier transgressions. "His criminal career was known only to two or three persons as criminal as himself," he wrote. And perhaps . . . well, if only he had not feared exposure and if only he could have avoided his "old comrades in crime," perhaps, just possibly, he could have overcome his past (as one item, a second-degree murder conviction and time served in California). After all, he did exude "great executive ability." He did have a "power over men that was remarkable"; he could appear the "fine person"; he could show off a "polished address" and display a "prescient knowledge of his fellows," with all these attributes "mellowed by the advantages of a good early education."

So cool, dispassionate, and effective at counseling others was he, that "he speedily became a general favorite."

At the same time, though, there was no one he feared more than Jack Cleveland, the same man he shot in the saloon at Goodrich's Hotel. Or so said Langford. "This man, who made no secret of his own guilty purposes, had frequently uttered threats against the life of Plummer, and never lost an opportunity publicly to denounce him. Their feud was irreconcilable."

Oddly, as old acquaintances with no love lost between them, they had arrived in Bannack together toward the end of 1862—after setting rival caps for the favors of a young lady living with relatives at a farm on the Sun River, some distance away. The fact that she ultimately choose Plummer as her husband did little to improve Cleveland's disposition—but only partly explains his hostile attitude. Cleveland's dislike for Plummer began much earlier, stemming from the days when Plummer was a town marshal in California busily pursuing Cleveland as a lawbreaker.

Upon shooting Cleveland (asserted Langford), Plummer took pains to find out if his slowly dying victim had said anything about their shared background . . . and was reassured when told nothing like that had occurred. As a former California habitue, Cleveland certainly knew about some or all of the three fatal shootings in which Plummer had been involved before pulling up stakes for, first Washington Territory then the future Montana. Bold and obnoxious, Cleveland had turned the tables on Plummer and "trailed" him "all the way from California," reported historian R. E. Mather in *Wild West* magazine. "During his pursuit," she wrote, "Cleveland had loaded up on whiskey and then boasted at saloons that he was the great hunter on the trail of his 'meat,' Henry Plummer."

Langford, for his part, saw no hope of reform or redemption for the future sheriff, who he argued should be considered "a very monster of inquities" and regarded as a man "stained with the guilt of repeated murders and seductions." Further, he and his criminal associates, his gang of "road agents," ultimately were responsible for 102 murders in the region, Langford alleged. Local newspaper editor Dimsdale, himself a vigilante apologist, in an earlier book of his own had assailed the Plummer gang as a network of spies, stool pigeons, fences, roadsters, telegraph horsemen, and officers, all headed by a "sadistic" chief. He also claimed that the gang was responsible for countless robberies and more than 100 murders.

Thanks to such allegations by Langford and Dimsdale, the legend was born that the vigilantes removed a vicious criminal ring from their corner of the future state of Montana . . . and perhaps, unlawfully, they did. As historians now point out, however, the vigilantes did so without lawful process and at the cost of depriving the accused of fair trial. In some cases they likely executed the innocent along with the guilty.

Whatever the full and true story, events moved rapidly after the Ives hanging just before Christmas 1863. In short order, one of the newly formed vigilante group's first victims implicated Henry Plummer as mastermind of the Bannack–Virginia City band of outlaws. As a result, the smooth-talking sheriff was seized on a cold January night in 1864 and hanged from a gallows that he had built himself at Bannack. Two of his deputies met similar fates just before him, all as prelude to the spree of nearly two dozen vigilante hangings over six weeks.

Soon after, the gold in Grasshopper Creek played out and the miners moved on. The Alder Gulch gold vein feeding Virginia City eighty miles away lasted much longer and thus sustained that small community for many years before it, too, played out.

Both towns wound up as mere shells of their former selves, with Bannack today occupying a Montana state park as a real-life ghost town . . . but a ghost town with an unusually dramatic past.

Additional note: Still standing in the old town are the red brick building that once served as Territorial Montana's first capitol, a two-story schoolhouse of wood, a church, the old jail (dirt floor, sod roof, barred windows, and very small cells), plus assorted log cabins and false-front store buildings all along the short main street—remnants of about sixty structures in all. Not far away, with a path leading to it, is Hangman's Gulch, the scene of Plummer's nighttime hanging in January 1864. A replica of the gallows provides a stark reminder. So does the ghost town's Outlaws' Cemetery not far away.

Virginia City, taking over from Bannack as territorial Montana's capital in 1865, fared better as the real center of Montana's gold rush. The town reached a peak population of ten thousand while the mines of the area produced eighty-five million dollars before playing out.

In recent years, millionaire rancher Charles A. Bovey restored much of the town's Lower Wallace Street historic section, replete with wooden sidewalks, old-timey street lamps, and false-front stores filled with antique goods. Again, the town includes a territorial capitol, plus the onetime home of editor Dimsdale's *Montana Post,* the Bale of Hay Saloon, and an old stone building used as a summer theater by the Virginia City Players to enact period melodramas. Once again, not far away is a historic cemetery of some note—a "Boot Hill" that provides the final resting place for some of Henry Plummer's gang.

Further Note: Calling the old ghost town the "toughest town in the West," Bannack State Park offers visitors an annual Bannack Days historical outing the third weekend of every July. Located twenty-five miles southwest of Dillon, Montana, Bannack is open to visitors year round as well.

☆
---

1 8 6 4
"No More Biscuits for You"
☆

A pioneer woman seldom remembered these days, Elizabeth Dyer Entriken, together with sister and brother-in-law Ann and William Bailey, cofounded the town of Bailey in 1864 as a spot on the map of mountainous Park County, Colorado, a segment of the Front Range of the Rockies just west of Colorado Springs. While the Baileys operated a tavern in their village for several years, Sister Elizabeth lived alone on the edge of the settlement for nearly fifty years.

She lived there "fearing nothing and welcoming any storm-bound wayfarer or dusty tramp, including Indians, with food and shelter," says an online history of the South Platte Ranger District, Pikes Peak & San Isabel National Forests, by Terence DeLay (http://www.fs.fed.us/r2/psicc/spl/history.htm).

But not even this independent and firm-minded soul was quite prepared for the day Ute chief Colorow and up to a dozen of his braves "dropped in," quite unannounced, "and gruffly demanded biscuits."

Obligingly, Elizabeth pointed them to her table and began baking biscuits, "two large pans full." Her guests "fell upon them hungrily and grunted for more." After the next batch disappeared just as quickly as the first, they asked for more. And after that, some more. Again and again, they wanted more. "No sooner would she bring in fresh pans and her back be turned than the biscuits would vanish," wrote DeLay.

Soon she was nearing the bottom of her flour barrel. And enough was enough in any case.

She minced no words in telling Colorow that no more biscuits were in the offing. "You're eating me out of house and home," she apparently said. "Not another biscuit do you get."

He at first seemed not to hear. "Hungry, hurry," he repeatedly growled.

But his hostess by now was adamant. The flour was nearly gone; she could not spare any more.

Then came the moment of truth. As the Ute chief reluctantly prepared to depart, he swung aboard a waiting pony—the exertion loosened the front flap of his shirt from beneath his waistband, and, lo, out tumbled a "cascade" of uneaten biscuits! Elizabeth's quick glance at his companions revealed they also boasted overstuffed, barrel-like shirt fronts.

Here was a moment fraught with potential trouble for a lone woman dealing with the often-mysterious, sometimes threatening rulers of the forest around her. It could be a moment of embarrassment for all, of anger and shrill accusations on her part . . . even of hilarity, since the chief and his overblown braves certainly did look a bit ridiculous.

Elizabeth Entriken had better sense, however, than to give in to any of the foregoing. "For a moment I was mad clear through, to think they had been 'stuffing' away my biscuits," she said later. "Then I had an almost irresistible desire to laugh. But I kept a grave face, told Colorow to remain on his horse and picked up for him all the biscuits he had dropped. He never thanked me, calmly stuffed them back into his shirt. However, he never again tried that trick."

More important, "He was grateful that I had saved his dignity, [he] came several times and ate biscuits and told me I was a 'heap good squaw' and his friend."

Even better, "None of the Utes ever bothered me, not even afterwards when the Indians grew ugly and the Colorado militia was called out against them."

★

1 8 6 4
In Search of Mount Whitney

★

In the far distance they had seen a towering peak that could be, must be, the highest in the land. Just fifteen miles to the south it beckoned like a siren. *Come climb me. Be the first!* Clarence King, easterner, tenderfoot fresh out of Yale, and Dick Cotter, a packer, had provisions that would last for six days.

Fifteen miles . . . six days. It could be done, couldn't it?

"Why not?" Cotter had shrugged when King made his startling proposal.

But look where they were that summer's day of 1864 . . . on a high, high ridge of the same Sierra Nevada range where they had been traipsing around as members of the California State Geological Survey. Well, maybe not *traipsing*, exactly. Nor carelessly, for this truly spectacular terrain could also be treacherous.

Really treacherous . . . as in life-threatening. Even so, albeit with a gulp and "not a dry eye in the party," they said good-bye to three companions, then set off for the beckoning peak that one day would be known as Mount Whitney, truly the highest mountain in the contiguous United States. King, brilliant, adventurous, often flamboyant, occasionally given to exaggeration, and yet later the first director of the federal government's Geological Survey agency, wrote about the leave-taking and the intended two-man assault on Mount Whitney in his book *Mountaineering in the Sierra Nevada.*

"Before he let go of my hand, Professor [William] Brewer asked me for my plan, and I had to own that I had but one, which was to reach the highest peak in the range," King wrote.

But looking about from the party's vantage point on the somewhat lesser Mount Brewer, King had to admit that he saw "as yet no practicable way."

Still, he and Cotter proceeded southward in hopes of climbing down a fairly friendly looking cliff from their high ridge. At the same time, Brewer and his remaining two companions resumed their trek upward, to the summit of his namesake mount. After a short while, they were mere microscopic dots in the distance. King and Cotter were quite alone and on their own now.

They soon found themselves looking over the edge of a sheer precipice with an apron of snow extending, almost unbroken, for perhaps three thousand feet. Wrote King: "We went to its edge and contemplated the slide." But it was "a fearfully steep angle." Maybe sliding down wouldn't be such a great idea after all. "We threw a stone over and watched it bound until it was lost in the distance; after fearful leaps we could only detect it by the flashings of snow where it struck, and as these were, in some instances, three hundred feet apart, we decided not to launch our own valuable bodies, and the still more precious barometer, after it."

That meant the only way to proceed would be to inch along the top of a cross ridge about four miles to the south that extended to the next range from the wall of Mount Brewer. "To do this, we had a rather lively time scaling a sharp granite needle, where we found our course completely stopped by precipices four and five hundred feet in height."

With no hope of negotiating the "fantastic pinnacles" lying ahead, they began to climb down the "most broken-up part of the eastern descent," no easy task either.

"The heavy knapsacks, beside wearing our shoulders gradually into a black-and-blue state, over-balanced us terribly, and kept us in constant danger of pitching headlong. At last, taking them off, Cotter climbed down until he had found a resting place upon a cleft of rock, then I lowered them to him with our lasso, afterwards descending cautiously to his side, taking my turn in pioneering downward, receiving the freight of the knapsacks by lasso as before."

In this way they spent half the afternoon descending perhaps a thousand feet. As sunset approached, they found themselves in a bowl, or "amphitheatre," covered with a thick layer of snow. A gorge below looked "utterly impassable." And at their backs, the wall of Mount Brewer "either rose in sheer cliffs or in broken, rugged stairway, such as had offered us our descent."

From here the cross ridge still offered the only hope of an exit, "and the sole chance of scaling . . . [it] was at its junction with the Mount Brewer wall."

But they still had to plod on through the snow and rocky "debris" on the floor of the bowl to reach that junction, a minor feat accomplished just before sunset.

With darkness now hastening down upon them, they of course couldn't try to scale the ridge until morning. But where to find shelter for the night in this desolate place? "A high granite wall surrounded us upon three sides, recurring to the southward in long elliptical curves. . . . A single field of snow swept around the base of the rock, and covered the whole amphitheater, except where a few spikes and rounded masses of granite rose through it, and where two frozen lakes, with their blue ice-disks, broke the monotonous surface."

Their only choice for a campsite was a "granite crevice" near one of the frozen lakes, "a sort of shelf just large enough for Cotter and me." Not quite realizing just how miserable the night would be, they supped on cold venison and bread while heating up a "tepid" cup of tea with a small fire fueled by a few shavings whittled from their wooden barometer case.

Naturally, when time came to sleep, it was cold and uncomfortable on their knobby stone slab. The night became increasingly cold. "The snow congealed, the brooks ceased to flow, and, under the powerful sudden leverage of frost, immense blocks were dislodged all along the mountain summits and came thundering down the slopes, booming upon the ice, dashing wildly upon rocks."

The two mountaineers were safe enough tucked into their shelf, "but neither Cotter nor I could help being startled, and jumping just a little, as these missiles, weighing often many tons, struck the ledge over our heads and whizzed down the gorge, their stroke sounding fainter and fainter, until at last only a confused echo reached us."

The next day, after rising at 4 A.M. to breakfast on more frozen venison, they "ascended a long steep snowfield with the aid of steps cut with Cotter's bowie knife," reports mountain-climbing author Paul Richins Jr. on his *Backcountry Resource Center* Web site, http://www.jps.net/ prichins/backcountry_resource_center.htm. They then "reached a narrow ledge leading up diagonally toward the top of a cliff."

But now they found themselves in a precarious, seemingly impossible position. "There was," recounted King (excerpted on the *Backcountry* Web site), "no foothold above us. Looking down over the course we had come, it seemed, and I really believe it was, an impossible descent; for one can climb upward with safety where he cannot downward."

After half an hour's study of their situation, it appeared their only hope now lay with a shelf thirty feet above them. If they could only reach the shelf, they could keep on their upward course. But how to reach that shelf?

The two climbers of course had noticed the two or three "spikes of granite" protruding from the edge of the distant shelf. How about if they lassoed one of them, then climbed the rope hand over hand, "sailor-fashion," King suggested to his companion. (Assuming, naturally, that the spikes would be "firmly connected with the cliff.")

Hence, for the next few minutes, two men with a precarious foothold on the side of a cliff vainly hurled their lassoes at a shelf of rock far above their heads.

It was a "very difficult undertaking," King observed, but at last, "I made a lucky throw, and it tightened upon one of the smaller protuberances."

Gingerly, first King (all of 150 pounds in his youth) then both men together hung on the rope to see if the lassoed outcrop would hold their weight. "Whether the rock moved slightly or whether the lasso stretched a little we were unable to decide; but the trial must be made, and I began to climb slowly."

For the next few minutes King climbed hand over hand, occasionally swinging against a smooth rock face absolutely bare of a foothold. Tiring about halfway up, he stopped to rest by "curling" his feet in the rope, then gave in to a dangerous temptation.

He looked down.

And what a sight! "Straight down, nearly a thousand feet below, at the foot of the rocks, began the snow, whose steep, roof-like slope, exaggerated into an almost vertical angle, curved down into a long white field, broken far away by rocks and polished, round lakes of ice."

Far from being terrified at the sight, King was exhilarated: "At that moment, when hanging between heaven and earth, it was a deep satisfaction to look down at the wild gulf of desolation beneath, and up to unknown dangers ahead, and feel my nerves cool and unshaken."

Minutes later, he had gained the distant shelf and was hauling up the knapsacks, "after which Cotter came up the rope in his very muscalur way without once stopping to rest."

Now they proceeded still upward, negotiating a zigzag shelf to a "thin blade of a ridge" connecting to the summit above, a ridge "so narrow and sharp . . . that we dared not walk, but got astride, and worked slowly along with our hands, pushing the knapsacks in advance, now and then holding our breath when loose masses rocked under our weight."

According to Richins, King and Cotter now were on the Kings-Kern Divide. "To their dismay a glance ahead revealed that the slope they now had to descend was even steeper than the one they had just come up. As for the ridge itself, it was terrifyingly narrow and unstable. Uncertain how to proceed, the two men exercised the time-honored choice of mountaineers in difficult situations, which is to sit down and eat lunch."

During their thoughtful lunch, they decided they still must go down . . . *somehow.*

The obvious way would be to lower themselves by rope from crevice to crevice. And the first *step*, so to speak, would be a sliding descent by rope to a notch forty feet below their luncheon spot. Once Cotter had followed King in that by-now-relatively-simple maneuver, they heaved and looped their rope to free it from its catching place above and, as a result, disconnected their only tie to the "upper world."

They could really be in for it now! In fact, that's exactly what Cotter said to King. But, wrote King, "our blood was up, and danger only added an exhilarating thrill to the nerves."

Their latest shelf was "hardly more than two feet wide." It was so smooth there was no place to fasten the lasso. Someone—King in fact—would have to crab his way down the face of the rock to the next ledge down, wrapped all the while in the lasso with his partner holding on to the rope for dear life. Cotter now braced his back against the cliff, "found for himself as firm a foothold as he could, and promised to give me all the help in his power."

Fine, but the outcome would depend largely upon King's own nerves and skill. Indeed, this may have been their most severe test yet. And so, gingerly again, King began a descent. "I made up my mind to bear no weight unless it was absolutely necessary; and for the first ten feet I found cracks and proturbances enough to support me, making every square inch of surface do friction duty, and hugging myself against the rocks as tightly as I could."

Even so, he would owe his life to a small alpine gooseberry bush not yet even in sight below him. What *was* in sight after a spell, about eight feet below, was the next shelf. Twisting and turning, while "hanging by two rough proturbances of feldspar," King looked desperately for another handhold.

Nothing. And worse, "the rock, beside being perfectly smooth, overhung slightly, and my legs dangled in the air."

> That shelf below, however, was more than three feet wide. . . . And I thought, possibly, I might, by a quick slide, reach it in safety without endangering Cotter. I shouted to him to be very careful and let go in case I fell, loosened my hold upon the rope, and slid quickly down. My shoulder struck against the rock and threw me out of balance; for an instant I reeled upon the verge, in danger of falling but, in the excitement, I thrust out my hand and seized a small alpine gooseberry bush, the first piece of vegetation we had seen. Its roots were so firmly fixed in the crevice that it held my weight and saved me.

Next, after the knapsacks were lowered, it would be Cotter's turn, with King holding the rope. The rest of the descent was difficult also, but after that, after successfully crossing the Kings-Kern Divide, King and Cotter found the going easier, notes the Richins Web site. Still intent upon climbing the Sierra's highest peak, "They climbed up smooth granite faces and hewed steps up fearfully steep slopes of ice to the summit."

But there, they found it wasn't the highest peak after all. "To our surprise," wrote King, "upon sweeping the horizon with my levell, there appeared two peaks equal in height to us, and two rising even higher."

The fact is, they were on Mount Tyndall, and they didn't have the supplies to keep going in search of future Mount Whitney. Instead, they had to turn back for their camp near Mount Brewer. "King's account of the return trip is as thrilling and undoubtedly as greatly exaggerated as the story of his climb of Mount Tyndall," says Richins. At the same time, however, "There is no slighting of his accomplishments . . . his round trip with Cotter through a virgin wilderness was clearly an extraordinary achievement."

Ironically, King would try twice more to be the first to climb Mount Whitney, failing to reach its summit each time (in one case, he was on the wrong mountain again), but in 1873, he finally did climb Mount Whitney, highest point in the United States—but too late by now to become its first conqueror.

☆ ☆ ☆

Additional note: Mount Whitney, the highest peak in the contiguous United States at 14,494 feet, was named for geologist Josiah Dwight Whitney, who founded the California Geological Survey (CGS), and it was the men of a CGS field party of 1864—Clarence King, Richard Cotter, James Gardner, and William Brewer—who apparently comprised the first group to spot the highest peak in a crowd of towering peaks in the Sierra range. When three fisherman later became the first to climb the peak, they tried to name it Fisherman's Peak, but King's field party of 1864 already had named it Mount Whitney, and that was the name that stuck.

Mount Whitney rises from California's Owens Valley on the eastern edge of today's Sequoia National Park, only eighty-five miles from the lowest point (279 feet below sea level) in the contiguous United States, Badwater Basin in Death Valley. Today a trail leading to the summit of the peak is such a magnet for would-be climbers that they must register in advance in order to meet the daily quota of climbers allowed on the mountain.

★

1 8 6 6
Today an Oregonian

★

As a young man, he spent six years traveling Europe and North Africa with a German prince. Fluent in four languages, he nonetheless turned his back on Old World culture and returned to the rough-and-ready life of the American frontier. Motivated, shall we say, by his genes, he became a mountain man.

After years of hunting and trapping, sometimes guiding, too, he helped lead the Mormon Battalion from New Mexico to California in 1846. After a period as alcalde (or mayor) of the San Luis Rey Mission, he joined the California gold rush. A decade or so later, however, now in his late fifties, he apparently held down the lowly station of a small-town hotel clerk in Auburn, California.

He left that job in 1866 to join the Montana gold rush but died en route of pneumonia at age sixty-one and was buried in Danner, Oregon. No wondrous fortune made, no great accomplishments achieved.

Today, his gravesite is to be found on the National Register of Historic Places . . . but what, by comparison with so many other frontiersmen of the West, had he ever done to become so notable historically? Certainly his claim to fame wasn't his six years spent under the patronage of Prince Paul Wilhelm of Wuertenburg, Germany. Nor, in actual fact, was it anything really significant he himself had done or accomplished all on his own.

Again, look to the genes. Sometimes called North America's youngest "explorer," he was Jean Baptiste Charbonneau. Through no fault or virtue of his own, he had been born in 1805 to the French-Canadian interpreter Touissant Charbonneau and his Shoshone wife, Sacagawea, at Fort Mandan near today's Bismarck, North Dakota. He then was carried to the Pacific Coast and back again as an infant "member" of the historic Lewis and Clark Expedition. Therein lies his fame, his chief mark in history . . . but there indeed was more to him than just that.

To begin with, in his very first weeks of life, a William Clark descendant not long ago noted, "This remarkable child withstood the hardships and fatigue, the hunger and the cold, as well as did the hardiest of the men." Delivering a dedication speech at Jean Baptiste Charbonneau's gravesite in 1971, William Clark Adreon of St. Louis, Missouri, a direct descendant of the expedition's co-leader, added that the infant explorer "was reported to have been ill only once[,] when Captain Lewis treated him for a high fever caused by a swollen throat and neck on May 22, 1806."

This came while the expedition was bogged down traversing the snow-clogged Lolo Trail eastward through the Bitterroot Mountains of western Montana. Possibly he had contracted the mumps or possibly he suffered from tonsillitis. In any case, his only treatment was the application of poultices of wild onions and a salve made from the resin of the long leaf pine, with beeswax and bear's oil mixed in. It took the child nearly two and a half weeks to recover . . . but recover he did.

Born not ten minutes after Meriwether Lewis gave Sacagawea rattlesnake rings crushed in water to speed up her labor, Jean Baptiste quickly became a great favorite of William Clark. He called the baby boy "Pomp" or "Pompy" for his precocious "little dancing boy" activity. Clark was so taken with the child that he offered to raise him and provide him a good education back in St. Louis once the expedition was all over. As further mark of Clark's esteem, he named an odd outcropping of sandstone on the south bank of the Yellowstone River "Pompy's Tower" (today, "Pompey's Pillar") for the little boy. Clark also scratched in his own name and the date, July 25, 1806—July 25 being his own birthday—into the sandstone formation. Carefully preserved under a glass shield today, Clark's etched name is considered the only still-existing "graffiti" left behind by the Corps of Discovery.

Just for good measure, Clark also named the nearby "Baptiests' Creek" for Sacagawea's child.

When Lewis and Clark returned to the Mandan villages in August 1806, the Charbonneau family stayed there—since Sacagawea was still nursing her baby, little Pomp could not very well go off with Clark just then. Three years later, however, he could . . . and, in effect, he would. After all, Clark had put it all down in writing: "As to your little Son (my boy Pomp) you well know my fondness for him and my anxiety to take and raise him as my own child. I once more tell you if you will bring your son Baptiest to me I will educate him and treat him as my own child—I do not forget the promis which I made to you and Shall now repeat them that you may be certain."

For that matter, Clark's generous offer included the boy's parents as well. "Charbono," Clark wrote with his usual abysmal spelling, "if you wish to live with the white people, and will come to me, I will give you a piece of land and furnish you with horses, cows, & hogs."

Touissant Charbonneau and Sacagawea briefly did try out the farmer's life in the St. Louis area, arriving in 1809, but unhappy with that choice, they returned to the north two years later. Left behind in Clark's enthusiastic care was their young boy Pomp.

Clark's descendant Adreon recited what happened next: "Clark enrolled him in a school taught by a Reverend J. E. Welch, a Baptist minister. Clark's account books for 1810–11–12 and 1820 list payments for tuition, books, lodging, firewood, ink and laundry." The boy, in the meantime, had grown to the point that his contemporaries described him as a "handsome youth, not nearly as dark as a full blooded Indian," said Adreon. "He was medium height, bright eyed and wore his hair long."

While still a teenager, he left St. Louis to take up more rustic residence at a traders village at the mouth of the Kansas River. It was there, in 1823, at the age of eighteen, that he came to the attention of the visiting Prince Paul of Wuertenburg . . . and, in a way, that was fitting, since Jean Baptiste's mother was "a Shoshone princess," whose father had been a chief and whose brother Cameahwait had been a chief. "These Indian men were leaders of their people—both died in battle protecting their people," Adreon noted.

Prince Paul obtained Clark's permission to carry Pomp across the Atlantic as a ward. "They traveled together for six years, to the capitals of Europe and many cities in France, Germany, and Northern Africa," added Adreon. "They returned in 1829 to St. Louis."

It had been a fabulous experience for the young frontiersman, who was all of twenty-four at this point, but now he faced the difficult task of deciding what to do next.

"Baptiste was classically educated, speaking four languages, but he was not trained to earn a living in the frontier village of St. Louis," noted Adreon. And so the son of Sacagawea turned northwest again, headed for "the big sky country," where, in the years ahead, he would leave "an enviable record as an interpreter and guide to many prominent leaders of the era of the opening of the west."

An explorer and trapper for the Chouteau Fur and American Fur companies at one time or another, he soon was rubbing shoulders with the likes of fellow mountain man Jim Bridger, the great Pathfinder—John C. Frémont, Kit Carson, Stephen Watts Kearny, and even his mentor Clark's son, Jefferson Kearny Clark. While many of his fellow frontiersmen were somewhat illiterate, Jean Baptiste became somewhat famous as a rough-and-ready mountain man who could recite Shakespeare by the evening campfire.

In 1846 he joined the famous Mormon Battalion as a scout for its difficult, six-month, seven-hundred-mile crossing of the Chuhuahan, Sonoran and California Deserts on a westward route from New Mexico to what is now San Diego. The battalion—at that point consisting of more than three hundred men accompanied by four women and six children—is considered the first party to cross those deserts by wagon (see pages 120–25).

At one point, Baptiste is said to have saved the day—and his own skin—in an unexpected encounter with three bears. By this account, the animals suddenly reared up to block his search for a safe mountain crossing for the party behind. Acting quickly, he managed to shoot one of the bears, killing it, and the other two warily backed off. As one result, Baptiste's companion travelers could enjoy safe passage. As another, they also could enjoy fresh bear meat.

With journey's end at San Diego, meanwhile, the Mormon Battalion had paved the way for "thousands of pioneers, treasure seekers and others who would follow the lure of California," noted the online magazine *DesertUSA*.

Baptiste stayed on in California, taking the alcade post at the San Luis Rey Mission. Troubled by the way some whites treated the Indians, he soon resigned . . . just in time to join the 1848–49 gold rush.

The next years of Baptiste's life are almost blank. Unsuccessful as a gold miner, he subsequently turned up as a clerk in the Orleans Hotel in the northern California gold town of Auburn. But that was in 1861, more than a decade since his initial response to the gold strike at Sutter's Mill. And now, five years later, came electrifying news again—gold again! This time in Montana.

And there it was once more, that same old wanderlust! He just had to go out on the trail one more time.

It was William Clark's descendant, Adreon, who provided a fitting epitaph for the son of Sacagawea and Touissant Charbonneau. "Was Baptiste Charbonneau a Canadian, an Indian, or an American by adoption?" Adreon asked in his graveside dedication speech. "Be that as it may, today he is an Oregonian, resting here forever at the end of the trail."

✮

1 8 6 7
When the Silver Ran Out
✮

Up the mountain and then down. Like so many others who settled the Old West, Eilley Orrum Bowers made the roller-coaster trip in both directions. But, ah, what heights she had reached in the interim!

Born poor in Scotland in 1826, she made her way to America, passed through two marriages to Mormons, and by the late 1850s was running boarding houses in Nevada's silver-crazed mining communities known as Johntown and Gold Hill, hard by the Washoe Valley on the eastern slopes of the High Sierra. Her first step up the dizzying slopes of success in the West came, according to some accounts, when one of her miner-lodgers, financially busted, gave her a ten-foot claim in lieu of his room rent. Other accounts say she paid for one or more small claims in the area herself. Either way, one Lemuel Sanford "Sandy" Bowers, perhaps one of her boarders also, just happened to own a ten-foot claim adjoining one of hers. Both, it soon turned out, gave access to the fabulous Comstock silver lode of Nevada.

Eilley and Sandy were married, and their combined twenty feet of plain-looking dirt and rock provided an income of fifty thousand to one hundred thousand dollars a month (accounts vary). In a short time, they became Nevada's first silver millionaires (or among that esteemed number), with Sandy boasting, "I've got money to throw at the birds." Eilley, for her part, was called "Queen of the Comstock."

Putting their boarding-house days well behind, they began construction of a grand sandstone-and-granite mansion in the Washoe Valley, on land Eilley had acquired as a result of her divorce from

Alexander Cowan, her second husband. At this point in life, Eilley was determined to create the most elegant mansion in the West, no expense spared. And that meant hiring a San Francisco architect to draw up the combined Georgian and Italianate design. It meant importing sandstone from California and stone cutters from Eilley's own dear Scotland (the granite came from the hills behind the grand home). It also meant grandiose travel to Europe, where the Queen of the Comstock reportedly sought a personal audience with Queen Victoria of England.

When that effort failed, the story goes, Eilley had to content herself with a sprig of ivy from Westminster Abbey. Returning to Nevada, she triumphantly planted the ivy and announced it was a gift from Queen Victoria herself.

More substantially, the grand new mansion benefited from the fine furnishings, paintings, statuary, and three-thousand-dollar Venetian mirrors Eilley also brought home. Among her proud acquisitions was a set of initialed silver flatware fashioned from the product of the couple's own silver diggings.

By the time the Bowers Mansion—as the grand edifice still is called—was completed in 1864, the couple and their only child, an adopted daughter named Persia, appeared to be sitting pretty at the pinnacle of yet another spectacular rags-to-riches story from the nineteenth-century American West. Unfortunately, the downward slide was about to begin.

In 1867 their silver vein ran out. In 1868 Sandy, only thirty-five, died of lung disease (silicosis). In 1870, Eilley's tightening finances forced her to sell their mine. In 1874 her twelve-year-old daughter, Persia, also died—of a ruptured appendix.

According to an Internet account furnished by the Women's Resource Center at the University of Nevada, Reno (UNR) (www .unr.edu/wrc/nwhp/biograph/bowers.htm), the youngster had been visiting at home—in the mansion—for a summer weekend, and Eilley had carried her back to boarding school in Reno. Eilley barely had returned from the round-trip journey when she received word to hurry back to Reno . . . but too late. Persia was buried next to her adoptive father on a hillside behind the Bowers Mansion. (*Note:* Years earlier, Eilley had lost two of her own children in infancy. At one time she was raising second husband Alexander Cowan's orphaned nephew Robert Henderson.)

Meanwhile, the widowed and financially strapped Scotswoman tried to turn the grand mansion into a hotel and resort. "Nighttime parties and summer picnics became a way of life for Mrs. Bowers," notes the Internet source written by Tamara Buzick. A seeming bonanza for Eilley was the fresh silver strike of 1873, called the "Big Bonanza," since it "brought new life to Virginia City and Nevada." With jobs suddenly on the increase again, money flowing again, "the people of Virginia City and the surrounding communities found the need to celebrate, and Bowers Mansion seemed the most likely place to party," notes Buzick's biographical sketch. "Afternoon picnics were commonly held during the summer months. The Miners Union, Knights of Pythias, the Pioneers, and many other organizations often sponsored large picnics. Thousands of local residents rode trains, brought their wagons and even walked to these grand affairs. Eilley always was considered the gracious hostess, but this did not help her financial situation."

Not even a third-floor addition designed to accommodate more lodgers would help. In 1876 the Bowers Mansion was sold at auction . . . Eilley had to move on. Before doing so, by some accounts, she poured lye on her ivy "from" Queen Victoria—presumably, if Eilley couldn't enjoy the ivied prospect, no one else would either.

Moving on to a sad and bitter end, Eilley became a crystal-ball-toting fortuneteller, first in Reno then in San Francisco. In her seventies and somewhat senile, she returned briefly to Reno in the summer of 1901 . . . and wound up in a county poorhouse. She kicked up such a ruckus, however, the county commissioners put her on a train to San Francisco "and bid her farewell." Somewhat less heartlessly, says Buzick, "A local lawyer was able to gather together about $30 in donations to help send her on her way."

In 1903, at the end of her down slope, the Queen of the Comstock, by now seventy-seven, died at the King's Daughters Home in Oakland, California, exactly as she had started out in life—poor.

Additional note: Eilley's grand mansion at 4005 Old Highway 395, Washoe Valley, Nevada, endured many years of neglect and ruin but came upon happier days in more recent years. Now fully restored and fleshed out with period furnishings, it is open to the public as the centerpiece of the Bowers Mansion Regional Park. Few of the Bowers couple's own furnishings are left, but one highlight is the personalized silver flatware Eilley ordered while on her shopping spree in Europe. Another is her daughter's wooden doll buggy. Meanwhile, sentimentalists may be happy to know that with the help of Henry Riter, a subsequent owner of Bowers Mansion, Eilley's ashes were returned to Nevada and buried behind the mansion next to her husband, Sandy, and daughter, Persia. Call (702) 849-1825 for visitation schedules and other information.

And the Spike Said . . .

MESSAGE FROM THE PAST: The golden spike at the time was worth an estimated $460. On its head were engraved the words, "the last spike." On the spike itself were engraved the words, "The Pacific Railway, first ground broke Jan. 1863, and completed May 10th, 1869. May God continue the unity of our country as this railroad unites the two great oceans of the world." It was one of those days, like Thomas Jefferson's first July Fourth, spent at Independence Hall in Philadelphia in 1776, when people make a note of even the temperature. And on this May 10, 1869, at Promontory Summit, Utah, the thermometer that afternoon registered 69 degrees in the shade. Reporting on the historic day's events was the *Deseret News* of May 19, 1869.

> The last tie has been laid; the last rail placed in position, and the last spike driven, which binds the Atlantic and Pacific oceans with an iron band. The electric flash [of the telegraph] has borne the tidings to the world and it now devolves upon us, the favored eye-witnesses of the momentous feat, to enter our record of the facts. The meridian hour has come and on the expansive and lofty plateau, at the summit of the Promontory, a scene is disclosed in the conception of which every exultant element of humanity is revivified. Never before has this continent disclosed anything bearing comparison with it.

The massive oaken-hued trains of the Central [Pacific] lie upon their iron path, confronted by the elegant coaches of the Union Pacific. A thousand throbbing hearts impulsively beat to the motion of the trains as the front locomotives of each Company led on majestically up to the very verge of the narrow break between the lines, where, in a few moments, was to be consummated the nuptial rites uniting the gorgeous east and the imperial west of America, with the indissoluble seal of interoceanic commerce.

Indian Captives All

However gossamer thin, there sometimes was a silver lining to the Indian captive stories repeatedly coming out of the untamed nineteenth-century West. Not exactly a happy ending, but in three such cases an ending happier than might have been expected.

The foreword to all Indian captive stories involving children was the ordeal of being ripped away from family members, usually after seeing them brutally killed. Then came a life of harsh assimilation into another culture, often accompanied by physical abuse and treatment as a slave. And finally, if and when rescue took place, there would be the difficulties of re-assimilation into white society.

Taken chronologically, consider these true sagas of Indian captivity, all involving the "gentler" but obviously *resilient* sex.

• **Cynthia Ann Parker** was about eleven years old when a large party of Comanches, Kiowas, and Kichais swooped down on her family's Fort Parker on the Navasota River in central Texas in 1836, killing several of the bastion's defenders and carrying away five captives in all. Three apparently were eventually released, but Cynthia and her six-year-old brother John stayed and, in effect, became Comanches.

Their family had moved to the Texas frontier from Crawford County, Illinois, less than two years before. . . . now, these young newcomers to the frontier were dragged off into an even more alien life than anything they had known back in the white society of Illinois.

An uncle, James Parker, risked three forays into Comanche territory in hopes of locating and rescuing his brother Silas's children, but with no positive results. Ten years after the abduction, Cynthia's name popped up in a newspaper article citing a chance encounter with the captive, by now a young woman at least twenty, by a trading group headed by Col. Leonard G. Williams. She was with a group of Comanches camped on the Canadian River. The Indians rejected Williams's offer to pay a ransom for her release. She stayed.

Sometime later, Texans learned that she was assimilated into the Comanche tribe and married to an Indian warrior named Peta Nocona. In time, they had three children, two of them sons . . . and one of *them* was destined to become a historic figure.

Meanwhile, a fully grown John Parker had fallen ill with smallpox on the Llano Estacado plateau in the Texas Panhandle and had been abandoned there by his Comanche comrades. He had with him, though, a Mexican girl he supposedly had fallen in love with during a Comanche raid across the border into Mexico, and she helped him through his crisis. He then abandoned his Indian life and returned to Mexico, where he became a stockman and rancher, according to the *Handbook of Texas Online.* He returned to Texas only for a stint of Confederate service in the Civil War. Reportedly, too, he tried in the mid-1840s to persuade Cynthia to return to white society, but she refused. (By some accounts, Zachary Taylor, hero of the Mexican War and later U.S. president, paid a ransom for the release of John Parker and fellow captive James Plummer. Apparently, too, Sam Houston secured the release of another Fort Parker captive, Mrs. Elizabeth Kellogg, with a monetary payment.)

In 1860, almost twenty-five years after the Parker children had been captured, a group of Texas Rangers raiding a Comanche camp on a tributary of the Pease River discovered that one of their "Indian" captives was a "non-English-speaking," blue-eyed white woman with a baby girl—Cynthia Ann Parker, subsequently so identified by another uncle, Col. Isaac Parker. She would go with him only on condition of being informed if her two sons were found. Her husband, a war chief among the Nocone Comanche, had been killed in the raid.

In 1861 the Texas legislature awarded her a one-hundred-dollar annual grant for a five-year period and named her uncle Isaac and another Parker family member as her guardians. None of that really mattered to the distraught woman, now separated from her sons and presumably not even sure if they were alive or dead. She tried several times to run away, back to the Comanche.

For a time she lived with a brother named Silas and for a time with a sister. She died in 1871, probably at age forty-six, and in her last years "she never saw her Indian family, the only family she really knew."

Silver lining (of sorts): Her son Quanah Parker, born about 1845 in the Wichita Mountain region of today's Oklahoma, grew up to become the last chief of the warring Quahadi Comanche, and as such, after a period as a leader of the tribe's fierce resistance to white settlement, he became a leader "in the tribe's adjustment to reservation life," notes the *Texas Handbook* Web site. His reversal from stubborn warrior to recognition that white settlement no longer could be held off led to his appointment by white officials as chief of the various Comanche bands pressed into reservation life in southwestern Oklahoma. "It was a fortuitous choice," notes the online *Handbook*, "for over the next quarter century, Quanah provided his people with forceful, yet pragmatic leadership."

• Also taken captive by raiding Indians, but in 1851 and, in this case, by Apaches (or, some say, Yavapais), was twelve-year-old **Olive Oatman,** born in Illinois and traveling west with her father, Royce; her mother; and six siblings. At the outset, the Oatmans had been part of a fifty-five-member group that left Independence, Missouri, on August 9, 1850, in twenty wagons. Their original goal was southern California, their chief pathway the Santa Fe Trail. Unfortunately, there had been disputes and differences of opinion along the way, and by February 1851 only two other families still accompanied the Oatmans through the dehabilitating Arizona desertscape, and *they* called a halt at Maricopa Wells west of Tucson. The Oatmans, pushing for Fort Yuma and the Colorado River, chose to go on alone. An unwise decision, it turned out.

"It was a ghastly journey," wrote Robert Benjamin Smith in the August 2001 issue of *Wild West* magazine. "The Oatmans had one yoke of oxen and two of cattle, and by now all the animals were dying in their traces. A contemporary newsman would later describe Arizona as 'a barren, deserted, dreary waste, useful only as a dwelling place for the coyote.' Royce Oatman could hardly have agreed more. Since leaving Tucson he had been on the edge of total breakdown, and by now only the calm assurances of his wife kept him going."

On the evening of February 18, just atop a hill on the west side of the Gila River, the Apaches, dressed in wolfskins, struck. Using short clubs, they bludgeoned to death everybody in the Oatman family but Olive, her sister **Mary Ann** . . . and a teenaged brother, Lorenzo, who appeared to be dead but wasn't. After looting the family goods, the Indians took the two girls and the family's pitiful-looking cattle back across the Gila as the start of a difficult trek across the desert terrain that didn't end until they reached a Tonto Apache village on the third day. There the two girls were greeted by the villagers with shrieks, cuffs, and spitting.

The two girls spent the next year near today's Congress, Arizona, as slaves. While the men of the tribe ate meat, the women constantly had to forage for yucca buds, wild onions, cactus root, prickly pear fruit, or other edible vegetation, wrote Smith. "It was a miserable diet for the Oatman girls, requiring terrible labor to maintain a bare subsistence, and it was made all the more bitter by the taunting behavior of the Apache."

Could life get any worse for them? Yes. After a year, they were sold to Mojave chief Espaniola near Needles, California, for two horses and three blankets. The ten-day trek to his village with little to eat on the way was bad enough, but then came a life of renewed slavery, poor diet, and finally a drought that left the Indians themselves with hardly enough food to subsist. Mary Ann died, probably of starvation. After that the Mojave went to war with the Cocopah, who lived seven hundred miles away. Olive's captors brought back a Cocopah girl as a prisoner . . . when she tried to escape and failed, they crucified her in front of Olive and riddled the victim's body with arrows.

Both Olive and Mary Ann, before her death, had been marked as Mojave slaves with tattoos of indelible blue cactus ink on their chins.

For Olive, at least, not all was lost yet . . . her brother Lorenzo, left for dead at the massacre site in 1851, had shaken off his temporary paralysis after a while, stumbled into the desert, and after two days of wanderings encountered some friendly Pima who helped him recover and return to civilization. For the next four years, he stayed in the California area and tried to interest various authorities in searching for his two captive sisters, but to no avail. Finally, an editorial in the *Los Angeles Star* stirred fresh attention to the Oatman case . . . coming forward was a Yuma who had heard of Olive's whereabouts. One thing led to another, and her release after five years of captivity was successfully negotiated.

Silver lining (of sorts): "Incoherent for several days after her release," noted Smith, then joyfully reunited with her brother, Olive soon was able to join him in telling her story to a writer whose subsequent book sold out three editions and made enough money to give both Oatman survivors a college education.

Moving to New York, and usually wearing a veil in public to hide the indelible tattoo on her face, Olive promoted the book with lectures. Freed in 1856, she married cattleman John Bryant Fairchild in 1865. They spent the next seven years in Detroit, during which time he reportedly did his best to round up and destroy all copies of the book telling her captivity story. After those seven years, they moved to Sherman, Texas, where he "made a fortune" in banking and real estate, according to the *Handbook of Texas Online*. "In 1876 Olive and John adopted a daughter," says the same source. "Though shy and retiring, Olive interested herself in the plight of orphaned children but rarely discussed her own youth as an orphan and Indian captive."

• Coming later than most Indian captive episodes was the case of the four **German** sisters seized near Fort Wallace, Texas, by Cheyenne Indians on September 11, 1874. The girls ranged in age from little **Addie**'s five years to big sister **Catherine**'s seventeen. In between were **Sophia,** twelve, and **Julia,** seven. Chief Medicine Water led the war party that killed and scalped their parents, John and Lydia German; their brother Stephen, and their two sisters, Rebecca and Joanna, on the spot, notes the *Texas Handbook* Internet site.

The German family had been trekking westward to Colorado by wagon when disaster struck just a day's journey from Fort Wallace.

After looting the wagon and setting it afire, the Cheyennes carried the four girls into the Texas Panhandle. As they traveled southward, they were "subjected to exposure, malnutrition, and occasional maltreatment," says the *Handbook* site. "Catherine, in particular, recalled instances of gang rape by young 'dog soldiers' and indignities at the hands of Cheyenne women, particularly Medicine Water's obnoxious wife, Mochi (Buffalo Calf Woman)."

After a short time, the two younger girls, Julia and Addie, were traded to a Cheyenne party led by Grey Beard, "who for the most part neglected them." Now one band, Medicine Water's, joined other Indian parties and moved down the west side of the Llano Estacado in Texas and New Mexico, and the other, Grey Beard's, headed down the east side. It was the latter band, encamped at McClellan Creek ten miles south of today's Pampa, that U.S. Army Lt. Frank D. Baldwin attacked out of the blue on the morning of November 10. Quickly routing the Cheyennes, he and his men "were astonished to find Julia and Addie German, both emaciated and near starvation." Army scout William "Billy" Dixon later would recall "how hardened scouts and soldiers turned aside to hide their emotions as the little girls sobbed out their story."

Now the army put out the word that peace with the Indians of the region would depend upon the safe return of the two older German sisters . . . and indeed they were released in March 1875 as a number of Cheyenne chiefs came in to an Indian agency to surrender. "The sisters pointed out to the officers the individuals who had murdered their family and those who had abused them, including Medicine Water and Mochi. These, along with others singled out for various crimes, were placed in irons and sent to Fort Marion, Florida, for incarceration."

Silver lining (of sorts): With Col. Nelson Miles, future army chief of staff, appointed their guardian, Congress established a ten-thousand-dollar endowment for the girls from Cheyenne annuities for their support and education. Each would receive twenty-five hundred dollars upon reaching the age of twenty-one. In the meantime, they were raised by Patrick Corney and his wife in Kansas—"all four girls eventually married and settled in Kansas, Colorado and California."

Shooting the Grand Canyon

MESSAGE FROM THE PAST: Here's a *real* cliffhanger for you. Not from some dime-store novel, but from real life in the Old, the Wild West. And can't you just picture it? A one-armed man plastered against a canyon wall, his last foothold too far below to reach . . . and no handhold above. This man is stuck. After all, a one-armed man beyond the bounds of all civilization . . . what can he possibly do? What *was* John Wesley Powell, on his way to shoot the Colorado River through the Grand Canyon, to do? For there he was, unable to go up or down.

Of course, like the hero in the dime-store novels of old, he did extricate himself from his grim predicament, but only with the help of the man above, who obligingly slipped off his trousers and lowered an empty pants leg for Powell to grab onto. Which he promptly did and, presto . . . was saved!

But what an amazing man, that Powell. Amazing at raising the funding for his post–Civil War explorations and then at his explorations of the Green and Colorado Rivers, especially of the Colorado in its wild coursing through the mile-deep Grand Canyon.

He lost that missing arm fighting for the Union in the Civil War, but that obviously didn't stop him from negotiating the great "shoot" that is the Colorado rushing through the Grand Canyon's deep, deep gouge in the earth. Just four years after the hostilities ended, John Wesley Powell and his party first rode the Green River into the Colorado, then paused to take stock and make ready for the plunge ahead. It was August 13, 1869, and just ahead lay the deepest canyon on earth.

We are now ready to start on our way down the Great Unknown. Our boats, tied to a common stake, are chafing each other, as they are tossed by the fretful river. They ride high and buoyant, for their loads are lighter than we could desire. We have but a month's rations remaining. The flour has been resifted through the mosquito-net sieve; the spoiled bacon has been dried and the worst of it boiled; the few pounds of dried apples have been spread in the sun, and reshrunken to their normal bulk; the sugar has all melted, and gone its way down the river; but we have a large sack of coffee. The lighting of the boats has this advantage; they will ride the waves better, and we shall have but little to carry when we make a portage.

We are three quarters of a mile in the depths of the earth, and the great river shrinks into insignificance, as it dashes its angry waves against the walls and cliffs, that rise to the world above; they are but puny ripples, and we but pygmies, running up and down the sands, or lost among the boulders.

We have an unknown distance yet to run; an unknown river yet to explore. What falls there are, we know not; what rocks beset the channel, we know not; what walls rise over the river, we know not. Ah, well! We may conjecture many things. The men talk as cheerfully as ever; jests are bandied about freely this morning; but to me the cheer is somber and the jests are ghastly.

With some eagerness, and some anxiety, and some misgiving, we enter the canyon below, and are carried along by the swift water through walls which rise from its very edge . . .

After a fairly routine journey of about fifteen miles on August 13, including stretches of deep, fast-moving water, rocky rapids, and at least one portage, Powell and his party camped overnight in a cave. The next day, however, they faced a foaming, racing set of rapids for a third of a mile, with no room on shore for a portage, no break in the towering walls of granite on either side.

> We step into our boats, push off and away we go, first on smooth but swift water, then we strike a glassy wave, and ride to its top, down again into the trough, up again on a higher wave, and down and up on waves higher and still higher, until we strike one just as it curls back, and a breaker rolls over our little boat. Still, on we speed, shooting past projecting rocks, till the little boat is caught in a whirlpool, and spun around several times. At last we pull out again into the stream, and now the other boats have passed us. The open compartment of the "Emma Dean" is filled with water, and every breaker rolls over us. Hurled back from a rock, now on this side, now on that, we are carried into an eddy, in which we struggle for a few minutes, and are then out again, the breakers still rolling over us. Our boat is unmanageable, but she cannot sink, and we drift another hundred yards, through breakers; how, we scarcely know. We find the other boats have turned into an eddy at the foot of the fall, and are waiting to catch us as we come, for the men have seen that our boat is swamped. They push out as we come near, and pull us in against the wall. We bail our boat, and on we go again.

Best Stagecoach Driver?

Mirror, mirror on the wall, who was the most legendary stagecoach driver of them all? Interesting question for any Wild West history buff . . . who might be tempted to name onetime stagecoach drivers **Wyatt Earp, James Butler "Wild Bill" Hickok,** or even **William "Buffalo Bill" Cody.**

Tempted but in the end to pass them up because each achieved his truly legendary status for reasons unrelated to his brief stint as a stagecoach driver.

So that decision leaves . . . well, let's see. How about **Donald R. "Cannonball" Green** of Kiowa County, Kansas, fame? Here was a man who not only drove stagecoaches, he owned and operated his own "Cannonball Stageline." Also going by the title "Colonel," he was known as a flamboyant presence who delighted in twirling his diamond-studded watch chain, who liked to boast that "Father Time" himself could not keep up with his "Cannonball."

Green helped to organize the town of Greensburg, Kansas . . . named after himself of course. And so taken with the town was the *Kiowa County Signal* that it was moved on June 1, 1888, to say, "Greensburg is the liveliest town in the state today, for money, marbles or watermelons." Meanwhile, Cannonball Green in 1889 was elected the county's first member of the Kansas State Legislature.

He ruffled a few feathers when he ejected teetotalling crusader Carrie Nation from his stagecoach after she snatched a cigar from his mouth and threw it away, but he still is fondly remembered today by his namesake town. "His fine stage coaches and speeding broncos blazed trails which railroads and highways later followed," notes the town's Internet Web site (http://skyways.lib.ks.us/towns/Greensburg/history.html).

For all that, though, Cannonball surely is not as well known—as legendary—as two more figures who held the reins for teams of horses dashing hell-for-leather along the hot, dusty, and rocky roads of the Old West—the famous **"One-eyed Charlie" Parkhurst** of California and **Henry "Hank" Monk** of California and Nevada.

To review Charlie's claim first, here was a true professional who drove stagecoaches for nearly twenty years, from the early 1850s to the late 1860s, largely in the area of Santa Cruz. Small in size, Charlie drank a bit, cussed a bit, chewed tobacco, and smoked cigars with the best of them. Successfully held up once, Charlie was ready for the next bandit that came along—this outlaw had to settle for a shotgun load in the chest. (Another version has it that Charlie shot a bandit known as "Sugarfoot" with a six-shooter.)

Called "one-eyed" due to a patch covering one eye, Charlie apparently was born in New Hampshire—in 1812, according to Richard Beal's book *Highway 17: The Road to Santa Cruz.* Various accounts say that Charlie was orphaned at an early age and ran away to Rhode Island from a relative's home or an orphanage while still very young. First becoming a stable boy then a driver, Charlie drifted westward to

California about 1850 or 1851. According to Mark McLaughlin's book *Sierra Stories,* Charlie adopted the eye patch after being kicked by a horse. In another injurious situation reported by McLaughlin (not only a raconteur of historical western stories but a weather historian as well), Charlie's lead horses one day stepped off the road while on a steep downgrade. The wavering coach then struck rocks along the roadside with a jolt that tossed Charlie—reins still in hand—onto the ground. Face-down, Charlie was dragged a short distance but "soon managed to steer the frightened horses back onto the road."

Since they did make heavy use of a whip, drivers such as Charlie often were called whips . . . and Charlie was expert enough with the lash to snap open an envelope with it "or cut a cigar out of a man's mouth," added McLaughlin. Charlie was known also to imbibe quite a bit, actually. He never drove the day after payday, it seems, due to a night spent drinking and gambling. Only 175 pounds in weight, Charlie nonetheless weathered an occasional fistfight.

After two decades of hauling mail, passengers, and their baggage— and no doubt a bit of freshly mined gold—Charlie had to give in to crippling rheumatism of the hands. That meant leaving the coaches to operate a stage station and saloon between Santa Cruz and Watsonville, California.

On November 3, 1868, with Ulysses S. Grant running for president, Charlie took time to vote . . . a unique and historic vote as events would turn out.

Charlie late in life indulged in cattle ranching and raised chickens at Aptos, California. But advancing age and cancer were catching up as Charlie eventually retreated to a small cabin near Watsonville.

Charlie died there on December 29, 1879, of cancer of the tongue, and only then was it discovered that "Charlie" had been a woman! Or, as stated in an obituary appearing in the *Sacramento Daily Bee,* "It was discovered when friendly hands were preparing him for his final rest that Charley Parkhurst was unmistakably a well-developed woman." Not only that, according to the Wells Fargo Internet site (http://www.wells-fargo.com/about/stories/charlie.jhtml), an examining physician reported evidence that *she* at some point in her life had been a mother.

Then, too, that vote back in 1868 may have rendered "Charlie" the first woman to vote in an American presidential election, since women's suffrage wasn't provided by the Nineteenth Amendment for another fifty-two years.

Before moving on to Hank Monk, meanwhile, another pair of notable drivers were **Billy Blackmore** and **"Baldy" Green,** both recalled by McLaughlin in his *Sierra Stories.* Ranking "as aristocracy on the Nevada frontier," McLaughlin wrote, stagecoach drivers were a colorful lot. "Most wore handsome gloves of the softest leather, finely stitched gray frock coats and fancy jewelry. Some drivers never spoke, others talked a little just to be sociable, while a few repeatedly told jokes just to see some Easterner bite. All had pride in their occupation and treated their horses like family."

A "crack whip" was Billy Blackmore, famous for ruining lodging-place beds in his sleep. Also noted for his attention to passenger comfort, Billy suffered nightmares about his careening, mountain-road stagecoach runs, it seems. Dreaming that his coach was thundering down a steep slope, perhaps barely in control, he was wont to mumble orders for his horses to stop—"Whoa, there! Whoa!" Naturally, he also stamped on the brakes . . . that is, the footboard of his bed. "Billy was a terror to landlords, who were forced to build special beds that he could not kick down."

As for Baldy Green, the story there was one of bad luck—he forever was being robbed on his runs. "His stage was held up so often that Wells Fargo concluded he either was in with the gangs or just plain cursed." Fed up with Baldy, Wells Fargo transferred him to a run "far out in the Nevada desert." He was so unhappy with that arrangement, he quit and took to hauling freight.

The real star of the Sierra drivers, however, was Hank Monk, described by McLaughlin as "most famous of all the men who ever handled the reins of a coach."

Indeed, so many are the Hank Monk stories to be found in various accounts that it is, as McLaughlin noted, difficult to distinguish the facts from the fictional. The truth is that he remained on his bouncing driver's seat for more than twenty years, despite his hard drinking and the wear and tear of a highly stressful job. "His record of transporting gold bullion without a loss was unsurpassed, as were the speed records he set racing between popular destinations. During one winter snowstorm, drifts covered the road, and Monk's stage was running late. In order to keep to his scheduled time, he drove for forty-eight consecutive hours."

Like so many legendary figures of the Old West, Henry Monk began life as an easterner . . . in Waddington, New York, March 24,

1826. By the early 1850s, now in his late twenties, he was driving the Sacramento-to-Auburn run for the California Stage Company, a power-house stageline then operating along twenty-seven hundred miles of road in California and Oregon. Once silver mining began in western Nevada, the Pioneer Stage Company opened a run between Placerville, California, and Virginia City, Nevada—"over a hastily cut road south of Lake Tahoe." Soon joining the Pioneer line, Hank Monk took over the route from Placerville to Genoa, Nevada. Surmounting the high Sierra, this was "one of the toughest rides in all the west," wrote McLaughlin. "Drivers on this rugged trans-Sierra crossing encountered washed-out bridges, ferocious blizzards, lashing rain and stage robbers."

Dressed to the nines—canary-yellow gloves, gray frock coat, wide-brimmed felt hat—and carrying a silver-handled whip, the trans-planted New Yorker quickly built a reputation as a skilled and daring driver. Amazingly, he continued to build upon that record even though he sometimes couldn't stagger out of the nearest saloon on his own . . . even though he sometimes was carried to his waiting stagecoach by willing helpers.

Despite such sorry risk to self and others, he was picked to be lead driver in a caravan transporting a visiting President Rutherford B. Hayes from Carson City, Nevada, to Spooner Summit, overlooking Lake Tahoe, in 1880. Hayes wanted to visit the Comstock mines en route to California, at that time the longest trip ever undertaken by an occupant of the White House. "The first coach carried President Hayes, General [William Tecumseh] Sherman, Secretary of War Alexander Ramsey, and Nevada Governor John H. Kinkead," McLaughlin wrote. "Sitting in the driver's seat holding the reins was Hank Monk, who had sobered up for the occasion. For once, Hank took it easy."

The happy result was a safe trip with no injury or mayhem perpetu-ated upon the presidential party.

The fact is, Hank Monk didn't need a safely delivered president to assure his own legendary niche in the lore of the West. He long before, in July 1859, had catapulted himself into the public eye with a famous, probably record-breaking journey on the roller-coaster run to Plac-erville with a lone passenger bouncing around inside the coach. He was Horace Greeley, well-known New York editor and a future presidential candidate (in 1872). Told that Greeley had to be in Placerville by 5 P.M., Monk needed no further urging. With a pledge to "get you there," he sent his team of horses bolting down a slope strewn with boulders. "They made the first twelve miles in fifty-three minutes. Greeley choked on the dust and tried to hold on. At Yarnold's [Toll House], Monk quickly changed the team of horses and off they charged. They hurtled around blind corners and along narrow mountain trails. The terror-stricken celebrity tapped Monk on the back. 'Driver,' he shouted into the wind, 'I'm not particular for an hour or two!' Greeley was a famous and imposing man, but Monk was unimpressed. He yelled, 'Horace. Keep your seat! I told you I would get you there by five o'clock, and by God I'll do it, if the axles hold!'"

They did, and he did. A relieved Greeley afterward bought Hank a brand-new suit. Meanwhile, stories about Greeley's breathtaking ride soon spread around the nation—Congress itself was treated in 1866 to a version ridiculing Greeley, who later lost his bid for president. Meanwhile, his onetime stagecoach driver managed to reach retirement age without major accident or injury, enjoying a number of years as a legend in his own time . . . and well beyond his death in Carson City from pneumonia in 1883.

☆ ☆ ☆

Additional note: Considering the all-but-sacrosanct schedules they strived to meet and the rough terrain traveled, it's a wonder the stagecoach drivers of the West didn't meet with lethal accidents on a regular basis. Less serious accidents, however, were commonplace. And no wonder. As McLaughlin noted, speed was a key to success as a stageline . . . and a matter of pride to the drivers. Even their passengers got into the act, often betting "to see which driver could make the best time." Thus "rival stages bounced down the narrow mountain roads, flirting with the steep cliffs." Curves were negotiated "at breakneck speed" (except when covered with ice). Hardier passengers enjoyed the thrills.

Fortunately for one and all, the coaches themselves were stoutly built. "The wheels and axles usually held together despite slamming into blocks of stone or lurching in and out of deep chuck-holes." The most widely favored of the western stagecoaches, incidentally, was the famous Concord coach, named for its very eastern birthplace, Concord, New Hampshire.

No matter how stoutly built was the coach, its human cargo was apt to bounce around inside with every bump encountered outside, sometimes so violently as to land on the floor. On the other hand, McLaughlin noted, "The ride for those clinging to the roof was the most exciting of all, and the most dangerous."

Once in a while, there indeed was a really bad accident. As also recalled in his *Sierra Stories,* a packed stagecoach jumped a cliff-side road on July 22, 1863, with nine passengers crowded inside and six hanging on for dear life outside. As some leaped for safety, the coach plunged into the Truckee River. The outcome was one man killed and various degrees of injury to most of the remaining passengers. One survivor, A. C. Wightman, was snatched up by the raging river waters, stripped of all his clothing, and whisked a hundred yards downstream before rescuers could come to his aid. In another case cited by McLaughlin, a stagecoach driver and all six of his horses were killed "when a stage flipped over and rolled 300 feet down a steep mountainside." All the passengers involved in that mishap somehow survived. Just one more miracle among the many encountered by those taking the risk of stagecoach travel across the mountains and deserts of the Old West.

Fond Farewell to Buffalo Soldiers

MESSAGE FROM THE PAST: In March 1869 Capt. (Bvt. Brig. Gen.) W. H. Penrose addressed a farewell letter to the black "Buffalo Soldiers" of the Tenth U.S. Cavalry Regiment and their white officers upon his relinquishing command of a column that took part in Gen. Philip H. Sheridan's winter campaign of 1868–69 against the Cheyenne and Arapaho. Penrose, also white, had led one of three columns driving the Indians toward a central column led by George Armstrong Custer, who then utterly destroyed Cheyenne Chief Black Kettle's encampment on the Wichita River in late November. Penrose and the men of the Tenth did not themselves grapple with the Indian foe, but one of the three lesser columns crushed a band of Comanches on the north fork of the Red River. Penrose and his men did contend with harsh terrain and wintry weather that killed as many as forty of their horses on one day and twenty-five on another. The farewell by Penrose after a tough task well done was a markedly fond one.

> You started from this post [Fort Lyon, Colorado Territory] on an important mission under many disadvantages. Your horses were in poor condition, and you were to march, without forage, to penetrate a raw and before unknown country. Hardly had you started when you encountered severe storms of rain and snow, accompanied by intense cold; you were without suitable and necessary shelter for such inclement weather; your horses perished day by day, you yourselves suffering from intense cold, many with frostbitten hands and feet; but through these hardships and difficulties you pushed nobly on, undaunted, undismayed, anxious to meet the enemy.
>
> But few commands have ever been called on to endure more than you have, and none have more cheerfully performed their duty.
>
> Although it was not your fortune to meet and engage the enemy, yet this movement was a part of a grand plan, emanating from that great soldier, Major-General Sheridan.
>
> You were instrumental in compelling a large force of the enemy to make a retrograde movement, and there appears to be no doubt that this was the identical force which Bvt. Major General Custer was thus enabled to encounter and destroy. Your efforts were therefore of material service in the winter campaign.
>
> Had you had the opportunity I am fully assured you would have maintained in battle the honor of the flag and your regiment.
>
> To the officers and men who so nobly stood with me in our most difficult task I extend my kindest, heartfelt thanks, and wherever you go my kindly interest shall be with you in all your undertakings. May success crown all your efforts.

By virtually all accounts, success *did* crown the efforts of both the Ninth and Tenth Cavalry Regiments in the West and Southwest. The black men and white officers of the two Buffalo Soldier regiments not only engaged the Indian enemy on many occasions, they also built forts, Oklahoma's Fort Sill among them; they carved out roads in the Southwest, explored uncharted terrain, located water sources, served as an emergency police force, and performed many other yeomen duties of benefit to the settlers of the West.

"For twenty-four years," wrote William H. Leckie in his book *The Buffalo Soldiers,* "these regiments campaigned on the Great Plains, along the Rio Grande, in New Mexico, Arizona, Colorado, and finally in the Dakotas. Their antagonists were the enemies of peace, order and settlement: warring Indians, bandits, cattle thieves, murderous gunmen, bootleggers, trespassers, and Mexican revolutionaries. All these they met many times, and with success, regardless of extremes of climate and terrain that ranged from the broken, rugged, and torrid Big Bend of Texas to the rolling plains, badlands and sub-freezing temperatures of South Dakota."

Their toil at building frontier forts, Leckie also pointed out, often meant they had laid the foundation for future cities, such as Fort Sill's neighboring Lawton, Oklahoma. Then, too: "Many a frontier official owed his life and his job to the support given him by these black men in blue, and many more farmers and ranchers slept soundly in their beds because a thin line of Negro troopers guarded them from harm."

Not every battle for the Buffalo Soldiers was an unalloyed success—prejudice and discrimination were tough enemies to beat. Typically, when the newly formed Tenth Cavalry first took shape at Fort Leavenworth, Kansas, the post commander forbade their appearance on the parade ground in company with all-white units. The Tenth's first commander, Benjamin H. Grierson, objected so strongly, he risked a court-martial . . . but won the day, according to Bruce J. Dinges in the book *Soldiers West.* At other times, the Buffalo Soldiers had to deal with local toughs in the frontier towns springing up alongside the very frontier posts manned by the protective "thin line" of black troopers.

For all their success in so many of their assignments, they didn't rate a great deal of public recognition until the latter half of the twentieth century. As Leckie wrote in 1967, "Three-quarters of a century have passed since the work of these regiments on the frontier came to a close, and their contributions still go largely unknown and unheralded." He went on to say that the Ninth and Tenth Cavalry were first-rate regiments by any standards one wishes to apply and "major spearheads in the settlement of the West."

★ Part 5 ★
Cowboys & Indians, Lawmen & Outlaws

Town Marshal for Five Months

"Died a martyr to duty," says the dusty tombstone in Abilene, Kansas. "[A] fearless hero of frontier days, who in cowboy chaos established the supremacy of law." And no, he wasn't Wyatt Earp or some other hard-bitten figure of Hollywood legend. He was plain old Tom Smith—Thomas James Smith—a New York boy who traveled west.

No tenderfoot, he was, in fact, a hardbitten type—an ex-cop from the big city. And he was a marshal, but in his case, a town marshal rather than a deputy U.S. marshal like Earp. And he did face down rebellious gun-toting lawbreakers . . . but normally with a heavy fist, rather than a six-shooter.

He had just been sworn in as town marshal of Abilene on a Saturday evening in May 1870, when minutes later he faced his first challenger, a loudmouthed cowboy named "Big Hank." Dark had settled in when the newly hired lawman found the drunken, gun-toting "Big Hank" barring his way down a main street of Abilene.

"You the new man who thinks he can run the town?" demanded the pugnacious cowboy.

Smith politely allowed that he was, although he did state his job description a bit more precisely. "I intend to maintain order and enforce the law," he said.

As both men knew, Abilene had a new gun ordinance in effect—no firearms to be carried inside the town limits. The hope of the town's elders was to bring a little peace and quiet to their community, which had grown wild and woolly ever since Texas ranchers began sending their beef cattle to Abilene in 1867 to meet the new Kansas Pacific Railroad line running through town.

"What are you going to do about the gun ordinance?" said Big Hank with obvious disdain.

"I'm going to see that it's obeyed," replied Smith. "I must trouble you to hand me yours."

"Like hell," growled Big Hank, not merely unwilling to part with his piece of iron but challenging Smith to do something about it. That of course had been the cowboy's objective all along—to test the latest lawman in Abilene, especially in the downtown "Lone Star District" near Mud Creek, where Texas cowboys fresh from a cattle drive tended to congregate and whoop things up with dangerous vengeance.

"Fighting, murders, drinking and gambling were daily features of the area named for the home of many of its visitors," wrote Sandy Wilson in the February 1995 issue of *Wild West* magazine. Among the one- to three-story buildings lining the streets, he noted, "The cowboys' wishes were the district's commands: it included saloons, hotels, boarding houses, outfitters such as H. H. Hazlett's and the inevitable two dozen or so sporting houses."

Tom Smith knew all this when he arrived in town early that last Saturday of May 1870. He had applied for the newly created job of town marshal earlier in the year, but Mayor Theodore Henry had turned him down because the New Yorker appeared too "soft-spoken and mild-mannered." What the mayor overlooked was the fact that Smith had spent several years as a New York police officer, no job for a shrinking violet. More to the point, Thomas James Smith had experienced the decidedly rough and violent life of the "Hell-on-Wheels" towns that sprang up in the pathway of the Union Pacific Railroad as it pushed westward in the late 1860s. He had survived the wild ways of one such rail town after another as its town marshal. (Most of those towns disappeared as quickly as the construction crews laid track beyond the next horizon, but one that remains on the western maps of today is Cheyenne, Wyoming.)

Now that the transcontinental railroad to Promontory Point was completed, Smith was back in Abilene and looking for a job. By then, Henry and the council were a bit more desperate. Henry still warned Smith that he would be wise to look the town over before signing the dotted line. The transplanted New Yorker did just that, then returned to the mayor's office at twilight. "I believe I can handle the town," he said.

Just how would he go about his potentially thankless task? "All the guns in town must go," answered Smith. "Whiskey and pistols are a combination beyond control. Might as well contend with a frenzied maniac as an armed and drunken cowboy."

This time impressed by Smith's quiet assurance, Henry asked him when he would like to begin. "At once," was the laconic reply.

Seconds later, Smith had been sworn in by the mayor, and minutes later he was walking back into the center of town.

He hadn't gone a mile before he encountered "Big Hank," long a bully of the weak-kneed, even of lawmen such as a town marshal. According to Wilson, rumor already was out that Abilene might have found itself a new law enforcement officer. "Hank had always bragged that no man would disarm him, and so far he had been right."

Stopping the new lawman and haranguing him, however, proved to be the cowboy's second mistake of the day. The first was spending the day in the saloons. Still another was misjudging his "soft-spoken, mild-mannered" adversary.

Once again refusing to hand over his pistol, then calling the new marshal unpleasant names, didn't help Big Hank's self-appointed cause either. Quick as a flash, Smith let fly with his fists. Twice. The second and final blow caught the slow-thinking bully on the side of the head. Down he went. For Smith it was a simple matter to pluck the man's six-shooter from its holster and order the chagrined owner out of town.

Word of the new marshal's feat quickly spread through Abilene—as welcome news for the community's law-abiding citizens and, on the other hand, as a sobering note for the ever-restless denizens of the turbulent Lone Star District. Noted Wilson: "Questions flashed through the saloons and camps. Could it be that law and some order had come to Abilene? Or would Smith be unable to repeat the episode?"

Inevitably, he would be tested again, this time by a drover named "Wyoming Frank," who appeared in town the very next day, sloshed down some whiskey, then went out and accosted the new marshal on the street. The badgering this time did not end until the two men had moved into a saloon, at which point the patient Smith struck. When Wyoming Frank did not fold quite so quickly as Big Hank, Smith used the butt end of his own gun on the drover's thick head.

With his latest challenger laid out on the floor, Smith helped himself to his weapon. Yanking Frank to his feet, Smith gave him five minutes to get out of town and warned, "Don't ever let me set eyes on you again."

The effect upon the onlooking crowd was electric. The bartender immediately told Smith that Frank was a coward who got what he deserved. Holding out his own weapon, the bartender said: "Here's my gun. Reckon I'll not need it so long as you are marshal." Seeing that the saloon patrons were unholstering their guns, Smith announced they could stash the weapons with the bartender until they left town.

Now Abilene really had something to talk about. A marshal who meant business—who could do business, a lawman's business. "The vast majority of cowhands were treading more carefully in the saloons and gaming halls," wrote Wilson. "Guns were rarely worn openly, and the wild, unbridled attitude of the past was curtailed considerably."

Even so, there were criminal elements in Abilene—real criminals, not hotheaded cowboys. These were "professionals" who preyed on the visiting cowboys—stole their money, cheated them, robbed them, even murdered them. They may have instigated an ambush that almost cost Smith his life that summer.

Called to investigate a problem in a home one night, Smith cautiously entered the house . . . only to see the lights suddenly wink out, followed by the roar of guns, and a fusillade of bullets strike the wall behind him. Luckily, he had had the presence of mind to drop to the floor as the lights went out. In seconds, the barrage ended, his assailants were gone . . . and Smith was unhurt. He vowed vengeance upon those responsible for the ambush, but he never did find out who they were. He really wasn't given the time.

Just weeks later, in early November 1870, while making an arrest of a murder suspect outside of town, Marshal Thomas Smith was shot in the chest by the suspect, Andrew McConnell, and then nearly beheaded by an axe-wielding companion, Moses Miles. A posse from the aroused town tracked the murderers down and brought them back to stand trial. Easily convicted, they served only fourteen years in prison for their crime.

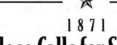

1 8 7 1
Close Calls for Sherman

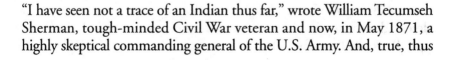

"I have seen not a trace of an Indian thus far," wrote William Tecumseh Sherman, tough-minded Civil War veteran and now, in May 1871, a highly skeptical commanding general of the U.S. Army. And, true, thus far on his inspection tour of the West Texas frontier, no marauding Indians had presented themselves. Surely, all those complaints by the region's settlers were exaggerated. Surely, too, any occasional Indian foray merely was to steal a few horses, Sherman also said.

Setting out for Fort Richardson in northwest Texas from the frontier outpost of Fort Griffin the morning of May 17, the nation's highest-ranking general and a small escort of seventeen black troopers and three officers entered a nine-mile stretch of largely open ground about midday. They had left the Brazos River behind and now were following the Butterfield Overland Mail route through Salt Creek Prairie, and again, not a trace did Sherman or any member of his party see of a hostile Indian. Members of the party laughed, allegedly, when one of the mounted infantrymen yelled, "I see an Indian!"

Arriving at Fort Richardson without incident that evening, Sherman wrote: "The road is across rather rough country and water is very scarce. Of course we saw no Indians."

Fact is, *they* had seen *him.*

More than one hundred hostile warriors were watching from a nearby height exactly as Sherman and his mounted escort followed the stage road through the flat bottom of the Salt Creek Valley below and moved on toward the eastern horizon . . . unmolested.

Led by four determined Kiowas, the mixed force of Kiowa, Arapahoe, Comanche, Cheyenne, and allies eyeing the Sherman party consisted of Plains Indians fed up with confinement to their Fort Sill reservation across the Texas border. Resenting the thin rations they and their people were granted there, they also hated the never-ending stream of settlers taking over their old hunting grounds. They were outraged also by the white man's steady extermination of their buffalo herds, for many generations a major source of food and clothing.

Three of the four were Kiowa chiefs already known to the white soldiers, but not the fourth. Sometimes understood to be the real power behind the more visible Kiowa leadership, the fourth man was Maman-ti ("Sky Walker"). He was a chief, yes, but he also was a medicine man who based his "magic" on communication with a screech owl somehow carrying the spirit of a deceased relative. Maman-ti wore a cured owl skin on his hand and manipulated it like a hand puppet—the owl skin, he told his followers, was the medium by which he received spiritual messages. Although Sherman didn't know it, he could thank such an ephemeral "message" to Maman-ti for holding back the restless warriors as the general's entourage passed right below their noses.

The next group to appear below the watching Indians, however, would owe no such thanks to the war party. Unfortunately for freighting contractor Henry H. Warren's muleskinners carrying corn westward to Fort Griffin, Maman-ti's "medicine" had dictated that the war party should attack the second party to cross the valley below, not the first. Accordingly, when the Warren wagon train appeared on the dusty Salt Creek Valley trail the next day, the Indians attacked.

Leading the warriors, in addition to Maman-ti, were the seventy-year-old Kiowa chief Satank ("Sitting Bear"), lusting for revenge since his oldest son had been killed in another Texas raid the year before; the famous fifty-year-old Kiowa warrior Satanta ("White Bear"); and the far younger twenty-two-year-old Addo-etta ("Big Tree"), known for his reckless bravery.

The twelve teamsters manning Warren's mule train were "all armed against the possibility of attack," noted Allen Lee Hamilton in *Wild West* magazine (May 1990). "But 12 stood little chance against 100."

Summed up the same historian for the *Handbook of Texas Online:* "They killed the wagon master and six teamsters and allowed five to escape. The Indians suffered one dead and five wounded. They immediately returned to the reservation."

If they were pleased with themselves, however, they—and thousands more of the Plains tribes—were about to rue the day of the murderous attack on Henry Warren's mule train.

First, though, Sherman would be disabused of his skeptical reaction to talk of Indian raids on the Texas frontier . . . and rudely so at that. He and Maj. Randolph Barnes Marcy, inspector general of the army (and George B. McClellan's father-in-law) were still at Fort Richardson the night of May 18 when a pitiful wreck of a man presented himself at the fort gates. The post commander, Col. Ranald Slidell Mackenzie, earlier in the day had confirmed settler reports of Indian depredations. Then, too, a delegation from nearby Jacksboro "presented notarized affidavits and testimonies listing a total of 129 murders committed in their country in the previous six years," wrote Hamilton. "The general listened thoughtfully to the citizens' reports but remained skeptical."

Now came a rude awakening. Minutes after midnight, the pitiful-looking survivor from the mule train attack staggered up to the fort entrance. "Thomas Brazeal, one of the surviving teamsters, stumbled, drenched and bleeding, into the fort after walking 20 miles in the rain and darkness on a badly injured foot."

As he explained, he and four others had escaped the Indian war party by fleeing from the wagons into scrub woods near Cox Mountain. Mackenzie and his men rode to the massacre scene the next day and found the mutilated bodies of the seven victims.

Sherman, of course, was furious and—realizing he and his party could have been the victims instead—shocked.

He moved on to Fort Sill, no longer so skeptical and in fact determined to take action then and there, since most of the recent Indian raids apparently were carried out by Indians from the reservation itself.

At Fort Sill, Indian agent Lawrie Tatum, a Quaker in place as part of the Grant administration's "Quaker Peace Policy," knew Satank and Satanta had been absent from the reservation—"he promised Sherman he would question the chiefs when they came in for their rations." When they did, four days later, on May 27, Satanta boldly admitted his role and boasted, "If any other Indian claims the honor of leading that party, he will be lying to you. I led it myself." As one "justification" for his actions, he cited rumors that a railroad was to be built across the Indian territory. He also said he needed to teach his warriors how to fight.

When he then named Satank and Addo-etta as fellow participants, the elderly Satank hissed in Kiowa to shut his mouth . . . but too late, the story was out.

Just days later, the three chiefs were "invited" to a council with a great warrior chief from Washington, with Sherman himself. The boastful Satanta arrived first, ushered to a seat on the front porch of Fort Sill commander Benjamin Grierson's private quarters. Greeting him there were Sherman, Marcy, Grierson, and two aides. With little prodding, Satanta repeated his account of the Warren wagon train raid.

Sherman's reaction of course was predictable: pure, cold fury.

To the Indian chief's apparent surprise, Sherman denounced the raid as cowardly—"and told the chief that if his braves wanted a fight, then he and the Army would be happy to oblige them."

At this, "Satanta realized that not all was well. He started to rise but one of Grierson's aides stuck a cocked pistol in his face and forced him to sit back down."

Events now developed at near-lightning speed. The elderly Satank appeared, accompanied by ten or so Kiowas . . . but several additional army officers joined them on the now-crowded front porch. Meanwhile, the young chief Addo-etta was dragged, "dusty and bleeding," into view by additional soldiers. He had been discovered in the reservation's trader's store. "He tried to escape by leaping through a window but was ridden down and captured."

Sherman then stated the obvious—they were under arrest for the murder of the seven victims of their raid on Henry Warren's wagon train. They would be taken to Texas to stand trial. Hamilton summed up the tumult that followed:

> The scene instantly became turmoil. Satanta stood and threw back his blanket, exposing a revolver in his belt, shouting that he would rather die than be taken as a prisoner to Texas. Others drew pistols and knives. Sherman snapped a command, the porch window shutters flew open, and a squad of troopers leveled their carbines on the Indians. A column of dismounted cavalry double-timed around the corner of Grierson's house and formed in two ranks facing the porch. The front rank knelt and both brought their weapons to the ready. Then a bugle sounded and the gates of the stables were thrown open—out galloped two troops of mounted soldiers. They encircled Grierson's house, cutting off any possibility of escape.

But that wasn't the end of it—Sherman was about to experience his second brush with death on the West Texas frontier.

First a Kiowa called Tene-angopte ("Kicking Bird"), long known as a peace advocate, stood up and told Sherman, "You and I are going to die right here."

As if to prove the case, the fierce Kiowa chief Giapago ("Lone Wolf") suddenly "galloped" up to the porch.

Parting his way through the startled soldiers, he elaborately dismounted, laid his two carbines and bow and quiver on the ground, then picked them all up again and "strode" to the porch, unimpeded. He gave one carbine to another Indian and the bow and arrows to a fellow chief seated among the Kiowas, one Setimkia ("Stumbling Bear").

Giapago then sat down in front of Sherman and, "gazing intently at him, very deliberately cocked his carbine."

Setimkia in the meantime had strung the bow and taken an arrow out of the quiver.

He now stood and shouted at his fellow Indians: "You are acting like women. I don't know what it will be like after death, but [I] am going to find out. I only want to kill the big soldier chief."

He then aimed his bow and arrow at Sherman while Giapago did the same with his carbine.

Finally, one of the officers reacted. Grierson bowled into Giapago, "knocked the weapon aside, and wrestled him to the porch."

As Satanta then reached for his revolver, the onlooking soldiers raised their guns, obviously ready to fire.

For tense seconds, it was a standoff.

But Satanta finally cried, "No! No! No!" and the Kiowas backed down. The three chiefs associated with the raid were jailed, pending trial back in Texas. Sherman decreed the others should be free to go, so long as they returned the mules stolen in the raid.

Days later, on June 8, Ranald Mackenzie was ready to take the prisoners to an awaiting Texas courtroom. They would be the first Indian chiefs to be tried for murder in the white man's civil courts.

But not the elderly Satank, who could not stand the thought of "being dragged back to Texas in chains." He was, after all, an honored warrior, a member of the elite *Koietsenko,* a society open only to the ten greatest warriors of the tribe, "each pledged to death before dishonor."

Singing the society's death song as the prisoner train moved out from Fort Sill, he kept his hands busy beneath his blanket . . . busy stripping the flesh off his wrists in order to discard his handcuffs. Then, goes the Hamilton account, with a war whoop, he threw off his blanket and attacked his guards with a knife he had managed to conceal, stabbing one in the leg and slashing at the other."

He was shot down immediately. The Tonkawa Indian scouts with Mackenzie's column scalped the Kiowa warrior-chief on the spot, and his body was left lying by the side of the road.

In Jacksboro, Texas, soon after, the two younger chiefs, Satanta and Addo-etta, were convicted of murder and sentenced to death by hanging. Supporters of the Grant administration's Quaker Peace Policy in dealing with Native Americans then created such a stir that Grant ordered Texas governor Edmund Davis to commute the death sentence to life imprisonment. That done, the two chiefs eventually—in less than two years' time—were paroled on promise to stay on their reservation.

Sherman was so angry he wrote to Governor Davis and said that if the two chiefs were to take scalps in revenge for their treatment, "yours is the first that should be taken."

More important, Sherman's army prepared for an offensive campaign against Indian marauders in place of the more defensive peace policy. And when Indian raids along the Texas frontier resumed in the summer of 1874, the army launched a retaliatory campaign by three thousand or more troops—the Red River War—that drove the Indians back into their reservation lands. Satanta was rearrested and returned to prison, where he took his own life by leaping from a window. The younger Addo-etta, on the other hand, released after the Red River War, became a peaceful farmer, a Sunday school teacher, and a church deacon.

Sherman long before had returned to Washington after his inspection tour of West Texas, just in time to turn down requests that he run for president. Appearing before a congressional committee, meanwhile, he laconically described the tense standoff with the Kiowa chiefs as "an angry council on Colonel Grierson's porch, at Fort Sill, which came near to resulting in a hand to hand fight."

★

1 8 7 2
Mercy in an Apache Fight

★

Kill or be killed was the endlessly repeated story in the Southwest as the white man fought the Apache, and the Apache the white man, with women and children often killed along with the men . . . except for the otherwise ugly day in 1872 when a four-year-old boy was spared, pulled to safety by one of his people's purported enemies.

It all took place among rocks and stone walls, with huge boulders pressed into the fight. The U.S. Army's Capt. John G. Bourke later described the scene he and his soldiers found after tracking a band of Apaches to their lair in a cliff side on the Salt River in Arizona one cold December night. "There was no moon," Bourke wrote, "but the glint of stars gave enough light to show that we were in a country filled with huge rocks and adapted most admirably for defense."

In the dark, his detachment, probably mounted infantrymen, had come across fifteen Pima ponies in a "grassy glade," their flanks rough with "hardly crusted" sweat, their hooves banged up by rocks, and their knees full of cholla cactus thorns. The soldiers could only conclude the ponies "must have been driven up the mountain by Apache raiders that very night."

Clearly, the raiders themselves must be close by. But where?

"There in front, almost within touch of the hand, that line of blackness blacker than all the blackness about us, was the canyon of the Salt River. We looked at it well, since it might be our grave in an hour, for we were now within rifle shot of our quarry."

Quietly feeling their way in the dark, a dozen of the best shots among the soldiers followed the Apache scout Nantaje along an invisible trail snaking down the face of the precipice, Bourke wrote in 1891 for *Century* magazine (his remarks also can be seen at the Eyewitness history Web site www.ibiscom.com). Their objective was a cave, and the purpose was to "get into place in front of the cave in order to open the attack."

But there was more to the quiet deployment of the troops, who were not lacking in number. "Immediately behind them should come fifty more, who should make no delay in their advance; a strong detachment should hold the edge of the precipice to prevent any of the hostiles from getting above them and killing our people with their rifles. The rest of our force could come down more at leisure, if the movement of the first two detachments secured the key of the field; if not, they could cover the retreat of the survivors up the face of the escarpment."

The first dozen men, the good shots, "slipped down the face of the precipice without accident," added Bourke, "following a trail from which an incautious step would have caused them to be dashed to pieces [below]."

Picking their way down the steep canyon wall for two hundred yards or so, they came "face to face with the cave and not two hundred feet from it."

The Apache raiders obviously had no idea they had been tracked down to their lair. "In front of the cave was the party of raiders, just returned from their successful trip of killing and robbing in settlements near Florence on the Gila River. They were dancing to keep themselves warm and to express their joy over their safe return."

The mounted infantrymen had arrived just in time to see half a dozen or so freshly awakened squaws "bending over a fire and preparing refreshments for their valorous kinsmen,"

Bourke noted, "The fitful gleam of the glowing flame gave a Macbethian tinge to the weird scene and brought into bold relief the grim outlines of the cliffs between whose steep walls, hundreds of feet below, growled the rushing current of the swift Salado."

If the Apaches thought only an eagle or mountain sheep could "intrude," how wrong they were!

Listen as Bourke narrates the scenario that ensued. Listen and picture, however grimly. Here were the Apache warriors, safely returned to their women and children . . .

> But hark! What is that noise? Can it be the breeze of the morning which sounds "Click, click"? You will know in one second more, poor, deluded, red-skinned wretches, when the "Bang! Boom!" of rifles and carbines, reverberating like the roar of cannon from peak to peak, shall lay six of your number dead in the dust.

Now began the real fight, just as the first rays of sunrise broke over the horizon. Now, with one of the "worst bands of Apaches in Arizona . . . caught like wolves in a trap," out of the cave and past its protective parapet of rock up front "swarmed the warriors." Now, by the "bucketful," the soldiers "poured in lead."

Naturally, there was no controlling who in or about the cave might suffer the consequences. "The bullets, striking the roof and mouth of the cave, glanced among the savages in the rear of the parapet and wounded some of the women and children, whose wails filled the air."

Asked twice to surrender and outnumbered three to one, the Apaches still would not. Nor would they allow their women and children to leave. Twice they had shrieked defiance to any thought of surrender.

The second time meant "their end had come."

The detachment of soldiers left at top of the cliff side, "to protect our retreat in case of necessity, had worked its way over to a high shelf of rock overlooking the enemy beneath, and began to tumble down great boulders which speedily crushed the greater number of Apaches," Bourke wrote.

The overall result of the early morning attack was seventy-six Apaches dead. "Every warrior died at his post."

Still alive, though, were some of the women and children who had sought protection to the rear of the cave. They were captured and taken on the military column's horses and mules to Camp McDowell, fifty miles away.

Among them was a four-year-old boy with a bullet crease extending from the top of his head to the back of his neck, "leaving a welt an eighth of an inch thick, but not injuring him seriously."

It seems that he had appeared, "absolutely naked," during the heaviest fighting. He ran out of the cave from the side of the parapet in front, then "stood dumbfounded between the two fires."

Without hesitation, Nantaje, the Apache scout who had gone down the cliff side first, "rushed forward, grasped the trembling infant by the arm, and escaped unhurt with him inside our lines."

The onlooking soldiers also reacted quickly. "Our men suspended their firing to cheer Nantaje and welcome the new arrival," wrote Bourke, then they resumed their deadly assault. In the end, seventy-six killed. One little boy rescued. Added Bourke: "Such is the inconsistency of human nature."

1874
Crucial Semicolon

Uh-oh, Texas in the news again. Very much in the news as downstairs in the old state capitol was one governor, feet dug in and refusing to leave quietly . . . and upstairs another duly elected governor, already sworn in.

Grounds for their dispute? A "semicolon" ruling by the Texas Supreme Court that appeared to nullify the upstairs governor's recent election. Not a missing semicolon, as some writers have averred, but an intrusive one.

Taking place in January 1874 was the Lone Star State's Coke-Davis Dispute, in which newly elected governor Richard Coke, a Democrat, wished to take over the reins of government from the highly unpopular Reconstruction governor, Edmund Davis, a Republican. Although Coke clearly had won the gubernatorial election of late 1873 by 85,549 votes to the 42,663 cast for Davis, the latter would not go quietly.

As a result, Davis, his chief followers, and elements of his newly created state police were sequestered on the first floor of the old state capitol at Austin, while Coke and members of the Fourteenth Texas Legislature, also newly elected, were camped out on the second floor. There, after obtaining a key, the lawmakers had occupied the legislative chambers and inaugurated their man as governor on January 15.

Outside, wrote columnist Jesse Sublett in the October 1997 *Texas Monthly*, "hundreds of blacks gathered on the Capitol grounds to show their support for Davis."

In fact, adds the *Lone Star Junction* Web site under the heading "Coke-Davis Dispute" (http://www.lsjunction.com/events/cokedavs. htm): "Austin was a land mine in early 1874. People from all over the state had gathered to witness the inauguration of Democrat Richard Coke as its next governor. At long last, this would mark the end of Reconstruction and radical military rule in Texas."

And true, elected governor in 1869 by a narrow margin, Davis had pushed a program of expanded political rights for blacks while restricting those of former Confederates. He also created the state police to enforce law and order and even suggested the possible division of Texas into three different states. Such measures, notes the *Handbook of Texas Online*, "encountered strong attacks from both Democratic and Republican opponents and added to the controversy surrounding Reconstruction in Texas." It didn't help matters that Davis, once himself a Democrat, had fought in the Civil War—in Confederate Texas—as a Union cavalry commander (the U.S. First Texas Cavalry).

Described as "tall, gaunt, cold-eyed" and a "commanding figure," Davis apparently was personally "incorruptible" as governor, wrote Ezra J. Warner in his book *Generals in Blue*. At the same time, added Warner, "[F]or his four-year term he was virtual dictator of the state, having absolute power of appointment over eight thousand state and local employees."

Then, too, added Sublett in his *Texas Monthly* account, "Davis also irked many ex-Confederates when he took out a notice in an Austin newspaper in 1871 urging people to buy pies from Mrs. Brown, an African-American, instead of those sold by Mrs. Warren, who'd lost two sons in the rebel army."

Finally, Davis won few converts in a state still imbued with a frontier mind-set when he commuted the death sentences of two Indian chiefs convicted of murder in the Warren Wagon Train Massacre of 1871 (see pages 242–48), although he was in that matter acting at the urgings of the Grant administration in Washington.

Richard Coke, meanwhile, was a much better fit for the white, male voters of the former Confederate state of Texas as he and Davis approached their election donnybrook of 1873. Not only was Coke a Democrat tried and true, not only had he fought *for* the Confederacy, rising from private to captain, he also had been kicked off the post-bellum state supreme court by Union Gen. Philip H. Sheridan as an "impediment to reconstruction." Sheridan's action as military governor of Texas immediately after the war probably guaranteed Coke a good percentage of his votes in the 1873 election.

In any case, with Coke apparently elected by a two-to-one margin, Davis took the view (a) that his term really didn't expire until April 1874, (b) the election of Coke was invalid, and (c), the spurious election had been invalidated by a ruling of the state supreme court, which, in turn, was based upon an intrusive semicolon found lurking in the brand-new state constitution of 1869.

In its Article III, Section 6, the foundational charter specifically said that elections would be held "at the county seats of the several counties until otherwise provided by law; and the polls shall be opened for four days."

Notice the key provision *until otherwise provided by law* and notice the semicolon immediately following the word *law.*

The words *provided by law* very clearly gave the law-making state legislature the right to change the county-seats provision stated in the constitution.

For the election of 1873, the lawmakers indeed had made changes. They decreed the poling would be held in precincts rather than county seats only, and they gave the voters only one day to vote, rather than the four contemplated by the constitution.

And there, exactly, was the rub—the one-day allowance versus four days.

The three-member state supreme court nullified the election by ruling that the lawmakers had no right to limit the four days of voting to just one.

But, but, but . . . it says, *until otherwise provided by law,* does it not?

Yes, but not all the way through the sentence, insisted the court, thanks to the intrusive, perhaps even unintended semicolon after the word *law.* That small punctuation mark, usually so innocuous as to deserve no mention whatsoever, in this case was the key. It meant, according to the court's view, that the second clause of the sentence stood alone, independently, and so it was a provision that was *not* liable to any change decreed by the lawmakers. Thus, an election with the polls standing open for only one day had to be invalid, under the terms of the state constitution, which called for four days instead.

Davis, emboldened by the court decision, asked the Grant administration to send Federal troops to enforce his defiant position, but the answer coming back from Washington was that his right to continue in office seemed too doubtful to warrant armed intervention. In the end, after a tense standoff of several days, Davis finally stepped down on January 19 rather than risk bloodshed over the succession issue. Or, as summarized by the *Texas Handbook,* "Davis refused to use the police powers of the state" to uphold the high court's semicolon ruling. Further: "Coke chose to ignore it and seized power from the existing government. . . . His takeover ended the Semicolon Court, since he immediately implemented the constitutional amendment, also passed in the disputed election, that increased the number of judges to five and allowed the governor to appoint new ones. Coke removed the sitting justices and appointed an entirely new court."

One result was a parade of Democratic governors of Texas lasting for more than a century. Coke, himself, once more was elected governor before moving on to the U.S. Senate. He also is remembered today as a chief founder of Texas A&M University and for that reason is sometimes called the father of Texas A&M. Davis, on the other hand, later lost election bids for governor again and for a seat in the U.S. House. He remained for many years chairman of the Republican Party's state executive committee.

1875
Model Indian Fighter

He was born in Staunton, Virginia, in the year 1851—and right there was a major problem. His timing.

Following the normal course of events for any starry-eyed boy who wanted a career in the military, in the army of his country, he grew up yearning to attend the military academy of his dream world, earn his commission, and join the U.S. Army.

Bad timing would not be the only obstacle ahead of Carter Page Johnson. The son of an itinerant teacher, he grew up in a time of war, in circumstances of family poverty. All that being the case, his father was forced to seek a free education for his son, a "State Cadetship" at the Virginia Military Institute (VMI).

With young Carter already accepted under that circumstance by VMI, an important step toward fulfillment of his boyhood dream. He entered VMI's cadet ranks in 1872 at the age of twenty, older than the norm, and he was graduated in 1875 as twenty-eighth in a class of forty-five. "The VMI class of 1875 was above average in the future successes of those who graduated," wrote Robert W. Wentz Jr., editor of the *VMI Alumni Review,* in its winter issue of 1990. "Eleven would become lawyers; five, physicians; five, educators; four, engineers; two, clergymen; and six, planters or farmers."

A close look at the list reveals that none joined the U.S. Army. None except Johnson, "the only member of his class who sought a military career," noted Wentz also. Johnson, in fact, would be the only VMI graduate to serve in the U.S. Army "from the period of time between the Civil War and the late 1890s," added Wentz.

That remains a distinction in itself, but Johnson was destined to accomplish more, much more—as an Indian fighter, a great artist's model soldier of the West, and late in life, Indian peacemaker.

First, though, he had to seek acceptance by the U.S. Army—U.S. Army as in *Union army,* that is. And in 1875, the year of Johnson's graduation, the army wanted no part of an officer produced by VMI, that "nest of vipers" whose Prof. Thomas J. "Stonewall" Jackson, whose many graduates, and even whose downy-cheeked cadets had fought the Union army so hard and effectively in the recently concluded war.

But Johnson was determined to become a soldier no matter what. To overcome the army's refusal to grant him a commission, he simply "packed away his VMI diploma and enlisted as a private."

Thus, in the backwash of a grinding war, Johnson joined sometimes unexalted company. Wrote Wentz on this score: "Without a foreign foe, the reduced ranks of the Army after the war attracted the dregs, the ne'er-do-wells, the loafers and the drifters. Limited in literacy and polish, they were assigned to the outposts of the west to protect the tide of settlers moving into the new territories."

In short order, the Virginian found himself stationed at Fort Robinson, Nebraska, found himself growing a fierce-looking, handlebar mustache, and campaigning against the Sioux, the Cheyenne, and the Nez Perce as a member of Company F, Third U.S. Cavalry. Unusually well educated by contrast with his fellow enlisted men, a good horseman and brave fighter, he moved up in rank from private to corporal to sergeant in short order as well.

Now his timing was absolutely right. In looks, demeanor, experience, reputation, location—and large curling mustache—Johnson was exactly the model soldier of the West that a young artist visiting from the East was seeking . . . Frederic Remington by name.

So it was, in the 1880s, that they became fast friends, that Sergeant Johnson, once from VMI's cadet ranks, became the lead figure in several of Remington's classic paintings of the Old West—leading the column in "Mile After Mile Rushed the Little Column," central figure in "Battle of War Bonnet Creek," leading the charge in "Through the Smoke Sprang the Daring Soldier," among others.

Johnson's career moved on in the meantime. In 1882 he finally received a commission as a first lieutenant. In 1883 he joined the black Buffalo Soldiers of the Tenth Cavalry in Arizona in campaigns against Geronimo, Dull Knife, and the Apache Kid. "At one point, Johnson was credited with having moved his unit over 800 miles in 17 days in pursuit of one elusive Indian war party—no small feat and a rival for the records set by Stonewall Jackson's foot cavalry," observed Wentz.

Reaching the rank of captain, Johnson apparently fought a war or two in the saloons of the West as well. In one such instance, he and two civilians exchanged hot words in an establishment at Maxey, Arizona. One of the men hurled a whiskey-filled tumbler at Johnson, hitting him square in the forehead and cutting it open. After a second missile struck Johnson in the nose, the assailant now reaching for a large beer mug, Johnson wielded his revolver and shot twice. The man died the next day, and Johnson subsequently was acquitted . . . on grounds of self-defense.

In time, Johnson served in the Spanish-American War of 1898, at one point fighting his way across the island of Cuba with Troop M of the Tenth Cavalry to deliver supplies to the leader of the Cuban rebels. He also would spend a tour of duty in the Philippines.

Reassigned to Fort Robinson again, he briefly returned to his native Staunton to take a bride, Rosa St. Clair Harrison. Now in his fifties, Johnson settled down and spent time developing a ranch near his duty post. It appeared the Indian wars were all over . . . but then came the Ute Uprising of 1906. Johnson was off to the wars again, only this time he rode into the Indian camp alone and negotiated the peace. As one result, he accompanied the Ute leaders to Washington for a meeting with President Theodore Roosevelt and received TR's personal instruction to resolve their problems amicably. Which, over the next two years, he did.

By the time of Johnson's retirement in 1910 after thirty-three years of service, the onetime cadet and U.S. Army private had reached the rank of major. More important, the VMI grad—his school's *only* military careerist in nearly four decades following the Civil War—had carved out a legendary career fully deserving a unique place in the nation's pantheon of remarkable military leaders and heroes.

The Body Was Hardly Marked

MESSAGE FROM THE PAST: On the morning of June 27, 1876, U.S. Army Lt. James H. Bradley, chief of scouts with Col. John Gibbon's column at the Little Bighorn River in Montana, was among the first soldiers to find the bodies of the 225 men killed by Sioux, Cheyenne, and other Indians in the massacre known ever since as Custer's Last Stand. It was a terrible scene, everyone of course dead, including the officer in charge, the U.S. Seventh Cavalry's Lt. Col. George Armstrong Custer and two of his brothers, one of them a civilian. Many if not all of the bodies were scalped and otherwise mutilated. But . . . not Custer's, despite wildfire rumors to that effect. Not according to Bradley, who gave this account in a letter published in the *Helena (Mont.) Herald* of July 25, 1876.

> Even the wounds that caused his [Custer's] death were scarcely discoverable (though the body was entirely naked) so much so that when I afterwards asked the gentlemen whom I accompanied [his fellow officers, presumably] whether they observed his wounds they were forced to say that they had not . . .
> Probably never did a hero who had fallen upon the field of battle appear so much to have died a natural death. His expression was

rather that of a man who had fallen asleep and enjoyed peaceful dreams than that of one who had met his death amid such fearful scenes as that field had witnessed, the features being wholly without ghastliness or any impress of fear, horror or despair. He died as he lived—a hero—and excited the remark of those who had known him and saw him there, "You could almost imagine him standing before you!" Such was Custer at the time of his burial, on the 28th of June, three days after the fighting in which he had fallen, and I hope this assurance will dispose of the horrible tale of the mutilation and desecration of his remains.

Actually, a Sioux may have cut off the joint of a Custer finger, a mutilation unnoticed by Bradley, suggested Dr. Lawrence Frost, a long-time Custer scholar, in his 1981 book *Custer Legends*. The Sioux warriors might have done far worse, but two Southern Cheyenne women who found Custer's body shortly after the fighting—and recognized him—discouraged the Sioux by saying the body was that of a relative of theirs . . . "so the Sioux cut off only one joint of a finger," summed up Frost. The two Cheyenne women, though, stuck a sewing awl into the dead man's ears. "This was done to improve his hearing," since "he had not heard" what the Cheyenne chiefs had told him when he smoked a peace pipe with them sometime beforehand. The chiefs had warned Custer then that if he broke promises of peace and fought the Cheyenne, the "Everywhere Spirit" would see to his death, added Frost's account, based in turn on the story a Cheyenne woman told Dr. Thomas B. Marquis, agency physician to the Cheyenne in the 1920s.

⭐

1 8 7 6
Who Killed Custer?

⭐

On the one hand, George Armstrong Custer once said that if he were an Indian, he would prefer to cast his lot to the "free open plains rather than submit to the confined limits of a reservation, there to be the recipient of the blessed benefits of civilization with its vices thrown in." On the other hand, he didn't hesitate to fight the Indians of the Old West. In 1876 his specific task as commander of the Seventh Cavalry was to help round up the Sioux and the Cheyenne and move them onto reservations.

Rashly, he advanced on a large village of 2,500 to 5,000 Indians in a valley along the Little Big Horn River, split his 650-man regiment into three elements, and ordered the attack. Instead of the 1,000 warriors he expected, however, the foe before him was probably the largest gathering of "hostiles" in the West—anywhere from 2,500 to 3,000 warriors. They turned on the central column, commanded by Custer himself, and killed all 225 men, Custer and two brothers among them.

Enter now White Bull, nephew of the famous Sitting Bull.

I charged in. A tall, well-built soldier with yellow hair and mustache saw me coming and tried to bluff me, aiming his rifle at me. But when I rushed him, he threw his rifle at me without shooting. I dodged it. We grabbed each other and wrestled there in the dust and smoke. It was like fighting in a fog. This soldier was very strong and very brave. He tried to wrench my rifle from me, and nearly did it. I lashed him across the face with my quirt, striking the coup. He let go, then grabbed my gun with both hands until I struck him again.

But the tall soldier fought hard. He was desperate. He hit me with his fists on jaw and shoulders, then grabbed my long braids with both hands, pulled my face close and tried to bite my nose off. I yelled for help: "Hey, hey, come over and help me!" I thought that soldier would kill me.

Bear Lice and Crow Boy heard me call and came running. These friends tried to hit the soldier. But we were whirling around, back and forth, so that most of their blows hit me. They knocked me dizzy. I yelled as loud as I could to scare my enemy, but he would not let go. Finally, I broke free.

He drew his pistol. I wrenched it out of his hand and struck him with it three or four times on the head, knocked him over, shot him in the head and fired at his heart. I took his pistol and cartridge belt. Hawk-Stays-Up struck second on his body.

Ho Hechetu! That was a fight, a hard fight. But it was a glorious battle, I enjoyed it . . .

On the hill top, I met my relative, Bad Juice [Bad Soup]. He had been around Fort Abraham Lincoln and knew Long Hair by sight. When he came to the tall soldier lying on his back naked, Bad Soup pointed him out and said, "Long Hair thought he was the greatest man in the world. Now he lies there."

"Well," I said, "if that is Long Hair, I am the man who killed him."

So said White Bull, according to the account labeled "Custer is Killed at the Little Bighorn" in the book *Eyewitness to America* (1997). The book's bibliography, in turn, credits *I Have Spoken* (1971), edited by Virginia I. Armstrong. And the same White Bull claim was advanced by the well-known historian Stanley Vestal in the February 1957 issue of *American Heritage* magazine . . . but not in the biography of the great Sioux chief Sitting Bull that Vestal originally published in 1932, *nor* in his subsequent biography of White Bull, which appeared in 1934.

Why not? Finding and interviewing the person who actually killed Custer would have been a coup for any historian worth his salt. And yet, noted Robert M. Utley, himself a distinguished historian of the West, Vestal in the original editions of his biography (*Sitting Bull, Champion of the Sioux*) never mentioned White Bull's claim . . . and yet later Vestal did. Exploring the issue in his own, much later biography of Sitting Bull, *The Lance and the Shield* (1993), Utley cited Vestal's explanation that he withheld the information while Sitting Bull's nephew White Bull was alive, for fear, as Utley summarized it, "[that] some hot-head might harm the old man."

And yet, observed Utley, there was no mention of the White Bull account in Vestal's notes. In a footnote in his biography of Sitting Bull, Utley wrote, "No serious student of the Little Bighorn today believes he [White Bull] is responsible [for Custer's death]."

So, if not White Bull, who *did* kill Custer at the battle of the Little Big Horn? Keep in mind that his body bore two potentially fatal wounds, their sequence unknown. One was a bullet wound in the left breast and the other in the left temple.

Those two injuries rule out suicide, lifelong Custer scholar Lawrence Frost asserted in his book *Custer Legends* (1981), since it would have been impossible for a right-handed man to shoot himself in either place. Furthermore, no powder burns were reported at either entry site.

On the other hand, Frost went on to throw cold water on the White Bull story. For instance, could White Bull have lashed Custer across the face while trying to hang on to his rifle at the same moment? Said Frost on this point: "This part of the story is a bit difficult to accept when one considers that Custer, who was admittedly the stronger of the two, had grasped White Bull's rifle with both hands, yet the Indian was able to retain it with one hand while he used the other to wield his quirt."

Or consider White Bull's statement that he wrenched Custer's pistol from his hand "and struck him with it three or four times on the head, knocked him over, shot him in the head and fired at his heart." If all that were the case, Custer's body should have been roughed up accordingly "Yet," wrote Frost, a podiatrist by occupation, "none of the many who saw Custer just before he was buried made any mention of any violence done his body other than the two bullet holes that killed him. Lieut. [James H.] Bradley, who was on the burial detail and gave a careful description of Custer as he appeared when found, stated that, 'Even the wounds that caused his death were scarcely discernable.'" (Actually, Bradley used the word "discoverable," rather than "discernable." See pages 257–58.)

Taken a step further, "It is difficult to believe that anyone struck across the face several times with a quirt, then pistol whipped three or four times, would not show evidence of abrasions or contusions."

Case closed? Assuming so, who killed Custer?

Frost suggested the Indians attacking Custer's command on the fatal hillside probably didn't even know he was there. For one thing, "Long Hair," as he was known among the Indians, recently had cut his hair short. For another, it was an extremely hot day. As a result: "The officers and men would have removed their outer clothing with its insignia. Perspiring and covered with dust from that sandy soil, identification would have been an impossibility."

As this analyst said also, the evidence is of little to no hand-to-hand fighting . . . rather, the Indians could shoot down the soldiers from afar, and in that scenario there is no telling whose bullets struck which targets. As for arrows, while they might have been identifiable to their owners, they often were lobbed over the dead horses the troopers used as a defensive wall. Thus, they were not aimed at a specific target that an Indian later could claim as his intended kill. In any case, there is no evidence that Custer suffered any arrow wounds. Summed up Frost: "The Indians greatly outnumbered the troopers. They had only to keep firing from a distance until the last soldier was accounted for."

Moreover, only two dead Indian ponies were found on the battlefield. If the Indians had ridden their mounts into the mass of soldiers on the hillside, "the defending troopers would have brought down a greater number of them."

Then, too, a Cheyenne chief later told Dr. Thomas B. Marquis, agency physician for the Northern Cheyenne in the 1920s, that the Indians themselves had no idea who had killed Custer.

1 8 7 6
Only Survivor

Who survived Custer's Last Stand? Did anyone? Down through the years, there have been claims and counterclaims, but longtime Custer researcher Lawrence A. Frost once noted that the "one survivor of the fight on Custer hill that rises above all contention" was a horse—Capt. Myles W. Keogh's horse ironically named Comanche.

A few other Seventh Cavalry mounts had survived the battle itself, but they were in such bad shape they had to be destroyed. That left only Comanche to be led away by the first troopers to reach the battleground. "It was Lieut. Henry J. Nowlan, Keogh's comrade in arms in the Pontifical Zouaves and the Civil War, who saw and recognized the animal. Covered with blood from numerous bullet and arrow wounds, Comanche neighed softly as if seeking some friends."

First thinking his old friend's mount also would have to be shot to end its misery, Nowlan took a closer look and "decided there was hope."

As a result, the horse was led—"slowly," to be sure—the fifteen miles to the steamer *Far West,* moored at the mouth of the Little Bighorn River, and there, "[H]e was carefully bedded down on grass at the extreme stern of the boat."

Then and there a new and thoroughly coddled life began for the only horse to survive Custer's Last Stand. "He became the special concern of the entire crew," wrote Frost in his 1981 book *Custer Legends.* "The horse responded rapidly to these attentions."

After arriving at Fort Lincoln on the Missouri River opposite today's Bismarck, North Dakota, Comanche quickly became the post pet. "Orders were issued by Col. Samuel D. Sturgis that no one was to ride Comanche under any circumstances, nor was he permitted to do any work, and that he was to be saddled and bridled and led by a trooper of I Company on every ceremonial occasion."

The next year for Comanche was one of convalescence . . . but also the beginning of an addiction, addiction to alcohol. Since the horse had become "intemperate," noted Frost, "he was given a whiskey bran mash about every other day. Convalescence soon became a pleasure."

In fact, the horse became a shrewd but harmless lush. He somehow divined the arrival of pay day. "Comanche became a regular visitor at the enlisted men's canteen on payday where the boys, willingly enough, treated their favorite to a bucket of beer. When the boys ran out of funds, he would visit the officers' quarters to panhandle."

He became "quite attached" to one man in particular, the post blacksmith Gustave Korn, who in turn gave Comanche "devoted care" during his period of recuperation. "He followed the trooper everywhere, even trotting down to Junction City and neighing in front of the house where Korn's lady friend lived."

This meant Korn had to come out and lead Comanche back to his stall. "It may have been jealousy."

But Comanche's otherwise idyllic life was fated to meet with an unhappy echo of Keogh's fate at the hands of the Sioux and Cheyenne at the Little Bighorn. Late in 1890, the horse's "pet human," Gustave Korn, marched off to battle the Sioux at Wounded Knee, South Dakota . . . and he did not return. Like Keogh, he had been killed. Back at their post, Comanche now entered a long downward slide. "He seemed to lose interest in everything except the panhandling of beer. On November, 6, 1891, he died at the age of nineteen."

Thus, he had been four at the time of Custer's Last Stand, and he had lived another fifteen years thereafter . . . and all that time at leisure, retired from active duty and fondly known in army circles as "second commanding officer" of the U.S. Seventh Cavalry.

1 8 7 6
A Pioneer Rancher Moves In

Just about everybody has credited him with inventing the chuck wagon, but the *Fort Worth Star-Telegram* went a considerable step or two farther by saying he, "with a handful of men, invented the American ranching industry." Not only that, said the Fort Worth newspaper, this innovative rancher's long life "was a virtual chronicle of Texas' nineteenth-century history and reads like an adventurous pulp fiction novel."

A living legend back then, added Jerry Flemmons in the newspaper account (see wysiwyg://206/http://www.virtualtex.com/history/fame/trail), he even today "is an essential fixture within Texas' mythology of cowboys and Indians, ranchers, cattle, horses and indomitable spirit."

He established one of the first major cattle-drive trails to market. He was the first to ranch in the Texas Panhandle's Palo Duro Canyon, managing and partly owning a spread that grew to 1.3 million acres grazed by more than 100,000 cattle . . . and by 250 buffalo as a hedge against the bison's complete extinction. His, in fact, would become the first cattle operation in the Panhandle, period.

Bareback on a mare named Blaze for the white splash on her face, Charles Goodnight, all of nine years old at the time, had ridden into Texas in 1845 with his family, which came from Illinois to settle in Milam County near Nashville-on-the-Brazos. Never spending more than six months, total, in school, the youngster was hired out to do farm work for neighbors from the age of eleven on. As a teenager, he briefly became a jockey, and when a bit older he went into the freighting business with a team of oxen.

By the late 1850s he and a stepbrother were raising and trailing a few hundred mostly wild cattle in the Brazos Valley region. They did well enough to provide their shared parents a new log-cabin home in 1858 at Black Springs, Texas.

After the stepbrother married, Goodnight "ran" the cattle pretty much on his own, but he also met Oliver Loving, who would become a key partner, fellow cattle pioneer, and good friend. At the outset of their relationship, Goodnight joined Loving in sending a herd to the Colorado gold camps. Before Goodnight and Loving would make more history together, however, Goodnight had to play out another historic moment, for he was the one who tracked down the Comanches "holding" the captive white woman Cynthia Ann Parker, now married to chief Peta Nocona and mother of Quanah Parker. Leading Capt. Jack Cureton's rangers to the Indian encampment in the last days of 1860, Goodnight took part in the attack that killed Nocona and "freed" a reluctant Cynthia Ann, who had grown up with the Comanches in the two decades since her capture as a young girl. Ironically, notes Flemmons, Goodnight later in life "would form a lasting friendship with her Comanche son, Quanah."

Before Goodnight and Loving could join forces again, the Civil War intervened. Goodnight and the Cureton Rangers now became part and parcel of the Texas Frontier Regiment, formed for homeland security against Indian marauders, bandits, and like threats. With his service over in 1864, Goodnight returned to his fledgling cattle business, which had *not* benefited from the turbulence created both by the Civil War and the continuing Indian "troubles" along the Texas frontier. Moving to fresh rangeland in Throckmorton County, Goodnight suffered a major setback when marauding Indians stole two thousand of his cattle in September 1865.

But he had his eye on a new market that was likely to pay higher prices than he could get in Texas for beef on the hoof—the Federal Indian agencies and U.S. Army posts in neighboring New Mexico. In the spring of 1866, he and Loving together had enough cattle to mount a major cattle drive, requiring eighteen hands to manage, into New Mexico. As a result, not only did they sell their beef at a good profit, but this time they made *real* history. Together they had established the Goodnight-Loving Trail, a pathway to be used by southwestern cattlemen for years ahead, while Goodnight alone had created the chuck wagon concept to keep the hands fed at all times "on the road," as it were.

They followed their own trail twice more to Fort Sumner, New Mexico, but on the third trip Loving was fatally wounded by Indian raiders. Goodnight conveyed his partner's body back to his family in Weatherford, Texas, for burial there and continued to turn over Loving's share of the proceeds from their partnership. In 1869, meanwhile, Goodnight began a ranch outside Pueblo, Colorado. The very next year, he married a schoolteacher from Weatherford, Mary Ann Dyer, and they spent the next six years at his Rock Canon Ranch near Pueblo.

Far from finished with life's business, Goodnight was an innovator here, too. He dabbled in irrigated farming and began an apple orchard. Keeping his hand in the cattle-drive business, he blazed a Goodnight Trail from Granada, Colorado, to Almagordo Creek in New Mexico and helped to found Colorado's first stock raisers' association. He also invested in a local bank, a meatpacking facility, various farmlands and city lots, even an opera house.

When overstocked ranges and the Panic of 1873 threatened to put an end to his many ventures, Goodnight saw the need to retrench and moved on with sixteen hundred of his longhorn cattle in search of a new homestead and ranch. He settled upon the virginal Palo Duro Canyon in the Texas Panhandle, itself virgin territory only recently "cleared of hostile Indians," as H. Allen Anderson points out in the *Handbook of Texas Online.*

He brought his cattle into the huge canyon in October 1876, but only after his cowboys drove the local buffalo fifteen miles back into the canyon, "to make room for the cattle." In effect, Goodnight was starting all over again. "Within the bounds of the present Palo Duro State Scenic Park, Goodnight constructed his first temporary living quarters, a dugout topped with cottonwood and cedar logs, with abandoned Comanche lodge poles as rafters. Subsequently, farther to the southeast in Armstrong County, where the canyon floor widened out to ten miles or more, the colonel [as Goodnight by now was called] built a comfortable three-room ranch house from native timber without using any nails. He also built corrals and a picket smokehouse at the site, which he affectionately dubbed the Home Ranch."

In the next few months, Goodnight formed a new partnership with a Colorado investor, John G. Adair, creating the JA Ranch with Goodnight holding a one-third interest and earning an annual salary of twenty-five hundred dollars for managing the spread. "During his eleven years with the JA," adds the Anderson account, "Goodnight devoted his time and energy to expanding the range, building up the herd and establishing law and order in the Panhandle. In the summer of 1878, he took the first JA trail herd, led by his famous steer Old Blue, north to Dodge City, Kansas, then the nearest railhead. The Palo Duro–Dodge City Trail, which he blazed, was well used in subsequent years by many Panhandle ranchers."

Now came a double set of historical ironies. The same Palo Duro Canyon in 1874 had been the setting of the final significant battle of the Red River War, in which the U.S. Army had fought rebellious Indian bands, Comanches among them, that had been terrorizing the frontier off and on for years. Taking the Indians by surprise in the huge canyon, Col. Ranald S. Mackenzie and his men shattered their strength in one fell swoop by capturing, and destroying, most of their ponies.

Now, nearly twenty years later, with the buffalo, an Indian mainstay, almost gone, the same Charles Goodnight parlayed a treaty with Cynthia Ann's son, Comanche chief Quanah Parker, to provide him and his tribe two beef cattle every other day in place of the buffalo . . . so long as the Comanches did no harm to the JA herd. The "beeves," of course, would come from the ranch in the canyon where the Indians had suffered their shattering loss to Mackenzie's troopers.

Meanwhile, Goodnight added the Quitaque (Lazy F) Ranch to his holdings, "reportedly [becoming] the first Panhandle rancher to build fences of barbed wire," and helped organize the Panhandle Stock Association, which he served as its first president. By the time his partner Adair died in 1885, the JA had grown to 1.32 million acres and more than one hundred thousand "of Goodnight's carefully bred" cattle. "In addition, Goodnight was a pioneer in the use of artificial watering facilities and the ownership of permanent ranges in fee. As an early believer in improvement through breeding, he developed one of the nation's finest herds through the introduction of Hereford bulls."

Then, too, "with his wife's encouragement, he also started a domestic buffalo herd, sired by a bull he named Old Sikes, from which he developed the 'cattalo' by crossing bison with polled Angus cattle."

In a new chapter, he sold out his interest in the JA in 1887, staying on as manager for another year before he and his wife built a new ranch house close to his namesake town of Goodnight, Texas, as nucleus for a much smaller ranch where they eventually kept not only their cattle and buffalo, but elk, antelope, "and various other animals in zoo-like enclosures, as well as different species of fowl." By now, too, they had launched Goodnight College.

Toward the end of Goodnight's more activist career at the JA, he suffered a near-fatal stomach ailment, made a few bad investments, and was "severely censured by the press" for his role as a leader of big-time cattlemen's interests. After the Goodnights retreated to their smaller spread near Goodnight, however, the same ranch became "a major Panhandle tourist attraction," while the couple's wildlife preservation efforts drew wide national attention. Buffalo from their herd "were shipped to zoos in New York and other eastern cities, Yellowstone National Park, and even to Europe."

But Goodnight, now in his sixties, remained active on a number of other fronts. "As a friend of Quanah Parker and other Plains Indian leaders in Oklahoma, Goodnight staged occasional buffalo hunts for former braves. He also exchanged visits with the Pueblo tribes in New Mexico, endorsed their causes in Congress, and gave one tribe a foundation buffalo herd. In addition, he grew Armstrong County's first wheat crop and conducted other agricultural experiments with the encouragement of pioneer botanist Luther Burbank; indeed, the colonel was often called the 'Burbank of the Range.'"

After fifty-five years of marriage, Goodnight's wife died in 1926, and he himself fell ill soon after. Ninety at the time, he was destined to recover and marry yet again. His new wife, whom he married on his ninety-first birthday in March 1927, was Corrine Goodnight, "a young nurse and telegraph operator from Butte, Montana, with whom he had been corresponding because of their mutual surnames." Learning of his illness, she had come to Texas and nursed him back to health, it seems. She was all of twenty-six when they tied the knot.

Selling his last ranch and buying a summer house in Clarendon, where he and Corrine married, Goodnight died on December 12, 1929, at his home in Phoenix, Arizona, where he spent the cold months of the year "because of his delicate condition." Until his death, adds Anderson's online account, "As a living frontier legend, he was often interviewed by Western authors and journalists, as well as such scholar-historians as Lester F. Sheffy, Harley T. Burton and J. Evetts Haley."

He left no children and in death he was reunited with his first wife by burial next to her in the Goodnight Community Cemetery.

★

1 8 8 2
Rising Above Disgrace
★

At West Point in the 1870s, Henry O. Flipper not only had to perform as well as his fellow cadets, he also had to endure their shunning. As one of his classmates later said, Flipper "behaved himself very well indeed, and was generally liked by his classmates, but no one openly associated with him, and anyone doing so could have been 'cut' from the Corps."

Even so, they reportedly cheered and gave him a standing ovation when he graduated.

Out west later, it was the reverse: good times, good friends, at first, but then apparent disgrace . . . and likely it was the race factor. But again, he would overcome . . . almost.

Flipper was an African American from Georgia. Moreover, he had been born a slave. His father belonged to a slave trader, and his mother was owned by a minister in an entirely different household.

Six African Americans had been admitted to the U.S. Military Academy at West Point, New York, before Flipper, but none had made it to graduation. For a time, Flipper's roommate at West Point was a fellow black. He didn't make it through.

For the next sixty years *after* Flipper's graduation from the academy, only two black cadets managed to emulate him.

"Truly," says a recent West Pointer, "Henry O. Flipper was a pioneer. In 1877, he became the first African American to graduate from West Point. It is almost impossible to imagine the additional burdens he must have endured in breaking this new ground. But his achievement does give us an insight into the fortitude and perseverance of this extraordinary man." So noted Louis Caldera, secretary of the Army, at a 1999 Pentagon luncheon honoring many of Flipper's descendants.

Way ahead of Caldera, though, was Maj. Gen. John M. Schofield, superintendent of West Point in 1877, the year of Flipper's graduation. "No white cadet had ever been burdened with the hope of an entire race on his shoulders," commented Schofield, who also pointed out that Flipper had endured the difficulties of his position "quietly and bravely." He had been forced "to stand apart from his classmates," noted Schofield, "as one with them but not of them."

Perhaps that was not entirely true, however. According to the biographical sketch on the Mobeetie (Texas) Jail Museum's Old Mobeetie Texas Association (OMTA) Web site (http://www.mobeetie.com), the slender black received a standing ovation when handed his diploma.

Shortly after that, it was down to business . . . in Flipper's case, down to business as the first African American to hold an officer's commission in the regular army. This young lieutenant was assigned to the fabled Buffalo Soldiers on the western frontier, where by Caldera's account, and those of most others as well, "He served with distinction at various posts and in several combat actions." Among the latter was the U.S. Cavalry's campaign in the Southwest against the Apache leader Victorio, during which Flipper led Troop A of the Tenth U.S. Cavalry Regiment as the regiment's first black officer.

At one point, noted William H. Leckie in his book *The Buffalo Soldiers,* Flipper led a group of couriers carrying dispatches ninety-eight miles in twenty-two hours. "His services in the Victorio War had won plaudits from both [Capt. Nicholas] Nolan [Flipper's company commander] and [Col. Benjamin] Grierson [regimental commander] and a bright career seemed assured," Leckie noted.

But at Fort Concho, Texas, later, added Leckie, "Clouds appeared on the horizon." The young black officer ruffled a few feathers of his white counterparts by spending time riding with "one of the few eligible young ladies at the post."

Such attentions "aroused the resentment of some of his fellow officers." Indeed, "Lieutenant Charles Nordstrom, who had previously enjoyed the young lady's undivided attention, was particularly incensed, and Flipper soon found the atmosphere about Fort Concho increasingly cool."

The trouble, when it finally came, arose at Flipper's next posting: Fort Davis, Texas. Flipper was appointed post commissary, but soon a $2,047 shortage in commissary funds turned up . . . and Lt. Col. William R. Shafter, the post commander, was quick to accuse Flipper of embezzlement and order his arrest. A subsequent court-martial found the black officer innocent of the charge but guilty of conduct unbecoming an officer. The crushing result: He was dishonorably discharged from the army.

For Flipper it was a blow never to be undone. Wrote Leckie: "To the end of his days Flipper maintained that he was the victim of a plot hatched by Colonel Shafter, Lieutenant Nordstrom, and Lieutenant Louis Wilhelm."

Victim or not, the army hadn't heard the last of Flipper . . . not by a long shot. If he could meet the challenge of his shunning experience at West Point, he could square his shoulders and endure this humiliation as well. But first, notes the Old Mobeetie Texas Association (OMTA) Web site, Flipper's request for review and dismissal of the sentence went up the chain of command until reaching the secretary of war, who agreed the sentence should be reduced. That recommendation went next to President Chester A. Arthur. . . . but, another blow, Arthur concurred with the decision to drum Flipper out of the army.

Now reporting to his temporary civilian job in an El Paso steam laundry every day, Flipper seemingly faced a bleak future, his career dreams shattered. He later said, "I was thoroughly humiliated, discouraged and heart-broken at the time." But he still was determined . . . determined now to "go forth in the world and by my subsequent conduct as an honorable man and by my character disprove the charges."

As a civilian, he in fact came close to that goal. Far in the future, Caldera in 1999 summed up Flipper's civilian career by noting that he "was widely admired as a man of exceptional intellect, competence, and integrity." More specifically, he became a "surveyor, civilian and mining engineer, author, translator, special agent to the Department of Justice, aide to the Senate Committee on Foreign Relations [as an expert on Mexico], and assistant to the Secretary of the Interior." Not a bad résumé for any nineteenth-century army officer, much less a cashiered African American!

Under Interior Department auspices, he worked with the Alaskan Engineering Commission and, notes the Mobeetie Web site, he "was responsible for the planning and construction of the Alaskan railway system." His U.S. Senate work came when he joined the staff of Sen. Albert Bacon Fall as an aide. Fluent in Spanish and considered an authority on Mexican land and mining law, Flipper at another point compiled *Spanish and Mexican Land Laws* (1895) for the Justice Department, notes the U.S. Army's Center of Military History (http://www.mil/cmh-pg/topics/afam/flipper.htm). Right after graduation from West Point, he had published the autobiographical book *The Colored Cadet at West Point* (1878). He also wrote a narrative of his life in 1916 that appeared later in historian Theodore D. Harris's 1963 book *Negro Frontiersman* and again in an expanded 1995 book by Harris, *Black Frontiersman.*

Then, too, declared Caldera in 1999, "Despite his mistreatment, Lieutenant Flipper remained a committed patriot. On the eve of the [1898] war with Spain, he sent a telegram to the Secretary of War offering his services to our nation. He made a similar offer when the United States entered World War I."

Unhappily, he would not in his lifetime overcome the full effects of what Caldera called "a great injustice." He noted that Flipper "labored tirelessly to clear his name," while "numerous bills seeking his exoneration were introduced in Congress." But none ever advanced beyond assignment to committee. When Flipper died in 1940 at the age of eighty-four, there was no significant change in his reputation . . . except for his remarkable civilian career. Now, Caldera observed, "the fight to restore his reputation was carried on by his family and by others who knew his story."And change, however belated, was in the offing.

• In 1972 Ray McColl, a white schoolteacher in Georgia, joined with Flipper's niece, Mrs. Irsle Flipper King, to begin a process of research and appeal that lasted four years.

• In 1976, reacting to their efforts, the Army Board for Correction of Military Records "granted Lieutenant Flipper a posthumous honorable discharge." The board, however, did not have the authority to reverse Flipper's conviction or to issue a pardon.

• In 1977, "Flipper's Ditch" at Fort Sill, Oklahoma, became a national engineering landmark. Not simply a ditch, it was a drainage system he perfected as a means of draining stagnant water blamed for the malaria that had plagued the army post for years. The pooled water, of course, provided a breeding ground for mosquitoes.

• In 1978 Flipper's remains were removed from an unmarked grave in Atlanta and reburied in Thomasville, Georgia, his place of birth, "with full military honors," notes Elliot Minor in the *Central Georgian,* a daily online newspaper covering central Georgia's African-American community (wysiwyg://54/http://www.thecentralgeorgian.com/in-retrospect-002.html).

• In the 1970s also, the West Point alumni—The Association of Graduates—placed a bust of Flipper in the academy library, next to a display recalling his days as a cadet and frontier soldier. "After a late night of research and study, it was truly inspirational for me to pause at that bust, to gaze upon the memorabilia in the display case, and to reflect upon how he persevered in the face of very difficult circumstances," said Caldera. He also noted that the academy alumni present an annual award to "the cadet who most exemplifies his [Flipper's] leadership, self-discipline, and perseverance."

• From 1989 to 1993, Gen. Colin Powell, the first African American to serve as chairman of the Joint Chiefs of Staff (and later, secretary of state), displayed a painting, *Tracking Victoria,* in his Pentagon office showing Flipper on horseback, pointing the way ahead for the troopers of the Tenth Cavalry.

• In the late 1990s, a new post office in Flipper's hometown of Thomasville was named for Flipper, as were a park in town and a room in the public library.

Finally, on February 19, 1999, President Bill Clinton officially pardoned America's first African American army officer. Recalling Flipper's court-martial and his subsequent appeals, Clinton commented, "A later Army review suggested he had been singled out for his race, but at the time there wasn't much justice available for a young African-American soldier." The 117 years since the day of Flipper's dishonorable discharge, the president added, was "too long to let an injustice lie uncorrected.

"The Army exonerated him in 1976, changed his discharge to honorable and reburied him with full honors. But one thing remained to be done, and now it will be. With great pleasure and humility, I now offer full pardon to Lt. Henry Ossian Flipper of the United States Army. "This good man now has completely recovered his good name."

Excitement Over Jesse James

MESSAGE FROM THE PAST: Jesse James, killer, robber and gang leader, began his ugly career as a member of the notorious Quantrill's guerrillas during the Civil War, then kept up his violent ways by killing nine or more persons and robbing banks, trains, and stagecoaches in the Midwest for nearly two decades. Despite all that criminal havoc, there were many who regarded him and his gang as Robin Hood–like folk heroes, among them the anonymous reporter for the Western Associated Press who wrote this graphic account of James's death in St. Joseph, Missouri, in April 1882.

A great sensation was created in this city this morning by the announcement that Jesse James, the notorious bandit and train-robber, had been shot and killed here in St. Joseph. The news spread with great rapidity, but most people received it with doubts until an investigation established the fact beyond question. Then the excitement became more and more intense, and crowds of people rushed to that quarter of the city where the shooting took place, anxious to view the body of the dead outlaw and to learn the particulars.

The body is that of a man of magnificent physique, who in the pride of health and strength must have been a commanding figure, six feet tall, and weighing 175 pounds, with every muscle developed and hardened by active life. It is a body that would fill with delight the surgeon seeking material for demonstrating anatomy. The features but little disturbed in death are not unpleasant, and bear the imprint of self-reliance, firmness and dauntless courage. To look upon that face is to believe that the wonderful deeds of daring ascribed to Jesse James have not been exaggerated. The hair is dark brown, the eyes half-opened, glazed, a cold steel gray, upon the upper lip a close-cropped mustache, stained by nasal hemorrhage, and the lower part of the face covered by a close brown beard about four inches long. Over the left eye is the blackened wound caused by the bullet of Robert Ford, the beardless boy whose cunning and treachery, animated by greed of gold, brought to an ignoble end the desperado who has so long snapped his fingers contemptuously at the law and its myriad of agents.

A superficial examination of the body would alone afford strong proof that the dead body is that of Jesse James. He has been literally shot to pieces in his daring exploits, and his old wounds would have killed any one cast in a less rugged mold. Two bullets have pierced the abdomen, and are still in the body. There is a bullet-hole in the right wrist, and another in the right ankle. Two more disfigure the left thigh and knee. The hands are soft and white and unstained by manual labor, and middle finger of the left hand has been shot away at the first joint. Hundreds of people have passed before the body, and while there is a unanimous expression of relief that the country was rid of so formidable a desperado, there were not a few who did not hesitate to condemn the manner of his taking off. Nevertheless, the young Ford brothers are undeniably the heroes of the hour. As they sat in the County Clerk's office this afternoon awaiting their call before the Coroner's inquest, then progressing in an adjoining room, they were the coolest and most unconcerned persons present, and the very last a stranger would pick out as the slayers of Jesse James.

✯

1 8 8 3
Tale of a One-Eyed Horse

✯

If the story had not come from the widely known and respected Royal Canadian Mountie Samuel B. Steele of nineteenth-century vintage, it would be a bit hard to believe—it in fact would be downright unbelievable. After all, a horse that fell seventy-five feet into a rocky river gorge from a cliff-side trail, broke a leg, then was shot five times, normally isn't expected to survive.

This one, though, did, according to Steele.

Also amazing is the fact that the steed's owner, Canadian engineer and rancher H. S. Holt, also survived a significant tumble from the cliff-side trail.

The incident took place back in 1883 near Golden, a mining boom town in the Canadian Rockies. "The trail along the side of the mountains near Golden was only suitable for pack animals," Steele reported. "It was very dangerous; at the highest part it was more than a thousand feet above the foaming torrent and [it was] bad enough anywhere."

Into this situation rode Holt with a party traveling from the Kicking Horse River to the Columbia. Holt's "spirited bronco," an otherwise fine horse, had had no experience in negotiating spidery mountain pathways. Worse yet, as the group reached the lower canyon on the Kicking Horse River, with Holt leading, "the trail was very bad."

When his horse jittered and slipped on a loose rock underfoot, Holt dismounted and did his best to persuade the animal to back up—"which she would have done had she been a trained mountain pony." Instead, his tremulous mount suddenly surged forward, giving her master such a jolt that he was knocked right off the trail. The cliff side at this point, said Steele, was "perpendicular," and the drop to the rocks below was seventy-five feet. Into this void went Holt, head over heels—literally.

"In falling he turned a complete somersault, landing on his stomach on the trunk of a dead tree which had been caught in the rocks on the side of the canyon." This, by later measurement, twenty-seven and a half feet down!

The horse, meanwhile, together with the loose rock, a monster chunk of at least eight hundred pounds, also fell from the trail but fortunately did not hit Holt's tree on the way down.

Holt's companions managed to rescue him with little complication. They lowered a lariat, he looped it under his arms, and they heaved him back up to the trail . . . considerably sore but otherwise not much worse off for the experience.

Still, he was sorry about his mount. "Looking down, he saw the horse lying on the rocks below; thinking her leg was broken and being unable to get down the perpendicular wall of the canyon, he concluded it was best to shoot her and proceeded to carry his idea into execution."

The terrain, the odd angle, and the distance all conspired to make it a very difficult shot, especially with a pistol instead of a rifle. "He succeeded in putting five bullets of his revolver into the horse's head without touching a vital spot."

At this point, the horse somehow regained her feet then fell into the river, "which was at that season and all summer a raging torrent." The hapless animal was carried downstream about half a mile and deposited on the opposite banks of the river.

There the horse stayed all night and part of the next day, until Holt sent his packers back to retrieve the saddle, bridle, and some papers from the saddlebags. His men found the bronco was still alive, although one of her eyes was shot out, three of her ribs were broken, and one leg was "almost cut off."

They built a sort of shelter for her with brush before leaving her lying on the riverside rocks. Soon, at Holt's instruction, they returned with some oats to feed the pitiful animal—"and give her a chance to recover, which, wonderful to relate, she did."

How's that again? *Recover!* From all that?

Yes, indeed, insisted Steele. The horse was sent to Holt's ranch in Alberta for a year or so, and then came the abortive Riel's Rebellion of western Canada. "[A]nd when the Alberta Field Force was raised for the suppression of the rebellion I saw a man, who had been employed as a mail carrier in the Rockies, in the ranks of the Alberta Mounted Rifles, riding a one-eyed horse, which he informed me, and so did others, was the animal which went over the canyon with Mr. Holt."

☆ ☆ ☆

Additional Note: The Kicking Horse River, none too surprisingly, acquired its somewhat quaint name through a horse-related incident, but not this one. No, on quite another occasion, it seems, an exploring party led by geologist James Hector came upon a major, fast-moving river in the Canadian Rockies. It was the late summer of 1858— August 29, in fact—when he and four companions came across a striking forty-foot fall—"where," he later wrote, "the channel is contracted by perpendicular rocks."

Just then, and wouldn't you know it, a pack horse trying to avoid fallen timber slipped off the trail and fell right into the stream . . . but luckily into a corner eddy and so no great danger. Even so, wrote Hector, the banks of the stream were so steep "we had great difficulty in getting him out." But they got a rope around the animal's neck and managed to pull him out.

With that chore finally accomplished, Hector turned to his own horse, which had strayed among the nearby spruce trees to nibble upon some greenery. When he approached and reached for the animal's trailing lines, however, the horse delivered a kick to the explorer's chest that knocked him unconscious for the next two hours or more. Still in pain when he came to, the geologist was unable to travel until two days later. He and his party continued to be dangerously short on solid food until one of them shot a moose on September 3.

Thanks to Hector's kicking horse, the stream today appears on the maps as the Kicking Horse River. More relevant to Canadian history, the incident occurred at the mountain pass later used by the Canadian Pacific Railway (CPR) to cross the Canadian Rockies, thus eventually to bind east to west and west to east—by way of Kicking Horse Pass.

Related note: Still another pass through the great mountain ranges of western Canada was named for the American railroad surveyor Maj. A. B. Rogers, who in the early 1880s was checking out the CPR's proposed east-west route through both the Rockies and the Selkirk Mountains. One day, attempting to ford a rushing mountain stream with Rogers aboard, *his* horse was knocked off its feet by the current and swept downstream—more graphically, "the horse rolled downstream," wrote the major's mountain guide Tom Wilson. Both horse and rider soon dried out from their unexpected bath, recovered their aplomb, and went on with the survey work at hand . . . but from then on that glacier-fed stream was known as Bath Creek.

1 8 8 4

Dude from the East

Tall are the tales—and at least partly true—still told in the Dakotas of the eastern dude who bought himself a ranch or two back in the eighties (1880s of course), took up residence in a log cabin, and started playing cowboy.

Have a heart, though. Give the bespectacled young man a wee measure of pity. Made a stunned widower just three years after his marriage, he took up residence at his ranch in the North Dakota Badlands just after his wife and his mother both died on the same day in the same New York townhouse. The young wife was overcome by Bright's disease the day after delivering her first child, Alice.

For the moment, he had no stomach for the life of wealth and ease that still could be his back in the East, where he served in the New York state legislature and had published a book.

So he came to the Little Missouri Valley in search of solace, some peace of mind, before moving on with his life. He always had loved the outdoors, thrilled to the tales of the West, even as an asthmatic boy.

If he loved the West, though, it didn't always love him.

Walking into a hotel bar at Mingusville near his ranch one cold evening in hopes of finding a cup of coffee, he instead found a drunk weaving about with two revolvers in his hands while the other patrons shrank away. In seconds the bespectacled tenderfoot became a verbal target for the drunk, who loudly informed the onlookers that "four-eyes" would stand the house to drinks. The dude didn't indicate any complaint as he calmly took his seat at a table and watched his would-be tormentor draw closer and closer.

With the drunk standing over him, however, the dude suddenly rose up and struck with both fists. The flurry of punches knocked out the drunk, his two pistols given up harmlessly as he hit the floor.

On another occasion, a second tormentor decreed and sent word that the easterner must pay a range fee to have his cattle graze on the second man's spread, even if no one else in the vicinity was asked to pay such a fee. This news came with the threat to exact the fee from the dude's hide, if need be.

In no time, the so-called dude was at the other rancher's door and telling him what he could do with his so-called range fee. Needless to say, no fee was charged or paid.

This was after the dude had gone on a hunting trip and shot an excited, charging grizzly bear right between the eyes.

The most remarkable story behind the dude's growing "tough guy" reputation had to do with a stolen boat—the dude's own, of course—taken from its customary place on the Little Missouri River. Ever resourceful, he had his men build another boat, then set off downriver among chunks of ice in pursuit of the thieves with two of his cowboys. Three days later, they found his first boat drawn up on the river shoreline. Nearby were the three culprits, a gang of horse thieves headed by the notorious Redhead Finnegan, it so happened. The dude and his men "landed and sneaked up on the thieves' camp and got the drop on them, in a tense confrontation," wrote Peter Collier (with David Horowitz) in a book about the easterner's family.

Now came a quandary. The dude and his men made three. The culprits made three, and there were two boats to take back upriver. How to split up?

The dude's solution was to borrow a horse from a nearby cowboy, ride fifteen miles to a ranch, hire a wagon, then return to the river. He ordered his men to take the boats back upriver while he took charge of the three prisoners. Armed with a Winchester rifle, he placed them in the wagon and took up position behind—walking—as the party set out for the distant town of Dickinson.

The trip took two days and two sleepless nights, with the "dude" trudging the entire way on foot.

Two years after beginning his restorative sojourn in the Badlands, he returned to the East, where he would stay—except for occasional visits over the next few years. After all, he did have a child awaiting him, the baby girl named Alice, along with an old friend from his childhood, Edith Kermit Carow.

Back east, the not-so-tender dude soon married Edith, distinguished himself as an organizer and leader of the "Rough Riders" in the Spanish-American War, as governor of New York, as vice president of the United States, and finally, as president.

He was Teddy Roosevelt. Citing the "strenuous life" of his two years in the Badlands as the basis for the rest of his life, he once said: "I never would have been President if it had not been for my experiences in North Dakota." It was there also that he proved the value of his own truism: "There were all kinds of things of which I was afraid at first. . . . But by acting as if I was not afraid, I gradually ceased to be afraid."

Additional note: Teddy Roosevelt's initial interest in ranching out west first took concrete form after he visited the Badlands to hunt buffalo in 1883. Smitten by the wide-open spaces of the Dakotas, he bought a share in the Chimney Butte Ranch, then owned by Canadians Sylvane Ferris and Bill Merifield.

Returning east, he promised to visit again soon, but none of the three possibly could have guessed at the Roosevelt family tragedy that would strike on the following Valentine's Day. The two Canadians, in the meantime, had built a one-and-a-half-story log cabin of ponderosa logs recovered from the nearby riverbanks, primarily for their new partner's use.

It was waiting there, about seven miles south of Medora, North Dakota, when the grieving widower made his retreat to the Badlands in 1884 and took up residence on his share of the ranch land, a spread named the Maltese Cross for its cattle brand.

The log cabin's pitched roof provided room for a sleeping loft, but TR actually slept in a ground-floor alcove next to the kitchen area. The downstairs otherwise consisted of one central room, and the windows were equipped with real glass.

After several months, the future president moved to the more isolated Elkhorn Ranch thirty-five miles to the north. His Maltese Cross cabin, though, continued as a center of operations and was used as a bunkhouse for his cowboys.

Years later, with Teddy Roosevelt settled into the White House, the old log cabin was launched upon a new "career" as a tourist attraction. Dismantled then rebuilt log by log, it was on view in St. Louis and in Portland, Oregon, for national expositions before returning home for the North Dakota State Fair of 1906. It then remained on the grounds of the state capitol in Bismarck until 1959, but in "crumbling" condition, according to a description appearing in the *Bismarck Tribune* in 1939.

Later, however, the cabin came into the protective hands of the National Park Service (NPS), was carefully restored, then moved to the NPS Visitor Center in the Theodore Roosevelt National Park adjacent to Medora, where it still can be seen today.

That "dude" who once lived in the small cabin, of course, was the same man who, as president, established the U.S. Forest Service, who designated sixteen national monuments (for one of them, the Grand Canyon National Monument, setting aside eight hundred thousand acres of Arizona land), and who persuaded Congress to approve five new national parks, fifty-one wildlife refuges, and various set-asides for national forest lands. As president, he supported the National Reclamation Act of 1902 establishing the U.S. Reclamation Service and giving the Federal government new control of major dam construction and irrigation fields—that is, of the major water resources of the West.

His use of the 1891 Forest Reserves Act expanded federal land reserves from forty million acres to almost two hundred million acres.

So enamored of the West was he that long before he became president, he wrote a number of books about the West: *Hunting Trips of a Ranchman* (1885), *Thomas Hart Benton* (1886), and the four-volume history, *The Winning of the West* (1889–96). In addition, a collection of articles he wrote for *Century* magazine appeared in book form as *Ranch Life and the Hunting Trail.*

(Incidentally, the book by Collier and Horowitz alluded to on page 279 is *The Roosevelts: An American Saga.*)

Walking from Cincinnati to Los Angeles

MESSAGE FROM THE PAST: One day in 1884 newspaperman Charles F. Lummis set out on a lengthy walk from Cincinnati, Ohio. By the time he reached Los Angeles, California, 143 days later, he had covered 3,507 miles . . . all on foot. While many were his adventures en route, one highlight for him was his climb up the steep, icy slopes of Pikes Peak in Colorado.

After getting up out of the canyon, and upon a southerly spur of the peak, I began to find trouble with the snow, which had drifted a couple of feet deep in the trough-like trail. There was no dodging it, however, for outside the one path all was loose, sharp rocks. At the wild, desolate timberline, where the last scrubby dwarf of a tree clung sadly amid the rocks, matters grew worse; for as soon as I rounded Windy Point, a savage, icy blast from the snow peaks of Sangre de Cristo fairly stabbed me through and through. My perspiration-soaked clothing turned stiff as a board in five minutes, and the very marrow of my bones seemed frozen despite the violent exercise of climbing. Worst of all, it was almost impossible to breathe in the face of that icy gale, though otherwise I have never felt any of the unpleasant symptoms, either in heart, lungs, or nerves, experienced by many at that altitude.

It was 3:30 P.M. when I stood panting at the door of the signal service station on the very crest of Pike's Peak—then, and perhaps still, the highest inhabited building on earth. It is 14,147 feet above the level of the sea—more than two miles higher than most of you who read this.

The day after his arrival in Los Angeles, Lummis began work as the first city editor in the employ of the *Los Angeles Times.* The excerpts here come from his subsequent book, *A Tramp Across the Continent.* Naturally, he would never forget the view from atop Pikes Peak.

Such a vista could only be where the greatest mountains elbow the infinite plains. Eastward they stretch in an infinite sea of brown. At their edge are the cameos of Manitou and Colorado Springs; the Garden of the Gods, now a toy; the dark thread of the Ute Pass, through which, in Leadville's palmy days, streamed the motley human tide. Seventy miles north is the cloud that is Denver. Fifty miles to the south, the smoke of Pueblo curls up from the prairie, falls back and trails along the plain in a misty belt, that reaches farther eastward than the eye can follow. A little pond-like broadening in this smoke-river shows the location of La Junta, one hundred miles away. West of south, in long and serried ranks, stand the Culebra and Sangre de Cristo ranges, while nearer tower the southern walls of the Grand Canyon of the Arkansas. Off to the west are the far giants of the Rockies in incomparable phalanx—for Pike stands in regal isolation a hundred miles from any peer. His sole companions are the 10,000 and 12,000 [foot] "foothills" that look up in awe to his lofty throne.

1 8 8 4
Sarah Winchester's Crazy House

Begun in 1884 and under construction, night and day, for thirty-eight years, with 160 rooms, 2,000 doors, 47 stairways, 47 fireplaces, 17 chimneys, 13 bathrooms, and 6 kitchens resulting, Sarah Winchester's rambling house in San Jose, California, never was finished.

Add up all her change orders over the years, an estimated five to six hundred rooms were built then torn apart to make way for new ones. That estimate may account for the ten thousand window panes also claimed on behalf of the amazing Victorian mansion on San Jose's Winchester Boulevard.

A lonely widow and heir to the Winchester Repeating Arms Company fortune, the eccentric Sarah Winchester just kept building and building—literally, twenty-four hours a day—after fleeing the sadness of her life in New Haven, Connecticut, where both her husband, Winchester Rifle scion William Wirt Winchester, and their only child, a weeks-old infant named Anne, had died, albeit fifteen years apart and, in his case, due to adult tuberculosis. Arriving in San Jose in 1884, she bought an unfinished, eight-room farmhouse in the Santa Clara Valley three miles west of town, hired squads of carpenters, and ordered them to start building . . . building and building in ceaseless, round-the-clock shifts.

Soon, the farmhouse was swallowed up. Turrets and towers rose. New room upon new room appeared, add-on to add-on. Floors multiplied, until the Winchester Mansion soared to seven stories at its highest point. And still she built . . . sometimes interior doors or stairs went nowhere, other times secret rooms and passageways were added as well as false cupboards a half-inch deep and upside-down posts and columns. Everything was beautifully, expensively decorated or furnished, with parquet floors and Tiffany-glassed windows.

What was going on? What was she doing? Even in often zany California this was eccentric behavior, to say the least. And . . . think of the money! Before it was all over, before the unfinished Winchester House ever could be finished, she had spent an estimated $5.5 million on her modifications, a bushel of money today, a phenomenal sum by the standards of *her* day. But then . . . the house covered six acres eventually, and as the Winchester heiress, she earned an estimated one thousand dollars a day. She could afford to indulge.

But why? On the one hand, her project certainly was a way to keep busy and possibly ease her grief . . . on the other hand, Sarah Winchester reportedly was told by a medium in Boston that she and her family were haunted by the spirits of those killed by Winchester repeating rifles, "the gun that won the West." To escape these bad spirits, she was told, she must go west and build a large home to appease them. "As long as construction of the house never ceased, Mrs. Winchester could rest assured that her life was not in danger," explains a magazinelike book published by the Winchester Mystery House, a major tourist attraction today. "Building such a house was even supposed to bring her eternal life."

The legend contends that she retreated to an inner séance room at night to find inspiration for the next set of instructions for her round-the-clock workmen. Whether that really was the case, she obviously was serious about the number thirteen. Everywhere in the never-finished house there were thirteens—stairs with thirteen steps, an Italianate porcelain sink with thirteen drainholes, windows with thirteen panes, thirteen ceiling panels in some rooms, thirteen windows in the thirteenth bathroom . . . thirteen hooks in the séance room, "which supposedly held the different colored robes Mrs. Winchester wore while communing with the spirits."

The overall result many have called a monstrosity, others considered it merely bizarre, still others a striking Victorian mansion of great beauty . . . if a bit unorganized on the whole. The interior without doubt is a hodgepodge, a labyrinth, an unfathomable mélange . . . but, who knows? Perhaps everything was built with a clear purpose all along. "When Mrs. Winchester set out for her Séance Room," said *The American Weekly* in 1928, "it might well have discouraged the ghost of the Indian or even of a bloodhound, to follow her. After traversing an interminable labyrinth of rooms and hallways, suddenly she would push a button, a panel would fly back and she would step quickly from one apartment into another, and unless the pursuing ghost was watchful and quick, he would lose her. Then she opened a window in that apartment and climbed out, not into open air, but onto the top of a flight of steps that took her down one story, only to meet another flight that brought her right back up to the same level again, all inside the house. This was supposed to be very discomforting to evil spirits who are said to be naturally suspicious of traps."

Certainly, by the turn of the century, nineteenth passing into twentieth, she had built a gigantic "trap," or collection of traps, that no one but she herself quite understood. According to the Mystery House book, she daily met with John Hansen, "her dutiful foreman," the morning after her nightly séance and conveyed the "new changes and additions."

All were of her own design and "while she sometimes drew up simple sketches of the building ideas, there were never any blueprints . . . or building inspectors!"

With money no object, with no apparent intention ever to finish her project, Sarah Winchester indulged her changes of heart a thousand times over. "John Hansen stayed with Mrs. Winchester for many years, redoing scores of rooms, remodeling them one week, and tearing them apart the next.

"It is doubtful whether Hansen ever questioned his boss. Mrs. Winchester may have been trying to confuse evil spirits, or simply making mistakes, but there were no budget ceilings, or deadlines to meet. This resulted in many features being dismantled, built around or sealed over. Some rooms were remodeled many times. It is estimated that 500 to 600 rooms were built, but because so many were redone, only 160 remain. This naturally resulted in some peculiar effects, such as stairs that lead to the ceiling, doors that go nowhere and that open onto walls, and chimneys that stop just short of the roof!"

Bizarre or not, the house that Winchester built in San Jose was no blight on the neighborhood. Not only was the interior a showcase of Victorian elegance, as the owners of today proclaim, but Sarah Winchester also planted stunning gardens around the ever-expanding house while also developing commercial fruit orchards on the 160-acre grounds. "After being picked and boxed in the field," adds the Mystery House book, "the fruit was dried in Mrs. Winchester's special dehydrator, which had a large coal furnace and could dry half a ton of fruit in thirty hours. Most of this fruit was sold at the market to supplement Mrs. Winchester's income."

A recluse suffering from arthritis in her later years, Winchester gave away considerable sums of her money—to various charities. "Orphanages and many other local charities benefited from her anonymous contributions. She welcomed the neighborhood children and let them play on the grounds, even inviting them in to eat ice cream or play the piano."

She reportedly slept in a different bedroom every night, and she had many to chose from. The massive San Francisco earthquake of 1906 caught and trapped her for several hours in a favorite one, the mansion's Daisy Bedroom (she loved daisies). It also "toppled" her seven-story observation tower and significantly damaged other sections of the rambling mansion. Her solution? "After having the structural damage repaired, she immediately ordered the front thirty rooms—including the Daisy Bedroom, Grand Ballroom, and [the three-thousand-dollar] front doors—sealed up." Sealed and never to be used again during her lifetime.

Thus it was in another bedroom that she died in her sleep one night in 1922 . . . and all work on her as-yet unfinished house stopped then and there.

Her will (in thirteen parts) left various monies to family and employees and a "substantial" sum to the Winchester Clinic of the General Hospital Society of Connecticut (today still a part of the Yale Medical Center in New Haven) for the care of tuberculosis patients.

In 1974 Winchester's house became a California Registered Historic Landmark and was placed on the National Register of Historic Places. No doubt she would have been pleased. Or perhaps *is*...

Additional note: Today the Winchester Mystery House has been completely refurbished. The rambling Victorian mansion is open to the public. Visitors not only can see the beautifully kept grounds and tour the inside, they can visit the Winchester Historic Firearms and Antique Products Museums also on the grounds. The Mystery House is on Winchester Boulevard in San Jose, between Stevens Creek and Interstate Route 280, an hour's drive south of San Francisco. For visiting hours and further information, call (408) 247-2000.

1885
Snowbound

In the sparsely populated and primitive Old West, a blizzard was a life-threatening danger . . . and not only in the mountains. Joe Gaston, who helped to develop and settle Hugoton, Kansas, in the mid-1880s, never forgot the blizzard that struck his flat-country area the night of a Christmas Eve dance. "That evening when I went after Bell McFadden for the dance," he recalled years later, "it was a clear and beautiful night." The dance was "a huge success," with twenty couples (and four babies) attending.

About 11 P.M., the ladies served a basket supper, and close to midnight, "someone came in and said it was snowing, so everyone made a dash for home."

That was fine for the folks who lived only two or three miles away, but Joe Gaston's "date," Bell McFadden, lived with her brother John in a dugout far out of town. The so-called dugouts of his era, Gaston explained, "were made by digging into the earth three feet, then timber three feet above the earth with dirt thrown over the tops and sides. A small light in the door and one end furnished all the light they had. They used buffalo chips for fuel, and carried water from our town, a distance of six miles."

The snowstorm that began shortly before midnight assumed blizzardlike intensity right away, presenting a real danger to anyone risking travel very far beyond the small town's safe perimeter. "It was snowing and blowing so badly we dared not try to make it," Gaston wrote in a memoir on file today in the Stevens County (Kans.) Public Library at Hugoton. He persuaded his date to spend the night with him—in a small barn "built for twenty horses" but now crowded with forty horses and twenty-five persons. Among the latter were seven emigrant families already camped in the barn with their eleven children. Obviously, Joe and Bell would be both safe and well chaperoned during their "overnight" stay in the barn. The only problem was, "It snowed and blowed for seven days." Even though the stranded settlers kept a cook stove going around the clock, it was so cold, "chickens roosting in the barn froze setting on the mangers besides the horses."

Finally, on the seventh day, the snow stopped. "[S]o I started to take Miss McFadden home, six miles west of town. Before we got there it began to snow and blow again and I got lost. About three o'clock we ran into another dugout, whose owner had left his name on the door, and we knew we were one mile from the McFadden claim. We could not stay in the dugout because we had neither food or fuel, so our only chance lay in reaching McFadden's."

The snow was blowing so hard the couple's two horses "would not face the wind." Joe had to lead them. Fortunately, about dark, he saw a light. It was the dugout at the McFadden homestead . . . he and Bell were safe, at least for the moment. "I have never seen a light that looked so good," he acknowledged in his memoir.

Later that night, though, John McFadden thought he heard a cry for help from somewhere outside the dugout. Joe prepared to brave the elements once again. "We fastened two clothes lines together and fastened one end to me and the other end to the house. I went out and circled the dugout and found Alec King, who had left in the morning for his homestead two miles north of where I found him."

The next day, with the morning temperature hovering at 10 below zero, Joe was trying to figure out a safe way to travel back into town, where he lived. He came up with an inspired scheme, although he had to wait awhile for results. "I put a collar on one of my horses and tied a note to it telling where I was, and told them to bring a saddle horse out for me. I turned the horse loose, and three days later they came for me from town."

Back in town at last, he joined with others standing on the roof of a barn, from which they could see "over three hundred head of dead cattle." Amazingly, "Some of them were frozen stiff standing in their tracks and hardly looked dead." Even more amazing, "Some were branded by Nebraska owners, the cattle having drifted three hundred miles in ten days."

More seriously, Joe and his fellow townspeople figured there must be more people trapped by the blizzard in their primitive homesteads out in the countryside and thus in real danger. "We organized parties and went out to look for people on their claims," he wrote. And sadly the worst fears of the potential rescuers from Hugoton were realized. "We found one family, a man, wife and three children, frozen to death in a small shack. They had just located [in the area] and had no fuel on hand. They had burned up everything that would burn except the outside boards of the house."

Pitifully, all five family members were found dead in bed, where, evidently, they had huddled together in a desperate and final effort to stay warm.

Then, too, atop the barn again, Joe and his companions saw something move in the tall grass poking above the snow cover in the sand hills outside of town. Mounting a saddle horse, Joe went out to look. He found a team of horses hitched to a wagon . . . an empty wagon. Obviously, someone had hitched up the horses and had started out in the wagon, perhaps seeking the safety of town. The horses were rigged with tight bridles that prevented them from lowering their heads— "therefore they were feeding in the tall grass." Their master, though, must be stranded somewhere out in the snow-covered plain.

"We took the team in, and a party of us started out in a sled."

The result was another heart-rending discovery. Following the wagon's track for about three miles, Joe's party found the body of a man lying face down, his knees worn "down to the bone" and his toes in the same condition. His would-be rescuers from Hugoton figured he had frozen to death while walking behind the wagon, and then, because his hands were frozen to the tailgate, he apparently was dragged for miles before being knocked loose.

Realizing he probably had a stranded family awaiting him somewhere out in the snow-covered landscape, Joe and his companions set out the next day to backtrack even farther along the wagon's path toward town. They traveled sixty miles north before they finally came across the man's wife and two children—alive! "The wife said her husband had gone to an abandoned claim one half mile away the day of the storm to get some lumber."

He never returned. "After he became lost the horses had drifted with the snow, and getting into the sandhills [near town] had saved them from being frozen, too." In fact, Gaston summarized, "Eleven persons in our county froze to death during the storm."

Life in the nineteenth-century West could be like that.

But spring would come, and in the spring following the Christmas Eve blizzard of 1885, "the town boomed." That was when the locals formally met to organize their county. "I helped take the census of the [proposed] county, and we had a lot more inhabitants and taxable property than was required to organize." A three-member commission was appointed by the governor to call an election and locate a county seat. Joe Gaston, obviously a take-charge sort of man, was appointed to the post of deputy sheriff.

☆

1 8 8 6
Nighttime Call on Geronimo

☆

Officially designated "A-1," he couldn't read or write. He once was arrested in a murder case. But no matter, he's on record . . . on the revered and book-length scroll of America's Medal of Honor winners.

He earned the nation's most coveted military decoration long before he bearded an angry, possibly drunken Geronimo in his own den. And now he lies buried, as he absolutely wished, in an unmarked grave below a piñon pine in a canyon in Arizona's White Mountain region.

A friend, adviser, and companion to Indian-fighter George Crook for many years, he stood tall, six feet one inch. He wore his hair long and black. His complexion, according to army records, was "copper." He was . . . but first, here's what the congressional summary of all Medal of Honor winners has to say about him:

Rank and organization: Sergeant, Indian Scouts.

Place and date: Winter of 1872–73.

Entered Service at: Camp Verde, Ariz.

Born: 1853, Arizona Territory.

Date of Issue: 12 April 1875.

Citation: Gallant conduct during campaigns and engagements with Apaches.

Engagements with the Apache, it says, yet . . . he himself was an Apache, and his burial site lies hidden away in the twenty-five hundred square miles of pine forest in Arizona's Fort Apache Indian Reservation. Choosing his own burial site at the end of a full life, he was interred by Apache ritual and tradition. And yet he fought with the encroaching white man against fellow Apache. Inconsistent? A betrayal of sorts?

Not really. The fact is, Alchesay (his only name for many years), while born an Apache and raised an Apache, was of the White Mountain Apache, once led by his uncle, a chief named Pedro, a far more peaceful band than, say, Geronimo's mostly Chiricahua Apache followers. "Comparing the White Mountain Apache people with Geronimo would be like comparing Iowa farmers with Al Capone," explained William Hafford in the *Arizona Highways* book *They Left Their Mark*. "In fact, many peaceful Apache of the Geronimo era were as fearful of the rampaging Geronimo and his followers . . . as were white settlers."

Chosen by Chief Pedro for future tribal leadership, Alchesay realized from his earliest days of manhood that the white settlers arriving from the East in greater and greater numbers were here to stay, Hafford also noted. "He envisioned a prosperous future for his people only if they learned to live cooperatively with the whites. He understood, also, that Apache warriors, while holding a well-earned reputation as masters of guerrilla warfare, could never prevail on a long-term basis against the overwhelming might of the U.S. military."

Alchesay was ready, then, when George Crook was sent into Arizona's rough terrain in 1871 to subdue the more murderous Apache bands in their home territory, ready to respond to Crook's dictum, "We must use Apache methods and Apache soldiers." And Crook, of course, followed his own advice to the letter. As *The American Heritage Book of American Indians* observed, "There being no solidarity among Apaches in general, Crook employed the warriors of conciliated bands to fight the bands that insisted on remaining hostile."

Meeting with the White Mountain Apache leaders, he won their trust, and deservedly so, as events later would show. Young Alchesay and several companions signed up as scouts for Crook and his command in their campaigns against the more rebellious Apaches. But "scout" in this case meant a good deal more than simply a guide, tracker, or point man proceeding ahead of his unit—as events turned out it often meant the men of the unit who bore the brunt of the fighting against a wily, vicious enemy.

Either "kind" of Apache of course was a formidable foe. "The Apache could cover 40 miles a day on foot, shambling along in his sloppy legginglike moccasins, or could reel off 75 miles a day on horseback, caring nothing about running his horse into the ground since his remount station was the nearest ranch," said the same *American Heritage* history. "He could live off the country, 'hilarious and jovial' while a civilized pursuer was perishing of hunger, thirst and sunstroke. He could travel as invisibly as a ghost, appear or disappear as silently as a shadow. The soldier on his trail only knew of his presence when the lethal bow or Winchester announced itself from a concealed and highly defendable position."

Meanwhile, Alchesay was with Crook for the latter's winter campaign of 1872–73—the period for which the Apache scout would earn his Medal of Honor. His citation doesn't go into detail or credit his extraordinary recognition to any one battle, but author Hafford cites a fierce encounter as typical of his performance during the entire campaign. This was the battle of Turret Mountain. "In late March, 1873, the Apache scouts, accompanied by white Army troops, were looking for an outlaw band of Tonto Apaches that had tortured and killed three settlers near Wickenburg. Alchesay and his scouts were put on the trail, but locating the ruthless gang was no easy task. Finally, the scouts captured a Tonto Apache woman who revealed the location of the hostiles. On March 27, Alchesay led his scouts to the top of Turret Mountain where the outlaws were hiding and, in a lightning predawn attack, killed more than 50 and captured 15."

Then, the very next month, Alchesay and his scouts struck at yet another frontier predator, this time at Deltchay, "leader of the last major renegade band in the area." Another flurry of action came in August 1874, when Alchesay and thirty fellow scouts "chased a band of renegades under Chappo and literally wiped out the outlaws," reported Hafford in the *Arizona Highways* book. Various "mopping up" operations continued until the spring of 1875. For the time being anyway, Crook's Apache campaign was over. He was now transferred to the Department of the Platte. In that same year, Alchesay was awarded his Medal of Honor . . . and discharged from service, along with his fellow scouts.

But what about Crook's side of the bargain struck between himself and the "good" Apaches . . . what about his promises of fair treatment when, in fact, settlers and outright criminals began to move into Apache country, killing their game, or, in the case of the unscrupulous, cheating them of supplies assigned to them by the government? What to think when people stole their lands . . . or when the government itself (the Indian Bureau) made decisions moving them from home-land reservations to new ones that they hated?

Those things did happen, and they in time would lead to a new Apache campaign. Crook really wasn't through after all . . . but not for lack of effort on his part to protect the Apache. "General Crook was an Indian fighter of skill and wisdom, and what was still more extraordinary, of an honesty as stubborn as one of his treasured pack mules," noted the *American Heritage* book. "He would no more break his word to the leader of a pack of ragged Apaches than he would break his word to a field marshal of England."

Paradoxical as it might seem, the Apaches were fortunate to have Crook as their primary enemy. At the same time, Washington was fortunate to have a soldier in the field as fair, understanding, and effective as Crook. "He realized that Apaches were not the hell hounds the frontier pictured, and they were not the saintly martyrs pictured by sentimental friends of the Red Man in the East. They were frightened people who were tremendously experienced at being the subjects of extermination, an experience that had made them the most polished masters of ruthless guerrilla fighting in the history of the United States," added the *American Heritage* history.

In Crook's absence after the mid-1870s, said author Hafford in his account, "the plight of the Apache took a slow but inexorable turn for the worse under the corrupt administration of the new Indian Agent Joseph C. Tiffany." What exactly could an unscrupulous Indian agent do? Plenty, it seems. "Through fraud and theft of the Apaches' food and clothing rations, Tiffany nearly starved and froze to death the peaceful reservation Indians."

For Alchesay and ten more of Chief Pedro's clan, however, worse was yet to come. Acting in the summer of 1881, Tiffany had them arrested in the murder of a government scout. They then languished in a jail at Fort Thomas without charges being filed against them, without trial, for fourteen months. According to Hafford also, they were held despite evidence indicating their innocence and "in the face of a government order to either try the men or release them."

Finally, after a Tucson law firm and newspaper rallied to their defense, a federal grand jury ordered the release of the long-suffering Apaches. Said the grand jury: "How any official possessing the slightest manhood would keep 11 men in confinement for 14 months without charges, knowing them to be innocent, is a total mystery."

Tiffany, the object of the jury's wrath, now "slithered off into obscurity," Hafford reported.

Still, not all was well in the historic land of the Apache.

As of 1882, Crook was back. Geronimo and the "wild-running" Chiricahua, striking from the Sierra Madres in northern Mexico, had gone on the rampage. By contrast, Alchesay, fresh from jail, "never displayed the slightest bitterness or resentment against the white community," wrote Hafford. Indeed, said a white contemporary of the tall Apache, "Without saying a word, he showed us all how to accept the difficulties of a difficult world." And now, for a second time, he joined Crook as close adviser, friend, and companion in the field.

The campaign against the wily Geronimo was neither easy nor quick, but by the spring of 1886 it appeared he was ready to give up his constant, wearing fight on the run. Arrangements had been made for a meeting near the Mexican border between the two leaders, Crook and Geronimo. "The conditions of the meeting, stipulated by Geronimo, gave the renegades a distinct military advantage."

It was after dark on March 25, 1886, when Alchesay and a scout named Kae-tenna went alone into the enemy's camp to persuade Geronimo to surrender, a tinderbox mission made all the more risky by the fact that the renegade Apache often was known by that time to be "in a high-voltage state of paranoia made worse by his conspicuous consumption of alcohol." The same often was true of his closest lieutenants. "Throughout the night, Alchesay talked with the exhausted, mostly drunk renegades—all of whom were armed to the teeth," wrote Hafford. "The next day, Geronimo agreed to surrender, and Crook credited Alchesay and his companion scout. 'Without their aid, surrender could not have been achieved,' he said."

Never mind that Geronimo and twenty of his warriors soon after obtained alcohol from an unscrupulous "whiskey peddler," got drunk, escaped, and remained at large another five months. While all that is true, the fact is that Alchesay again had proven his great courage—and his considerable persuasive skills—by negotiating Geronimo's first surrender.

With peace settling on the traditional Apache land, Alchesay, long since made chief of his clan, turned to cattle-raising for an occupation. "He also made lasting friendships with many whites," wrote Hafford.

One special such friendship was with Lutheran minister Edgar Guenther, who established his church on Fort Apache Reservation land that Alchesay obtained for him. The two men often hunted and fished together—"and worked as a team to further the interest of the Apache people."

By Hafford's account also, the minister's son, Arthur *Alchesay* Guenther, later pastor of the same church, would recall two critical times when Alchesay proved a real friend in need to the elder Guenther. The first time came during the worldwide flu epidemic of 1919. The Reverend Guenther was exhausted from traveling the reservation to minister to the sick. "The chief [Alchesay] urged him to rest," recalled the younger Guenther, "but Dad just kept going. Finally, Alchesay exercised his tribal authority, and with the forceful demeanor of a great chief, officially banished my father from the reservation. He and my mother went to Oceanside, California, and stayed there until my father's health returned."

The other time that Alchesay came to the rescue was when the family barn burned down with Guenther's first car, a Model-T Ford, inside. Alchesay and the reservation superintendent persuaded Guenther to get away for a few days, to go on a fishing trip with them.

While he was gone, related the minister's son later, "wagon loads of Apache people arrived at the church." As soon became obvious, they came with a purpose. "Lumber was hauled over from the tribal sawmill, and by the time the fishing party returned, a new barn, freshly painted, was standing at the site of the fire."

The younger Guenther knew Alchesay as a tall, stately man in his seventies. "He took me horseback riding many times. Sometimes he took me for walks, always holding my hand."

But why would Alchesay carry the official designation "A-1"? The younger Guenther remembered that also. "Way back when General Crook came to the reservation, the government assigned identification numbers (much like Social Security numbers) to the people.

"Alchesay got the first number, A-1. When I was a kid, and because I was named after him, my nickname was A-1."

Alchesay was so close to the elder minister and his family, he officially opened the door to Guenther's newly built Lutheran church when it was completed in 1922 and spoke briefly to the Indians and whites attending that first worship service. Symbolically given a key to the church, he asked with dying breath in the late summer of 1928 to have it placed in his hand and buried with him. And it was.

★

1887
Disappearance of Mysterious Dave
★

In the Old West there were shootouts and there were . . . well, there was this mysterious shooter named Dave Mather. He was an outlaw and a lawman, a friend of Wyatt Earp, a man who floated from Mobeetie, Texas, to Las Vegas, New Mexico. Mather was a lynch-mob leader, a Dodge City drifter, a probable cattle rustler, a con man, a deputy sheriff, a deputy marshal, an assistant marshal . . . a murdering back-shooter, and a compiler of a thoroughly untidy résumé that ended with his disappearance after a brief sighting in Lone Pine, Nebraska, during the summer of 1887. But first he had a hand in two of the most spectacular shootouts ever reported.

Before that, however, Mather could be as mean and lowdown as anybody with a gun. There was a shootout when he was a deputy marshal, of all things, in little Las Vegas, New Mexico, when the gang led by Tom Henry—"a band of tough, swaggering youths," per Leon Claire Metz in his book, *The Shooters* (1976)—came riding into town. The local city marshal, Joe Carson—in other words, Mather's boss—confronted the potential hotheads at the door of a saloon and told them that under city law they had to check their guns with the bartender. According to Metz, they "snickered" at the notion, "so Carson and Mather came charging through the saloon door a half-hour later and that's when the lights went out."

As they went out, guns boomed in the dark. Carson was so "riddled with bullets" he hardly had time to fall before he was dead.

Tom Henry apparently had done some of the shooting, and of course there were the others with him to consider as well. They were John Dorsey, James West, and William "Big" Randall. But it turns out neither Randall nor West would be much of a factor anymore. "The gunmen," wrote Metz, "unfortunately concentrated on the wrong man." Carson may have gone down under the fusillade of shots, but not Mather, and his guns "were booming too."

In seconds, Mather had killed Randall, had shot West "twice through the body," and had "put a bullet through Henry's leg."

Odd behavior for an occasional outlaw himself?

Just wait, this case of no honor among thieves gets worse . . . and worse.

A doctor hurrying to the scene said the badly wounded West should be taken to a hospital, but Mather, thought to be a New Englander originally, and possibly a descendant of the fire-breathing Puritan preacher Cotton Mather, was having none of that. As far as he was concerned, West was going to jail; let him linger there.

That was in mid-January. On February 6, fugitives Dorsey and Henry had been found at Mora, New Mexico, Metz wrote, and were returned to Las Vegas and its jail, where their companion West still lingered. That night Mather led a lynch mob to the jail. The mob took the trio to a windmill in the town plaza. "A rope dangled from high above."

This wouldn't be pretty, but it wouldn't unfold exactly as planned, either.

West, begging for mercy, went first. Bleeding and carried to the grim place on a litter, he really was strung up . . . only his hands were not tied and he was able to slip them beneath the loop of rope forming the noose and pull himself up. He was screaming for his mother and then, "as his ill-fitting trousers dropped low on his waist, he cried, 'Please button my pants.'"

If anyone in the crowd was by now developing second thoughts over such a sorry spectacle, it was too late. "At this moment, Joe Carson's widow began shooting at the prisoners."

The fact is, there would be no hangings after all.

Under this latest fusillade, both Henry and Dorsey fell to the platform, but neither one was dead . . . yet. "Writhing in agony" from his latest gunshot wounds, Henry "crawled to the platform's edge and begged someone to shoot him through the head."

As if that were a signal, all three prisoners—all of whom were less than twenty-one years old—were, "within seconds," according to western writer Metz, "full of holes." And whose fault was that? "A coroner noted dryly the next day that the dead men had met their just fate from the hands of parties unknown."

Far from blameless in the matter, Mather "not long afterwards" drifted on . . . and on, his road to a historical vanishing act to be marked by at least one more shooting.

But first, a look at his activities up until now.

Was he born in Connecticut or Massachusetts? Since sources differ, New England is a good compromise, while his birth date seems agreed upon as 1845.

Was he really a descendant of Cotton Mather, though? Maybe.

He went west, but where and when?

According to Metz, "Mysterious Dave," as he later was known, first turned up in 1873 in Arkansas, where he acquired a slight reputation as a cattle rustler. No known convictions.

The next year he made the scene in Dodge City, Kansas, soon to be a notorious cow town, but at the moment a mecca for buffalo hunters. There he gambled and from there he did some buffalo hunting himself. He was knifed in a gambling dispute, recovered, and became "a part-time peace officer around Dodge."

Moody, sometimes drunk, but always a deadly shot, "he was no great charmer to the eye," either. "He stood about five-foot-nine, had a slender build, dark complexion, brooding eyes, and a so-called 'killer mustache' (the droopy kind)."

Sitting and drinking alone in the saloons many an evening, he had an odd but effective way of checking to see if he were sober enough to continue. Out on the street just beyond the swinging saloon doors stood a fire bell. Borrowing his gun from the bartender about every half an hour, Mather took aim at the bell and fired off a shot. "If the bell rang, he was still sober. If he missed, he paid up and went home."

Meanwhile, he befriended Wyatt Earp, and in 1878 they moved to Mobeetie, Texas, the first real town in the Texas Panhandle and another rendezvous for buffalo hunters, according to the Internet site maintained by the Old Mobeetie Texas Association. Once known as "Hidetown" then "Sweetwater" or "Sweet Town." it became the Wheeler County seat in 1879.

Here, until run out of town by the sheriff, Earp and Mather ran a con selling gold-painted bricks as the real thing for one hundred dollars each. "According to the yarn Mather and Earp glibly wove, these gold bricks were from an old, recently discovered Spanish mine that the Indians had sealed up after slaughtering the priests and soldiers," explained Metz. "Now these priceless pieces of treasure were being sold at bargain rates in order to obtain enough money for a new expedition into the remote area."

The jig was up for Earp and Mather when the town sheriff bought one of the bricks and realized it was all a sham.

That is when Mather, alone, shoved on to Las Vegas, New Mexico, "a railroad and cattle center and one of the toughest towns in the territory." Among the notorious gunslingers and outlaws occasionally passing through, or even staying a while, were Billy the Kid, Jesse James, Dave Rudabaugh, and Doc Holliday, the latter accompanied by girlfriend "Big Nosed Kate." According to the Las Vegas history sketch maintained on the New Mexico Highlands University Web site (http://www.nmhu.edu/region/lvhist.htm), Holliday stayed long enough to open a dentistry practice here and to run a saloon and gambling hall before moving on to Tombstone, Arizona, for his role, at the side of the Earp brothers, in the famous shootout at the OK Corral. (No relation to the Las Vegas, Nevada, of today, incidentally, this Las Vegas owed its birth to settlement by fifteen Spanish families, then became a way station on the historic Santa Fe Trail from Missouri to Santa Fe, New Mexico. The present-day Highlands University in town traces its start to the New Mexico Normal School, established here in 1898. As another note of distinction, says the university Web site, the town gave Teddy Roosevelt twenty-one of his Rough Riders for the Spanish-American War and then, afterward, "hosted the first Rough Riders reunion, attended by the soon-to-be President himself.")

Settling momentarily in New Mexico's Las Vegas, Mather may have "sometimes held up a local train or stagecoach," speculated Metz, but "he nevertheless was employed as a deputy marshal." Then in mid-January 1880, "came his first test as a lawman." That was when the Henry gang had pulled into town and gone to the Close and Patterson Saloon without turning in their weapons.

As mentioned previously, they remained in town rather permanently . . . but Mather left after a while. He apparently drifted back to Dodge then Colorado then south to San Antonio. "In Texas he tried to pass counterfeit money and the sheriff chased him out of the county."

He may have spent time in El Paso, but he soon showed up in Dallas . . . "and became involved with Georgia Morgan, a black madam." When he left a few weeks later, it was with "pockets full of her jewelry."

Mather returned to Dodge City, where he became both an assistant marshal and a deputy sheriff. By now, Dodge had become best known as a cow town rife with saloons, dance halls, and brothels, but a reform movement had been under way here for a time . . . with some of the reformers themselves becoming saloonkeepers. A magnet for the likes of Bat Masterson, Wyatt Earp, and Luke Short and still the scene of shootings, Dodge continued to offer a lot of work for an honest lawman.

Mather and fellow assistant marshal Tom Nixon, himself a dance hall co-owner, mixed it up one day in July 1884 over the attentions that Mather apparently had been giving Nixon's wife, an invalid. By some accounts, Nixon shot and wounded Mather. By the Metz account, they "tangled in a darkened hallway," but neither one was wounded, even though Nixon rushed outside to claim he had "killed" Mather.

None of these activities proved beneficial in any way to Nixon, who just days later was shot in the back by Mather. That is to say, Mather made sure there was no margin of error when he "walked up behind Nixon in a saloon and emptied a revolver into his back." And yet "a jury figured Tom got what was coming to him, and acquitted Mather."

Somebody must have had a few reservations, since Mysterious Dave Mather now was asked "to move on." This he did, "becoming a wayward drifter across the plains and mountains of the West." After appearing at Lone Pine, Nebraska, in the summer of 1887, he left no footprints . . . he simply vanished from the pages of history.

☆ ☆ ☆

Additional note: As a legal footnote to the story of Mysterious Dave, a Dodge City jury did find him responsible for the death of a sleepy greyhound dog that was struck by a stray bullet when Mather shot Nixon in the back. As cited by Leon Metz, however, the jury finding was that the dog "came to its death by a bullet fired from the gun in the hands of Dave Mather, known as Mysterious Dave, and that the shooting was justified as any dog should have known better than go to sleep in a Dodge City saloon."

1 8 8 7
"Stovepipe" Johnson Pursues His Dream

Every man has his dream, but few have ever overcome so much to achieve it as Adam Rankin "Stovepipe" Johnson, early Texas mail-coach driver, Indian fighter, surveyor, Confederate general and raider extraordinaire, and founder of a Texas city once known as "Blind Man's Town."

Johnson began life quietly enough in Henderson, Kentucky, but left home and a job at a local drugstore in 1854 at the age of twenty to sample the adventurous life of a Texas frontiersman. Arriving in still wild-and-woolly Burnet County of the Texas hill country's Highland Lakes region, he soon established himself with the Butterfield Overland Mail service as a driver and station contractor well able to fight off Indians or other would-be predators. Also trained as a surveyor, he knew good land when he saw it, and one day he saw a sight he would never forget—Marble Falls on the Colorado River, a staircase waterfall of one step after another of pink granite that looked like gleaming marble. Close by, in fact, was a huge dome of tons of pink granite.

One look was all that young Johnson needed to settle upon his lifelong dream. He would found and build a city on the spot. With the river and falls as a source of power, his town was sure to grow and attract industry.

As he began assembling the land he would need to found his town, one plot after another, he knew he could not fail. Settlers would come flocking as soon as he was ready with enough land to advertise. Some years earlier, another entrepreneur, named Charles S. Todd, had tried to start "Todd's Village" at the same site, but his effort fell through. Undeterred by that bit of local history, Adam Johnson married, settled upon a homestead in nearby Burnet, started a family (there would be six children in all), and kept assembling his projected town's real estate.

But on the eve of the Civil War, he experienced his first numbing setback: All his land certificates proved to be worthless.

Perhaps it was fortunate that the start of the Civil War just months later provided an all-consuming diversion . . . but if so, fortunate only for the moment.

Going with the Confederacy, like his adopted state of Texas, Johnson soon was riding hard as a scout for the legendary cavalryman Nathan Bedford Forrest, but Johnson himself in short time would display the stuff of legends. When U. S. Grant closed the Union vise on Fort Donelson on the Tennessee River in 1862, Johnson was among those who escaped the trap with Generals Forrest and John B. Floyd.

Later in the same year, by now commander of his own hard-riding Texas Partisan Rangers, Johnson earned his colorful nickname of "Stovepipe" by capturing the Ohio River town of Newburgh, Indiana, "at the point" of two stovepipes mounted on a wagon and disguised as a cannon. To the embarrassment of a much larger Union detachment on hand, Newburgh "fell" to his twelve men and phony gun with not a shot being fired.

For that exploit and various other blows to the Union cause, Johnson would earn the undying enmity of many Union officers, especially those exasperated by the fruitless pursuit of Johnson's guerrilla-like group in Tennessee and Kentucky, often *inside* Federal lines. In fact, the day was coming (in 1864) when Union Brig. Gen. Hugh Ewing, a foster brother to William Tecumseh Sherman, would issue an order stating that a captured Johnson (and any of his men) should be shot "on the spot."

More fondly to be sure, one of Johnson's own troopers, Thomas S. Miller, years later observed: "Paladin of old was not more daring and heroic than this Southern knight on the field of battle. No man in the Southern army, no matter how high his rank, displayed more military skill. . . . He was literally the 'Swamp Fox' of Kentucky."

Also galling for Johnson's Union opponents, when "Stovepipe" accompanied Confederate raider John Hunt Morgan on his bold foray into Indiana and Ohio in midsummer of 1863, Johnson managed to escape the Union forces that closed in on Morgan at Buffington Island. The city planner from Texas simply swam across the Ohio River with his men. Morgan was taken prisoner (but later broke out of the Ohio State Penitentiary in a truly spectacular escape).

Still the partisan raider a year later, Johnson finally hit a rocky road of his own. While leading an attack on a Union encampment at Grubbs Crossroads, Kentucky, he was accidentally shot and terribly wounded by his own men. Quickly and easily captured, he was held for months as a prisoner. Fortunately, his captors did not shoot him outright, but he did finish out the war—and defeat of the Confederacy—as a prisoner at Fort Warren.

Returning to central Texas afterward, Johnson still carried his dream, even if achieving it would be far from easy. Refusing to give it up, however, the badly wounded war veteran bided his time and over the next thirteen years carefully retraced his former steps around Marble Falls. He roved the area in a carriage driven by a son as he revisited the old plots, all of them still etched in his memory. He juggled and purchased land here, land there, until eventually he had assembled the real estate needed to carry out the dream. By 1886, he was ready—he owned half the acreage in the area's original land grant and had established control of the rest. Now he laid out the lots for his proposed Marble Falls, formed an investment company with nine partners, and in 1887 began selling land at $75 to $750 a parcel.

"Soon the town was a thriving cotton center," notes today's Marble Falls Chamber of Commerce (www.marblefalls.org/history.htm).

Meanwhile, following a destructive fire in 1881, a new state capitol was under way at Austin. "Granite Mountain," the 866-foot dome of pink granite Johnson had first seen as a young man, offered bright prospect of just the stone the builders needed to satisfy their visions of a handsome new capitol. The owners of Granite Mountain were willing to provide the granite free of charge . . . but how to ship it to Austin, fifty miles distant? There was no rail line between the granite and an existing railroad at Burnet.

Enter, at this point, city-founder Johnson. "Immediately Johnson went to Austin and announced to the state legislature that he would give seven miles of right of way for a railroad from Granite Mountain to Burnet and assured the state that his fellow land owners would follow," says the chamber history. "The land contributions came in and a narrow gauge railroad was completed in 1885, using convict labor."

As one thing followed another, adds the chamber account, stone from Granite Mountain was used in buildings "all over the state, the nation and the world." Despite a century of quarrying, moreover, "[T]he size of this huge mass has changed very little. There are centuries worth of granite left in this quarry, which is the largest of its kind in the United States."

Moving to Marble Falls after years at Burnet, Johnson and his wife, Josephine, built a handsome home—nowadays the Liberty Hall Guest Haus hostelry—with a gorgeous view of the falls. In the 1950s a river dam obliterated that vista with the creation of today's Marble Falls Lake as both a power source and recreational asset. In his day, however, Johnson enjoyed descriptions both of the falls and of his burgeoning new city . . . descriptions furnished by his wife and children because he himself could not see either one.

During his six postbellum decades as a city founder and a major Texas personality, Adam Rankin Johnson, once famous as "Stovepipe" Johnson, was blind, thanks to that errant rifle shot in 1864 by one of his own men that destroyed both of his eyes. That severe handicap never stopped him from pursuing his old dream. Nor did it stop him from compiling a well-respected Civil War memoir, *The Partisan Rangers of the Confederate States Army.* Indeed, said his onetime trooper Miller, "Perhaps no man has led a more cheerful and happy life."

When that life ended in 1922, fittingly enough, funeral services for Johnson were held in the senate chamber of the state capitol at Austin, with burial in the State Cemetery nearby.

☆

1 8 8 8
Still Another Vanishing Act

☆

One of the most famous outlaws of the Old West never shot anyone, so far as is known . . . unless he did so during his reported Civil War service with the Company B of the 116th Illinois Infantry.

Famously genteel, never violent, indeed always quite the gentleman, he did brandish a shotgun and he did stop and rob at least twenty-seven stagecoaches, according to Wells Fargo, which ought to know, since all twenty-seven were Wells Fargo stages.

Best known to Wild West history buffs as "Black Bart," he apparently was known to his friends as Charles E. Boles, alias Charles E. Bolton, a diminutive (not quite five feet eight inches in height), neatly dressed, deep-voiced man with graying hair whose habit before a robbery was to leave his Room #40 at San Francisco's Webb House hostelry at 37 Second Street, take an evening boat to the inland port of Stockton, and then simply walk forty miles the next day to reach the mountains that evening. "The next day," onetime Wells Fargo agent James E. Rice wrote in 1920, Black Bart "would rob a stage and the only evidence he would leave would be a 'poem' in which there was some humor and occasionally a vulgar line. He was therefore known as the poetic robber." He signed his verses "the Po8."

His robberies ran from 1875 to 1883 and always took place in the mountains of northern California. "His M.O. [modus operandi]," says the Wells Fargo Web site (http://www.wellsfargo.com/about/stories/ch3.jhtml) "was to suddenly appear on lonely stage roads wearing a light-colored duster and a flour sack over his head with a derby hat perched on top of it. Armed with a shotgun, he'd order in his distinctive deep voice, 'Throw down the box!' He was extremely efficient at collecting all the loot in the treasure boxes and never once bothered with the small stuff like the passengers' valuables."

One time, says the Wells Fargo account, "when a panicked woman tossed him her purse, he gentlemanly returned it to her and said, 'Thank you, madam, but I don't need your money. I only want Wells Fargo's.'"

In fact, his target always was Wells Fargo, and it wasn't long before the stagecoach company's chief of detectives, James B. Hume, was spending a good deal of his time on the case. Writing in the June 1982 issue of *American History* magazine, John Stanchak pointed out that while Hume was a noted "pioneer in scientific detection," he in this case "had to fall back on a detective's first line of information-gathering, footwork." Thus, "Instead of pounding city pavements, he trooped up and down northern California hills talking to farmers, examining crime scenes, and measuring distances. By late 1882, this footwork paid off, giving Hume a detailed but surprising picture of Black Bart and the way he carried out his work."

That image was of a man in his fifties—old for an active stage robber—who was a likable, urbane dinner companion, was "magnificently mustachioed," and a tireless hiker who once, apparently with no horse at his disposal, robbed "two different coaches thirty miles apart in a 24-hour period."

For all his hard work, though, chief of detectives Hume had no idea who the gray-haired robber was or where he lived.

Hume did know, of course, that the very first robbery had taken place on July 26, 1875, near Copperopolis in Calavera County on the Sonora-to-Milton run. Black Bart, as the thief styled himself in one of his early poems, stepped out of the bushes as the stage creaked its way up a steep grade. He always wore a long coat or duster, his feet were bound in rags, and he wore a sack with eyeholes over his head and face. The striking thing about this first robbery was his use of cleverly placed sticks poking out of the roadside brush like so many guns held by hidden confederates. Stagecoach driver John Shine allegedly was convinced he was being held up by several robbers, but he discovered it was all a ruse after Black Bart took his loot and disappeared into the nearby countryside.

As Stanchak reported, "The phantom gang feature was dropped from the nervy bandit's repertoire after the first hold-up."

Ironically, Bart's career as a stage robber came to an end after he returned to the scene of his first robbery in November 1883. Not right after . . . but soon. What tripped him up was a dropped handkerchief with a laundry mark from a San Francisco laundry.

He had stopped the Sonora-to-Milton stage on the same hill as before, but with no fake guns in the bushes this time. The more significant difference was the fact that the driver this time had an armed companion who had jumped from the stage minutes before the holdup to do some hunting. He returned just as the robbery was ending. As Black Bart stepped back into the brush with a stolen bag of four thousand dollars in gold coin, the driver grabbed his friend's rifle and fired a shot at the departing bandit. He missed, but his companion then took the weapon, fired again, and apparently struck the fleeing highwayman. Bart "stumbled and fell."

But when the driver and his companion dashed into the brush to find him, he was gone . . . vanished again, and obviously only slightly wounded if at all. Still, he had left behind some vital items: his derby hat, a straight razor, his binoculars, "and some buckshot wrapped in a handkerchief." It bore the laundry mark FX07.

It was only a matter of weeks until Hume and his men tracked down the missing bandit by visiting dozens of San Francisco laundries.

They found one establishment that catered to a supposedly well-to-do man in the mining business who "belonged" to the same laundry mark: FX07. He went quietly.

In fact, he pled guilty to a single count of stage robbery (his twenty-eight robberies had netted him an estimated eighteen thousand dollars, by the way, a tidy sum for those days even in gold-fevered California), and he was sentenced to serve six years in the state penitentiary at San Quentin, a light sentence possibly taking into account his relatively advanced age of nearly sixty. Furthermore, he was able to return most of the money he had stolen, Stanchak noted, and "[H]e had never harmed anyone in the course of a robbery." As indicated by the load of buckshot carried in his handkerchief, it may also be that he never loaded his shot-gun, added Stanchak.

Released in just four years for good behavior, the notorious if somewhat aged bandit attracted a crowd of inquiring reporters. Asked if he would be writing any more poetry, he apparently laughed and said, "Didn't you just hear me say I'm through with crime?"

Shortly after his release from prison in January 1888, Black Bart disappeared for good.

---------------- ✯ ----------------

1 8 8 8
County Seat War

---------------- ✯ ----------------

On the ground next to nineteen-year-old Herbert M. Tonney lay four bodies. He himself was wounded and playing dead. All this shooting, all these deaths were the result of a "county seat war" between the proponents of two rival towns in southwestern Kansas!

So heated was the rivalry that the advocates of one town, Hugoton, now had gone so far as to gun down anyone they associated with the rival town of Woodsdale. And, by the way . . . all murders notwithstanding, Hugoton, Kansas, today *is* the county seat.

"I knew that my turn must come pretty soon," Tonney recounted after the "Hay Meadow Massacre. "It was Chamberlain who was to be my executioner, J. B. Chamberlain, chairman of County Commissioners of Stevens County, and always prominent in Hugoton matters. Chamberlain was about eight feet from me, or perhaps less, when he raised his rifle deliberately to kill me. There were powder burns on my neck and face from the shot, as the woman who cared for me on the following day testified in court.

"I saw the rifle leveled, and realized that I was going to be killed. Instinctively, I flinched to one side of the line of the rifle. That saved my life. The ball entered the left side of my neck about three quarters of an inch from the carotid artery and about half an inch above the left clavicle, coming out through the left shoulder. I felt no pain at the time, and indeed, did not feel pain until the next day. The shock of the shot knocked me down and numbed me, and I suppose I lay a minute or two before I recovered sensation or knew anything about my condition. It was supposed by all that I was killed, and, in a vague way, I agreed that I must be killed; that my spirit was simply present listening and seeing."

There was even more murderous action to come. Having shot Stevens County sheriff John M. Cross and three other members of a hastily organized "posse" from Woodsdale, one or more of the Hugoton advocates now went around making sure everyone of the shooting victims was dead . . . *really* dead.

"Someone came to me, took hold of my foot, and began to pull me around to see whether I was dead. [Sam] Robinson wanted to make sure. Chamberlain, my executioner, said, 'He's dead. I gave him a center shot. I don't need to shoot a man twice at that distance.' Either Chamberlain or someone else took me by the legs, dragged me about and kicked me in the side, leaving bruises which were visible for many days afterwards. I feigned death so well that they did not shoot me again. They did shoot a second time each of the others who lay near me."

The multiple shootings took place at a so-called hay camp on the northeast shore of Wild Horse Lake, described by Harry E. Chrisman in the *Hutchinson (Kans.) News* of June 28, 1961, as "a wet-weather basin that is totally dry in dry years." More to the point, the shooting scene was in a lawless no man's land between Kansas and Oklahoma, later to become the Oklahoma Panhandle. It would be difficult to find a court claiming jurisdiction. Indeed, the Hugoton "shooters" made no attempt whatsoever to harm the three haymakers who witnessed the execution-style killings.

The episode was the climax to a months-long rivalry between Hugoton and Woodsdale for county-seat status. As explained by Chrisman in his newspaper article "Blood Spilled in Kansas 'County Seat Wars,'" the founders of Hugo, later Hugoton, laid out their town in 1885, only to see two lawyers, Sam Wood and J. C. Price, come along and establish Woodsdale, "six miles north and two miles east of Hugo, across a belt of sandhills." The newcomers then offered lots for free to woo away Hugoton's potential populous. The Hugoton crowd, on the other hand, used fake names in a census count to meet the state's minimum population quota to achieve county status, according to shooting survivor Tonney.

Meanwhile, Wood and Price conducted their own census, came up with lower figures, then set out for the state capital of Topeka to present their case to the state authorities. Before they could get there, however, a "posse" from Hugoton arrested them. "The Hugoton posse took the two lawyers to No Man's Land to hang them," added the Chrisman account. Perhaps, but since it didn't happen, that's speculative. It couldn't happen right then because a Woodsdale posse swung into action and, in an ambush, freed the men and arrested the Hugoton crowd, its members then released on bond. All these events took place in 1886.

As one thing continued to lead to another, Woodsdale hotel owner Sam Robinson ran for county sheriff, lost to Cross, then defected to the other side. The reason, other than pure pique, soon became obvious. "Hugoton then made Sam Robinson its city marshal and gave him two town lots to which he moved his hotel," wrote Chrisman. As other accounts explain, he moved the two-story building itself.

In the spring of 1888, the situation escalated as a Woodsdale justice of the peace issued a warrant for the arrest of Hugoton city marshal Sam Robinson for pistol-whipping a deputy sheriff during a meeting at the St. Nicholas Hotel in nearby Voorhees, Kansas. "The arrest attempt," Chrisman added, "sparked a fight between Hugoton partisans and the Woodsdale group, Winchester rifles and shotguns making their appearance for the first time. More than two hundred men were involved in the action.

"Luckily, no one was killed in the skirmishing which took place, both in Hugoton streets and in the sandhills."

Next, with neither side backing down, came a crisscross of posses plunging into the nearby no man's land. First, learning that Robinson and others were on an outing at a ranch in the lawless strip, Woodsdale sent a posse to arrest him. He fled.

The next day, he joined up with a Hugoton posse that "had come out to rescue him," reported Chrisman.

That same day, county sheriff Cross also crossed into no man's land with his rather small contingent of just three men, plus the nineteen-year-old Tonney. Having heard that Robinson was cornered in "the Strip," Cross intended to arrest him. By nightfall, however, he and his weary "posse" of four encountered the haymakers alongside Wild Horse Lake and took up their invitation to camp there overnight.

"After all were in their bedrolls asleep," added Chrisman, "Sam Robinson and his posse rode in.

"Awakening the sheriff's posse, Robinson asked for their guns. When the Woodsdale posse had been disarmed, Robinson lined them up in a row."

Then came the methodical shooting of Cross and his companions, as described by lone survivor Tonney in a 1977 publication from Keys, Oklahoma, *The Old Timers News Yearbook*. Fortunately for Tonney, the assailants soon rode off, leaving him for dead . . . but taking the haymakers with them. They safely would be dropped off later at a small town called Niagara. Tonney's recollection: "The haymakers were now in trouble, and said they could not go on putting up their hay with the corpses laying around. Robinson told them to hitch up and follow the Hugoton party away. They did this, and after a while I was left lying there in the half-moonlight, with the dead bodies of my friends for company."

After twenty minutes or so, Tonney bestirred himself—"I found I could get on my feet, although I was very weak." He examined the bodies of his companions then found a nearby buffalo wallow of "filthy water." Filthy or not, "I led my horse there, lay down in the water and drank a little of it." Mounting his horse, he rode "about fifteen or sixteen miles along a trail, not fully knowing where I was going."

The haymakers, meanwhile, had rushed to Voorhees with news of the shootings, and Tonney now met a constable from that town proceeding to the murder scene. Since the Hugoton crowd might return at any time, the constable hid Tonney in a cornfield. "This, no doubt, saved my life, for the Hugoton scouts were soon down there the next morning, having discovered that one of the victims had come to life."

When two wagons "with ice" were sent from Woodsdale to pick up the bodies, "these Hugoton scouts met them and made them ride through Hugoton so that the assembled citizens of that town might see the corpses."

Tonney was taken to a doctor as both towns now prepared to defend themselves. "After my arrival at Woodsdale, it might have been supposed that all the country was in a state of war, instead of living in a time of modern civilization. Entrenchments were thrown up, rifle pits were dug, and stands established for sharp-shooters. Guards were thrown out all around the town, and mounted scouts continued to scour the country. Hugoton, expecting that Woodsdale would make an organized attack in retaliation, was quite as fully fortified in every way."

Fortunately, the governor called out the state militia to maintain order, charges were brought, a trial was scheduled, the situation gradually simmered down . . . although not with justice done, by any means.

Chrisman noted that a federal district court in Paris, Texas, many miles from the scene, returned indictments against thirty Hugoton citizens, indictments largely based on Tonney's account. In a trial begun on April 4, 1890, six Hugoton men were convicted and sentenced to be hanged, county commissioner Chamberlain among them.

Hugoton marshal Sam Robinson, however, not only "had fled the county," he was sitting safely in a Colorado prison on a robbery conviction. Meanwhile, since most of the convicted men were Civil War veterans, a public furor arose on their behalf, but it was the U.S. Supreme Court they late could thank for granting their demands for a new trial, due to questions about the federal court's jurisdiction in the case.

Meanwhile, Sam Wood of Woodsdale faced a civil proceeding in Stevens County Court at Hugoton, and on June 23, 1891, he turned up at the church serving as the courthouse and was shot in the doorway by the judge's armed guard, Jim Brennan, Chrisman reported also. Wood died on the spot in front of his wife.

"Brennan was never tried; though a half-hearted attempt was made to do so, no jury was found who would try him in Hugoton," added Chrisman's account. "Without Wood's brilliant leadership, Woodsdale shivered and died, became another ghost site. Hugoton remained the county seat."

Also mentioning other "county seat wars" in western Kansas, Chrisman said the coming of the railroad spelled a very welcome end to them. "By 1890," he wrote, "the railroads had laid their tracks across the western counties and those towns favorably situated lived, many of the others died. Many towns moved, bag and baggage to the railroads, often, as did Liberal, starting completely new towns.

"So with more or less permanent town sites established along railways, came the end of the county seat wars in Kansas. It had not happened too soon."

Additional note: Tonney, as chance would have it, ran into his would-be killer Chamberlain years later in a Leavenworth restaurant. Describing the encounter as a "singular experience," Tonney said that Chamberlain and a friend sat down at the same table that Tonney himself was using. "My opportunity for revenge was right there. I did not take it. Chamberlain and his friend did not know who I was. I left the matter to the law, with what results the records of the law's failure in these matters has shown." No one, added Tonney, ever went to prison for any of the murders committed in the name of the Stevens County Seat War.

Record-setting Structures

One ornate structure, completed in 1888 after six years of construction work, was the seventh largest building in the world. Another, the first of its kind built west of the Mississippi River, took fifteen years to reach completion . . . a third took twenty-two years. Still another became the largest domed structure by volume in the United States. Yet a fifth qualified as the world's fifth tallest dome built of masonry.

Aside from a few domes, what do all these imposing structures have in common? Every one of them—and quite a few more—are among the state capitols dotting the West in often magnificent and splendiferous style.

For instance, the seventh largest building in the world at the time of its construction in the 1880s? Who built it? Wouldn't you know, it had to be that big, brawny, sometimes swaggering western state with a proud history of independence from absolutely everyone . . . that is to say, who else but the Lone Star State of **Texas?**

Six years in the making and faced with pink granite from Marble Falls, Texas, the truly splendiferous capitol at Austin sends its dome soaring to 309 feet 8 inches in height, a full 7 feet higher than the dome's model adorning the U.S. Capitol in Washington. While the exterior walls are of pink granite, the interior walls and dome are of Texas limestone, noted Willis J. Ehlert in his 1993 book *America's Heritage: Capitols of the United States.* Crowning the lantern housing atop the dome, Ehlert points out, is a sixteen-foot statue, the Goddess of Liberty, "holding the Lone Star in her raised hand." Inside, "The rotunda rises four floors to a sky-blue ceiling with the Texas Lone Star in the ceiling." Further, "The Capitol's south foyer floor memorializes the twelve major battles fought on Texas soil. In the center of the rotunda floor is a terrazzo design of the 'Seal of Nations,' showing the five nations that have ruled Texas. Around the Seal of the Republic of Texas are the Great Seal of the United States, the Seal of the Confederacy, the Seal of Mexico, the fleur-de-lis of the French coat of arms, and the Seal of Spain."

Texas did have earlier capitols, three of them right in Austin, but the last such structure in Austin had been ruined by fire. To design its replacement in the 1880s, Texas hired then fired architect Elijah E. Myers of Detroit, who early in life gave up law studies to become a carpenter and joiner. It's not clear whether he ever completed architectural school, but using the pseudonym "Tuebor," he submitted the winning entry in the design competition of 1881 for the new Texas capitol and was hired to oversee the project for twelve thousand dollars.

Originally planning a square dome, he decided on round instead. Other changes came along, too, but his real downfall stemmed from his delays and the apparently unreal illnesses he repeatedly claimed. The Texas capitol board fired him after five years on the job and turned to Pomeranian-born builder Gustav Wilke of Chicago, already the chief subcontractor on the project, to finish it over the next two years.

He did so, using Myers's plans, which were extensively studied during renovation work in the 1980s, one hundred years later. Myers came to his Texas job after designing Michigan's capitol in the 1870s and before moving on to Colorado, to carry on with its capitol, notes *The Handbook of Texas Online.* He had designed an Idaho territorial capitol no longer in existence and a Utah capitol "that was never built."

Modeled upon the nation's Capitol in Washington, the Renaissance Revival structure in Austin, when completed in 1888, boasted "392 rooms, 18 vaults, 924 windows, and 404 doors," according to the Texas *Handbook.* It cost $3.7 million to build, with convicts quarrying the pink granite from Marble Falls, Texas (see pages 300–303). The original goddess statue of zinc, raised to the top of the dome in 1888, had to come down for restoration work in 1985, a tricky task accomplished by a helicopter. Now housed on the capitol grounds in a special structure, the first Goddess of Liberty has been replaced on the dome by a new statue "cast of aluminum in molds made from the original zinc statue," notes the *Handbook.* "The entire cost of more than $450,000 was raised from private donations."

Standing to the right of the capitol's main entrance is a thirty-five-foot structure, a dome on top of arches, mounted in turn upon four large pillars, and all a monument to the defenders of the Alamo. On the pillars, says the *Handbook,* "are engraved the names of the heroes of the Alamo." Such is the occasional inexactness of history, however, that "forty names on this monument are inaccurate."

Construction of the **Colorado** capitol in Denver, meanwhile, was begun in 1886 and took twenty-two years to complete—"because the builders were determined to use mostly state materials," said Ehlert in his *Capitols* book. Like the Texas structure, Colorado's domed edifice "resembles the basic Classical design of the nation's capitol in Washington." A western capitol that took even longer to complete—from a start in 1893 to completion in 1928, thirty-five years in all—is the **Washington** State Legislative Building in Olympia, its completion attributable to "disputes about size, plans, and location," wrote Ehlert. The final product, he added, "is the tallest domed masonry state capitol in the United States and the fifth tallest in the world." The Washington state dome rises to 287 feet and at the time of its installation was "the fourth largest dome in the world."

A domed state capitol begun even while the U.S. Capitol itself was still under construction in Washington is **California**'s handsome center of government in Sacramento, a structure begun in 1861 but not completed until 1878. Even so, California's is the oldest state capitol west of the Mississippi. "Set in a park of ten city blocks, it is surrounded by over 400 varieties of exotic trees and plants," noted Ehlert.

Built many years after California's capitol, **Wisconsin**'s striking governmental edifice in Madison boasts "the largest dome by volume ever built in the U.S. and the third largest dome by volume in the world." **Iowa,** though, can claim a unique distinction all its own on the dome front—its state capitol in Des Moines sports a central dome plus smaller domes mounted on each corner of the building.

Every state has its own nickname, state bird, flower, animal, etcetera, along with wonderful and symbolic heroes, many of them evoked by various statues, monuments, and other adornments seen at one state capitol or another, such as a rendering of Wisconsin's state animal, the badger, protruding from a pediment over an entrance to the state capitol. But only **Oklahoma** can boast a symbolic oil derrick standing near the front steps. Not only that, but the Sooner State's Greco-Roman styled state capitol building in Oklahoma City is "the only state capitol building with an oil well under it."

Called Petunia One, the well was tapped in 1941, wrote Ehlert, and at one time it produced six hundred barrels of oil a day. The massive four-story capitol building itself offers no dome . . . but then, with an oil derrick rising from a petunia bed in front, who's going to notice?

Meanwhile, the Oklahoma capitol is unique in one more way: It is the only state capitol in America designed to have a dome that never got its dome.

Kipling Survives a Colorado Passage

MESSAGE FROM THE PAST: Traveling through the American West in 1889, Rudyard Kipling found a lot to complain about. His resultant book, *From Sea to Sea* (no "Shining" included), "probably stands as the most brilliant piece of invective ever unloaded on late-nineteenth-century American life," noted editor Frederick R. Rinehart in his 1993 collection of pieces titled *Chronicles of Colorado.* As Rinehart noted, Kipling did not spare Colorado from that same invective. Perhaps it had something to do with the hailstorm that apparently was his greeting.

> The heat was stifling. We quitted the desert and launched into the rolling green plains of Colorado. Dozing uneasily with every removable rag removed, I was roused by a blast of intense cold and the drumming of a hundred drums. The train had stopped. Far as the eye could range the land was white under two feet of hail—each hailstone as big as the top of a sherry-glass. I saw a young colt by the side of the track standing with his poor little fluffy back to the pitiless pelting. He was pounded to death. An old horse met his doom

on the run. He galloped wildly towards the train, but his hind legs dropped into a hole half water and half ice. He beat the ground with his forefeet for a minute, and then rolling over on his side submitted quietly to be killed.

When the storm ceased, we picked our way cautiously and crippledly over a track that might give way at any moment. The Western driver urges his train much as does the Subaltern the bounding pony, and, 'twould seem, with an equal sense of responsibility. If a foot does go wrong, why there you are, don't you know, and if it is all right, why all right it is, don't you know. But I would sooner be on the pony than the train.

And now a few words on the American personality.

And he is versatile—horribly so. The unlimited exercise of the right of private judgment (which by the way, is a weapon not one man in ten is competent to handle), his blatant cocksureness, and the dry-air-bred restlessness that makes him crawl all over the furniture when he is talking to you, conspire to make him versatile. But what he calls versatility the impartial bystander of Anglo-Indian [India, as in the great subcontinent Kipling usually wrote about] extraction is apt to deem mere casualness, and dangerous casualness at that.

The railroads apparently were a typical product of that unwelcome versatility—casualness.

Take up—you can easily find them—the accounts of ten consecutive railway catastrophes—not little accidents, but first-class fatalities, when the long cars turn over, take fire, and roast the luckless occupants alive. To seven out of the ten you shall find appended the cheerful statement: "The accident is supposed to have been due to the rails spreading." That means the metals were spiked down to the ties with such versatility that the spikes or the tracks drew under the constant vibration of the traffic and the metals opened out. No one is hanged for these little affairs.

We began to climb hills, and then we stopped—at night in darkness, while men threw sand under the wheels and crowbarred the track and then "guessed" that we might proceed.

Rather than meet his Maker half asleep, Kipling, a future Nobel Prize winner, bestirred himself, went forward to a club car, and:

[I] was rewarded by two hours' conversation with the stranded, broken-down, husband-abandoned actress of a fourth-rate, stranded, broken down, manager-bereft company. She was muzzy with beer, reduced to her last dollar, fearful that there would be no one to meet her at Omaha, and wept at intervals because she had given the conductor a five-dollar bill to change, and he hadn't come back.

He eventually did, with the proper change. Meanwhile, Kipling persevered while the train crossed the Rockies, climbing, climbing, climbing, then, on the down side, dashing into a tunnel here, another there, and out again, at one point flying around a curve "on one wheel chiefly, the Gunnison River gnashing its teeth below." Just after clearing Black Canyon and another gorge, nine thousand feet above sea level:

[W]e came most suddenly round a corner upon a causeway across waste water—half dam and half quarry pool. The locomotive gave one wild "Hoo! Hoo! Hoo!" but it was too late. He was a beautiful bull, and goodness only knows why he had chosen the track for a constitutional with his wife. She was flung to the left, but the cow-catcher caught him, and turning him round, hove him shoulder deep into the pool. The expression of blank, blind bewilderment on his bovine, jovine face was wonderful to behold. He was not angry. I don't think he was even scared, though he must have flown ten yards through the air. All he wanted to know was: "Will somebody have the goodness to tell a respectable old gentleman what in the world, or out of it, has occurred?"

The good news is, more or less like the dispossessed bull, Kipling survived his travel through Colorado.

1 8 8 9
Case(s) Dismissed

When California's U.S. Sen. David C. Broderick agreed to meet California Supreme Court Justice David S. Terry in a duel stemming from a public exchange of insults, it was unfortunate for Broderick that Terry was allowed to chose the weapons. Broderick wound up with an unfamiliar European pistol having a hair trigger. Thus, his weapon went off as he was lifting it into firing position. With his one round lodged in the ground at his feet, he then stood there quietly, at Lake Merced near the San Francisco–San Mateo County line the morning of September 13, 1859, while Terry took his turn at will and with no further risk to himself. He could have desisted at that point, but he didn't. He fired, his bullet struck Broderick in the chest . . . fatally.

Broderick, once a stonecutter and the son of an immigrant Irish stonecutter who had worked on the U.S. Capitol, thus became the only member of the U.S. Senate ever to have been killed in a duel.

Ironically, Oregon Sen. Edward Dickinson Baker, a Lincoln ally chosen to speak at Broderick's funeral, himself was destined to become the Senate's only battlefield fatality ever—as he led his men straight into awaiting Confederate guns in the battle of Ball's Bluff near Leesburg, Virginia, in 1862.

And Terry, no stranger to violent scenes, later fell to gunfire as well—not because of his Civil War service as a Confederate general, but years later as a result of slapping a member of the U.S. Supreme Court in the face. That ugly incident, too, happened in California . . . at a train station in 1889.

David Colbreth Broderick was born in Washington, D.C., in 1820, but the family moved to New York in 1823. "Broderick learned his political art in New York City's Tammany Hall," notes a historical U.S. Senate Web site (http://www.senate.gov/learning/min_3e.html). "In 1849 the antislavery Democrat joined the gold rush to California and settled in San Francisco, where he made his fortune in real estate."

He advanced politically as a leader in the Democratic Party's antislavery wing, becoming first a state senator, then presiding member of the state senate. Next eyeing a seat in the U.S. Senate, he managed to hold up the reelection of Sen. William Gwin, a member of his party's proslavery faction, for nearly two years. Broderick was able to do this because in those days the legislature rather than the voters named the state's senators. Many members of the same legislative body, not-so-incidentally, attended its sessions armed with pistols or at least knives.

In 1857 Broderick and Gwin worked out an agreement giving Broderick a full six-year term in the Senate and Gwin the four years still left to the state's other Senate seat. "Broderick's price was full control of California's federal patronage appointments," says the Senate

Web site, but, "President James Buchanan, Gwin's proslavery ally, ignored this agreement and continued to grant patronage to Gwin, who continued to distribute it."

With the new state of California unspared in the hot national debate over slavery, feelings were running high as the 1859 elections approached. Broderick and Justice David Terry, long a proslavery Gwin ally, exchanged verbal sallies, with Terry at one point asserting that Broderick was aligned with the black leader Frederick Douglass, rather than with that other Douglas who was a U.S. Senator and party leader, Stephen Douglas of Illinois. Broderick in a fateful response to one of Terry's attacks, countered with a remark basically saying that Terry was dishonest. "I have hitherto spoken of [Terry] as an honest man," Broderick said, "as the only honest man on the bench of a miserable, corrupt Supreme Court, but now I find I was mistaken. I take it all back. He is just as bad as the others."

Their illegal duel, fatal to Broderick, was the result. Before dying three days later, he said, "They have killed me because I was opposed to a corrupt administration and the extension of slavery."

The San Francisco chief of police apparently had tried to stop the duel by arresting both participants the morning of September 12 and charging them with disturbing the peace. But they went ahead with their encounter the next morning instead. While eulogizing Broderick and deploring his death as a great loss to the community, the *California Police Gazette* in the immediate aftermath (September 17, 1859) also moaned: "When will we [in California] cease to be so terribly scourged and take our place among the enlightened of the age? If not soon, we will cease to exist as a people, for strife and bloodshed will annihilate us."

Perhaps the editors were thinking, in part, of the same Justice David Terry's role in another violent incident, when, back in 1856, he had stabbed a local vigilante leader in the neck, nicking the man's carotid artery. Charged with attempted murder, Terry managed to win acquittal. Now, after he had slain Broderick in a highly suspicious, possibly rigged duel, charges were brought against Terry again, but he again won dismissal, this time in a Marin County court. As one further result, however, Terry reportedly was so despised in San Francisco that he had to relocate to Stockton.

It wasn't long before the Civil War erupted, changing lives even in distant California. Terry, a giant for his time at six foot three and well over two hundred pounds, joined the Confederacy, rose to the rank of brigadier general, was wounded at Chickamauga, but recovered and after the war returned to his law practice in Stockton.

A few years later, he married a much younger and flamboyant woman who had been party to a notorious divorce case and in fact was his own client. At one point during the extended and complicated legal proceedings in both the state and federal courts, Terry's wife came before Terry's old judicial and political enemy Stephen Field, who had served on the California high court at the same time as Terry. Long since elevated to the U.S. Supreme Court by Abraham Lincoln, Field briefly was back in California and sitting for the moment as a federal circuit judge.

When the sixty-six-year-old Terry's feisty young wife became so obstreperous in the courtroom that Field ordered her removed, Terry tangled with the U.S. marshals trying to carry out the order. He punched one in the face and tried to pull out a knife as other deputies "jumped into the fray," noted Paul Kens in his 1977 biography *Justice Stephen Field*.

As a result, Field sentenced his old companion and enemy from their days on the California Supreme Court to six months in jail and the wife to three months.

The next time Field returned to California—the summer of 1889—he was accompanied by a bodyguard, David Neagle. "Neagle was said to be the stuff of old westerns—a small man who, in his early days in Tombstone, Arizona, had built a big reputation as a quick gun," wrote Kens. On August 13, Neagle and Field were on a train from Los Angeles to San Francisco when David Terry and his wife boarded at Fresno.

The train stopped at Lathrop the next morning, and passengers alighted for breakfast "in the stationhouse," the Terrys and Justice Field included.

When Terry spotted Field at his table, he approached and, depending on the varied accounts that came out of the incident, either struck Field two sharp blows in the face or "merely brushed Field with an open hand." Both Field and Neagle claimed it was the former.

Whichever, Neagle reacted instantly . . . pulled his gun and fired two quick shots. Terry died on the spot.

The informally appointed bodyguard could have faced a homicide charge in the state courts, but before California could proceed, federal officials procured his release on a writ of habeas corpus granted by a federal court. The state fought the issue all the way up to the U.S. Supreme Court, which in the end voted six to two to uphold the writ and keep Neagle out of California's custody. Field, wisely enough, did *not* take part in the decision.

⭐ Part 6 ⭐
Sliding into a
New Century

1 8 9 6
In Pursuit of Dreams

Wild and woolly all right was this western clime during its gold boom, which, like the fevered California gold rush, attracted a flood of fortune seekers, hardbitten types, harmless characters, and quite a few human cockroaches. As often was the case in California, just getting there was half or more of the battle. But off the gold stampeders went anyway, nearly at the moment they heard the word.

Among those who wasted no time reacting was the mayor of Seattle, Washington, W. D. Wood. He was attending a convention in San Francisco when the news came in: *Gold in the Klondike!*

Without returning home, the story goes, Mayor Wood tendered his resignation from office by telegraph and set about raising a stake of $150,000 to buy an oceangoing steamer as the start of a shipping company. The May 1, 1998, issue of the *Klondike Weekly* (http://www.yukonalaska.com/klondike/bystate.html), notes that his ship, the *Humboldt,* was overloaded and quite a bit delayed in departing from San Francisco for the north. To get his ship on its way with the maximum paying cargo aboard, Wood contrived to "leave behind some fifty thousand pounds of his passengers' personal baggage."

That would never do, a number of the victimized passengers decided . . . before actually trying to hang the former mayor "on the dockside." Fortunately, "Cooler heads prevailed, and the ship was reloaded."

Lurking back in Chicago just about that time was one of the Klondike "cockroaches," Lambertus Warmolts. Advertising himself as a knowledgeable guide familiar with the rough Yukon country, he talked thirteen residents into paying five hundred dollars each for him to lead them into the fabulous northern gold fields. They were drawing close when he "abandoned camp" with their money and left the Chicagoans on their own. "The Chicago group pushed on to Destruction City in the Northwest Territories of Canada, where most of them died of scurvy. Only a few of them ever made it to Dawson City."

Still another cockroach of the Yukon and Alaska, a legend in his own time at that, was Jefferson Randolph "Soapy" Smith, a slippery con man, murderer, and gang leader whose career in crime apparently began in Colorado. Born in Georgia on the eve of the Civil War, he drifted west as a young man and took up the well-known shell game. You know, three walnut shells and a dried pea hidden underneath one of them. Watch the man move them around on a smooth surface and, for a fee, try to guess where the pea went. Guess right and you get a prize . . . except that the slight-of-hand artists plying the shell-game trade always make sure the pea isn't there.

It sounds fairly innocent . . . and at least short of mayhem and murder. But Soapy started up (or down) the ladder to serious crime by doing just that—plying the shell con in Colorado. Specifically, it may have been at Leadville, once a wild-and-woolly boom mining community itself. According to a town history posted on the Internet (http://www.leadville.com/history/soapy.htm), he and a partner operated their shell game on the corner of Harrison Avenue and Third Street.

Escalating their "game," they next planned to sell paper-wrapped soap bars to unwary bar patrons after "demonstrating" there was money hidden under the wrappings. "He ["Soapy"] then walked inside one of the local saloons, where his silent partner 'bought' one of the bars of soap from Smith, and upon opening it (in front of the other patrons) was 'surprised' to find a crisp one hundred dollar bill under the wrapping! Needless to say, soap sales escalated at a phenomenal rate for 'Soapy'." And hence his nickname.

Needless to say also, it wasn't long before Soapy had to leave town in a hurry, eventually moving on to the gold fields of the north.

By the time of the Klondike boom in 1897, he was well settled in Skagway, Alaska, at the center of a far-reaching web of one hundred or more confederates who preyed on the gold-fevered new arrivals. His cohorts did more than simply entice the newcomers into "traditional," if somewhat crooked, gambling halls or dens of prostitution. "His men met newcomers at the docks posing as clergymen, newspaper reporters, knowledgeable old-timers and freight company representatives," recalls the *Alaska Gold Rush Trails* Internet site (http://www.gold-rush.org/ALASKA/stories/Ala03n.html). Soapy's operatives then found a thousand and one ways to fleece the newly arrived innocents. In one such con, Soapy and Company offered an "army enlistment tent" where the inquirer was told to strip for a physical, only to have his clothes and valuables stolen while he met with a phony doctor.

Soapy's minions also infested the two overland trails leading to the gold fields—the White Pass and the Chilkoot. There they were known to set up tents and invite weary travelers in for a bit of warmth . . . and a spot of fixed gambling, even the good old shell game again. For that matter, neither outright robbery nor murder was beyond the Soapy gang's modus operandi. So ubiquitous was the gang's presence on the White Pass Trail that no less an organization than the Canadian North-West Mounted Police once had to shift to the Chilkoot in secret while attempting to deliver $150,000 in newly collected customs fees to a waiting vessel at Skagway. Even then, the Mounties had to hold off gang members at gunpoint while traversing the final stretch to the docks.

The day finally came when Soapy overreached himself. "He and his thugs fleeced a miner of $2,800 in gold," recalls the Alaska Gold Rush Trails site. When he complained, fed-up citizens of Skagway formed a vigilante committee headed by former Oregon schoolteacher Frank Reid, now the town engineer. Reid confronted Soapy Smith, shots were exchanged, and Smith was killed and Reid was fatally wounded.

On the other hand, the Klondike gold rush produced its share of spectacular good luck stories. Clarence Berry, for instance, was a bartender at Fortymile in the Yukon Territory when an acquaintance asked him for a loan in order to keep prospecting. "Berry obliged," reports the *Klondike Weekly*, in return for a half interest in his borrower's claim on Eldorado Creek. As a result, "Berry took a million and a half dollars out of the Klondike and, unlike so many, died with his fortunes intact." Not only that, he became owner of the Brooklyn Dodgers and New York Giants baseball teams.

Others found alternate ways to make their fortunes. Upstate New York native Joe Ladue, considered the chief founder of Dawson City in the Yukon, worked and prospected in the American West before drifting up to the Yukon Territory in 1881, traversing the Chilkoot Pass on the way. Two years later, realizing the area's miners needed finished wood to build their sluice boxes, he established a sawmill at Sixtymile River. When gold turned up in the area of the Klondike River, he moved to its mouth, laid out the outlines of a town, then set up a new sawmill. This was in 1896, and he began selling lots at five to twenty-five dollars each. Then the gold rush erupted in earnest. By midsummer of 1897, the next year, he was selling his lots at eight hundred to eight thousand dollars each. "Joe Ladue was always one step ahead of the rush—whatever was needed he supplied, building a general store and saloon, expanding the mill continually, and then organizing the huge Joseph Ladue Gold Mining and Development Company Ltd. for further expansion" says the *Klondike Weekly* of July 12, 1998.

He apparently did it all in a hurry, because by December 1897 he returned to New York and married Anna "Kitty" Mason. They bought a 250-acre farm in his hometown of Schuyler Falls, New York. In due course, they were dinner guests of President William McKinley . . . shortly before McKinley was assassinated in Upstate New York.

Money from Ladue's Yukon assets "kept pouring in," but "the years in the north had been hard on him physically." He had tuberculosis, and a stay in Colorado Springs failed to halt the ravages of the lung disease. "In the spring of 1900 he returned to his farm at Schuyler Falls, and on June 27, 1900, the founder of Dawson died at home, less than three years after obtaining his hard-won riches." He hadn't quite reached his forty-fifth birthday. Anna later remarried and lived to 1948.

Meanwhile, A. J. Goddard and his wife spent the entire winter of 1897 carrying two steamboats into the Yukon by way of the snow-and-ice-clogged White Pass Trail—piece by piece. Their goal was to carry the first cargo down the river in the spring. Their achievement was an early steamboat service linking the gold fields and the Pacific.

Speaking of the same overland trail, another former mayor responding to the siren's call of the Yukon was George Brackett, once the chief official of Minneapolis. In the fall of 1897, "he witnessed the carnage and horror of the White Pass trail," notes the *Klondike Weekly*. "Scarcely a single horse survived of the three thousand that were used on the trail." So what did he do? He constructed a wagon road along the mountainsides. When it was completed, the gold "stampeders" who made use of it that winter were happy to pay his toll.

Another good luck story, combined with more hard work, was that of a onetime muleskinner from South Dakota, Dick Lowe. His good fortune came strictly from the gold. Some years earlier, he had found gold in the Black Hills of the Dakotas and started up a transportation company, but "Indian trouble" forced him to move on. Shifting his base to the Yukon, he laid claim to a tiny piece of land on Bonanza Creek while working with a surveying team. He tried to sell, then rent it out, but no one was interested.

He then began prospecting it himself . . . and found gold! His small plot produced half a million dollars' worth before he was through, "the richest claim per square foot ever staked in the Yukon."

Lady Luck of course was besought and her absence bewailed on a daily basis in places other than the rippling creeks hiding the precious yellow metal. Lady Luck was the mistress of big-time (and little-time) gamblers infected with their own brand of gold fever . . . and one of these was Harry Woolrich. He had the touch, a Midas touch with the cards, many thought. And many handed over a stake, asking him to play for them, usually at the Dawson City Monte Carlo Dance Hall and Saloon. If he won, he kept half the proceeds. If he lost, it was their money that was lost . . . not his.

One fabled night, he won sixty thousand dollars, renounced gambling, and prepared to leave on the next steamer out. But the steamer was delayed. He went back to the gaming tables for one more round . . . and "twenty-four hours later, the boat long gone, Woolrich had lost his fortune and his ticket out of the Yukon."

The co-owner of the same Monte Carlo establishment, by the way, was "Swiftwater" Bill Gates, who had struck gold at the supposedly unlucky thirteenth Eldorado claim. His first strike enabled him to buy out more claims, and he became one of Dawson City's richest men. He was a womanizer and was famous locally for bathing in champagne.

Meanwhile, not all the women who flocked to the gold fields were dance-hall girls or prostitutes. Far from it! Martha Munger Purdy and her husband, Will, Chicago blue bloods, set out for the Klondike in 1898 but split up when he decided upon Hawaii instead. As a result, Martha and her brother slogged through the notorious Chilkoot Trail. As she later noted about one day on the trail: "I cursed my hot, high buckram collar, my tight, heavily boned corsets, my long corduroy skirt, my full bloomers, which I had to hitch up with every step."

As events turned out, she had been two months' pregnant while on the Chilkoot. Assisted by two prospectors, she delivered her backwoods babe in a log cabin across the Klondike River from Dawson, wrote Ken Spotswood in *Women of the Klondike,* an article developed for the Yukon Anniversaries Commission in 1997 (also available at http://www.yukonalaska.com/klondike/women.html).

Rather than return to her wealthy parents, "She went on to manage a sawmill, and had staked a claim on Excelsior Creek which later proved rich and made her financially independent." After divorcing Will Purdy, she married George Black, a Dawson City attorney who became commissioner of the Yukon and the Yukon's member of the Canadian Parliament. When illness forced him to step aside, she ran for election in his place, and at the age of sixty-nine "became the second female MP [Member of Parliament] to serve in the House of Commons."

Among the more harmless characters who graced the gold fields was a gray-haired, blue-eyed woman who responded to Skagway newspaperman Emer J. White's advertisement for paper sellers. Giving her name simply as Barbara, she said she was a widow living with a daughter in Butte, Montana, but she had been visiting a friend in Seattle. When it was time to return home, she "impulsively" came north and visited Skagway first. "All my life I've wondered what it would be like to be out among complete strangers and make my own way," she told the newspaperman. So there she was, ready at age seventy-six to go it alone.

White had his doubts, but he gave her the job, half-expecting to be arranging her way home in a week's time. But . . . not quite. She sold her newspapers "like a pro." After receiving her first earnings, she bought a piano box "and made it her home on a vacant lot."

By that summer's end she had earned $1,350 and agreed to go home for the winter. Her daughter wrote later to say her mother arrived safely and to thank White. "Barbara" herself later wrote to ask if her job—and the piano box—would be available in the spring.

So far as is known, she never returned. As Ken Spotswood observed, she had turned a dream into reality . . . as did many thousands who flocked to the Klondike, the Yukon, Alaska, and Northwest Canada in the 1890s, among them good people, lucky people, the unlucky, the bad, and many an odd character.

Small Town Roll Call

A few towns and other locales of the West and their stories:

No connection with trucks or trucking, little **Truckee,** California, tucked away in the eastern foothills of the Sierra Nevada, derived its name from the Paiute chief who helped out the first westbound emigrant group to take wagons over the magnificent mountain range. After Chief Truckee pointed them to the Donner Pass in the fall of 1844, the Stephens-Murphy-Townsend Party of fifty men, women, and children was able to make the dangerous crossing . . . but not without considerable risk and effort.

They managed to retain five of their eleven wagons by taking them apart and hauling the pieces up the steep slopes by rope. Before they could complete the task and head down the western side of the mountain range, however, snowstorms struck and blocked the way. With a few men going ahead to find help, most of the party encamped on the south fork of the Yuba River. A baby, destined to be named Mary "Yuba" Murphy, was born during the emigrants' stay by the river, and in the end all fifty members of the Stephens Party survived.

Both the town of Truckee, often the coldest site in the nation, and the adjoining Truckee River are named in memory of the friendly Paiute and his guidance.

In Arizona, meanwhile, lies a town named for an incident in a poker game—**Show Low.** Only in Show Low, we're willing to bet, can you take a stroll down a main street called the Deuce of Clubs . . . named for the winning card in the winning hand that gave the town its name. It was Indian scout Col. Croyden E. Cooley who drew a fourth deuce in his poker game with his friend Marion Clark.

Meanwhile, **Greensburg,** Kansas, named for local stagecoach proprietor Donald R. "Cannonball" Green, has a truly unique claim to fame—it's a well dug in 1887 and 1888. Not just any old well, but supposedly "the world's largest hand-dug well." Anyone ready to scoff at such a claim can always join the three million or so visitors who troop to the site of the Big Well every year. What they find is a truly gigantic well 109 feet deep and 39 feet across. A metal stairway takes visitors down into this large hole in the ground for a really close look.

Begun in August 1887 to provide water for the newly established town and a small railroad line, the well was dug by transient workers, area farmers, and local cowboys. Their "equipage" consisted of shovel, pick, half-barrels, pulley and rope . . . and mules. Some of the workers set off for the work site before dawn every day, returned home about eleven o'clock at night, then tended to their farm chores before going to bed. "Other crews quarried and hauled native stone to be used as casing of the well," notes the Big Well Web site (http://www.bigwell.org/

bigwell/html). The stone was hauled into town by wagon from the Medicine River twelve miles away—on roads that "were little better than cattle trails."

The finished well was considered "a masterpiece of pioneer engineering." Adds the Web site: "The sinking of the well was accomplished as the stone casing, which acted as a keystone, was lowered into the ground. . . . As the digging progressed, the wide shaft was braced with rough two-by-twelve-inch planks that reached from wall to wall in a wagon-wheel type support. The soil was shoveled into half barrels and the barrels hoisted to the surface. The braces were later sawed off."

No one under twenty-one years in age was allowed to work in the well—the construction project was considered too dangerous for young, inexperienced hands.

Although the railroad soon bypassed Greensburg, the well gave the town water for fifty years.

Covered up for some time but then reopened in 1937 as a historic attraction, the well was designated a national museum in 1972. The American Water Works Association then named it an American Water Landmark in 1974.

Lincoln and **Fremont,** Nebraska, like many other villages, towns, and cities, owe their names to famous personages such as Abraham Lincoln or John C. Frémont. Even tiny **Brownville,** Nebraska (population two hundred), obviously owes its name—and founding—to a man named Brown . . . a rather obscure Richard Brown who turned up in the mid-1850s and built himself a log cabin in a wide-open stretch of land alongside the Missouri River. Oddly enough he came from **Oregon**—that is, a small town in Missouri named Oregon.

As for a somewhat larger town in the same state—in this case a county seat—**Kirksville** was named for Jesse Kirk. Rather obvious, you say? True . . . except for the "how come" explanation that Kirk swapped a fine turkey dinner for the right to name the town after himself!

Another town with an unremarkable-appearing name is **Florence,** Arizona . . . and in respectable, unexciting fashion, it was named for the sister of an early mayor. There is, however, no clue in that pedigree to one unforgettable moment in the town's history, courtesy of a local minister, the Reverend Barney Regan, who in the 1880s ran not just a saloon in Florence—but a "clean" saloon, *Arizona Highways* magazine reported in 1937. Apparently he meant a saloon with no drunks, no card cheats, no loose women, and no smutty jokes.

Then one morning appeared a rather disrespectful, rebellious cowboy armed with a pistol and spoiling for trouble. Pushing inside the saloon door, he took one shot at the mirror behind the bar . . . and that was all. One shot. "Quick as a flash, Rev. Mr. Regan jerked out his own pistol and killed him."

The funeral was held the next morning . . . with the same Reverend Regan officiating and preaching the sermon.

At other times, other locales, choosing a town name was so tedious! Consider the folks of today's **Rolla,** Missouri, when, back in 1857, the time came to name the town growing up near farmer John Webber's acreage, thanks in large part to the railroad warehouses locating there.

Let's call the town Hardscrabble, Webber suggested. No, argued a railroad man, let's call it Phelps. Naw, said a proud Carolinian, let's make it Raleigh—only he pronounced it Rolla. And Rolla it thenceforth would be, according to local legend.

In California, meanwhile, is the old mining town called **Georgetown**—named, naturally, for an early settler named George. But which "George" is a question still debated today. One George was a sailor named Phipps who led a group of fellow mariners finding "a fortune" in gold in a stream just below the town site of today, according to the El Dorado County Visitors Authority. But there also was a popular miner in the area named George Ehrenhaft.

"At any rate, Georgetown received its name from a George!" says the Web site text. And typically of its day and age, the mining community consisted of "tents, shacks and canvas structures lining the camp creek." Everything looked rosy and the camp was "booming"—until 1852. That's when a major fire destroyed the tent city that had mushroomed in gold-rich Empire Canyon. Georgetown residents then decided to abandon the canyon and build themselves a town of brick and stone structures with iron, fireproof doors, all a short distance away from the original gold works. They also made sure the new town's streets were wider than before, "to keep any future fires from jumping." Thus, "When they were finished, Georgetown was a thriving and beautiful town. It quickly rose to prominence as one of the richer camps in the area region and came to be known as 'the Pride of the Mountains'."

Not to be forgotten in any roll call of western towns is **Bartlesville,** Oklahoma, not only the home of the first major oil well drilled in Oklahoma, but also a namesake town . . . named for the remarkable and inventive (but usually forgotten) local storeowner J. H. Bartles.

It is no surprise to learn that Bartles founded Bartlesville . . . but then he went on to found **Dewey,** Oklahoma, and relocate his store in the new town. The move took five months, but the creative Bartles was able to keep his store open for business the entire time it crept along a road he built from one town to the other . . . crept along as a team of oxen strained to pull it forward, inch by inch, on giant, rolling logs.

Dewey, of course, was Adm. George Dewey, whose fleet seized Manila during the Spanish-American War, and the Dewey Hotel in Bartles's Dewey was popular with pioneer Oklahoma oilmen who liked to gamble in the hostelry's Tower Room. The town today also is home to the Tom Mix Museum.

Puyallup, Washington, is no joke to the people who live there and love it—it's named for the local Puyallup Indians, and to them, it seems, the word meant "generous people." Nice.

Gig Harbor, Washington, on the other hand, is named for an event—for the day explorers in a gig needed shelter from a storm and found it in the small bay in front of the future site of the town named, essentially, for their conveyance.

In Colorado, someone thought better of keeping **Uncompahgre** as a town's tongue-twisting name, and named it **Delta** instead. At one time, the shape of the town site resembled the Greek letter Delta at that.

Meanwhile, it also seems that a local merchant's wife can be held responsible for **Marysville,** Kansas (population thirty-four hundred). As well remembered by many travelers on the Oregon Trail, back in the mid-1800s Mary Marshall's husband, Frank, operated a ferry that carried westbound settlers across the Big Blue River here. More recently, the town has become the black squirrel capital of the United States, thanks to the escape of several rare black squirrels from a traveling carnival in 1912. Marysville has the distinction, in fact, of being the only U.S. locale where black squirrels live—and propagate—in the wild.

Fascinating Women
of the West

By Ingrid Smyer

AT THE BEGINNING WAS a dream, a dream that the vast unexplored spaces beyond the Mississippi River would become a part of the United States. Under President Thomas Jefferson, that vision, his vision, of a nation stretching across the continent became a reality.

It happened, not through war, but first through the purchase of an area of 828,000 square miles of land from Napoleon's France for fifteen million dollars (plus considerable interest, as it turned out). Then came the incredible eight-thousand-mile expedition to the Pacific and back, well beyond the perimeters of the Louisiana Purchase, led by Meriwether Lewis and William Clark. And here was the first glimpse, the first confirmation of the vast possibilities and resources that lay beyond the Mississippi and Missouri Rivers. Here was confirmation of prairies, mountains, rivers, that would fill out the grand vision of an America stretching from sea to sea.

And among the handful of explorers blazing this momentous trail was a woman!

Sacagawea was her name. A teenager, a Native American woman with a papoose on her back. She was a valuable guide for the expedition, an ambassador to her own people, a translator . . . and the first known woman to make the arduous journey from midcontinent over the mountains to the Pacific.

Lewis and Clark had been instructed by Jefferson to note the flora and fauna along the way, to befriend the Indian tribes encountered, to learn all they could about the native tribes' customs and habits—what they ate, what they wore, their traditions, their family relationships, and not the least of Jefferson's interests, their willingness to trade. As the Corps of Discovery then traveled through the wilderness, its members not only met Indians but also the occasional white man already there reaping the fur resources of the West and Northwest. What they were, though, were mostly French-Canadians who had learned to live among the tribes, often as traders. One such man was Touissant Charbonneau, husband of Sacagawea.

And soon, on the heels of Lewis and Clark, came the American fur-trappers—the rough-and-ready mountain men. Realizing the opportunity, they rushed into the snow-covered mountains in search of beaver pelts, mostly for fashionable men's hats, and rarely did these rugged individualists return to the structured world they had left behind. For these first Americans to follow in the steps of Lewis and Clark, all of them men, the West offered untrammeled freedom, space . . . time.

Ever after, going by the image we have inherited today, the Wild West was a man's domain.

Not necessarily so . . . even if Hollywood from its fledgling days of the early twentieth century did see the gold to be mined in "moving pictures" depicting an epic—but largely male—story of the West. The "Western" of course became a mainstay of the movie industry for decades, and as such an icon of the collective American memory. To be sure, there was the occasional mountain man, but the more frequent and popular images were of unshaven poker players at a round table, of gunslingers quick on the draw, of the U.S. Cavalry and the Indian foe and, more ubiquitous than any other image of the West, of the vaunted cowboy in a saloon, on the range, on a dusty street, just out there . . . somewhere. Still, all men.

In the early black-and-whites, we could always tell the good guys from the bad by their ten-gallon hats, couldn't we? White hats for the heroes and black for the villains. And naturally there always was the damsel in distress, and who should come to her rescue but the dauntless hero in his white hat (or in soldierly uniform presumed to be blue). Saves her, he does, then more often than not, rides off into the sunset, free to pursue his next adventure. Didn't we say, a man thing!

Later, about the time of technicolor, came the more romantic approach—white-hatted hero rides off into the sunset *with damsel*. Or, imagine this: He doesn't ride off at all. He sticks around. Hints of marriage are in the air. Imagine, marriage! Woman joins man in conquest of the West.

Even history books have been ever so slow to reach a Technicolor stage of their own, to ease the emphasis on the role of men in the settlement and development of the American West. Sooner or later the full picture will emerge, and women no longer will be waiting in the wings for discovery. Thanks to the mid-twentieth century's interest in women's studies, a clearer, more realistic representation has been evolving.

The beckoning West indeed was wild and dangerous, but never mind. Women joined the westward march anyway, even if they usually started out as an "adjunct" to a man. They were indeed wives, mothers, sisters, but still they went, and in great numbers. The total number of women headed west during the nineteenth century probably will never be known precisely, but just about any journal or diary written by a westbound traveler mentions women . . . or was penned by a woman. By 1852 the register of westbound travelers passing through Fort Kearny on the south banks of the Platte River, a segment of the famous Oregon Trail, showed a count of 7,021 women and 8,270 children. As that count alone confirms, the lure of the West acted upon both genders—emigration was a family activity. The vast nineteenth-century migration from the settled East of the United States to new frontiers to the west was conducted by thousands of families disillusioned with urban crowding or the tired soil of once-fertile farmlands back east. Or it simply was the lure of wide-open spaces, of being on their own, of improved economic conditions . . . sometimes, for the sheer adventure of it all, they simply packed up and left home for the storied West.

In many cases, the pioneers heading west were responding to a family tradition that said each new generation will move on, always to the west, to the latest frontier to be conquered. Descendants of America's largely English settlers of colonial days found the eastern territories of their forebears becoming more and more crowded . . . filling up. It soon became traditional for the next generation to move farther west and start afresh, even as their earliest forebears had done. And what vast, limitless expanses did beckon! "Why delay marriage, why limit children, why divide a patrimony, why cling to the family hearth, when the limitless resources of the West seemed there for the taking," wrote Kathleen Neils Cozen in *The Oxford History of the American West* (1994).

Other groups filling out the westward-ho ranks were newer arrivals, such as the Irish and Scandinavians escaping natural calamities in the Old World. Germans came in large numbers, while there also was a steady trickle of Eastern Europeans.

Even though these newcomers carried their own cultural traditions with them, the conditions the westward-bound emigrants experienced, one and all, assured that there would be a recurring sense of the frontier spirit felt by all . . . that all would have shared in a uniquely *American* experience, teaching *American* values, and leaving behind a heritage of those values.

The restless spirit and mobile nature of these westward migrants tended to create a sense of justification for settling the vast new territories—often Indian-occupied lands—at will, in the name of "manifest destiny," the doctrine that held it only inevitable and indeed necessary for an expanding United States to absorb *all* the territories stretching sea to sea between the bottom of the continent and the Canadian border to the north.

Justification or not, husband and wife headed west, with the women sharing the new conditions all the way. Were they "liberated"? Well, on the trail west, they got the same vittles, rode in the same covered wagons, waded through the same mud, coughed up the same trail dust, slogged through the same snow, climbed the same mountains, forded the same streams, fought off the same Indians, lived under the same stars, and in the end arrived at the same wondrous or, often, bitterly disappointing destination as their menfolk.

And sometimes, don't forget, they also died on the trail west, just like the menfolk succumbing to disease, accident, or Indian attack. For the women, though, add childbirth as a travel risk the men did *not* share.

At the end of the trail, at the new homestead, a good bit of the sharing ended . . . roles changed. Suddenly, the women were confronted with maintaining a home under extremely primitive conditions—the new "home" at first might be a tent made of animal skin or canvas from the covered wagon, or it might be a sod hut. It likely was on an isolated plot far from any neighbors, cut off entirely—no mail for months at a time—from the folks back east. The man of the family was busy clearing their land, plowing the fields, starting up a log cabin as their abode, hunting to feed the family, starting a business.

Life in the West was not the same as in the settled lands left behind, and with such drastic change there came new attitudes, new expectations . . . new ways of thinking, true. But what about the old values and ways of thinking? As pointed out by Lesley Poling-Kemper in her book *The Harvey Girls,* men all too often gambled, drank, made deals, drank again, lost quickly acquired fortunes, or just plain lost themselves in the crowd, while women "transplanted traditional views of the 'woman's sphere' in their new communities." In short, the women were busy civilizing the West even while they were surviving the West.

Everything happened so fast, too. Consider that in 1829 Dr. Isaac Galland and his wife, **Hannah,** arrived in Iowa. The baby girl she soon delivered apparently was the first Anglo baby born in Iowa. After the Black Hawk Purchase Treaty of 1832 removed the unfortunate Sauk and Mesquake tribes from eastern Iowa, wrote Glenda Riley in her book *Prairie Voices,* "the trickle of migrants became a deluge." By 1846, less than twenty years after the birth of the Galland couple's child, Iowa had become a state. By 1870 its population had soared to 1.2 million, and the U.S. Census Bureau declared the Iowa frontier to be closed.

Meanwhile, statehood or no, frontierlike conditions still existed in Iowa long after 1846. The massacre of white settlers at Spirit Lake by the Sioux in 1857 provides a painful case in point . . . and serves to remind us today of the squeeze between Indian rights and the white nation's feeling of manifest destiny. Today we tend to look upon those early settlers judgmentally, but many of the emigrants heading west "believed that they had the right—even the God-given mandate—to displace Native Americans from their homes and land," wrote Glenda Riley.

Despite the many stories of disasters that could befall the unwary newcomer, those already in the West, Iowa included, felt it important to attract more and more settlers. They subscribed to the theory that more is better, that new emigrants would enhance business and become partners in establishing community and even statehood. And many of the newest arrivals in the promised land certainly did send back glowing reports. "Our land is beautiful, though there are few trees," wrote **Gros Svendsen** in 1863 to relatives in Hallingdal, Norway, after traveling to Iowa's Emmet County with her husband, Ole. "We have good spring water nearby. Best of all, the land is good meadowland easily plowed and cultivated."

Ole went off to fight in the Civil War in 1864, serving under William Tecumseh Sherman and leaving Gros to run their new farm. One way for her to make ends meet was to churn butter and sell the excess to neighbors. Because the early school system in the county was inadequate, she taught her children both in English and in her native Norwegian while also becoming a community scribe for the less educated adults. Her work on the farm and attending to the needs of neighbors never seemed to end, but she found time for her true enjoyment on summer evenings—sitting outdoors and blowing an alpenhorn.

Ole returned from the war unscathed, and together they increased their farm holdings and brought in good crops. They were active in the local Lutheran church and the community . . . the future looked bright. In 1870, however, times were not good, agricultural prices were low, grasshoppers had damaged the crops, and the Svendsens found themselves in debt. With the help of relatives back in the Old Country, Ole and Gros never experienced abject poverty, but they had many mouths to feed . . . life was a struggle.

In her thirties, Gros looked at a photograph of herself and saw what she thought was an old woman. After the birth of her tenth child in 1878, Gros died. Though her life story may seem insignificant today, her letters and diaries—and those of so many other pioneer women of the West—today are an invaluable legacy allowing real glimpses of their day-to-day life on the prairie, among the hills, in the mountains and their valleys, on the distant coast . . . on the ranch, too.

For a look at the ranch life, Texas seems the place to start, and **Molly Goodnight,** wife of the man credited with "inventing" the chuck wagon (see pages 263–68), makes a good study. Born in Tennessee in 1839, Mary Ann—known as Molly by almost everyone—moved to Belknap, Texas, in 1854 with her family. Left in charge of five younger brothers after the deaths of both parents when she was about fifteen, she taught school to help support the family. By the time she met Charles Goodnight, she had honed her abilities to cope with the hard frontier life.

Charles and Mary—as he called her—were married in 1870, and they settled down on his ranch in Colorado. When the going got tough for the young couple in the drought and financial panic of 1873, they returned to Texas, driving their herd before them. That proved no problem for the hardy Molly—she simply drove a team and wagon loaded with supplies while Charles, one of her brothers, and their ranch partners, John Adair and his wife, helped keep the herd in line.

According to Joyce Gibson Roach in the *Handbook of Texas Online,* Molly pitched right in to help build the two-room cabin that would serve as the Goodnight home after they arrived at the site of their new ranch in the Palo Duro Canyon in the Texas Panhandle. The Adairs eventually returned to their home in Ireland, leaving the Goodnights to maintain the Texas ranch on their own. It was not long before their JA Ranch was well known throughout the high plains. And Molly, as first lady of Palo Duro Canyon, often the only woman on the ranch, became doctor, nurse, spiritual comforter, sister, and mother to the ranch hands. It is easy to understand why the cowboys of the high plains enshrined her as "Mother of the Panhandle."

She rode the range on horseback, feeling perfectly at ease, especially after her husband had a two-horned sidesaddle designed for her. It was while riding the range that she was horrified to find baby buffalo left to die in the wake of commercial buffalo hunters who had shot and skinned the adult buffaloes. Almost an endangered species by the 1880s, the buffalo desperately needed an angel of mercy . . . like Molly Goodnight, who now made saving the buffalo her personal cause. Rescuing and raising the orphans, Molly led the way in establishing the Goodnight buffalo herd, which soon became well known throughout the world.

As the Texas Panhandle continued to gain in population, as its towns expanded, schools, churches, and like institutions needed a helping hand as well. Molly again came to the rescue. In 1898 she helped establish Goodnight College. No wonder that when Molly died in 1926, by then in her eighties, her headstone was engraved with this message: "Mary Ann Dyer Goodnight, One who spent her life in the service of others."

No matter how many traveled west in the nineteenth century, there always was a shortage of women, especially in the gold fields of California and nearby environs. When that intelligence reached Europe, and France in particular, it wasn't long before several boatloads of mademoiselles of "good character" arrived in San Francisco. They were quickly hired by the city's burgeoning saloons and gambling houses and paid the exorbitant sum of $250 a month to rake in the winnings of the male customers or to serve them drinks at the bar. The feminine newcomers were highly valued since they gave the establishments a touch of class—and guaranteed a steady flow of male customers. Before the first month was up, it turns out, many of the newly arrived young ladies had rings on their fingers and were taking a walk down the aisle.

Since this kind of news spreads fast, however, it wasn't long before women of "easy virtue" also came flocking to the California gold fields.

And there was gold of a sort to be mined by these "ladies of the evening," but not exactly by panning for it in the California stream beds. One noted prostitute claimed to have earned fifty thousand dollars in just a few months. Meanwhile, as women arrived from all corners, the difference between "good" and "bad" became clearly defined. The "good" women, such as "schoolmarms," were practically enshrined. Prostitutes were the "bad," and of course were among the first females to reach the myriad of hastily established mining camps.

Before real family units began to arrive in the far West, in most cases fresh from their overland wagon trains, it was strictly a man's world. And why not . . . hadn't its first American arrivals been, for the most part, young, single men seeking adventure and fortune as they struggled and sometimes fought their way across the vast, super-challenging territory lying west of home? Whether they had come as scouts, explorers, trappers, soldiers, surveyors, or miners, wasn't this a macho environment where a man was judged by how fast he could draw a gun, how much whiskey he could put away . . . how quick he was to display the tough-guy chip sitting on an easily "offended" shoulder?

Naturally, the men didn't have all the comforts of the home left behind. Tents, sod houses, even caves often were their only shelter.

Meanwhile, by midcentury, there were only two women for every one hundred men in the West. But now the single women started appearing in that same West, themselves attracted by the lure of possible adventure and fortune . . . and with plenty of male company a sure bet. Prostitution sprang up beyond gold-fevered California—in other hot spots and boom towns as well. Holladay Street in Denver, Colorado, became known as the "wickedest thoroughfare in the West." Here, wrote Ann Seagraves in her book *Soiled Doves,* "Approximately one thousand ladies of the evening plied their trade in the elegant parlor houses, brothels and shabby cribs which lined both sides of the street." Poor Ben Holladay, the freight and stagecoach mogul for whom the street had been named! After his embarrassed heirs petitioned the town fathers to change the name, it became Market Street, but whatever the name, it was still business as usual . . . the same business as before.

To this notorious strip came **Mattie Silks,** a pretty young farm girl from Kansas who, at the tender age of nineteen, already had reigned as a successful madam—in fact, as described by Seagraves, she already had been "a glamorous madam in a high-class parlor house." By 1876 she had worked her way west from Springfield, Illinois, to one boom town after another, until she and her "girls" reached Denver. "Within a brief period, Mattie, who had always been a successful businesswoman, had what was considered the 'carriage trade;' the money was rolling in!"

Certainly *not* the typical madam, Mattie had a creamy complexion, blue eyes, and blonde hair curled and piled upon her head. She wore fancy clothes of the latest fashion, her dresses lined with special pockets, one for her gold pieces, the other for her small, ivory-handled pistol. But Mattie wanted it all. She wanted a steady lover all her own.

Enter unlikely married man Cort Thomson, a "cocky little foot-racer who wore pink tights and star-spangled blue running trunks." Never mind that he had a wife and daughter stashed away somewhere, he and Mattie immediately hit it off—as a result, she had her "steady," and he had her money to spend on gambling, whiskey and, eventually, other women. He bought Mattie a gold cross covered in diamonds—financed with her own money, of course. No matter, she indulged in her Cort, even if he arrived at her parlor sitting astride his horse and riding up the front steps and through the door to demand more money. She simply would smile indulgently and "shower him with coins." The affair continued for years, but in the end Mattie—like generations of women before and since—wanted more. What she wanted, she got, too . . . when Cort's wife died, he and Mattie married. A few years later, his daughter died also, leaving to him the care of a granddaughter, a responsibility he refused to accept. But Mattie, apparently having a motherly instinct to satisfy, stepped forward to adopt the child and see to her care.

Nothing, it seemed, could turn aside her love for the futile little fop, nor he from her charms . . . and generosity. When he died in 1900, to leave behind a grieving widow of fifty-four, the funeral that followed "was extravagant," wrote Seagraves, "and her tears were many." The estimate is that through the years of their relationship he had borrowed or spent more than fifty thousand dollars of Mattie's money.

More happily, Mattie married again. She stayed on in Denver until her death in 1929 at the age of eighty-three . . . then to be buried next to Cort Thomson, "the only man she ever loved." Prostitution by then had long passed its heyday on old Holladay Street, with few to remember the petite young woman from Kansas with curls piled atop her head, come to Denver in those bustling days after the Civil War to seek her fortune as an unusually astute madam. Indeed, Mattie during her professional "career" probably saw nearly two million dollars pass through her hands. She had lived lavishly, however, and had only a small estate—a few pieces of jewelry, some property and four thousand dollars in cash—to leave her second husband and adopted daughter.

If "thar's gold in them hills," there was silver, too, and **Nellie Cashman**—that was her real name—meant to get her share. An Irish lass from County Cork, Nellie had arrived in Boston at the age of five with her widowed mother and younger sister. Working as a bellhop in a fine Boston hotel, she luckily caught the eye of a hotel guest named Ulysses S. Grant, and he urged her to go west, recalled Bob Katz in his article "The Angel of Tombstone" appearing in the online magazine

DesertUSA (http://www.desrtusa.com/mag98/may/papr/du_cashman. html). Needless to say, what the Union hero of the Civil War had to say would make an impression upon Nellie, described as both pretty of face . . . and, as the West was about to find out, pretty tough, too.

Taking Grant's advice, she soon developed a wanderlust leading her to San Francisco and then on to some of the most boisterous mining camps in the West. Often seen in men's trousers and a fur hat, she first stopped in the Pioche mining district near Nevada's silver-rich Virginia City. She saw that the miners, however rough, tough, or gruff, needed decent food and housing—the boarding house she opened filled quickly with grateful and hungry miners. A few years later, hearing of a gold strike at Dease Lake in northern British Columbia, not far from the Juneau, Alaska, she and some of her miner friends pulled up stakes and headed north.

It was here, in the winter of 1874–75, that Nellie became an "angel of mercy."

She had left camp for a trip to Victoria, British Columbia, to buy supplies. No sooner had she done so than a blizzard trapped the miners at their diggings—no one could get through, yet they needed supplies, especially food. But Nellie knew exactly what to do. As reported by Don Chaput in the March 1998 issue of *American History Illustrated* magazine, "She immediately purchased supplies and sleds, hired six men, sailed to Fort Wangell, Alaska, and headed inland through heavy snows." Now, mind you, she was no spring chicken—Nellie, in fact, was well past thirty, and a member of the "weaker" sex besides. Nonetheless, she and her band of six, plus pack animals loaded with fifteen hundred pounds of vital supplies, punched their way through snow sometimes ten feet deep to reach her stranded miners.

Arriving just in the nick of time with both food and, as it happened, desperately needed medicines, she then had to nurse perhaps one hundred miners sick with scurvy. "If Nellie had done nothing else for the rest of her career," wrote Chaput, "that incident alone would have guaranteed her a place in mining lore and tradition."

But no, there was more to come. Four years later, Nellie had left the snow country for the hot, dry desert to open a restaurant in the new railroad town of Tucson, Arizona Territory. The lure of the mines soon had her on the move once more, this time to the legendary town of Tombstone. She arrived there in 1880, right after the storied Earp brotherhood blew into town.

Her "angel" reputation already was known even in this desolate corner of the world, but it was her own determination that got things done. A lifelong and devout Roman Catholic, Nellie was able to persuade the owners of the Crystal Palace Saloon—Wyatt Earp among them—to allow the celebration of Sunday Mass there until she and others could raise the funds needed to build a church. Thanks in large part to her talent for persuasion, the money came forth, and Tombstone's Sacred Heart Roman Catholic Church soon was a reality.

Nellie, though, could be just as brave as she was persuasive. When mine owner E. B. Gage was about to be lynched by angry miners, Nellie charged into the mob in her buggy and carried Gage away before the scattered hotheads could react. More sedately, to be sure, she also helped to establish the town's first hospital, raised funds for the Salvation Army, the Red Cross, and amateur theatricals.

This lady entrepreneur always was able to support herself, and at times very well. Nellie owned or managed six different enterprises during these years, worked at mining herself, and bought and sold both silver and gold claims. Among other activities, she ran a boot store and opened another restaurant famous for its good food. According to the *DesertUSA* account, she "served 50-cent meals, advertising that 'there are no cockroaches in my kitchen and the flour is clean.'"

Still, Nellie Cashman always had in mind the "Big Bonanza," and when news came in 1883 of a gold strike in Baja California, Mexico, Nellie's restless spirit urged her on once again. Organizing a prospecting expedition, she had no trouble enlisting twenty-one leading citizens of Tombstone, among them future U.S. Sen. Mark Smith. Taking a train, sailing across the Gulf of California, trekking inland over Baja deserts, and almost dying from lack of water and the terrible heat, they failed to find any gold.

As if this disappointment weren't enough, Nellie learned upon her return to Tombstone that her widowed younger sister had died . . . and left five young children to be raised by Nellie, their closest relative. Naturally, she pitched in as their surrogate mother . . . and took them with her as she spent the next five years wandering the mining camps of Wyoming, Montana, New Mexico, and Arizona. The online *DesertUSA* adds that "under her care" all five children grew up to become "successful and productive citizens."

Never one to put down permanent roots, Nellie in 1898 headed north again, this time to a gold strike in the Yukon. She opened another restaurant and supply store there, and the miners flocked in, not only to enjoy her offerings but also because she was known to give out free cigars. Soon, though, Nellie was moving ever farther north, to establish mining operations of her own in the Koyukuk wilderness just sixty miles below the Arctic Circle. Legend has it that once, in her sixties, she crossed more than seven hundred miles of the snow-covered Arctic terrain by dogsled.

One of the great and most colorful figures of the Klondike, she settled down at last in Victoria. By now it was 1923, and, when interviewed that year by a reporter for the *Arizona Star,* she was asked why she never had married. "Why child," Nellie replied, "I haven't had time for marriage. Men are just a nuisance anyhow, aren't they? They're just boys grown up."

Nellie Cashman, "Angel of Mercy," died in Victoria just two years later.

Many women of the West never had a choice in the matter—they often were the children of newly settled pioneers, or they were born in the prairie schooners lumbering westward over the plains and mountains. Or, like **Berthenia Owens,** born on February 7, 1840, in Van Buren County, Missouri, they simply were carried West as small children.

She and her parents, Thomas and Sarah Damron Owens, left Missouri as part of the "Great Migration" of 1843, traveling all the way to Oregon, where they settled on the Clatsop Plains at the mouth of the Columbia River. Here she thrived and grew up . . . several times over, in fact, as her life took surprising and unconventional turns. And through it all she proved a resourceful and enduring woman.

One of nine children and a second daughter, Berthenia as a child always was a tomboy, and she "gloried in the fact," wrote Cathy Lucetti and Carol Olwell in their book *Women of the West.* Her father was known to call her his "boy." She in fact regretted that she was not a boy because she "realized very early in life that a girl was hampered and hemmed in on all sides simply by accident of sex."

Tomboy or not, with a new baby appearing every two years, she became the family nurse. Her mother had little time away from her pioneer chores to devote to each new arrival, and as a result, left Berthenia in charge of the little ones. All the children were taught self-reliance at an early age, and by age fourteen all the children were expected to do a full day's work.

By 1853, needing more land for their father's cattle, the family removed to southern Oregon, where there was abundance of grazing range. After the crops were harvested that year, the family prepared to spend the winter in Portland, then a very small town on the Willamette River. But who would drive the cattle southward? Berthenia, of course, was her father's choice, together with brother Flem and a hired hand, who, Berthenia said, was not half their equal. "Father said we were worth more than any two men he could hire," she added.

Soon settled in for the winter, the family was glad to welcome visitors. As fate would have it, one who came calling was Legrand Hill, whose family had come to Oregon the year before. It was arranged by the family that Berthenia, now fourteen, would marry Hill in the spring.

The wedding took place on May 4, 1854, with family and close neighbors in attendance. The groom's contribution to the marriage was a 320-acre farm four miles away, which he recently had bought on credit for six hundred dollars. As their home, it boasted a small cabin of round logs with the bark still on them. Berthenia brought to the marriage linens and feather bedding from her mother. Thanks to her father's generosity, she wrote, "My cooking utensils were a pot, tea-kettle and bake oven (all of iron), a frying pan and coffee pot, churn, six milk pans, a wash tub and board, a large twenty or thirty gallon iron pot for washing purposes, etc., and a water bucket and tin dipper."

She did not go unwillingly, by any means. "My soul overflowed with love and hope," Berthenia later remembered. "My happy, buoyant nature enabled me to enjoy anything, even cooking out of doors, over a smoky fire." To her it really didn't matter that they didn't have a fireplace or stove at first, for they had most of what they needed. Her practical nature appreciated their simple furniture—such as their bed, which had been made by boring three holes in the log wall in one corner, then attaching the rails. Built in this manner, a pioneer bed required only one steady wooden leg. Their table, she also recalled, "was a mere rough shelf, fastened to the wall, and supported by two legs." Three shelves along one wall served as a cupboard for their small supply of dishes—mainly tinware, "which in those days was kept scrupulously bright and shining." And she had one real treasure that she had bought with her own money before she married, a set of German silver teaspoons.

It was a new beginning for both, and the newlyweds had a great chance for a happy life together. "It was sweet, smiling spring—the season that I loved best," Berthenia wrote. She added, "The hills were bedecked with the loveliest wild flowers, for the variety and abundance of which the Umpqua valley is especially noted."

Two years later a baby boy was born and named George. This brought great joy to the mother, but by now Berthenia realized that her husband was lazy and irresponsible. Already they had lost the nice little farm through his neglect. Legrand was either out hunting or simply not doing any work. Berthenia finally told her father and mother of her predicament. Her father broke down and cried, saying that there had never been a divorce in their family. He hoped that she could make her marriage work. But if it didn't, she and baby George would be welcome back home.

As if her husband's laziness—he had lost a second farm and moved his little family into a tent on low-lying land and made ill-advised investments—and irrational behavior were not bad enough, he began to severely discipline the little boy, who was not old enough to understand. One day she could stand it no more—the final climax was when he threw the baby on the bed and rushed out in a fit of rage.

She always remembered how dismal her future seemed after the divorce, even though she was back in the loving home environment her family offered. "I could scarcely read and write," she added, "and four years of trial and hardships and privations sufficient to crush a mature women, had wrought a painful change in the fresh, blooming child who had so buoyantly taken the duties and burdens of wifehood and motherhood on her young shoulders."

But her pioneer spirit and energy would see her through, even when things seem the darkest. "I realized my position fully, and resolved to meet it bravely, and do my very best."

Thus began the transformation of a semiliterate teenager to a determined and successful physician. She raised her son and after she saw that he had a fine education, he became a doctor. And Berthenia herself took up medical studies at the University of Michigan. She obtained her medical degree in 1880, at the age of forty.

On July 24, 1884, she and Col. John Adair, a childhood friend whom she had not seen since she was thirteen, were married in the First Congregational Church in Portland, Oregon. The couple adopted a child in 1891 whom they named John. She practiced medicine in Yakima, Washington, until she closed her office on October 10, 1905. After her retirement she remained active in many causes—she lobbied for the Women's Christian Temperance Union, and she campaigned in favor of more exercise, shorter skirts and against sidesaddle horseback riding by women.

After a long, vigorous, and successful life marked by a rare divorce and, even rarer, by winning a doctor's degree at the age of forty-plus—a woman, mind you!—she died on September 11, 1926, at the age of eighty-six.

Another woman who had no choice in her westward move, but who would use it to great advantage, not only for herself but for many others, was a young slave girl named **Bridget "Biddy" Mason,** born on a Mississippi plantation in 1818. Her owner, Robert Smith, a Mormon convert, took Biddy and her three daughters on a two-thousand-mile trek across the continent to the Utah Territory, recalls the Southern California Historical Society's Web site (http://www.socalhistory.org/biddymason. htm). On the long journey, Biddy was responsible for herding the cattle, preparing the meals and serving as a midwife. Another slave, Hannah, was in the group that arrived in Utah in the year 1851.

After a short stay in Utah, Smith moved with his slaves to San Bernardino County, California, to which Brigham Young had dispatched members of a start-up Mormon community. This, too, would be only a sojourn since in 1855 Smith decided to return to the South. He wanted to take Biddy, Hannah, and their twelve children and grandchildren with him to the slave state of Texas, where he planned to establish his new home. Having lived in a free state since her arrival in San Bernardino in 1852, Biddy had experienced new ways, had seen a more open approach to the slavery issue . . . and, most important, had no desire to return to the old system of legal slavery.

Biddy and Hannah took Smith to court with a plea for their freedom. Clyde A. Milner II, in *The Oxford History of the American West,* explained that the case was decided by a judge in Los Angeles who took "special note of Robert Smith's desire to relocate four of the children born in the free state of California, to the slave state of Texas," and granted the mothers and their children their freedom.

Exhilarated by the fresh oxygen of freedom, Biddy now took the full name of Biddy Mason and settled in Los Angeles. She quickly found work as a nurse and domestic in homes at $2.50 a week. A frugal woman who saved her money, she soon purchased her own home as well as two additional lots in the city, then became an astute real estate investor. Through the years her house on South Spring Street became a haven for needy travelers, and she became a great supporter of quality education for African American children.

Biddy's charity took her to many areas of the city—she visited jail inmates and was always ready with a helping hand for all races. During a devastating Los Angeles flood in the 1880s, she not only prepared emergency foods and distributed them to the victims, she also paid the bill.

Beyond her newfound freedom, her wealth and open heart to the needy, Biddy Mason achieved a far-reaching first. In 1872, she and her son-in-law, Charles Owens, founded and financed the First African Methodist Episcopal Church of Los Angeles.

When she died in 1891, says Albert Greenstein's account on the historical society Web site, she was buried in an unmarked grave in Evergreen Cemetery. "Nearly a century later, on March 27, 1988, in a ceremony attended by Los Angeles Mayor Tom Bradley and 3,000 members of the First AME Church, a tombstone was unveiled which marked her grave for the first time."

Then there were those women who used the pen to make an impact on the Wild West. "As soon as I began, it seemed impossible to write fast enough," explained **Helen Hunt Jackson,** author of the once-famous novel *Ramona,* a historical romance.

Jackson, born Helen Maria Fiske in 1830 in Amherst, Massachusetts, was a friend and classmate of the town's celebrated poet Emily Dickinson. She wrote poetry and children's books, as well as novels and essays, using the pen name of H.H.H. But then came a visit to the Southwest. Jackson immediately was caught up in the history of the area, a fascination that led her, in 1879, to a lecture in Boston by the Ponca chief Standing Bear. After hearing his description of the forced removal of his people from their homeland in Nebraska, her interest became her cause and passion. Overnight she turned into a near zealot in her pursuit of money and helpful petitions on behalf of the Ponca Indians.

Her campaign soon led to a book, *A Century of Dishonor,* published in 1881. She sent a copy to every member of Congress with a grim admonition printed on the cover: "Look upon your hands: they are stained with the blood of your relations."

But not even that effort had much impact.

Defiant still, she traveled to southern California to spend several months of 1882 and 1883 touring impoverished Mexican barrios and isolated Indian settlements. As she had suspected, the Indian population was dwindling. Jackson was horrified to learn that in southern California in 1852 there were an estimated fifteen thousand Indians living on mission lands, and at the time of her visit three decades later there were fewer than four thousand. Stunned, she resolved to write a book exposing the horrible conditions she had seen. Her hope was that it would have a similar impact on the nation that Harriet Beecher Stowe once had with *Uncle Tom's Cabin*, according to the Southern California Historical Society's Web site account by Albert Greenstein (www.socialhistory .org/Biographies/hhjackson.htm).

For this book, H.H.H. decided to write under her own name. (*Note:* She had been married twice. Her first husband, an army captain, died an accidental death, and her second husband was William S. Jackson, a banker and railroad executive.)

Set in southern California, *Ramona*, published in 1884, told the sad love story of an Indian named Alessandro and a beautiful Mexican Indian girl, Ramona. Jackson's historical romance was an overnight success, the most popular American novel of its time, but much to her chagrin, the public reacted to *Ramona* very differently from what she had anticipated. Instead of picking up on her theme of needed reform, the general public found a gentle, romantic ideal of an earlier time in which the Indians happily did the bidding of kindhearted Spanish missionaries and landed gentry.

Sadly, the author died on August 12, 1885, less than a year after publication of her immensely popular book. *"My Century of Dishonor* and *Ramona* are the only things I have done of which I am glad," she had told a friend. "They will live, and . . . bear fruit."

She died, but her *Ramona* does live on, even today. Not only did her novel inspire early California tourism, movies, and songs—the 1920s hit *Ramona* is still available today in music shops—but it also led to the long-running outdoor *Ramona Pageant* staged annually in Hemet, California. And, notes the Greenstein online account, "[T]he name Ramona can be seen on street signs and commercial establishments throughout Southern California."

Another romantic icon of the West was created by the innovative restaurateur Fred Harvey, who imported hundreds of clean-cut young women to staff the chain of restaurants he opened at railroad stations along the Santa Fe rail line from Kansas to New Mexico. Not only did his "eateries" furnish the rare commodity of good, wholesome food for the weary traveler, but the "**Harvey Girls,**" as they were called, "never looked dowdy, frowsy, tired, slipshod or overworked," wrote Elbert Hubbard in the *Leavenworth (Kans.) Times* in 1905. Arriving from the East, these select single "girls" lived in dormitories and served most of their meals when the trains came in.

No surprise then that Englishman Harvey sometimes was called "Civilizer of the American West."

Among the best-known women of the West were the legendary **Calamity Jane** and the sure-shot **Annie Oakley,** but neither was typical of the hundreds of thousands of women who pioneered and peopled the West with hardly any comparable fanfare. Annie Oakley (real name, Phoebe Anne Mauzy or Mosey or Mozee), a wonderful shot and a mainstay of Buffalo Bill's Wild West show, was born in Ohio and never lived in the West. For all her prowess with a gun, she strictly was a theatrical creation. Calamity Jane (real name, Martha Jane Canary), on the other hand, lived in the West after leaving her native Missouri. Many are the stories—and contradictions—about her life from then on, but it does seem she served as an army scout, often dressed as a man, could shoot and ride hard with the best of them, and spent time in Deadwood, South Dakota, where she was known as a friend, if not lover, of James "Wild Bill" Hickok until he was shot and killed during a card game. She also was the heroine of an 1878 smallpox outbreak in Deadwood, to which she returned to die in 1903 after some years in Texas as the wife of a man named Burke. She is buried in Deadwood near Hickok's grave.

Two other women, though, are worth a closer look, one whose peoples were native to the West, and the other whose life story paralleled the exploration and settlement of the West.

SACAGAWEA

Fascinating, well, yes. Mysterious, certainly. A legend, that too. A heroine, absolutely. She was all of these and more.

Known as Bird Woman, Snake Woman, Grass Woman, or just Indian woman, and on occasion referred to as "Janey" by William Clark, by any name Sacagawea was an asset, even a vital link, and the only woman—a teenager with a papoose on her back at that—to travel with the Corps of Discovery.

The spelling of her name has many versions. Lewis and Clark sometimes wrote it as Sakakawea; researcher Grace Raymond Hebard, "hunting in the crannies of time" for the lost years of the Indian woman's life, titled her book, *Sacajawea*. The latter spelling derives from numerous attempts to decipher the mystery of her name. According to Irving W. Anderson in the summer 1975 issue of *We Proceeded On*, "Shoshoni advocates claim her as 'Sacajawea' (pronounced sak'a-ja-we-a), a form of her name which has become widely popularized both in spelling and pronunciation, especially in the far West." This spelling means "boat pusher" or "boat launcher" in Shoshone (sometimes spelled Shoshoni), which contradicts Lewis and Clark's tendency to call her "Bird Woman." To settle the spelling question, Anderson points out, Lewis and Clark scholars, the U.S. Geographic Names Board, the National Park Service, and the National Geographic Society, among others, have adopted *Sacagawea*.

Although her name and her part in the great continental exploration story are well known throughout the United States, she has become a bona fide folk heroine in the West, where lakes, rivers, and even mountains bear her name. National Park sites, historical sites, and tourist centers in the West feature books, statuettes, and other materials portraying Sacagawea's story and her *supposed* likeness . . . but only supposed. Since nowhere in the Corps of Discovery's journals is there a physical description of the Indian woman and since no sketches or painting of her are known to exist, her appearance in various pictures and statuary is the creation of the artist.

Who was this Native American we call Sacagawea?

She was born to the Shoshone, or Snake Indians, who lived in the Rocky Mountains at the headwaters of the Missouri in what is now Idaho. Little is known of her early life, except that when she was about twelve, she and several other girls were captured by a Hidatsa raiding party. She was carried to the villages of the Mandan and Hidatsa on the Knife River near present-day Bismarck, North Dakota.

Totally unknown to this child of the wilderness in the middle of the North American continent, her fate was settled when Thomas Jefferson bought the land known as Louisiana from France, doubling the size of the fledgling American nation. Her fame was assured when the president commissioned an expedition under the leadership of Meriwether Lewis and William Clark to explore this newly acquired territory and the land beyond it, all the way to the Pacific Ocean.

On May 14, 1804, Lewis and Clark's Corps of Discovery set out in a small fleet of boats on the Missouri River just above St. Louis, the start of a journey that would take them eight thousand miles on rivers, across plains, over mountains, and through valleys to the Pacific and back. It became certainly the most exciting travel drama in the history of America.

Meanwhile, French-Canadian fur trader and gambler Touissant Charbonneau had been busying himself around the Hidatsa-Mandan villages, buying or winning young squaws as his slaves or "wives." One account claims that he won two young squaws in a bet with the warriors who had captured them in Shoshone country four years earlier.

By late October 1804, the Lewis and Clark fleet, after months of rigorous upstream travel on the Missouri, had reached the Mandan villages—one on the west bank and, a shade farther upriver, a second village on the east. Nearby lived the Mandans' neighbors and allies the Hidatsas. As the two captains knew from their research, the Mandan villages were the center of the Northern Plains trade and attracted Indians from all around, especially in late summer and early fall. Thus the villages should be teeming with representatives from many tribes, as well as white fur trappers and traders—men from the British Hudson's Bay and North West companies, even an occasional hardy trader all the way from St. Louis.

It was here that the American explorers made their winter quarters. From their first encounter, relations with the Mandans looked promising but the captains were taking no chances—they built a fort as their winter headquarters and defensible safe haven. Many Indian tribesmen came to observe and to visit with the busy Americans.

Among the visitors were Charbonneau and his two wives. He offered *his* services as an interpreter to the explorers and was hired, but only because Lewis and Clark realized his Indian wives could be invaluable as the real translators. The result, as events turned out, was a translating *team*—Indian girl to Indians, then Indian girl to Touissant, then Touissant to a French-speaking member of the corps, and that person to Lewis and Clark. They would take along the French-Canadian, but only one wife could go.

Charbonneau chose his fifteen-year-old wife, Sacagawea, who was six months' pregnant. And wouldn't she turn out to be an essential addition to the company as its pathway led through the very territory occupied by her native tribe, often along trails she had known as a child! Not only would she become an interpreter but also a vital guide and even ambassador as the corps threaded its way through the mountains and to the sea far beyond. Even to tribes unfamiliar to her, the presence of a woman and child in the party would signal its peaceful nature.

But first there was a baby to be delivered. It was a cold winter's day in February 1805; a slight snow had fallen the night before, and conditions were primitive as the young Indian woman was about to have her baby. The father had gone off to hunt with some of the other men and would return with horses loaded with meat.

A clear picture of the event of Monday, February 11, was written in the explorers' journals: "We sent down a party with sleds, to relieve the horses from their loads; the weather fair and cold, with a N. W. wind. About five o'clock one of the wives of Charboneau was delivered of a boy; this being her first child she was suffering considerable, when Mr. Jessaume [another French-Canadian in the vicinity] told Captain Lewis that he had frequently administered to persons in her situation, a small dose of the rattle of the rattlesnake which had never failed to hasten the delivery. Having some of the rattle, captain Lewis gave it to Mr. Jessaume, who crumbled two of the rings of it between his fingers, and mixing it with a small quantity of water gave it to her. What effect it may really have had it might be difficult to determine, but captain Lewis was informed that she had not taken it more than ten minutes before the delivery took place."

The fine healthy baby boy, named Jean Baptiste, soon become America's youngest explorer. Although he was not yet seven weeks old, he was strapped to his mother's back when the corps, thirty-three in number with the inclusion of the small Charbonneau family, set off in April 1805 to resume the journey to the Pacific . . . at this point still proceeding upstream and northwesterly, but mostly westerly, on the Missouri River.

Rather than become a burden to the two captains and their men, the young mother proved useful far beyond simple domestic chores such as making camp every evening. She displayed her fortitude and courage only a few weeks into their journey, when she, her husband, and several corps members were sharing a pirogue rigged with sails. For reasons never explained, Charbonneau—once disparagingly described by Lewis as "perhaps the most timid waterman in the world"—was in charge of the sails. Clark and Lewis were watching from shore when a sudden squall struck, and Charbonneau panicked.

If the boat capsized, the captains knew, they would lose the invaluable records and supplies it held. As water poured into the buffeted, careening craft, one of the men in the boat yelled at Charbonneau to turn the boat into the wind, but he couldn't, or wouldn't, listen. And now vital maps, journals, instruments, and medical supplies began to float overboard.

Ashore and helpless, Lewis was furious. He was about to plunge into the chill waters, swim out, and try to save what he could. Meanwhile, the men in the pirogue were bailing frantically to keep it afloat. It had shipped so much water it was threatening to sink, with the loss of everything aboard. One of the men turned his gun on Charbonneau and threatened to shoot unless he righted the boat. This shocked the French-Canadian so much that he at last managed to run down the sail, thus allowing his companions to paddle the barely floating craft to shore.

Throughout the ordeal, Sacagawea remained perfectly calm in her perch at the stern of the pirogue, from which vantage point she was able to reach out, sometimes daringly so, and retrieve various articles as they floated by. Wrote a greatly relieved Clark in his journal that night, of May 14, 1805: "By four o'clock in the evening our instruments, medicine, merchandise, provisions, were perfectly dried, repacked, and put on board the perogue. . . . The Indian woman, to whom I ascribe equal fortitude and resolution with any person on board at the time of the accident, caught and preserved most of the light articles which were washed overboard."

Soon after the dramatic incident, Lewis wrote in his journal for May 20: "About five miles above the mouth of Shell river, a handsome river of about fifty yards in width discharged itself into the Shell river on the starboard or upper side. This stream we called Sahcagerweah."

Sacagawea was able to teach the explorers a few survival tricks. Since it wasn't healthy to live solely on the meat provided by the group's hunters, she pointed out the berries that were safe to eat and places to find them. When food was scarce, she led her companions to places in the woods where they could dig for edible roots.

Soon after the party reached the Great Falls of the Missouri, however, Sacagawea became very ill. Clark, the medical man of the group, bled her, as was the custom of the day. He wrote in his log that evening that he had moved her to a section of her boat less exposed to the sun to keep her cool. Lewis, in turn, took a small canoe to meander back and forth along the river in search of a sulfur spring, having heard that sulfur had good effects as treatment for fever and pain.

He found some and tried it on Sacagawea. It seemed to help but while awaiting the results, he logged his concern both for her and his expedition: "This [her fever and illness] gave me some concern, as well as for the poor object herself, then with a young child in her arms, as from her condition of her being our only dependence for a friendly negotiation with the Snake Indians, on whom we depend for horses to assist us in our portage from the Missouri to the Columbia river."

Feeling much better after the sulfur water treatment, Sacagawea came across some white apples and ate too many, after which she also gorged upon dried fish. When a fever then laid her low again, Lewis furiously turned on her husband and blamed him for allowing her to overindulge so soon after her illness.

In any case, good health soon returned to the young mother . . . but now still another peril threatened. After making camp along the riverbank one day, Sacagawea, her baby, Charbonneau, and Clark were almost lost. Just as they arrived at a nearby falls, a huge black cloud opened in the skies above. Clark led them to a nearby ravine with an overhanging rock to escape the downpour. As they prepared to wait out the storm, however, torrents of rainwater came gushing down the ravine, carrying a wall of rocks and mud and sticks right toward them. Clark grabbed his gun and started up the bank as the water reached his waist. Charbonneau had his wife by the hand but was so frightened that he hardly moved. Clark then pushed Sacagawea, who held the infant in her arms, ahead of him as they scrabbled up the steep bluff to safety. All made it out of the threatening ravine, but with nowhere else to seek shelter, they were left standing in the rain. Clark's black servant York by now was with them as well, having gone to look for them in the same ugly storm. Lewis, who witnessed the frightful scene, later wrote in his journal: "[O]ne moment longer and it would have swept them into the river just above the great cataract of 87 feet, where they would have inevitably perished."

Such were the adventures of this very young Indian woman, who by now had been kidnapped from her own native people as hardly more than a child, then sold like chattel to a hard-drinking, older trapper, then endured a painful childbirth, survived a near-fatal fever, weathered a serious relapse, escaped rushing waters, and occasionally suffered a beating from her husband. Yet she sustained herself through it all and cared for an infant in the face of severe privations and hardships . . . and endured all with grace and dignity.

If she were long overdue for a little respite, a moment of happiness, it was about to come. Not even the most creative Hollywood screenwriter could have sold this script: First, the travelers approached a landmark familiar to Sacagawea, a large rock formation called Beaver Rock because it resembled the animal. She assured the expedition leaders that they had reached the land of her people. The place in which the party made camp that night, farther along the trail west, was the same spot where she had been abducted by Indian raiders so many years before!

But wait, Hollywood, there's even more to come.

Lewis and Clark now divided the group into two parties to search for Sacagawea's tribe, which, she said, was close by. Riding ahead with two men, Lewis several days later glimpsed an Indian on a horse. The horseman was stopped some distance away and simply stared back, making no response to any of the explorers' overtures.

Another day passed, and Lewis again spotted Indians, this time young girls and a woman. Through sign language he convinced them that he was friendly and wished to visit their village. As the girls led him to the village, a group of men rode toward them. The leader was the same man Lewis had seen the day before. He was the Shoshone chief Cameahwait.

Meanwhile, Clark and his group, which included Sacagawea, were searching for Lewis. Suddenly Clark saw Sacagawea "begin to dance and show every mark of the most extravagant joy." A jubilant crowd approached the small party. One of the women rushed up to Sacagawea and hugged her. The two women had been abducted by the same group of raiders and now recognized each other.

Soon Clark and Lewis were invited to join Cameahwait in his tent. Anxious to get on with the horse trading, the two explorers readily accepted. They entered his tent, but there was little conversation until Sacagawea was sent for.

She entered the tent and sat down demurely, ready to perform as interpreter. When her eyes fell on the chief, "[S]he instantly jumped up, and ran and embraced him, throwing over him her blanket and weeping profusely."

Cameahwait was her brother.

Sacagawea was an Indian princess! The scene already was a screenwriter's dream, with a wonderful set of characters and a plot for the ages, but there was more to come. Her brother told her that all her family were dead except for him, a younger brother who was not there at the time, and a son of her eldest sister. She decided at once to adopt the young boy. After all this news she attempted to carry on as interpreter but her emotions overpowered her.

This occurred in the late summer, and Lewis and Clark were anxious to get going. There were mountains looming ahead, mountains that *must* be crossed before snow set in. To move on they needed horses. On August 22, the serious bargaining began.

Lewis later bewailed the price they had to pay for the horses. Even with Sacagawea's influence, the ponies were tired and sore old nags. The Shoshone were better bargainers than the Americans.

After much delay the Corps of Discovery was ready to climb the next mountain, literally. Before the explorers at last was the Continental Divide—they were ecstatic to see that, from here to the Pacific, the streams flowed westward. On the far side of the mountain ranges, they would leave their horses with friendly Nez Perce Indians. Finally, they built canoes and floated down the Clearwater River to the Snake and finally to the Columbia.

Food had not been a major problem east of the mountains, since elk, buffalo, and deer were plentiful. To the west of the mountains, there were fish—along the Columbia River salmon were especially plentiful. The area tribes dried their catch on wooden scaffolds. In bartering for food, Sacagawea again was helpful as the corps' translator. To vary the diet of fish and roots, however, the corps experimented with a new source of food, readily available from the native tribes along the way. Having become accustomed to eating horseflesh by this time, corps members "felt no disrelish" when presented with the new dish: *dog*.

Even though, as a Shoshone, Sacagawea would have none of this, the captains bought the dogs from the Chopunnish of the Nez Perce nation, who had plenty of dogs kept as pets and guardians but never used as a food source. When the Indians learned that the strange white travelers from the east were using the animals for food, they soon ridiculed the white men as dog-eaters.

Meanwhile, both Lewis and Clark made numerous entries in their journals about the "interpreters wife"; they often cited her contributions but never gave a clue as to their feelings about her. And neither are *her* feelings revealed in the journals. In the book *The Making of Sacagawea*, author Donna J. Kessler suggested, "Sacagawea clearly remains in the background, a person whose existence is defined by her functionality within the context of their mission."

Meanwhile, the men and Sacagawea temporarily found the travel easygoing as they floated down the Columbia at the rate of thirty miles a day. On November 7, after a disagreeable and wet night, fog lifted to reveal the tidal estuary created by the Pacific Ocean. It wasn't quite yet the ocean itself, but it was enough to mean a triumphant outcome to their months-long quest. Clark's journal entry for that day, if mistakenly saying it was the Pacific itself, nonetheless revealed the elation they all felt, and rightly so: "Ocien in view! O! the joy."

The next few weeks, however, would not prove any vacation for the tired, ragged travelers, who looked more like half-starved Robinson Crusoes in rotten clothes than triumphant men representing the president of the United States. Rain, strong ocean tides, and high winds hindered their search for an appropriate wintering site.

Returning to camp one day, Clark found a group of Chinooks, among them two chiefs, visiting with Lewis. One of the chiefs wore a beautiful robe made from two sea otter skins. Both Lewis and Clark wanted the robe and offered the Chinooks various articles for a trade. But nothing would do until the chief noticed Sacagawea's belt of blue beads. In no time, the blue-beaded belt had been swapped for the robe. And what did Sacagawea get in return? Noted Clark in his journal: "We gave the squaw a coat of blue clothe for the belt of blue beads we gave for the sea otter skins purchased from an Indian." No reference there to the "squaw's" feelings about the loss of her blue beads, which normally were highly valued by Indians.

A time came, however, when Sacagawea's opinion again counted. After much scouting of the territory at the mouth of the Columbia for a wintering site, Lewis favored a spot near the oceanside beaches where salt could be made from seawater. He also argued the weather would be colder farther upstream on the Columbia. Clark didn't care about the salt, even though the rest of the men craved it. But Lewis also pointed out that by being near the coast they might be able to flag down passing ships, and that would solve their supply problems for the winter. With · both captains then agreed, they called for a final decision by vote of the entire company. That meant both Sacagawea and Clark's slave York had an equal vote with the men, a moment historically touted as the first fully democratic vote in America, since it included both a woman and a black man.

They named their winter quarters Fort Clatsop for the usually friendly Indians of the area. During the long dreary winter to come, no ships came to relieve the seasonal doldrums, but one day some Clatsop told them of a beached whale a few miles south. Clark gathered some of the men to find the whale and collect some blubber and whale oil. Enter yet again Sacagawea. This time she spoke her mind and actually had her way! As Lewis summed it up in his log: "The Indian woman was very impo[r]tunate to be permitted to go, and was therefore indulged, she observed that she had traveled a long way with us to see the great waters and that now that monstrous fish was also to be seen, she thought it very hard she could not be permitted to see either."

While there is no record of her reaction to the "big fish," she did see it.

She also made tribal history as probably the first of her people ever to see the Pacific Ocean. Thus in so many ways we can say of this remarkable young Indian woman: She went, she saw, and to a great extent she conquered.

New Year's Day 1806 dawned with a great report of guns, a brave start to the new year even though breakfast for the corps offered no better vittles than its scanty Christmas dinner a week before. The weather was wet, windy, and cold, but the men of the Corps of Discovery still could celebrate success of their own—all were alive and relatively healthy if not completely well; they had traveled across two-thirds of a continent and found a passage to the Pacific. And now all eyes turned east as they anticipated spring and the return trip to civilization.

On that return journey, Lewis and Clark were again indebted to the Shoshone Indian woman who had traveled so long and so well with them. She was incredibly valuable to them in so many ways, and her infant son proved to be a good little traveler, too. As the explorers again passed through Sacagawea's native country, she was able to show them a new pathway through the mountains, a gap she remembered from her childhood. A few days later Clark referred to her as "the indian woman who has been of great service to me as a pilot through this country."

The Indian woman, the interpreter's wife, the squaw, the Snake Indian woman, "Bird Woman" . . . by any name, Sacagawea had proven herself throughout the arduous journey by a combination of courage, wilderness-wise savvy, cleverness, and general fortitude. When they returned to the Mandans' village, Sacagawea, her nineteen-month-old son and Charbonneau remained when the Corps of Discovery moved on. Clark was reluctant to part with little "Pomp," as he called Jean Baptiste. In fact he offered to take the boy to St. Louis with him when he was old enough to leave his mother (see pages 212–16).

In the end Touissant Charbonneau was paid $500.33 and given 320 acres of land for his services. Sacagawea was given nothing material . . . but surely, until her early death in 1812, she at least enjoyed a deep personal satisfaction over her role as the only woman on such a momentous journey. Perhaps in her quiet way she knew that someday she would be seen as a true American heroine.

JESSIE BENTON FRÉMONT

"Two for the price of one," was the rallying cry for the partisans of Bill and Hillary Rodham Clinton when *he* was campaigning for the White House. Not so surprising coming from a late-twentieth-century presidential campaign . . . but how about the fervent mid-nineteenth-century campaign shout "Frémont and Jessie" so often heard from the cheering supporters of John Charles Frémont? Nominated at the June 1856 convention in Philadelphia by the fledgling Republican Party, Frémont mounted one of the most passionate campaigns in American history. The candidate had already gained hero status, along with the fond nickname "Pathfinder," for his famous explorations of the Wild West. Now Frémont, with his wife, Jessie, by his side, ran a moral campaign against slavery, alarming to southerners and to many potential converts to the Republican side, but with enormous support in New England and the Midwest.

The enthusiastic supporters sang songs such as "Oh, Jessie Is a Sweet Bright Lady" (to the tune of "Comin' through the Rye") and "wore ribbons proclaiming 'Frémont and Our Jessie' or 'Jessie's Choice,'" noted Pamela Herr and Mary Lee Spence in their book, *The Letters of Jessie Benton Frémont.*

America took its politics seriously in the mid-nineteenth century—with strong sectional differences and strictly as a man's domain. Women were in the background . . . but not the outspoken, strong-willed Jessie. Her candidate-husband not only was delighted, but in all probability needed to have this energetic, intelligent woman campaigning by his side.

To find a woman of such prominence in a political campaign was unprecedented, and yet there she was, quite an inspiration for other

American women to become involved in a national campaign. At rallies, reporters spotted more and more women in the cheering crowds. "A new feature—four hundred ladies," as one reporter put it after a rally in Buffalo, New York. Also noted by Herr and Spence: a reporter at a large Massachusetts rally found "a multitude of the sisters of Jessie who, by their presence, inaugurated a new and happy era in the history of out-door political meetings in this section."

The stand that the Frémont campaign took on the slavery issue and the enthusiasm shown over Jessie's role led woman's-suffrage leaders—such as Susan B. Anthony, Lucretia Mott, and Elizabeth Cady Stanton—to rally around the Republican banner. But it was the female half of the Frémont team that the women were most excited about. "What a shame that women can't vote!" exclaimed abolitionist Lydia Maria Child. "We'd carry 'our Jessie' into the White House on our shoulders, *wouldn't* we?"

Jessie was also an asset for her husband while working behind the scenes at such thankless chores as answering his huge daily mail, whether political or personal. When the *New York Evening Post* needed information on her husband for a biographical piece, she traveled south to do research on his background. She played down his illegitimacy—already well known, it was a stigma John carried all his life, especially during his presidential campaign. The report Jessie wrote was not the first time she had used her writing skills for her husband. In fact it was her ability to put her husband's words to paper early in their marriage that had honed those very skills, a valuable asset years later when she started her own writing career.

Jessie Benton Frémont might have grown up a typical southern belle, considering her many childhood vacations spent at Cherry Grove, her maternal grandparents' Virginia estate that was worked by slaves. James McDowell, her Scots-Irish grandfather, had emigrated to America and settled in the Blue Ridge Mountains early in the century. His daughter Elizabeth, Jessie's mother, married the well-known U.S. Sen. Thomas Hart Benton of Missouri. Another politician in the family was McDowell's son, James Jr., uncle to Jessie and governor-elect of Virginia as of 1842.

Jessie's father was born and raised in North Carolina. He left the university at Chapel Hill in disgrace over an episode of petty theft, then ardently turned to the study of law in Tennessee, where he eventually began his career in politics. Later he moved to the bustling city of St. Louis on the Mississippi River (just below the mouth of the Missouri) and established himself as both a lawyer and newspaper editor. Elected to the U.S. Senate from his newly adopted state, he distinguished himself in Washington, where he served from 1821 to 1851 and then was sent back to Congress by Missourians to serve in the House of Representatives for one term beginning in 1853. He favored western expansionism, and because of this strong interest his home was often the gathering place for people of like mind. One of them, on his frequent visits to the nation's capital, was the young U.S. Army officer John Charles Frémont.

Jessie Ann, the second of four sisters and older than two brothers, was born in 1824. Aptly named for her grandfather Jesse Benton, she was a tomboy who quickly became a favorite of her father. She was bright, energetic, and full of a curiosity that was only partially satisfied by the books in her father's library. As she would later write in her memoirs, some of her fondest early memories were of the times her father "deposited her in the Library of Congress under the watchful eye of the Librarian while he went on to the Senate."

Jessie was only eleven months old when she made her first journey by steamboat to visit her paternal grandmother, Ann Gooch Benton, then widowed and living in St. Louis. During Jessie's childhood, too, the family made many trips down the Mississippi to New Orleans and up the Missouri to the bustling river towns of her father's constituency. When Congress was not in session every other summer, the senator would take his family to St. Louis. It was on these steamboat rides that an otherwise sheltered and privileged young Jessie saw a more free-wheeling side of life that encouraged her bent for adventure. She much preferred the newer, more open West to the restrictive life at the Cherry Grove plantation in Virginia, where children had to follow a schedule. Here, when guests arrived, she and her sisters were expected to present themselves properly attired in white starched linen dresses and lace-trimmed pantaloons, with dainty slippers on their feet and ribbons tied in their hair. But on the muddy Mississippi she saw men dressed in fringed deerskins, she saw riverboat gamblers, cocky gunslingers, and heavily powdered and rouged "ladies."

Back at the Benton home on C Street in Washington, Jessie was an eager listener to visitors such as the fabled William Clark. More frequent visitors were politicians of various stripe, diplomats, scientists, and, from Missouri, a newer, more rugged type—hearty westerners. Perhaps her love of the Wild West began there in the capital city and was reinforced by visits to the boom town of St. Louis. In both environments she gained knowledge of the vast land beyond Missouri and an understanding of the need to find new routes to the far West—thus to tap its resources. While at the McDowell plantation in Virginia, on the other hand, she saw a system she could not accept and later could not condone.

Jessie was placed in a boarding school at age fourteen, along with older sister Eliza . . . and predictably, Jessie hated Miss English's Female Seminary in Georgetown, a favorite for the daughters of diplomats and senators. In Jessie's view it was an unappealing "Society School." Her ardent wish was to remain at home and close to her father. "I meant to study and be his friend and companion," she later wrote. In fact, this bold and daring young lady defied tradition by chopping back her long wavy auburn hair in hopes that her father would be too embarrassed to send her back to the school in such a condition. Obviously displeased with his favorite daughter, he nevertheless relented and she did not return to school.

She may have disliked the society school, but it was here, at an afternoon concert, wrote Jessie's biographer Pamela Herr, that she met John Charles Frémont. He had been invited by her sister Eliza, who no doubt had met the young member of the newly formed Corps of Topographical Engineers on one of his frequent visits to the Benton home.

To Jessie, still a semisheltered but restless teenager, here was a romantic figure straight off the pages of a swashbuckling novel. The young surveyor had just returned to Washington in late 1839 from two seasons in the wilds of the West exploring routes to California; he now was preparing maps of the area. His talk of life on the prairie, the nights spent around the campfire with French-speaking explorers, his descriptions of buffalo herds so thick they looked like a moving dark sea, all must have set the young Jessie's heart racing.

He obviously felt the spark, too. When they first met, he later recalled, "She was then in the bloom of her girlish beauty and perfect health." Herr's 1987 biography of Jessie includes even more flowery terms: "She made the effect that a rose of rare color or a beautiful picture would have done." But beyond her outward beauty and "a soul so white," he recognized her quick mind and appreciated her tenderness and warmth. This meeting of the twenty-seven-year-old hero of the

West with the intelligent and beautiful sixteen-year-old daughter of a U.S. senator left Frémont with a glow that "changed the current and color of daily life and gave beauty to common things."

For Frémont, the attraction had to be enhanced by the stability and prestige felt by anyone sharing the warmth of family life at the gracious Benton home near Capitol Hill, replete with sweeping lawn and walled gardens. Jessie herself later cited fond memories of winter evenings by the "dark mahogany furniture gleaming in the fire-light" or the "glitter of the tea-equipage, the fragrance of the large plants of rose-geraniums, and the delicate bitter of chrysanthemums." For Frémont, this beautiful, cultured, and intelligent maiden offered a way of life he had never known. For the starstruck young senator's daughter, the dashing explorer offered promise of glorious adventure.

Senator Benton, though, thought otherwise, and understandably so. After all, the lieutenant in the Topography Corps, for all his celebrated status as a western explorer, was of a dubious background that was *not* enhanced by the cloud of an illegitimate birth. Further, the young man had no money to speak of.

With the help of officials in the War Department, the influential senator hurriedly hatched a devious plan to separate Frémont from Jessie, whom the senator quite appropriately liked to call "Imagination." Quite suddenly orders appeared whisking Frémont away to Iowa to survey the Des Moines River, and Jessie was hustled off to a cousin's wedding in Virginia.

All for naught! Both were back in the capital by August . . . but apparently willing to promise they would wait a year or more before talk of marriage.

All for naught again! While the family was busy planning Jessie's launch in society, the young lovers were meeting secretly. Jessie, wearing her first Paris gown, was presented at a grand White House ball given by the new president, John Tyler, in honor of the princely son of French king Louis Philippe. With the impetus of such an evening, the powerful and determined Senator Benton hoped, surely his beautiful, bright, and willful daughter would turn her thoughts to a more suitable young man.

All for naught indeed! Just a few days after the ball, Jessie and John were secretly married in Washington—by a Roman Catholic priest, since none of the Protestant ministers they contacted was willing to risk the well-known wrath of the senator from Missouri.

So began a lifelong love story between the dashing young man and his beautiful child-bride, not just one but both of them very much from the pages of that swashbuckling novel. The fact is, they now were off on a real-life adventure that would capture the imagination of the bustling Wild West, the nation, and the world for half a century.

Jessie certainly found romance and adventure (and some hard times, too) with her new "Pathfinder" husband, described by biographer Hess as tall with olive skin and gray-blue eyes showing the "natural dash of his French father." But there's no getting away from the additional fact that marriage to Jessie Benton gave her new husband access to political power and all the connections of the Benton family.

At first the powerful Senator Benton refused to accept the marriage. But as the loving father to a favorite daughter, he soon relented. As chairman of the Senate Committee on Military Affairs, which controlled funds for the Topographical Corps, he saw to it that his new son-in-law would be named its head. That boost, if nothing else, enabled the still-young Frémont to continue and greatly expand a spectacular career as a major explorer of the American West, followed by roles as conqueror of California, as one of that state's first senators, as the first Republican presidential candidate, as a significant mine and railroad developer, as a Union general during the Civil War, and finally, as governor of Arizona Territory.

Clearly the senator helped, and clearly Frémont himself deserves great credit for his many accomplishments. But it's clear also that Jessie deserves credit for *her* major role in the Frémont story . . . which really was a *Jessie* and John story.

Given the nature of her husband's line of work, Jessie hardly had time to adapt to her role as a married woman before he was off to the wilds again—this time to explore the far reaches of the fast-developing Oregon Trail and the Wind River Mountain Range in Wyoming. From the very moment of their marriage in 1842, Jessie was by his side in all endeavors . . . except the daring expeditions themselves. Still, there were ways to share in his work, and her first such contribution was to finish the report on his Des Moines River survey of 1841.

With that task done, and John gone on his latest travels west, Jessie was restless. At her father's suggestion she returned to his library to continue the self-education she had taken upon herself as a child. Already pregnant, she was happy to fill the lonely hours with useful work of her own . . . perhaps guessing even now that this probably would be but the first of many separations to come, given the nature of her husband's work.

But Jessie was not one to sit around by herself for very long. If she could not directly share in her husband's explorations, she would share in some of the adventure or, as she might have sometimes said, the *hardship,* to be found in traveling out west in her own way . . . but of course always to join or be close to him. Thus she frequently made the long, long trip to the West Coast, across an entire continent from Washington, including repeated travel through Panama that proved especially treacherous for her.

Few of the couple's letters to each another survived their daughter Lily's decision after Jessie's death to burn such highly personal messages, but Jessie's other letters gathered by Pamela Herr and Mary Lee Spence allow wonderful insights into the personality and thoughts of this remarkable woman as she poured out her heart to friends and acquaintances. The same epistles provide a marvelous descriptive account of life in the far West, from its El Dorado days of gold fever to real settlement to the turn-of-the-century sophisticated city of the Golden Gate.

In letters to her dear friend Elizabeth Blair Lee in Washington, Jessie revealed both the occasional good news and many of the ordeals of the Frémont family. Her second child, a boy named Benton in honor of her father, was born on July 24, 1848. He died just ten weeks later. The Frémonts at that moment were on the last leg of a journey up the Missouri River to a point where John would be leaving the family behind for another frontier expedition.

As if this were not enough to bear, the grieving parents already were smarting from Frémont's 1848 court-martial conviction, stemming from his zealous role in California's successful bid for independence from Mexico. President James K. Polk had suspended the sentence, but it all seemed so unfair. After all, Frémont—apparently under secret orders to take military action in the event of war with Mexico—first had joined hands with the California settlers staging the Bear Flag Revolt at Sonoma, then had joined with U.S. Navy Com. Robert F. Stockton in fighting the Mexicans and capturing Los Angeles, then, in January 1847, joined U.S. Army Gen. Stephen W. Kearny in recapturing Los Angeles.

Caught between two superior officers at odds, Frémont was appointed governor of the newly won territory by Stockton, but then he was arrested by Kearny on charges of mutiny, disobedience, and conduct prejudicial to military order. After being found guilty of the latter two charges, he resigned from the army despite Polk's intercession.

Meanwhile, in the few short years between their marriage of 1842 and the Bear Flag Revolt of 1846, John Frémont had become a household name across America. His report on the Oregon Trail–Wind River Range Expedition of 1842, written with Jessie's help, received wide circulation. The next year he set out across Wyoming and Idaho, made his way into Oregon, followed the Columbia River to Vancouver, then turned into Nevada, crossed the Sierra Nevada into California's Sacramento Valley, continued south to Los Angeles, turned east again to cross parts of Arizona and finally reached Utah. His report on this truly spectacular trip of 1843–44, again written with Jessie's helpful input, made Frémont a national figure and hero.

Now, as Jessie once again said her good-byes to her husband in the late summer of 1848, she must have noticed that he no longer was the young Pathfinder but a graying thirty-five-year-old private citizen heading an underfunded, unsponsored expedition. And she, too, was no longer the optimistic young woman who had once looked eagerly to the future. Her heart was heavy for her husband; she was in despair over this ill-timed separation and still pining for the lost infant. On a brighter note, however, she was to meet him in California in the spring.

And what a spring, what a year, it would be for California! "Gold" was the magic word. Not only the West but the East too was awash in tales of the gold. After all, it was just over a year since John Sutter's sawmill builder-partner James W. Marshall had discovered little nuggets of gold in the tailrace of their mill on the south fork of the American River. Young, old, and in-between, men of all types were arming themselves with picks, shovels, and pans and heading west, every one of them confident that a pot of gold was waiting at the end of the rainbow.

Boarding ship in New York for passage to San Francisco by way of the Panamanian isthmus, Jessie was not filled with those expectations. As much as she longed to see her husband—and to see the shining coast of California for the first time—she had been warned of the dreadful hardships imposed by the ship-to-shore-to-ship crossing at Panama. Even with the reassurance of a male protector accompanying her, her daughter Lily, and a maid, Jessie felt a sense of dread. The protector was her sister Sara's husband, Richard Jacob, who, needing a sea voyage to restore his health, volunteered to travel with the distaff trio.

It was a cold gray day as the *Crescent City* chugged out of the harbor that March morning, a dismal omen for the long journey ahead. As Jessie's father bid her farewell, according to Herr's biography, she heard someone whisper to him, "It is like leaving her in her grave."

Crowded aboard the ship were about 350 passengers, all men, except for Jessie, six-year-old Lily, their maid, and an Irish woman traveling with her husband. Perhaps this was one reason why Jessie at first kept to her stateroom . . . perhaps it was because nothing seemed to be going right. Little Lily constantly was in tears and clinging to her mama's skirts, the hastily hired maid turned out to be a thief and had to be locked in her cabin, and brother-in-law Richard was so seasick he was totally helpless and bedridden. Not seasick herself, Jessie was delighted finally to accept the captain's suggestion that she come up on deck, and for the rest of the journey she stayed there. She loved the fresh air and later wrote, "I had never seen the sea, and in some odd way no one had ever told me of the wonderful new life it could bring."

In Panama, however, the unavoidable overland trip across the steamy jungle from one ocean to the other delayed the Frémont party longer than any of them imagined. Richard was so ill he had to return home, but Jessie was determined to press on without her would-be protector. Once in Panama City on the far side of the isthmus, after a twenty-mile trek, Jessie fortunately could stay at the home of Señora Arce Zimena, whose nephew Jessie had known when he was Panamanian ambassador in Washington. What a blessing this was, for Jessie now was stricken with so-called brain fever, actually a respiratory malady causing her to cough up blood. After recovering, she thought more and more of returning home herself, especially after receiving word that her husband also had suffered a severe illness while on his latest expedition and was being nursed back to health by his friend and fellow explorer Kit Carson. But the determined Jessie decided to press on. And on June 4, 1849, she at last sailed through the narrow strait that her own husband had named the Golden Gate.

Standing by the rail of her ship, Jessie anxiously scanned the many boats coming to meet the steamer. But disappointment hung as heavy as the damp sea air upon her shoulders when she realized that her husband was not aboard any of them. A local merchant, William Howard, did arrive, per John's instructions, and took her to what was probably the best hotel in town—the Leidesdorff, a handsome structure garnished with verandas and gardens. A surprised Jessie found her spacious hostelry equipped with a luxurious carpet, elegant furniture, and even a piano . . . but no wood for a fire. Still-developing California, it seemed, was a land of startling contrasts—luxuries here, biographer Herr noted, but basic needs found wanting there.

As Jessie waited for her husband, she stayed busy receiving guests anxious to meet the wife of the famous California citizen. Her visitors couldn't wait to fill her in on the local gossip, just about all of it relating to the gold. . . . the gold, gold, and more gold. As Jessie could see for herself, signs of the incredible new wealth were all around as the buoyant forty-niners came to town fresh from the mining camps and intent on spending sprees. But gold was not the only means to wealth. Land speculation and the sale of supplies and luxuries shipped in from ports around the world also were creating a new moneyed class.

When John finally arrived ten days later, they had so much to tell each other. John reported "their" sawmill was turning out greatly needed lumber and soon would be profitable.

As his really electrifying news, however, she learned that Las Mariposas, a seventy-square-mile ranch in the Sierra foothills near Yosemite Valley that John had bought before the gold rush, was itself a font of gold, real gold. In the days ahead, reported Augusta Fink in her book *Monterey County,* workers at Rancho Mariposa "regularly" were sending the Frémonts one-hundred-pound buckskin bags containing twenty-five thousand dollars' worth of gold each.

Suddenly, though, Jessie fell ill and started coughing up blood. Her Panama fever had returned! It was decided that a move south, away from the fog and winds blowing in from the bay, would hasten her full return to health.

Taking a steamer once again, the travel-weary Jessie, along with Lily and John, arrived at the quaint coastal town of Monterey. Here, in a sleepy village still with a touch of old Spain about it, not far south of San Francisco, Jessie found the medicine she needed—rest, warmth, and sunshine. As an ironic touch, the Frémonts were able to rent a wing of the adobe villa of Señora Jose Castro, wife of the general who had opposed Frémont and the Bear Flag revolutionaries in northern California just three years earlier. Aside from an American military garrison, however, Jessie found a village populated only by women, children, and old men; all the young men had gone in search of gold.

The boatloads of men arriving every day along the coast of California, loading their pack mules with whatever food they could get their hands on then disappearing into the hills, left little for those back at the ranch. But Jessie found a special and helpful friend—the American military governor, headquartered at Monterey, was tending a vegetable garden and would bring her offerings from his patch from time to time. And Señora Castro, the proud owner of the only cow in town, gave the concerned mother a cup of milk a day for Lily. Despite the challenge of finding enough food and the difficulty of keeping house and cooking without help, Jessie relished life in Monterey.

The temporary Frémont abode offered nicely appointed rooms decorated with Jessie's special flair. With the bags of gold steadily arriving from the strike on their ranch, she felt justified in ordering fine silks for drapes and a matching cushion cover for an elegant bamboo sofa, along with chairs and carved tables, all imported from China and shipped to Monterey by steamer. Her cozy home offered a restful view of the bay at the front and a hillside of pines at the rear—this, plus the delightful weather, all contributed to Jessie's recuperation.

When political organizers came to the little capital town, the Frémonts graciously offered their home as a convenient meeting place—with no hotels or decent restaurants in the town, it was the best place for the political organizers to meet. Beyond the convenience, though, these were men intent upon achieving statehood for California, and any talk of possible U.S. Senate contenders always seemed to include Frémont at the top of the list.

Ironically, Frémont's chief rival had traveled to California on the same ship as Jessie just weeks before. As recalled in Augusta Fink's Monterey history, William Gwin of Tennessee had come to California for the express purpose of becoming one of the prospective state's first senators. By the time the first California constitutional convention was convened in Monterey, Gwin was a delegate from San Francisco. John and Jessie moved back to San Francisco to begin his campaign for the Senate.

Frémont had solved their housing need in the frantically growing boom town on the bay. Since money suddenly was no object for the Frémonts, thanks to the gold flowing so freely from their ranch, he ordered a prefabricated house from China. Quickly and easily assembled by fitting together the smooth wooden parts, it turned under Jessie's adroit hands into yet another cozy home for the family. Situated in Happy Valley, then a rapidly growing area where the housing mostly consisted of tents, the Chinese prefab one day would give way to the famous Palace Hotel on the same site.

At Happy Valley, Jessie was in her element, no longer just waiting for her husband to return from his latest expedition or waiting for events to find their way to her, now she herself was a part of the bursting *newness* all around. *She* could make things happen. No longer constrained by eastern conventions, she delighted in the openness of the bustling city's informal life, in the excitement of gold-rush California.

As Frémont's campaign for the Senate gained momentum, Jessie found herself immersed in the man's world of politics, and she thrived on it. Moreover, the men gathering at their home headquarters were quite impressed with her political savvy. One such man, wrote biographer Herr, found Jessie "the better man of the two" and characterized her as "far more intelligent and more comprehensive."

In a year's time, both Gwin and Frémont achieved their goal of becoming the first senators from California. Just before Christmas 1849, with the distant U.S. Congress expected to admit California as a state any moment, Frémont had returned to their Monterey abode, where Jessie anxiously awaited news of the election . . . the election of the would-be state's first two senators.

And he brought her great tidings—she was elated to hear that the legislature had elected him senator on the first ballot.

Once again it was time to travel! On New Year's night they boarded a steamer and were on their way east. Once again Jessie crossed the Panama isthmus, but this time she would not be a frightened and lonely young woman with a little girl in tow as she traveled into the unknown. She was returning as the wife of a gold-rich senator from the new state of California! More than rich and somewhat famous, more even than a woman of substance, Jessie now was a woman whose inner strength had bestowed a true sense of her own worth. Her California experiences—the challenges she had met and conquered—gave her new courage and independence. Now she was ready to meet the East head-on.

But first the Frémont family had to endure a Panama crossing that proved even more dreadful than Jessie's first trip through the infamous isthmus—Jessie again fell ill, this time with malaria. No matter how brave and persevering, she had to be drugged with opiates and carried to the home of Señora Arce. The kind and hospitable Señora once again set up her home to accommodate not merely one but three very sick Frémonts. It would be a full month before they were well enough to bid the gracious and good señora good-bye.

The rift between the North and South was widening by each passing day when the Frémonts finally arrived in the nation's capital in early 1850. In Congress feelings were running so high, Jessie's father, Thomas Benton, had been threatened on the floor of the Senate for his strong antislavery stand by a pistol-brandishing Mississippi Sen. Henry Foote. As the infuriated Benton dared his colleague to shoot, their fellow senators managed to intervene and calm the two.

Political quarrels aside, Jessie was delighted to find the social scene in high gear. Hosts were careful, however, to make sure that bitter opponents on the slavery issue were not on the same guest list. Restored to her usual vitality and health (and only in her thirties), the still beautiful wife of the senator from California was enjoying the attention lavished on her famous husband and herself. They were the center of the social circuit that season, which Jessie would later label as the "high tide" of their life.

While the Frémonts' social life was in full swing, their respective families were pitted against each other politically. Jessie's father was adamantly against the extension of slavery into new states, while her uncle, James McDowell Jr., recently elected as a Virginia congressman, took the opposite southern view.

But nothing could dampen Jessie's happiness at being home again, seeing old friends and meeting new. How could she ever forget teas at the British Embassy, dinners with the Prussian ambassador, gatherings at the salon of Massachusetts Sen. Robert Winthrop, where she met the famous orator Daniel Webster and the poet Henry Wadsworth Longfellow? Or the long lunches with childhood friend Harriet Williams, who had married the much older Russian ambassador Count Alexander Bodisco? All too soon, however, this "high tide" ebbed. Taking his Senate seat the day after California officially became a state on September 9, 1850, Frémont, holder of the state's short senate term, announced that the family would have to rush back to California so he could campaign for the next full term.

Another dreadful crossing of the Panama isthmus once again brought on Jessie's own brand of fever, but she coped, and soon—on November 21, 1850, a full month since boarding ship in New York—the Frémonts were back in San Francisco. Gone for less than a year, even these boom-town veterans were stunned to find the old bawdy town of tents, saloons, prostitution houses, and "residential" hovels had become strikingly "larger, richer, and more garish," according to

Herr. Nonetheless, Jessie decided Stockton Street was the desirable and fashionable place to live, even though it was near the main plaza and its bars and brothels. For Jessie, pregnant again, a new home and hearth spelled a return to domesticity.

But not for her politically minded husband. With the nation's political storms buffeting even distant California, Frémont was finding it more difficult now to line up like-thinking men behind his candidacy. His votes in Washington reflecting his antislavery convictions didn't sit well with the proslavery members of his own Democratic Party. In the meantime, father-in-law Benton, also suffering the vicissitudes of politics, threw himself wholeheartedly into battle for another term in the Senate, but this time lost. (Refusing to give up, he later won a seat in the U.S. House.)

All such worldly pursuits notwithstanding, Jessie was blessed on April 19, 1851, with the arrival of a healthy, vigorous baby boy. Named for his father, John Charles Jr. made theirs a complete little family of mother, father, daughter, and son, thought Jessie with a healthy dollop of pardonable pride. She also was very pleased with herself as little Charley's sole nurse. Hoping to ease her husband's hurt feelings over failure to gain his party's nomination for the next Senate race, Jessie was quite ready to settle down to a quiet family life.

It was not to be. At least not for now. Always seeking ways to improve their finances, especially since he had incurred enormous legal expenses connected with their Las Mariposas ranch, John announced the need for more travel—but this time to Europe. Of course, that meant once again taking the steamer from San Francisco, once again braving the crossing of the isthmus, once again sailing up the East Coast to New York . . . but this time continuing on to Europe. John's restlessness no doubt precipitated the journey, but in truth he needed to meet with his investors in London and to squelch rumors of financial problems at Las Mariposas.

Just before the decision was made to go to Europe, Jessie had witnessed fires raging through the tinderbox wooden houses that comprised the majority of San Francisco's structures. John had been away at the ranch during the fires, which were thought to have been purposely set. As the supposed arsonist struck one more time, Jessie had to flee with her children to the hills and watched their own home go up in flames. Fate was kind, though, and neighbors managed to salvage almost all the family's possessions.

Grateful for this and undaunted, Jessie was determined to settle into another house in the bustling city. Instead, she now faced again the Panama crossing, likely to be more difficult with a ten-month-old baby in tow.

To Jessie's happy surprise, they fared much better at this crossing. She and baby Charles both came through in fine fettle, even if she did have to pay an old sailor a few gold pieces to run the rats and roaches out of their cabin on the steamer to Panama.

The Frémonts would be far more luxuriantly quartered aboard the side-wheeler *Africa* for the crossing of the Atlantic to England, noted biographer Hess. Already excited over her first ocean crossing, Jessie was thrilled to find a hero's welcome awaiting the famous Frémonts in Liverpool. Still walking on air, they were ensconced in the posh accommodations provided by the Clarendon in London. All this, of course, was part and parcel of the lifestyle associated with the very rich, but the fact was, their ranch was in heavy debt and other loans John had accumulated while in the topography corps were still outstanding.

Jessie's social calendar was filled with teas here, salons there, plus invitations for weekends at elegant country estates. To top it off, she was presented to Queen Victoria.

But then the Frémonts' London bubble burst. To their utter embarrassment, John was arrested and jailed on the complaint of a creditor.

Jessie immediately called on one of John's investors, who, unbeknownst to her, had quarreled with her husband over the management of their mutual financial interests. Going to the investor's door, she insisted on seeing him despite the lateness of the hour and the fact that he had retired. She demanded bail for her husband, but the man refused. The next day a wealthy American living in London came to the rescue.

The Frémonts quickly were on the move again. Understandably anxious to escape the London disgrace, they crossed the Channel and took the train to Paris. Here they rented a house on the Champs-Elysées. Once more in elegant surroundings, Jessie again was swept up into a social whirl. Befriended by the Comte de la Garde, the Frémonts were invited to receptions given by Louis Napoleon.

On February 1, 1853, the supposedly "complete little family" underwent revision as a baby girl was born to the American couple in Paris. She was given the name Anne Beverley for John's mother. Then, too, came exciting news about their beloved American West. Congress had authorized western surveys for a transcontinental railroad. Informed that he would not be asked to lead a survey, John decided it was time to go home anyway.

By June of that year, the Frémonts were back in Washington with the new baby to show off to relatives—along with two French maids acquired in Paris. But tragedy struck again, just weeks after they had settled into Washington life. Jessie had taken the fever-ridden baby Anne out to the Maryland home of her friends, the Blairs, in hopes that the fresh air would help the ailing child. But in the end she and her friend Lizzie watched helplessly as the five-month-old drew her last breath.

During this period, Frémont was raising money for a private expedition, since he failed to win appointment to one of the government surveys. With the help of his father-in-law, however, he was able to organize a private exploration of the western wilderness once again. As he disappeared over the horizon the following year, Jessie remained in Washington, only to experience one family loss after another. First her mother died, and a few months later she had to stand with her grieving father and again watch helplessly as their Washington home, her childhood home, filled with all the family treasures and memories, went up in flames.

One happy event did brighten the horizon for the family: Another baby boy was born to Jessie on May 17, 1855. He was named Francis Preston Blair, for their good friend and political ally. Even though joyful over the fine healthy baby, Jessie herself became ill with neuralgia, which was so painful that she had to take opiates for relief. When she finally felt well enough, she and the children spent that summer on Nantucket Island.

It was to this happy beach abode that Frémont came with the startling news that both the Democrats and Republicans were making overtures to him as a possible presidential candidate. But . . . which way to go? It was a question broadly pondered across the nation. The old Whig Party was divided, the Democrats had to keep the southern wing—favoring slavery and its extension into Kansas and Nebraska—in the party, and the brand-new Republican Party was an unknown. One thing was sure—to join the Republicans would mean a break with the family, both with the southern branch and with Jessie's father.

In 1856 Frémont became the Republican Party's first presidential candidate. The North was excited about his antislavery stance, and at rallies in the West he attracted huge crowds. Jessie's appearances of course drew women in unprecedented numbers. They saw her as a courageous woman who could hold her own in the political sphere, and as a mother and homemaker with exciting pioneering frontier experience behind her as well. She hadn't exactly walked west or ridden a covered wagon, but she had been there, she had undergone her own hardships, and she radiated the very spirit of the frontier.

Popular as Frémont was, and with Jessie an added asset, the bachelor Democrat Buchanan won the election, albeit by a narrow margin. With that, the Frémonts bid politics and the East good-bye for a time. First, though, Jessie paid a farewell visit on her ailing father. A few days later they sailed out of New York, again en route to Panama. Thankfully, the crossing of the isthmus no longer called for a grueling trek through jungles, but instead offered a ride by train. The track Jessie had seen being laid during her earlier trips now serviced a comfortable train that carried passengers swiftly between the Atlantic and Pacific shores.

While the Frémonts were still at sea, two days out of San Francisco, Jessie's father, the longtime Washington personality and once-powerful senator, died at his home in Washington. It was April 10, 1858.

As the family passed through the Golden Gate, the travel-weary Frémonts were glad to be on dry land once more, but wasted not a minute before setting out again by boat up the San Joaquin River, changing to a rickety stagecoach for the two-day trip, and finally arriving at Las Mariposas, their ranch in Bear Valley. The family entourage consisted of John, Jessie, their teenaged daughter Lily, young Charley, baby Frank, plus Nina, a teenaged daughter of John's deceased brother Horatio Francis Frémont, plus Douglas Fox, or "Foxy," a teenaged boy from England, plus the two French maids.

The travelers were not so exhausted that they failed to take in the magnificent scenery on the last leg of the journey. Frémont, crossing the Sierra Nevada into California in the winter of 1844, had noted "the purity and deep-blue color of the sky," an observation that still held true nearly two decades later. But Jessie on this trip along Bear Valley now added her impressions as they rode through the wildflowers bobbing and waving among swales of natural grasses. As their party passed beneath the shading pine and oak, she noted that everything presented "a beauty and fragrance that I have never met before."

Even while settling in at the ranch with lively children to keep her occupied, Jessie was smitten with remorse for having left her ailing father, although he really had urged her to go on with her family to

California. When her guilt and grieving sapped her strength to the point of making her ill, John delayed a business trip to San Francisco to stay by her side and comfort her. Despite all, after barely a week's stay in the beautiful valley, Jessie wrote to Lizzie to say things were going well and that Lily, with a horse of her own, was teaching the boys to ride bareback. And she reported that her neighbors were friendly.

For all the cheerful tone in her letter, things were not nearly as wonderful as they could have been. John's financial troubles still dogged the couple. A dispute over mining claims had aroused the resentment of local miners. On a different level, the mistress and children of the ranch had to be on constant guard outdoors against lurking bears and rattlesnakes, even in their own vegetable patch. But it was the disputing miners and their claims on Mariposas land that proved the greatest nemesis of all.

When John bought the sprawling property in 1847 for a mere three thousand dollars, he received what was known as a "floating" grant. "In 1855, when the [California] Supreme Court in a split decision finally confirmed John's title to Las Mariposas," Herr explained in her biography of Jessie, "he drew its boundaries shrewdly—unscrupulously, some said—stretching them far up into the foothills to include rich mines claimed and worked by others." To the neighbors Jessie once considered friendly, all of them either settlers or miners, Frémont's boundary claims looked like outright theft. Some angry miners formed a league called the Hornitos and planned to act on a recent California Supreme Court ruling that any mine left unattended, even temporarily, was free for the taking. Such a decision of course would be a temptation for the unscrupulous to drive off rightful mine owners then claim the "abandoned" property for themselves. . . . exactly as did happen.

In his book *More Than Petticoats*, Erin H. Turner reported that the Hornitos were not above resorting to violence to achieve their own ends. Sometimes the legitimate mine owners were bribed to abandon their mines, thus leaving them for the Hornitos to claim as their own. Or, if that tactic failed, the rightful owners were driven off.

One evening when John was away protecting his mines, a Hornito on horseback delivered an ultimatum to Jessie that she had twenty-four hours to leave her home or see it torched and hear that John was killed. Jessie, well aware of the desperate situation, had thought through what she would do if the Hornitos should come calling. She knew she had to send word to the governor in Sacramento for help. Someone had to ride across the valley with the message. But who? Lily immediately vol-unteered, but Jessie wouldn't hear of that. Far too dangerous for a young girl. Instead she turned to young Foxy, the visiting English teenager, as the obvious choice for the long ride. But first Jessie devised a way to muffle the sound of his horse as he galloped past the Horni-tos. Gathering some rags, she saw that the horse's hoofs were tightly wrapped, and Foxy was off.

Jessie wrote to her friends the Blairs that she was overcome with fear for John. What she didn't say was that she lived in fear for all in the family. As Herr noted, Jessie also wrote: "Whenever Mr. Frémont was in sight I was very brave."

Actually, she proved to be quite the brave soldier without her hus-band by her side. Rather than sit and wait for a response to the message carried by Foxy, Jessie marched into Bates Tavern in Bear Valley, the headquarters of the Hornitos, and told the outlaws that what they were doing was against the law. "You may come and kill us—we are but women and children, and it will be easy—but you cannot kill the law," she declared.

Frightening as the miners' siege was, it finally was resolved in favor of the Frémonts, and Jessie added another notch of courage and self-confidence to her belt. And if she had always longed to have John by her side, she now was rewarded to find he was more content, less restless for the wilderness, and less seeking of adventure to prove his mettle.

As their finances somewhat improved, John found them a house by the sea in San Francisco, on the tip of Black Point, where Fort Mason now stands before a panoramic view of the bay. A thrilled Jessie wrote to Lizzie that they had found their marvelous refuge where she and John could now write his memoirs. "The flapping of the sails as the schooners round this point and the noise of their paddles as the steamers pass are household sounds," Jessie wrote.

The house was one of five clustered on the point, providing Jessie a virtual colony of new friends. Here, too, Jessie played hostess to the luminaries of the day. At her parties, often held in the garden, one would find Bret Harte, Herman Melville, the popular new Unitarian clergy-man Starr King, handsome Sen. Edward Baker of Oregon (in town to campaign for his friend and former law partner, Abraham Lincoln), or Carleton Watkins (later to become a famous landscape photographer). Once again, these were heady days for Jessie, who reveled in her role as mentor to the talented and famous.

Far to the east, though, the dark clouds of civil war were gathering, as the North and South failed to resolve their differences. John had gone to Europe on business, and once the war erupted in April 1861, he returned to accept a commission as a major general in the Union army. In July 1861 the Frémonts arrived in St. Louis, where John's command was headquartered

After the war (and Frémont's lackluster performance as a Union general), the Frémonts purchased a huge stone mansion on the Hudson near Tarrytown, New York. Here they planned to settle into quiet country living. They named the estate Pocaho, and Jessie again began to lay in her elegant appointments. John was often away on business, once more trying to bolster their fading fortune. Jessie, realizing the extent of their money problems, now became directly involved in his business affairs. She wrote letters and attended meetings with lawyers and bankers in shared attempts to settle their financial dilemma. With success still eluding their best efforts, Jessie responded to their dire need for income by contacting *New York Ledger* editor Robert Bonner to propose writing articles about the famous and near famous she had known. He was quite amenable to the idea. Thus began her twenty-year writing career.

Jessie first wrote a series of personality pieces under the title Distinguished Persons I Have Known, for which she was paid four hundred dollars each. With her husband's old traveling companion Kit Carson included among the western folk heroes she depicted, the stories were very popular, but Jessie tended to play down her writing talent as simply a pastime or hobby. If truth be known, however, she was thrilled—if quietly so—to gain recognition on her own. And like other women writers of her times, she was exhilarated by the power of earning money.

Moreover, no matter how modest her pose, the money she brought in was a great boon to the family coffers, which continued to deteriorate. In addition to her articles for the *Ledger,* Jessie wrote for *Harper's* and *Wide Awake,* a popular children's magazine. In May 1874, however, she was humiliated to realize the family could not pay the monthly mortgage on their home. Not long after, a tax collector was at the door to begin evaluating their possessions. They were forced to sell almost everything—some land in California, boats, horses, books—and in the end, Jessie had to part with her cherished painting of the Golden Gate by Albert Bierstadt.

As the Frémonts now moved around New York to various rented abodes, Jessie found her writing a solace, even at a cramped desk in a cheerless room. In these surroundings, however, she would turn out some of her best work. Even so, by 1878 the Frémonts were financially desperate. And now it was Jessie making the political rounds, in search of some kind of a federal appointment for John. Willing to help, it turned out, was Rutherford B. Hayes, who had supported Frémont's bid for the presidency back in 1856 and now was himself newly settled in the White House. He offered the nation's vaunted Pathfinder the governorship of Arizona Territory at the grand salary of twenty-six hundred dollars a year.

And so, Jessie dearly hoped, yet another beginning—and vindication of sorts for the onetime hero of the West. And so too, once again the Frémont entourage—now consisting of Jessie, John, Lily, Frank, their Irish maid Mary, and their beloved staghound Thor—crossed the continent for points west. But . . . what a change it would be from the months-long journeys by steamer, across Panama, and by steamer to California. This time they arrived in San Francisco on September 12, 1878, after traveling only a week by train, a conveyance that at the same time allowed them wondrous vistas of the country's majestic and still largely unspoiled countryside of green forests, golden plains, purple mountains, and sparkling streams.

As a once-familiar thrill also, their arrival in the West brought out throngs of well-wishers who still remembered the great explorer and conqueror of California. In the city of the Golden Gate, wrote Herr, "a committee of the Society of California Pioneers escorted them to the swank Palace Hotel, where they were given a lavish corner suite as guests of its flamboyant millionaire owner, William Sharon." By the time the well-feted couple arrived in Prescott, Arizona, to address the demands of John's governorship, they were exhausted. Four days later they attended a gala supper and dinner in their honor, which was written up in the local *Arizona Miner* as "the most brilliant social event that ever transpired within the boundary of Arizona."

But here the glamour once again faded quickly. Jessie found the heat oppressive and her duties as governor's wife equally pressing, although she was invigorated to some degree by the weekly history class she taught at the public school—"to an audience of awed adolescents dressed in their Sunday best to hear the celebrated Mrs. Frémont," wrote Herr.

A year later, Jessie was back in New York to promote John's latest mining schemes. And after a few more years, the Frémonts left Arizona for good, no richer than when they arrived. Returning to New York, the curtain on their shared life beginning to ring down, they still were financially strapped. All that glittering wealth that once seemed theirs forever somehow had vanished. Facing this fact, Jessie was more determined than ever to write and to write well. She began a series of historical sketches that she simply called "fireside" history, because, she said, writing conventional history would be too much for her. When *Souvenirs of My Times,* a collection of the series, was published in book form, it was well received. And though she was encouraged by the critics to write her own memoirs, she continued to produce what she called her "harmless puddings." Still, she did bring in the money.

Jessie and John finally settled down to write *his* memoirs. Lily, too, became involved in the process, having learned to type and thus created a clean, readable version of the longhand drafts. *Memoirs of My Life,* a 650-page book on the life of Frémont, up to and including the conquest of California, published in 1887, was the result. Just two years before, the dying Ulysses S. Grant's memoirs had earned his heirs half a million dollars—that gave the Frémonts hope that their memoir would prove a boon for them as well. Alas, yet again, it was not to be.

In 1890, thankfullym the financially needy Frémont was restored to the rank of major general on the army's retirement list and thus allowed to draw a helpful pension. Still, the family's circumstances offered no panacea.

The next step down for the once-glamorous couple and their daughter was a move to a rented cottage in New Jersey. Here, John's health deteriorated, and the two women became ill as well. Seeking a way out of their dilemma, Jessie swallowed her pride once more and went to see the president of the Central and Southern Pacific Railroads, whom she had charmed when she was in the bloom of youth and they had been co-passengers on the way to Panama on the old *Crescent City.* He made arrangements for the Frémont family to travel on his railroad to California.

This time the tired little family meant to make California their home "to the end of his days," as John said when making a speech at the annual flower festival upon their arrival in Los Angeles. But John still continued on his quest for wealth, traveling to New York from time to time while Jessie was making a life for herself in golden California.

On a final last trip to New York in 1890, though, John became ill and died with their son Charley by his side. "Father is dead," read the telegram that the son sent his mother.

He had been a legend as well as a husband and father, and now his widow was left to grieve, not only the loss of the man who had been the center of her life, but the humiliations brought on by unsettled debts—as well as controversy over his proposed burial in California. When the California legislature refused funds to have the body shipped to California for burial, Jessie had to accept that he would be buried in New York, but she could be glad at least that it was across the river from Pocaho, the grand estate on the Hudson where they once had found happiness together.

For months Jessie continued to grieve. She became so thin she could hardly walk alone. Lily, never married, was a great solace as Jessie gradually regained strength. Part of the healing process was California itself. "I took naturally to tomatoes, olives and the sea," she once remarked. And gradually, as in years past, Jessie flowered in the bright sunny state where she always had found warmth and welcome, the place she had lived in and loved for the greater part of her life. By 1895, when she was seventy, she was content with her life in Los Angeles. Part of her security she owed to her close friend and benefactor Caroline Severance, a leader in the women's rights movement who had raised funds to buy Jessie and Lily a house of their own. Jessie very much enjoyed the Friday Morning Club, a progressive women's group founded in 1891 by her friend Caroline. The widow of John C. Frémont delighted for a time in her own good health and simple pleasures such as her daily rides on the electric cable car system taking passengers all around the town. Such were Jessie's quiet final years until her death on December 27, 1902, with her faithful daughter Lily at her side. She was seventy-eight years old.

Epilogue: 1906
Appendix: Chronology
Index

Epilogue: 1906

MESSAGE FROM THE PAST: If the U.S. Census Bureau could declare the frontier was gone, dead, as of 1890, didn't another integral organ of the West—its heart, its soul?—die when the earth twitched at 5:13 A.M. on April 16, 1906, and brought brash, teeming San Francisco either crashing down in little pieces or made into kindling for the huge fire that erupted within minutes? Hundreds died, 225,000 were left homeless, 28,000 buildings were brought down or burned up in the fire . . . and along came Jack London to describe the spectacle as quite possibly no other writer ever could.

> The earthquake shook down in San Francisco hundreds of thousands of dollars worth of walls and chimneys. But the conflagration that followed burned up hundreds of millions worth of property. There is no estimating within hundreds of millions the actual damage wrought. Not in history has a modern imperial city been so completely destroyed. San Francisco is gone! Nothing remains of it but memories and a fringe of dwelling houses on its outskirts. Its industrial section is wiped out. Its social and residential section is wiped out. The factories and warehouses, the great stores and newspaper buildings, the hotels and the palaces of the nabobs, are all gone. . . .
>
> Within an hour after the earthquake shock the smoke of San Francisco's burning was a lurid tower visible a hundred miles away. And for three days and nights this lurid tower swayed in the sky, reddening the sun, darkening the day, and filling the land with smoke.

Clearly, it had been an incredible scene, an event beyond imagination. Only "a minute" after the quake, said London, "the flames were leaping upward." The quake had cut electrical lines, overturned trains, and toppled buildings, but worst of all, broken open and ignited the gas mains.

In a dozen different quarters south of Market Street, in the working-class ghetto, and in the factories, fires started. There was no opposing the flames. There was no organization, no communication. All the cunning adjustments of a twentieth-century city had been smashed by the earthquake. The streets were humped into ridges and depressions and filed with debris of fallen walls. The steel rails were twisted into perpendicular and horizontal angles. The telephone and telegraph systems were disrupted. And the great water mains had burst. All the shrewd contrivances and safeguards of man had been thrown out of gear by thirty seconds' twitching of the earth crust.

In just twelve hours, wrote London, half the heart of San Francisco was "gone." He was out on the bay, he said, watching as the fire built and built.

It was a dead calm. Not a flicker of wind stirred. Yet from every side wind was pouring in upon the city. East, west, north and south, strong winds were blowing upon the doomed city. The heated air rising made an enormous suck. Thus did the fire of itself build its own colossal chimney through the atmosphere. Day and night this dead calm continued, and yet, near to the flames, the wind was often half a gale, so mighty was the suck.

In the end, there was no measuring the staggering loss. For the American psyche, it was a disaster comparable only with Pearl Harbor and the terrorist attacks on the World Trade Center and the Pentagon on September 11, 2001.

An enumeration of the buildings destroyed would be a directory of San Francisco. An enumeration of the buildings undestroyed would be a line and several addresses. An enumeration of the deeds of heroism would stock a library and bankrupt the Carnegie medal fund. An enumeration of the dead—will never be made.

But the city, the state, the nation, so shaken in 1906 would go forward anyway and, while mourning for what had been, they, their peoples, nonetheless would regird themselves for the many tasks ahead . . . as indeed we have seen our nation do so many times in the past.

Appendix: Chronology

THE AMERICAN WEST IN THE NINETEENTH CENTURY

*A Chronology of Events with Reference to the People Who
Made Them Come About*

1800–1809

1800: The Spanish secretly transfer the Louisiana Territory to France but retain the lower Mississippi and the Southwest. **1801:** Thomas Jefferson, chief motivating force behind exploration of the American West, becomes president. Meriwether Lewis named the president's private secretary. **1802:** Spain temporarily closes New Orleans to American shipping. **1803:** Jefferson secretly asks Congress to fund an expedition up the Missouri River to find a northwest passage to the Pacific. France sells the Louisiana Territory (828,000 square miles) to the United States for $15 million. Preliminary plans for an expedition are made; Lewis is assigned to lead, and he enlists William Clark. **1804:** In May, Lewis and Clark lead the Corps of Discovery up the Missouri River on an expedition destined to take 28 months and cover 8,000 miles. **1805:** After wintering in present-day North Dakota, the explorers move west in April, accompanied by a Shoshone guide named Sacagawea, her infant son, and her French-Canadian husband. Jefferson enlists Thomas Freeman to lead a similar exploratory probe into the Spanish Southwest. By year's end, Lewis and Clark reach the Pacific Ocean near today's Astoria, Oregon, and encamp for the winter. **1806:** In March, Lewis and Clark begin the return journey. In May, Freeman and Peter Custis set out on the Red River for an expedition into the Southwest; they are turned back after 600 miles by the Spanish. In the fall, Zebulon Pike passes Pikes Peak in Colorado but fails to climb it. Lewis and Clark return to St. Louis. One of their men, John Colter, becomes one of the first "mountain men." **1807:** Pike, like Freeman, searches for the headwaters of the Red River, stumbles onto the Rio Grande, is detained by the Spanish at Santa Fe, but later is released. His report, issued in 1810, stirs up public interest in the lands west of the Mississippi. Colter joins with fur trader Manuel Lisa, who establishes the first fur-trading post, Fort Raymond, at the mouth of the Bighorn River. The era of beaver-trapping mountain men begins. **1808:** Colter explores the Bighorn and Wind Rivers and walks the grounds of today's Yellowstone National Park, the first white to

389

do so. A legend is born (in 1809) after his footrace of five to six miles, utterly naked, to escape a Blackfoot war party that had captured him and killed a companion. **1809:** A distraught, "deranged" Meriwether Lewis kills himself on the Natchez Trace.

1810–1819

1810: In the mountains, the Blackfoot drive off Andrew Henry after he builds a trading fort at the Three Forks of the Missouri. John Jacob Astor forms the Pacific Fur Company with plans to operate on the Pacific Coast. **1811:** Astor and Russians begin activities in the far West—Astor opens operations at Fort Astoria on the mouth of the Columbia River, and the Russians extend their chain of small Northwest colonies by establishing Fort Ross on Bodega Bay above San Francisco. **1812:** The War of 1812 begins. Zebulon Pike is a casualty. **1814:** Formal end of the War of 1812; the battle of New Orleans is fought in early 1815. Lewis and Clark's journal published. **1819:** Spain retains Texas; Florida becomes a U.S. territory by treaty.

1820–1829

1820: Stephen Long's U.S. Army expedition into the Rocky Mountains passes Pikes Peak, which is scaled by a member of Long's party, botanist Edwin James. Long's subsequent description of the area just east of the Rockies as the "Great American Desert" discourages would-be settlers. Slavery goes west with the Missouri Compromise allowing Maine and Missouri into the Union as nonslave and slave states, respectively. **1821:** The Santa Fe Trail from Independence, Missouri, to Santa Fe, New Mexico, is based on trader William Becknell's pioneering trip in search of new trading partners among the Spanish. Moses Austin wins a land grant from the Spanish in Mexico for a settlement of 300 families in Texas. Mexico revolts, throwing off Spanish rule. **1823:** After Moses Austin dies, Stephen F. Austin leads colonizing efforts in Texas. **1824:** Famed mountain man Jedediah Smith, traverses the South Pass running through the Rockies in western Wyoming, finds a fur paradise in the Green River Valley. Jim Bridger and Etienne Provost come across the Great Salt Lake independently of one another; Bridger takes honors as the first white to see it. The Bureau of Indian Affairs is established as part of the War Department. **1825:** The first annual rendezvous of fur traders is held at Henry's Fork on the Green River. For the next fifteen years, the most important fur trading will be done at these annual meetings of mountain men, Indians, and fur traders. **1826:** Jedediah Smith blazes the first overland route into California, going by way of south-central Utah, northwest Arizona, and the Mohave Desert—no pathway for the faint-hearted. **1827:** Smith turns back across the Sierra Nevada for the annual rendezvous then heads back to California; he loses half his men to Indian attacks in the Mohave. **1828:** Smith, traveling into Oregon, barely escapes another massacre. **1829:** Mexico refuses to sell Texas to the United States for $5 million.

1830–1839

1830: Accompanied by William Sublette, Jedediah Smith leads an early wagon train through the Rockies by way of South Pass. Joseph Smith publishes the Book of Mormon and establishes the Church of Latter-day Saints. Mexico, perturbed by the number of Anglo-Americans pouring into Texas, imposes limits on immigration.

1831: Jedediah Smith is killed by Indians on the Cimarron River in the Southwest. No rendezvous for mountain men is held. **1832:** Artist George Catlin travels with mountain men and fur traders to produce an extensive portfolio of classic Indian portraits. **1833:** Texas seeks separate statehood under Mexican rule; President Antonio López de Santa Anna refuses but eases immigration strictures. Samuel Colt patents his famous revolver. Like Catlin, artist Karl Bodmer travels among Indians and depicts their way of life. **1834:** The Indian Affairs Bureau is made into an independent department. Mountain men William Sublette and Robert Campbell establish the Fort Laramie trading post on the North Platte in Wyoming. It will be a major stop on the Oregon Trail. **1835:** Mountain men lose their market as demand for beaver-pelt hats lessens. To the south, restive Texans revolt against Mexican rule. At year's end, the Texans drive the Mexicans out of San Antonio. **1836:** On March 6, the Alamo falls; every defender is killed. Mexican troops massacre 300 prisoners after Goliad surrenders. Sam Houston's small army defeats and captures Santa Anna at the San Jacinto River in an eighteen-minute battle. Texas becomes an independent republic with Houston as president. Missionaries Marcus and Narcissa Whitman, on their way to the confluence of the Snake and Columbia Rivers in Oregon, cross the Rockies with another missionary couple; the two women are the first white women to do so. **1837:** The slavery issue undermines efforts in Congress to annex Texas. **1838:** Mormon leader Joseph Smith and his followers wander as far west as Missouri and Illinois; they are dogged by public controversy and opposition. The beaver-fur market shrinks dramatically. "Pathfinder" John C. Frémont begins explorations of the West.

<h3 style="text-align:center">1840–1849</h3>

1840: Last rendezvous of mountain men on the Green River, although huntsman William Drummond Stewart finances a final rendezvous in 1843. Texas-Mexico hostilities escalate. **1841:** Recent California arrival and would-be empire-builder John Sutter buys the Russian Fort Ross colony, takes pieces back to his own Fort Sutter at the future site of Sacramento. John Bidwell leads another early wagon train across the Rockies and into California; he then goes to work for John Sutter. **1842:** With Kit Carson as his guide, John C. Frémont crosses the Rockies at South Pass then explores the Wind River Mountains in western Wyoming. Mexican troops hit San Antonio hard in Dawson's Massacre. Texas capital briefly removed from Austin. **1843:** Year of the "Great Migration." Missionary doctor Marcus Whitman, on a return trip to Oregon, helps to lead 1,000 emigrants west in more than 100 wagons, the real jump start to years of emigration on the Oregon Trail. Frémont and Carson explore from Salt Lake to California by way of the Sierra Nevada then press into the Great Basin and the Wasatch Mountains of Utah and then to Colorado. The subsequent government report is a bestseller. **1844:** Mormon leader Joseph Smith is killed by a mob at Carthage, Illinois; Brigham Young assumes leadership of the Mormons. Expansionist-minded James K. Polk elected president. **1845:** Texas is admitted to the Union despite Mexican warnings of war. Mexico rejects U.S. offer of $40 million for California, New Mexico, and Texas. **1846:** Mexican War erupts. In California, Frémont briefly joins the Bear Flag Revolt against Mexican rule then joins U.S. forces fighting California's Mexican defenders. The final American victory is achieved in January 1847. Brigham Young's Mormons move farther west, wintering near today's Omaha, Nebraska. The

Donner Party is trapped by wintry weather in the Sierra Nevada; some die, others turn to cannibalism. **1847:** Mormons arrive at Salt Lake, establishing the Mormon Trail. The Mormon Battalion, recruited for the Mexican War, blazes a southern route from Santa Fe to California. Capture of Mexico City ends the Mexican War. Frémont is briefly governor of California then court-martialed while his superiors feud. In Oregon, Cayuse tribes in despair over a measles epidemic blame the pioneers and massacre fourteen at the Whitman mission station on the Columbia River. **1848:** In January, James Marshall finds gold at Sutter's mill on the south fork of the American River, fifty miles northeast of Sutter's Fort. The resulting gold rush does not happen until the next year. The Guadalupe-Hidalgo Treaty officially ends the Mexican War and awards Texas, California, New Mexico, and other Southwest lands to the United States. **1849:** The California gold rush attracts more than 80,000 newcomers, triple the territory's population, in just one year.

1850–1859

1850: California becomes a state. Mining towns boom and die. Fantastic fortunes are made overnight. **1851:** James Savage may be the first white man to see the Yosemite Valley. The federal government and the Plains Indians try to reach a compromise as tidal waves of settlers cross through Indian lands. **1853:** The Gadsden Purchase gives the United States a swath of land on the northern Mexican border from Texas to California for $10 million. **1854:** The Kansas-Nebraska Act replaces the Missouri Compromise of 1820 and allows a choice between slavery and its prohibition in each territory. The antislavery Republican Party is formed. Strife erupts in Kansas over slavery. **1856:** In Kansas, fanatical abolitionist John Brown raids proslavery settlers; proslavery raiders attack the town of Lawrence. Frémont is the first presidential candidate of the Republican Party; he loses to James Buchanan. **1857:** Troops are sent to impose federal law in Mormon-dominated Utah Territory, especially against polygamy. Paiute Indians and a Mormon group led by John D. Lee blamed for Mountain Meadows Massacre of non-Mormon wagon train emigrants in southern Utah. **1858:** The so-called Mormon War is called off after federal pardons are issued. A nonstop stagecoach makes history by traveling from St. Louis to Los Angeles, 2,600 miles in 20 days. **1859:** Gold found in Colorado and silver in Nevada; boom times ahead for each. Oregon becomes a state.

1860–1869

1860: Abraham Lincoln elected president. Pony Express riders begin mail runs from Missouri to California—10-day delivery time is routine on a one-way route covering 1,966 miles. **1861:** Civil War erupts. Kansas becomes a free state. Completion of the coast-to-coast telegraph ends the Pony Express. **1862:** Congressional action authorizes construction of a transcontinental rail line by the Central Pacific and Union Pacific Railroads. In addition, newly passed Homestead Act gives settlers 160 acres of public land (i.e., unclaimed) if they live on it and improve it for five years. Union forces defeat Confederates at Glorietta Pass after earlier Southern victory at Valverde. **1863:** Lincoln issues Emancipation Proclamation. Quantrill's raiders, Frank and Jesse James among them, sack Lawrence, Kansas. **1864:** Nevada becomes a state. Navaho defeated and held prisoner after raiding New Mexico settlements. Sand Creek Massacre of Cheyenne; 200 men, women, and children reportedly killed. **1865:** Civil War ends. Lincoln assassinated. Mark Twain's "Celebrated Jumping Frog of Calaveras County" is presage to a stream of literature of and from the West. **1866:** Lakota and allied tribes massacre troops from Fort Phil Kearny on the Bozeman Trail in northern Wyoming; known as the Fetterman Massacre. Start of the Goodnight-Loving cattle trail from Texas to New Mexico. The James brothers rob a bank in Liberty, Missouri. **1867:** Coming up from Texas on the Chisholm Trail are the first of many cattle drives to railheads in Kansas, this one to Abilene. **1868:** George A. Custer attacks the Cheyenne on the Wichita River in Oklahoma; women and children are among those killed. **1869:** Completion of the transcontinental railroad at Promontory Point, Utah. John Wesley Powell rides the Colorado River through the Grand Canyon. Wyoming recognizes a woman's right to vote.

1870–1879

1870: Utah gives women the right to vote. Bret Harte's short stories create western stereotypes. **1871:** Anti-Chinese riot in Los Angeles. Apache chief Cochise surrenders then flees. John D. Lee and others charged with murder for Mountain Meadows Massacre. **1872:** Publication of *Roughing It,* a humorous depiction of life in the West by Mark Twain. The federal government sets precedent by preserving the lands making up future Yellowstone National Park. **1874:** Custer's announcement of a gold strike in the Dakota Black Hills begins a rush into Indian lands supposedly protected by the Fort Laramie Treaty of 1868. **1875:** Lakota Sioux leaders warn government negotiators they will protect their land in the Black Hills if the government does not. **1876:** The Lakota War breaks out. Custer and 225 soldiers are killed at the Little Bighorn River in the massacre known as Custer's Last Stand. Colorado becomes a state. **1877:** Congress repeals the Fort Laramie Treaty, opening up the Black Hills to miners and others. Lakota leader Crazy Horse surrenders; later he is arrested then killed by a single soldier. John D. Lee is convicted and executed for the Mountain Meadows Massacre. **1877:** Chief Joseph and the Nez Perce surrender after an incredible four-month odyssey in the Northwest. Brigham Young dies. Gunfighter John Wesley Hardin, claiming more than forty notches on his gun, goes to prison for killing a deputy sheriff.

1880–1889

1881: Lakota chief Sitting Bull, who orchestrated the victory over Custer at the Little Bighorn, returns from Canada and surrenders. End of the last great cattle drive to Dodge City, which in the past fifteen years was the destination for probably two million Texas longhorns. Billy the Kid killed by Pat Garrett. In Tombstone, Arizona, shootout at the OK Corral, the Earp brothers versus the Clanton gang. **1882:** Jesse James killed by Robert Ford. **1883:** Teddy Roosevelt travels west to hunt buffalo; his western experiences in the early 1880s result in conservation measures two decades later. **1886:** Apache chief Geronimo surrenders after years of guerrilla fighting in the Southwest. **1888 :** The "Great Die-up" describes a winter of blizzards after a dry summer; hundreds of thousands of cattle die. **1889:** The Indian Territory (Oklahoma) is declared open to settlers at noon on April 22; thousands take part in the expected land rush—the "Sooners" are those who jump the gun and get their land *sooner.* Meanwhile, the "Ghost Dance" messianic creed spreads among the tribes of the West. Four more states admitted to the Union: North and South Dakota, Montana, and Washington.

1890–1899

1890: Wyoming becomes a state. In developments blamed on the Ghost Dance and government efforts to stop its spread, Sitting Bull is killed when Indian police try to arrest him. At the battle of Wounded Knee Creek, South Dakota, 178 Sioux, women and children included, are killed in the ugly last battle of the Indian Wars. Congress creates Yosemite National Park. **1892:** The Dawes Act opens almost two million acres of Crow lands to white settlement in Montana. Naturalist John Muir founds the Sierra Club. **1893:** Historian Frederick Jackson Turner declares the American frontier closed. Only two thousand buffalo remain in the West. **1896:** Utah becomes a state. A gold strike on Bonanza Creek in the Klondike, adjoining Alaska, opens another gold rush . . . the last gold rush in the West. **1899:** A final outburst from the era of the outlaw bands is led by Robert Parker and Harry Longbaugh, otherwise known as Butch Cassidy and the Sundance Kid, who rob their way across the West before fleeing to South America in 1901.

Index